AF530811

Very truly yours
Wiley Britton.

THE CIVIL WAR ON THE BORDER

A NARRATIVE OF OPERATIONS IN MISSOURI, KANSAS, ARKANSAS AND THE INDIAN TERRITORY DURING THE YEARS, 1861-62 BASED UPON THE OFFICIAL REPORTS OF THE FEDERAL COMMANDERS LYON, SIGEL, STURGIS, FREMONT HALLECK, CURTIS, SCHOFIELD, BLUNT, HERRON AND TOTTEN, AND OF THE CONFEDERATE COMMANDERS McCULLOCH, PRICE VAN DORN, HINDMAN, MARMADUKE, AND SHELBY

BY

WILEY BRITTON

MEMBER OF THE AMERICAN ASSOCIATION FOR THE ADVANCEMENT OF SCIENCE

WAR DEPARTMENT—1861-1862

VOLUME I.

THIRD EDITION, REVISED

G. P. PUTNAM'S SONS

NEW YORK — 27 WEST TWENTY-THIRD STREET

LONDON — 24 BEDFORD STREET, STRAND

The Knickerbocker Press

1899

Reprinted by Kansas Heritage Press 1994

1-878882-09-0

For information on other titles by Kansas Heritage Press contact
Kansas Heritage Press
P.O. Box 503
Ottawa, Kansas 66067

PREFACE.

In the following pages I have endeavored to give an account of the most important military operations and events in Missouri, Arkansas, Kansas, and the Indian Territory during the years 1861 and 1862. I have called the work "The Civil War on the Border," because during the period mentioned the most important military operations in Missouri and Arkansas were in the western parts of those States, and also because the Federal army operating in that section after the summer of 1862 was known as the Army of the Frontier. This designation of the army was quite appropriate, because until Kansas was admitted into the Union as a State in 1861, Western Missouri and Western Arkansas bordered on Kansas and the Indian Territories. Having served with the Federal army in that section during the entire war, and having participated in the operations and witnessed most of the events described, I have been able to write largely from observation. But that the work might be historically accurate, I have compared my data with the official reports published by the Government, and eliminated every thing that conflicts with official data. In such of the events described as are not covered by official data, I have drawn my accounts of them from the statements of eye-witnesses and participants, or from personal observation. The official reports are very meagre, except as to the larger operations, and give a very incomplete account of the war in that section. As a rule, the officers were so much occupied with the pressing duties of the hour that they gave little thought to the importance of preparing careful reports of their operations. But it has been possible by combining official data with personal observations and statements of participants in the operations and events described, to give a tolerably complete account of the conflict in that section during the period covered. In giving numbers engaged in actions and casualties on each side, I have almost invariably taken the official reports as a guide. Any one who has read the accounts of both sides of any given conflict will doubtless have noticed that there is a strong tendency for each side to magnify its own achievements and to belittle the achievements of its adversary. And probably there was scarcely an action in that section that the officers and troops on each side did not magnify their own achievements and exaggerate the strength and casualties of their opponents. A Confederate officer sometimes, for example, reported that he killed more of the enemy than the Federal commander reported that he had men in action. Instead, therefore, of accepting such exaggerated accounts, the commanding officers on each side have been permitted to state, as far as practicable, the strength of their respective forces engaged in the different actions and the casualties they sustained. While much has been written on the late war, no one that I am aware of has hitherto undertaken to give an account of the operations extending over that section during the period covered by this volume.

WILEY BRITTON.

WASHINGTON, 1890.

CONTENTS.

XXVI.

XXVII.

XXVIII.

XXIX.

XXX.

XXXI.

THE CIVIL WAR ON THE BORDER.

CHAPTER I.

THE CAPTURE OF CAMP JACKSON.

IMMEDIATELY after the election of Mr. Lincoln the secession leaders of Missouri commenced agitating and scheming to get the State pledged to the policy adopted by the extreme Southern States. If these States passed ordinances of secession severing their relations with the Union, then it was proposed that Missouri should do likewise. A majority of the members of the State Legislature were in favor of the Union and opposed to secession, but Claiborne F. Jackson, the Governor-elect, was in full sympathy with the Southern leaders in their secession schemes, and, it was generally believed, would do every thing in his power to assist them in taking the State out of the Union should the other Southern States go out. As the impending conflict became more imminent he talked of neutrality,—of the State occupying a neutral position,—but the Unionists were not inclined to place much reliance on his professions. Very soon after his inauguration in January, 1861, he and his advisers commenced shaping political affairs so as to take the State out of the Union. But as a majority of the Legislature were opposed to secession, he was, to some extent, checked in his treasonable designs. Still, as he was the regularly elected Governor of the State, his power for mischief was very great. He had all the machinery of the State under his control, and, as he was the commander-in-chief of the militia, he was able to organize it almost entirely in the interest of the secession movement. In organizing camps of instruction for the militia throughout the State, it was given out that the militia organization was solely for home protection. This statement looked plausible enough to men of undecided political views who were drifting along with the popular current, and, as a consequence, thousands of such men over the State went into the militia organization known as the *State Guard.* There is no doubt but that large numbers of men joined this force who would have preferred, when they found it was too late, to have cast their fortunes with the Union.

The excitement continued to increase, as one after another of the Southern States seceded, and the security for life and property became more precarious. The secessionists grew more intolerant and abusive toward Union men, and in many instances urged that they should be compelled to leave the State. In many localities it became the fashion to characterize Union men as abolitionists, and to tolerate abolitionists was to tolerate men who would probably soon be encouraging the slaves to leave their masters. It frequently happened that those who showed the greatest anxiety for the security of slave property were men who had never owned a slave and who probably never would have owned one. As the seceded States had been capturing the forts and arsenals, the arms and ammunition, and the Government property within their limits, the secession leaders in Missouri commenced advocating the taking of the arsenal and all United States property within her limits. There were large quantities of ordnance stores, such as arms, ammunition, and equipments, stored in the arsenals at Liberty and St. Louis, and if these could only be seized they might at once be put into the hands of the State Guard, which was under the command of the Governor, and which was officered by men of his own choosing.

Frank P. Blair and other prominent Union men of St. Louis kept the Government at Washington advised of the situation in Missouri, and even before the inauguration of President Lincoln, Lieutenant-General Winfield Scott directed General Harney, commanding the Western Department, to look to the defences of the St. Louis Arsenal, and, if necessary, to order up all the troops from Jefferson Barracks.

About the middle of February the Washington authorities became apprehensive that the secessionists were intending to make an effort to seize the St. Louis Arsenal, and so advised General Harney. Being on the ground, he kept himself informed of their movements, and, from the professions of the leaders, was not at first inclined to believe that they contemplated the seizure of the Government property in St. Louis. But he changed his mind when Governor Jackson established a military camp of instruction in St. Louis, and when General Frost, commanding a brigade of the State Guard at this camp, commenced drilling daily almost in sight of the arsenal. Thus the secessionists daily grew bolder, until it was an open secret that they intended shortly to seize all the Government property in the city. Shortly after the inauguration of Mr. Lincoln, it was determined that the St. Louis Arsenal should be under the immediate command of an active and efficient officer whose loyalty to the Government was beyond question. Captain Nathaniel Lyon, Second United States Infantry, who had recently been ordered to reinforce the troops at the arsenal, and who had impressed the leading and uncompromising

Union men of St. Louis as being a thorough soldier, actively loyal to the Government, and as possessing a high sense of honor in regard to maintaining the dignity and honor of the National Flag, was, on the recommendation of Congressman Frank P. Blair, of St. Louis, assigned, by direction of the Secretary of War, to the command of the St. Louis Arsenal. It was soon evident that the honor and interests of the Government were not likely to suffer at any point where Captain Lyon directed affairs, if his efforts were properly seconded. He carefully watched the movements of the secession leaders, and made preparations to meet any demonstration they might make.

Though intense excitement prevailed all over the State, and companies and battalions of the State Guard were being organized in nearly every town, yet St. Louis was the chief point of interest in the State. The secession leaders were very desirous of getting possession of not only the city, but also of the post-office, custom-house, arsenal, and all Government property. As the excitement continued to increase they became so outspoken in regard to their plans that General Harney, the Department commander, on April 16th, deemed it expedient to ask for instructions from the War Department for his guidance. After reporting the small available force of regular troops under his command to meet a possible attack, he stated that the arsenal grounds and buildings were completely commanded by hills in their rear and within easy range; that he had information, which he deemed reliable, that Governor Jackson intended very soon to erect batteries upon those hills, and also upon an island opposite the arsenal, and, in the event of the State seceding, demand the surrender of the arsenal. The public mind was constantly so inflamed by passing events and by the discussion of the situation, that a collision was liable to occur at any moment between the State and United States troops.

In the approaching contest the Union men were placed at a disadvantage all over the State, inasmuch as they could not organize for their own defence under the laws of the State. General Harney was continually receiving information of outrages being committed against the persons and property of Union citizens in different sections by secessionists, and yet he was unable to redress these wrongs or afford adequate protection to those thus wrongfully treated. As every thing that the Government did was regarded by the secessionists as a cause of irritation, and as the public property was then in imminent danger of seizure, Frank P. Blair soon saw the necessity of enlisting into the volunteer service of the United States a force of five to ten thousand men from Missouri, to protect the public property and the lives and property of Union citizens in the State. And through his efforts authority was obtained from the War Department for Captain Lyon to receive and muster into service, until further orders, all the men offered, not to exceed ten thousand. Before the end of April he had accepted and sworn in three thousand three hundred men and armed and equipped them for service at the arsenal. The Union men all over the State now began to take courage when they saw that the Government was in earnest in regard to affording them protection. They held mass-meetings in different parts of the State and passed resolutions pledging themselves to support the Government in the crisis now upon them.

On the 21st of April, General Harney was relieved of his command of the Department of the West, by the Secretary of War, which left the direction of military affairs at St. Louis in the hands of Captain Lyon. There was no reason to doubt General Harney's loyalty to the Government, but as he had not acted with such energy and firmness as the Union men believed the occasion required, his removal was demanded. He was anxious to avoid a conflict with the State authorities, and no doubt believed their assurances and professions of peaceful intentions, even though the drilling and arming of the militia had a hostile aspect. The Unionists felt that the hot-headed secessionists would take every possible advantage of the honest purposes of the faithful soldier, and that it would be better to have an officer in command who would not hesitate to suppress every treasonable design before it acquired power to do great mischief.

Governor Jackson convened the Legislature in extra session on the 2d of May, "for the purpose of enacting such laws and adopting such measures as may be deemed necessary and proper for the more thorough organization and equipment of the militia of the State, and to raise the money and such other means as may be required to place the State in a proper attitude of defence." This action of the Governor and secession leaders, it was generally understood, was taken with the view of forcing the State out of the Union. Even while professing a desire for neutrality to General Harney, Governor Jackson was negotiating through his agents with the Confederate authorities at Montgomery, Ala., for arms and ammunition to put into the hands of the State Guard for the purpose of capturing the St. Louis Arsenal. Furthermore, if not by his direction, yet by his tacit permission, the Liberty Arsenal in Clay County, near Kansas City, was taken possession of by organized companies of secessionists from Jackson, Lafayette, and Clay counties, and several pieces of light artillery and all the small-arms, ammunition, and equipments taken therefrom and distributed to the State Guard companies of that section. There was also much talk about a secession force organizing for the purpose of attacking and capturing Fort Leavenworth, Kansas, to get possession of the large quantities of arms and ammunition and other Government supplies stored there. General Harney, having been advised of the imminent danger of capture of the public property at Fort Leavenworth, at once ordered a force of infantry and artillery from several of the Western forts to march there with the least possible delay.

The extra session of the Legislature convened at Jefferson City on the 2d of May, but passed no important measures until after the Camp Jackson affair. Governor Jackson had directed General D. M. Frost to go into encampment with a brigade of State militia near the city of St. Louis, for the purpose, as he alleged, of having the troops under instruction, that they might acquire greater proficiency in the military drill. But Captain Lyon and Colonel Frank P. Blair, who were watching the movements of the secessionists, knew that most of General Frost's command were strong secessionists, and that it was daily receiving supplies of arms and ammunition, some of which had been captured from United States arsenals in other States, and that its attitude was daily becoming more and more threatening. It was also rumored that General Frost intended attacking the arsenal as soon as he deemed his force strong enough to make success reasonably certain. Though in a communication to Captain Lyon he stated that his command was not occupying a position of hostility toward the United States, yet all his actions and preparations indicated the contrary. The principal avenue of his camp was named "Davis," and another "Beauregard"; besides he had been receiving from the Confederacy and under its flag, large supplies of war material, most of which had been taken from United States arsenals in the seceded States. On the night of May 8th, a steamer arrived from Baton Rouge with a large supply of military stores, including muskets, ammunition, and cannon, addressed to a firm in St. Louis who were known to be strong Union men, but to whom no delivery of the stores was made or attempted to be made, their address being used merely as an artifice to prevent suspicion and close scrutiny when the boat's cargo should be examined by United States officers at Cairo. All the pieces of artillery were packed in boxes of heavy plank and marked "Marble," and the shot and shells were put into ale barrels. In fact, the intentions of General Frost were notorious, notwithstanding his professions of loyalty to the United States. In the face of all that had taken place he certainly presumed extraordinary stupidity on the part of Captain Lyon. But Captain Lyon had not been so backward as the actions of the secessionists had presupposed.

During the last few weeks he had organized, armed, and equipped about three thousand five hundred men, or five regiments of Missouri volunteers, and, including regular troops, he had upwards of four thousand men under his command. He had visited General Frost's camp in disguise and knew what was going on. He therefore determined that the secession leaders should go no further in organizing an army in his presence, to seize Government property and overturn the authority of the United States, without meeting resistance. Having made such preparations as he deemed necessary to meet the coming issue, on the afternoon of the 10th of May, he marched his entire force of infantry and artillery, with the exception of three or four hundred men left to guard the arsenal, through the city and arrived at Camp Jackson, situated in the western part of the city, at what is known as Lindell's Grove, and took up such positions as completely commanded the camp. His batteries, planted on the heights overlooking the camp of General Frost, were well supported by the infantry, with muskets and bayonets brightly gleaming, so that the whole array made an imposing appearance. It was the first warlike demonstration the people had ever witnessed, and thousands of men, women, and children left their homes and places of business to witness the impending conflict between the opposing forces, for it was asserted by the secessionists that

General Frost's command would fight to the last man before surrendering to Captain Lyon.

The troops and batteries having taken their proper positions, and every thing being in readiness to commence an attack, Captain Lyon addressed a communication to General Frost, demanding an immediate surrender of his command, "with no other conditions than that all persons surrendering under this demand shall be humanely and kindly treated." He also stated in this letter that General Frost's command was regarded as hostile toward the Government of the United States; that it was for the most part made up of those secessionists who had openly avowed their hostility to the General Government, and had been plotting for the seizure of its property and the overthrow of its authority; that said command was openly in communication with the so-called Southern Confederacy, which was at war with the United States; that he, General Frost, was receiving at his camp, from the said Confederacy, and under its flag, large supplies of the material of war, most of which was known to be the property of the United States, and that the extraordinary preparations being made plainly indicated none other than the well-known purpose of Governor Jackson, which had in view an attitude of hostility to the General Government and co-operation with its enemies.

General Frost hastily called together his staff and a few other officers for consultation. They saw Captain Lyon's batteries frowning down upon them from the neighboring heights, but within easy range, and the Federal soldiers recently raised occupying the elevated positions in line of battle or coming into line in columns of companies. It required but the word to let loose Jove's thunderbolts upon treason's big boasting warriors. General Frost had heard for several days of Captain Lyon's intention of attacking his camp, but did not expect it so soon. What should he do? His command was mostly composed of men who had been very violent in their expressions toward the Government and its friends, and a terror to all Union citizens. When the Government had but few troops in the city, they could hardly be restrained from attacking the arsenal and seizing other Government property. There was now an opportunity of gratifying their thirst for blood and glory. Should they satiate that thirst? Captain Lyon had given them half an hour to decide. Before the time had expired, however, General Frost sent a reply to Captain Lyon, stating that as he was wholly unprepared to defend his command from the proposed unwarranted attack, he was forced to comply with the demand for its surrender. Thus the whole brigade surrendered without firing a shot, and after being disarmed, the officers and soldiers were enclosed by a single file of Federal troops and marched as prisoners to the arsenal, where, the next day, they were released; the officers, with one exception, on their paroles of honor, and the enlisted men on their oaths not to fight against the United States during the war.

That they had been compelled to fight or surrender before completing their preparations for offensive operations, made not only the officers and men of General Frost's command, but also the secessionists throughout the city, boil over with indignation. Many of the violent secessionists in the city, when they heard that Captain Lyon had marched out with a large force of regular and volunteer troops to attack General Frost's camp, seized rifles, shot-guns, pistols, or whatever other weapons they could lay hands on, and rushed to the assistance of the State militia; but when they arrived in the neighborhood of their camp, they found it impossible to pass through the Federal lines. For the first time the boasters of treason and rebellion were beginning to feel the weight of the firm hand of the Government.

Just before six o'clock the troops and prisoners were in column and on the march to the arsenal, but shortly after the rear of the column had got in motion, or had left Lindell Grove, a halt was ordered. The people from the city were now in large crowds, covering the grounds in the vicinity of the camp and the vacant spaces and fences near the streets through which the troops were marching. The troops had halted but a few moments, when several discharges of small-arms were heard near the head of the column, and men, women, and children were seen fleeing in the greatest terror and dismay. But fortunately no one was hurt. A mob of hot-headed secessionists, who had just come out from the city, attacked the advance of the Federal troops. Scarcely had quietness been restored at the front of the column, when volley after volley of musketry was heard from the extreme rear-ranks, and men, women, and children ran wildly and frantically from the scene, leaving some twenty-five persons killed and wounded on the ground. The secession mob had again attacked Captain Lyon's troops, and the soldiers returned the fire with fatal effect. Some of the killed and wounded were innocent people, as is nearly always the case at the outbreak of a mob. The secessionists tried to make it appear that the firing into the crowd by the soldiers was unjustifiable and uncalled for. The greatest excitement prevailed throughout the city during the night, but Captain Lyon had every thing in readiness to punish the mob severely should they make further attack on his troops.

Large quantities of war material were captured from General Frost at Camp Jackson. Besides tents and baggage and camp equipments, there were 6 brass field-pieces, three 32-pounders, 1 mortar, 3 mortar beds, 1,200 muskets, 25 kegs of powder, 30 to 40 horses, and a large supply of shot and shell, which had recently been taken from the Baton Rouge (Louisiana) Arsenal. All the property thus captured, Captain Lyon had brought to the arsenal, and he detailed two regiments of Missouri volunteers and two companies of Regular troops to take possession of Camp Jackson.

CHAPTER II.

RIOT IN ST. LOUIS.

THE capture of General Frost's command did not at once convince the secessionists of St. Louis that the Government was henceforth determined to act with firmness, and that their violent demonstrations would bring upon themselves consequences of the most serious nature. A conflict resulting in bloodshed and loss of life was necessary to teach them a sense of moderation. The next evening after the Camp Jackson affair, as some 1,200 Home Guards, mostly Germans, who had during the day been sworn into the United States service, and armed by Captain F. D. Callender and Lieutenant Rufus Saxton at the arsenal, were returning to their station in the northern part of the city, crowds of secessionists collected on the streets through which they were marching, and hooted and hissed them, and fired into their ranks, killing one soldier and wounding several others. When the head of the column reached Seventh Street, the soldiers suddenly turned, and levelling their muskets, fired a volley down the street, killing and wounding ten persons. In the affair four soldiers and two citizens were killed and six citizens wounded. In a few moments immense crowds collected on the street of the bloody scene, and the excitement rose to a pitch never before witnessed in the city. But no further outbreak occurred. The firmness of Captain Lyon had had the effect of making the violent secessionists more considerate and cautious in their actions. Perhaps more than half of the people of St. Louis were loyal to the General Government, and it was evident that a still larger force could be organized if necessary to meet an extraordinary emergency.

By direction of the Secretary of War, General Harney resumed command of the Department of the West on the 11th of May, the day after the capture of Camp Jackson. As he was regarded as more conservative than Captain Lyon in the administration of affairs, General Frost addressed him a communication, protesting against the action of Captain Lyon in demanding the surrender of his command, and requesting that the property captured be restored to the State. In this protest General Frost stated that every officer and soldier of his command had taken with uplifted hand an oath to sustain the Constitution and laws of the United States, as well as to honestly and faithfully serve the State of Missouri against all her enemies. In view of the fact that a large portion of the munitions of war captured by General Lyon had recently been seized from United States arsenals in the seceded States and sent to General Frost, it was regarded by the Unionists as rather brazen-faced in him to ask that the captured property be restored to him as the property of the State. Though General Harney reported to Washington that Captain Lyon's conduct in the capture of Camp Jackson had his entire approval, yet his reappointment to the command of the Department and his presence in St. Louis had a tendency to complicate affairs, for the secession leaders believed that by promises and assurances they could keep him from taking any decisive action until they got strong enough to defy him. The riot in St. Louis on the day of his assuming command and the excited state of the public mind induced him to issue a proclamation in which he appealed to the people to pursue their usual avocations, to abstain from the excitement of public meetings and discussions, and to obey the laws. The secessionists wanted him to disband or change the location of the Home Guards in the city, but he stated in his proclamation that he had no authority to do it.

After the surrender of Camp Jackson, Captain Lyon was elected Brigadier-General of the command which he had organized, and through the representations of Honorable Frank P. Blair and some other prominent Union men of St. Louis, he acted under special authority from Washington. Though he consulted with General Harney in many things, his command was quasi-independent.

The news of the capture of General Frost's command was received at Jefferson City between five and six o'clock on the evening of the 10th of May, and the Legislature was in session. The news created the wildest excitement in that body, and in a few moments members were seen hurrying to and fro without any apparent purpose. The military bill which was pending passed both houses in less than twenty minutes, the act to take effect on its passage. A few hours afterward another despatch was received stating that it was the battery of the Southwest Expedition which had been demanded and surrendered. This was regarded as a secession success, and the excitement subsided. The two houses of the Legislature met in their respective halls again at half-past seven o'clock, and continued in session until half-past nine. The citizens and members of the Legislature had generally retired for the night, when, shortly after twelve o'clock, despatches were received confirming the first report of the surrender of Camp Jackson and the killing of citizens. The whole town was soon aroused by the ringing of bells, and members of the Legislature were hastily summoned to the Capitol. The two houses at once went into secret session, which continued until half-past three o'clock. The excitement was probably heightened by a terrible thunder-storm which prevailed at the time, for the vivid and almost continuous flashes of lightning momentarily blinded many of those who were hurrying to and fro through the streets. A despatch was received that two thousand troops were getting ready to leave St. Louis for Jefferson City, and this news increased the excitement. In consequence of this report the Osage Bridge, over the Osage River, about eight miles below Jefferson City, was burned to prevent trains with troops from coming through, and the State treasure and twelve thousand kegs of powder were removed to a place of safety. The military bill created a fund for arming and equipping the militia, and the whole military force of the State was put under the command of the Governor, and *the officers and men were required to take an oath to obey him alone.* General Harney, in his proclamation of May 14th, charactized this bill "as an indirect secession ordinance, ignoring even the forms resorted to by other States." He also said that its most material provisions were in conflict with the Constitution of the United States. He also called attention to the seizure of the Liberty Arsenal, and of the arms unlawfully taken from the United States Arsenal at Baton Rouge, and surreptitiously passed up the river in boxes marked "Marble," and received into the camp of General Frost.

General Harney was assured by good citizens, and no doubt believed, that his proclamation had produced a tranquillizing influence. It probably had among certain classes, but the secessionists continued their war-like preparations over the State without abatement, and Union men were being constantly driven from their homes. Though a great many men throughout the State of undecided views sympathized with and felt inclined to support the General Government in the coming issue, yet they felt apprehensive that it might disturb, or permit to be disturbed, the status of their slave property. In view of the general uneasiness on the subject, a prominent citizen of St. Louis, Mr. Thomas T. Gault, addressed a letter to General Harney for an expression of his sentiments. The General replied that he had no special means of knowledge on the subject, but that, from the statesmanlike views of the President, and the fact that Northern generals had recently returned slaves, who had sought refuge in their camps, to their proper owners, he did not believe it was the intention of the General Government to interfere with the institution of negro slavery. This statement was immediately published by all the leading papers in the State, and was received by many, who had not yet pledged themselves to secession, as quite satisfactory. General Harney being a citizen of Missouri, and a soldier of a high sense of honor, a statement of this kind had great weight with many of the thoughtful and intelligent men of the State. But all his earnest efforts to restore peace and quietness and a feeling of security throughout the State were unsuccessful, so that, on the 21st of May, he signed an agreement with Major-General Sterling Price, of the State Guard, having that end in view. This agreement was published along with another proclamation of General Harney's to the people, calling upon them to observe good order and to respect each other's rights. A good many thought that this agreement would be faithfully carried out on both sides, that it would have a good effect, and that the calamities of war would not afflict the people of the State. But, as General Price was in command of the State Guard, and acting under the orders of the secession Governor, Jackson, the Union men knew that he would not give a very attentive ear to their grievances, and under no circumstances call upon General Harney to use United States troops to assist in protecting them in their lives and property. In a letter to the Secretary of War in regard to organizing several regiments of Missouri volunteers, Frank P. Blair wrote that "the agreement between Harney and General Price gives me great disgust, and dissatisfaction to the Union men."

Really the Unionists were now worse off than before the agreement, for the secessionists could now oppress them without fear of being called to account. Numerous complaints of Union citizens were soon coming to General Harney, from different sections of the State, of aggressions committed upon them by secessionists. General Harney called General Price's attention to these complaints, giving him the localities where the outrages were alleged to have been committed. General Price had an investigation made, but, of course, found nothing wrong, the aggressions having been made by irresponsible parties. General Harney saw the effect of the agreement, and he also doubtless saw that he had placed himself in a position in which he could not afford adequate protection to the Union citizens without an infringement of the agreement. Representations of continued outrages upon Union citizens reached the President, as well as reports that General Harney had not acted as vigorously as he might have done. He was therefore again relieved of the command of the Department of the West on May 31st, for the last time, and we may now take leave of him, as he does not appear upon the scene again in connection with military operations in Missouri. He was a true soldier in every sense of the word. Though he believed that Missouri could be kept steadfast to the Union without appealing to the sword, no one acquainted with his character can, with justice, accuse him of being wanting in sympathy and loyalty to the General Government. He had, in the Mexican and Indian wars, during a period of nearly forty years, served his country with distinguished ability, scarcely equalled by any other officer in the army. This last time he was relieved he felt that the Washington authorities had not full confidence in him, and he was profoundly moved, for, in a letter to the Adjutant-General of the Army, he closed with the words: "During a long life dedicated to my country, I have seen some service, and more than once I have held her honor in my hands; and during that time my loyalty, I believe, was never questioned; and now, when, in the natural course of things, I shall, before the lapse of many years, lay aside the sword which has so long served my country, my countrymen will be slow to believe that I have chosen this portion of my career to damn with treason my life, which is soon to become a record of the past, and which I shall most willingly leave to the unbiassed judgment of posterity."

General Harney having been removed, the command of the Department of the West devolved upon General Lyon. The change was welcomed by the Unionists and regretted by the secessionists. Both parties now looked forward to an uncompromising policy and to vigorous measures toward upholding the authority of the Government. As matters continued to assume a threatening aspect throughout the State, and as the secession leaders knew that General Lyon had too little confidence in their professions of loyalty to the Government to spend much time parleying with them, Governor Jackson solicited an interview with him, which was granted, for the purpose of arriving at some plan by which the horrors of civil war might be averted from the State. Accompanied by General Sterling Price and Colonel Thomas L. Snead, the Governor met General Lyon, Colonel Frank P. Blair, and Major H. A. Conant, on the part of the United States, in St. Louis on the 11th of June, and had a four hours' conference, but without agreeing upon a plan of pacific measures which would be satisfactory to both parties. Governor Jackson submitted a proposition to the effect that he would disband the State Guard, break up its organization, disarm all companies which had been armed by the State, repress all insurrectionary movements within the State, repel attempts to invade it from whatever quarter and by whomsoever made, and protect all citizens equally in all their rights without regard to their political opinions; that he would, if necessary, invoke the assistance of the United States troops to carry out his pledges, and that he would maintain a strict neutrality, if the Federal Government would undertake to disarm the Home Guards, which were being organized and armed throughout the State, and pledge itself not to occupy with its troops any localities not occupied by them at that time. General Lyon and Colonel Blair were convinced that it would be about as reasonable to expect lambs to go unharmed guarded by wolves, as to expect Union men to be fully protected in their rights by the secession State authorities. General Lyon in reply expressed his views with modesty but with frankness, as a servant of the Government, and thought the Governor's proposition would at once overturn the Government's privileges and prerogatives; and that if it withdrew its forces entirely from the State, or pledged itself that they should only occupy their present positions, secret measures would be resorted to for the purpose of providing arms and effecting organizations which, upon any pretext, could put forth a formidable opposition to the General Government; and that even while arming, combinations could doubtless form in certain localities to oppress and drive out loyal citizens to whom the Government was bound to give protection, but which it would be helpless to do, as also to repress combinations, if its forces could not be sent into the State. Arkansas had already seceded and offered troops to the Confederate Government; and these troops, as well as those from other seceded States, might be used to invade Missouri in carrying out the secession programme, and in such an event, under the limitation proposed, the General Government could not take posts on the borders of the

State to meet and repel such force. He thought that the Government could not shrink from its duty, nor abdicate its corresponding rights, and only upon the basis laid down, in his opinion, could the rights of both the General and the State governments be secured, their legitimate functions exercised, and peace maintained.

The representatives of the General and the State governments at this conference being unable to agree upon a plan which would restore peace and security throughout the State, Governor Jackson returned to Jefferson City, and on the 12th of June issued his proclamation, reciting the terms of his proposition made to General Lyon, and calling into active service fifty thousand of the State militia for the purpose of repelling invasion and for the protection of the lives, liberty, and property of the citizens. To array the passions and prejudices of all classes against the General Government, in his proclamation he referred to General Lyon's action in the Camp Jackson affair, and his energetic action in suppressing the riot in St. Louis on the 11th of May, as a series of unprovoked and unparalleled outrages inflicted upon the peace and dignity of the State, and upon the rights and liberties of the people, by wicked and unprincipled men professing to act under the authority of the United States Government. After enumerating other grievances and alleged wrongs committed by the General Government, he further said: "While it is your duty to obey all the Constitutional requirements of the Federal Government, it is equally my duty to advise you that your first allegiance is to your own State, and that you are under no obligations whatever to obey the unconstitutional edicts of the military despotism which has enthroned itself at Washington, nor to submit to the infamous and degrading sway of its minions in this State." There was now no longer any question in regard to the position the State authorities of Missouri intended to assume towards the General Government. This proclamation of Governor Jackson threw down the gauntlet of open rebellion, and the Government was obliged to meet the issue or confess its weakness by abdicating its rightful authority. The citizens of the State were so equally divided in their political sentiments in regard to the question of Union or Secession, that clear-headed men should have felt some doubt of the possibility of so uniting the conflicting elements as to secure a permanent peace while the storms of war were raging across their borders. A great issue was involved, and Missouri, occupying a position between belligerent sections, her people divided in their sympathies as they were, could not justly be expected to remain idle spectators to the contest that was daily assuming more formidable proportions. Every thing pointed to the probability of the State being the battle-ground of the armies operating west of the Mississippi River.

CHAPTER III.

THE ROCK CREEK AFFAIR.

FOR nearly twenty years prior to the breaking out of the war, Independence had been the most important town of Western Missouri. A good many wealthy and influential men lived there. It was the point from which the large wagon-freight trains started out with goods and supplies for Santa Fe and Salt Lake, and for the Government forts and trading-posts in the Territories westward to the Rocky Mountains. Traders and trappers from among distant Indian tribes brought their furs and buffalo-robes there for sale or shipment East, and returned to the far-off wilds of the West with outfits and supplies. The town also has a local history, as being the place where the Mormons first settled, and from which they were expelled by the people of Missouri in 1838. The site of the city and the surrounding country have been considered by the Mormons ever since their expulsion as their Holy Land, to which they expect to return in the future. They have owned and kept fenced several acres of land within the city limits, on which they propose to build their temple when the faithful of their religion become strong enough. The town is beautifully situated on a high ridge four miles south of the Missouri River, and is in the centre of a fertile region, where blue grass grows luxuriantly upon all the uncultivated lands.

In the struggle between the Free-State and Pro-Slavery men of Kansas Territory, the prominent men of Independence did every thing in their power to shape the affairs of the Territory so as to make it a Slave State when admitted to the Union. When, therefore, Mr. Lincoln was elected President and the Southern States commenced passing ordinances of secession, the men of Western Missouri who had taken an active part toward making Kansas a slave State threw the weight of their influence into the cause of secession. Nearly every one was of opinion that the country was drifting into war, and those in favor of secession at once commenced preparations for casting their fortunes with the South. In the latter part of the winter and spring of 1861, two companies of light infantry, known as the Blues and the Grays, one company of cavalry, and one company of light artillery were organized at Independence, and devoted much of their time to instruction in the military drill and school of the soldier. The artillery company, commanded by Captain Starke, had two field-pieces, one of which was known as the "Old Sacramento," having been captured from the Mexicans by the Federal forces under Colonel A. W. Doniphan, First Missouri Mounted Infantry, at the battle of Sacramento during the Mexican War. These companies were at first independent, but were subsequently, when Governor Jackson made a call by proclamation for State troops, transferred to the State Guard.

The discussions in Congress concerning compromise measures were eagerly watched by every one interested in the coming conflict. Most of the secessionists, however, were opposed to any compromise that would limit the extension of slavery. Several of the extreme Southern States had passed ordinances of secession, and had commenced organizing troops to oppose the authority of the United States. Fort Sumter had been fired upon, and finally reduced and forced to surrender to General Beauregard. This triumph at the beginning of the crisis encouraged the secessionists throughout the Southern and slave States. The gauntlet of rebellion was now thrown down, and every day brought news of exciting interest: of the capture, in some of the Southern States, by State troops, of United States arsenals containing cannon, small-arms, ammunition, and materials for arming and equipping the new levies flocking into the hundreds of recruiting stations throughout the South. Political leaders harangued the people at every town and place of public meeting on the situation and grievances of the South, and intense excitement prevailed in every part of the State. Every one possessed of the military spirit was soon thirsting for war, though few had calculated its terrible consequences. Many officers of the Regular Army of the United States of Southern birth were constantly sending in to the Adjutant-General of the Army their resignations, and joining the State forces of their respective States, or accepting commissions under the new Confederate Government. In many instances, without waiting for the acceptance of their resignations, these officers left their stations, and putting themselves in communication with the Confederate authorities, offered their services to the so-called Southern Confederacy. Among those who had recently resigned their commissions in the United States Army, with the view of accepting service under the Confederate Government, was Captain Holloway, of Jackson County, Missouri. He had received his commission from Governor Jackson as colonel of a regiment in the State Guard before his resignation as captain in the United States Army had been accepted. Immediately after he returned home to draw his sword against the Government which had educated him in the military profession, and which he had sworn solemnly to support, he took charge of the three military companies which had been organized at Independence. He also had authority from the Governor to organize the State Guard in that Congressional district into regiments and brigades, as far as practicable.

Reports of exciting events in different parts of the country filled the newspapers, and the war feeling among the secessionists increased. A camp of instruction was to be established near Independence. Colonel Holloway sent out orders to the different company commanders in Jackson, Cass, Lafayette, and Clay counties, to bring their companies with as little delay as practicable to Rock Creek, near Independence, where a camp or rendezvous had been established. A few weeks, however, before the establishment of this camp at Rock Creek, Captain Henry L. Route, commanding a volunteer company of secessionists in Clay County, sent word to the leading secessionists of Jackson, Lafayette, and Clay counties, that if a sufficient number of men from these counties would come over and join him, he would lead them and take the arms, ammunition, and other ordnance stores from the Liberty Arsenal. Although there had been rumors for several weeks that the secessionists were intending to seize the arsenal, the Department commander did not take the precaution to send a force of Regular troops there to protect the Government property. It was generally known that only one ordnance sergeant stood in the way of those wishing to seize it. In response, therefore, to Captain Route's request, some two hundred unorganized secessionists from the counties named, during the night of April 20th, crossed the Missouri River at Sibley, about six miles below Independence, with their teams, and joining Captain Route on the north side of the river, proceeded to the arsenal, and took therefrom all the United States property. It was of course useless for the ordnance sergeant in charge to offer any resistance to the mob, for they were all armed with guns and pistols.

In the seizure of the arsenal the secessionists secured a large amount of war material with which to arm and equip the companies recently organized in that section. They took four six-pounder brass field-pieces mounted, two nine-pounder iron field-pieces not mounted, forty boxes of Mississippi rifles, about forty boxes of smooth-bore muskets, about the same number of boxes of carbines, and several boxes of pistols, besides large quantities of artillery and small-arms ammunition. The cannon, small-arms, ammunition, and other Government property thus taken was distributed mostly to the military companies of Jackson and Clay counties. The distribution was not satisfactory to the Lafayette County secessionists, because their county did not share equally with the former. This exploit of seizing the Government property at the Liberty Arsenal made the secessionists of this section bolder than ever, and the leaders who had participated in it heard, through Joseph Ervin, who had a contract with the Government for transporting army supplies from Kansas City to Fort Union, New Mexico, that a large number of arms and large quantities of ammunition and other army supplies were at Kansas City and ready for shipment, and that if they, the secessionists, wanted them, they must come at once and get them. After this information was received no time was lost, and in about a week after the sacking of Liberty Arsenal, Captain T. W. Arnold's company, the Grays, from Independence, commanded by Lieutenant Whitehead, left town the early part of the night and proceeded to Kansas City, and took from the Choteau warehouse on the levee all the arms, ammunition, and equipments that Mr. Ervin had ready for shipment to Fort Union. The carbines obtained at this seizure of Government property were sent to Cass County to be put into the hands of the secession companies that were organized there. As soon as it was known that the Liberty Arsenal had been sacked by the secessionists, Colonel Van Horn, a prominent Union man, and editor of the *Kansas City Journal*, telegraphed the commanding officer of the United States forces at Fort Leavenworth the fact, whereupon the commanding officer sent a company of Regular cavalry to Liberty. After staying at Liberty for two or three days, the company of Regular cavalry was ordered to Kansas City, and arrived there the day after Lieutenant Whitehead had taken the Government property from the Choteau warehouse.

Immediately on his arrival at Kansas City, the commanding officer of the company of Regular cavalry commenced to fortify his camp by throwing up breastworks on a bluff in the northwestern quarter of the city. Seeing that the United States troops were fortifying and intending to hold Kansas City, Colonel Holloway despatched orders to the commanding officers of companies in his district not already notified, to report, with as little delay as possible, to the camp or rendezvous on Rock Creek, near Independence. The companies from Jackson County reported in a few days, and the companies from Cass, Johnson, Lafayette, and Clay counties in a week to ten days. In all, there were twelve to fifteen companies assembled at Rock Creek for the avowed purpose of capturing or dislodging the company of Regular cavalry which was entrenched at Kansas City. Major Prince, commanding the United States forces at Fort Leavenworth, having been made acquainted with the hostile movements of the secessionists under Colonel Holloway at Rock Creek, moved down to Kansas City with three companies of Regular infantry, two companies of Regular cavalry, and two pieces of field artillery. After stopping there a few days and closely observing the movements of the secessionists, he sent Lieutenant D. S. Stanley, with a detachment of forty men under a flag of truce, to Colonel Holloway, to ascertain the intentions of the camp of armed secessionists under his command. Having taken possession of the Government property at the Liberty Arsenal, and that at Kansas City which was ready for shipment to Western forts, without meeting with resistance, the secession leaders seemed to think that the Government would passively allow them to carry out their traitorous schemes to an almost unlimited extent. And it was also reported that they intended, soon as they became better organized, to take possession of the large quantities of arms, ammunition, and other Government property stored at Fort Leavenworth, Kansas.

Lieutenant Stanley proceeded leisurely with his detachment of Regular cavalry about eight miles down the Kansas City and Independence road until he came in sight of Colonel Holloway's camp, and halted his men about three hundred yards from it. He then rode forward, with a sergeant carrying the flag of truce, until he met Colonel Holloway and his adjutant, Lieutenant McClanahan, both mounted. Colonel Holloway and Lieutenant Stanley saluted each other courteously, as was the custom with officers of the army, and the latter at once made known his mission. They had been in conversation but a short time when Lieutenant Stanley noticed that several companies of cavalry of Colonel Holloway's command, under Colonel Chiles, were making movements on each side of the road that threatened to flank him and cut him off. He called Colonel Holloway's attention to these movements, but the Colonel assured him that there was no danger—that he had ordered his men to keep their positions during the conference. Continuing the conversation for another moment, Lieutenant Stanley noticed again that the hostile movements of the secessionists had not ceased, but were becoming more threatening, whereupon he remarked to Colonel Holloway that his men were surrounding him, that he could stay no longer, and then turned and galloped back to his men and returned to Kansas City. Colonel Holloway and his adjutant turned at the same moment and were riding back toward the camp, when they were mistaken for the Federal advance, and were fired upon by their own impetuous men and killed. When Colonel Holloway turned around from the conference with Lieutenant Stanley, he saw that his men were not keeping their positions, and commenced to motion them back with his hand, which motion being understood by them as coming from the Federal commander, drew the fire that killed him. After the volley that killed Colonel Holloway and his adjutant was fired, scattering or random firing continued for about ten minutes, during which time seventeen men and officers were slightly and mortally wounded. Captains Harbaugh and Stonestreet died of their wounds. After the death of Colonel Holloway, and after the killed and wounded were gathered up and taken to Independence, Colonel Weightman, next in rank, assumed command of the secessionists and moved all the companies that night, about ten o'clock, through Independence to a point on a bluff on the east side of the Little Blue, seven miles east of Independence. Here some temporary earthworks were thrown up commanding the approaches from the west, but in a short time the command had decreased considerably in numbers by the men returning to their homes.

Lieutenant Stanley, on his return to Kansas City, reported to Major Prince the hostile movements of Colonel Holloway's command. The next morning, having put every thing in readiness for active operations, Major Prince marched his command of two companies of cavalry, three companies of infantry, and two pieces of field artillery down to the secessionists' camp, for he had not yet heard of their retreat, and the extent of the casualties of their blunder. Arriving on the ground of their recent camp, and finding that they had retreated, he continued his march to Independence. Before entering town, however, he halted his command and ordered his men to load their muskets and fix bayonets, evidently expecting that the populace or the secession companies would make some hostile demonstration. He entered town, the cavalry marching in front in columns of fours, the drum corps next playing "Yankee Doodle," the infantry next marching in platoons, and the two six-pounder field-pieces brought up the rear. The whole command, with the Stars and Stripes borne at the head of the column, marched around Court House Square and back to Rock Creek where the secessionists had recently rendezvoused, and where Major Prince encamped for the night, and returned to Kansas City the next morning, having met with no resistance. Colonel Holloway was very popular among the secessionists of Western Missouri, and his death was regarded by them as a great misfortune to their cause.

For a week to ten days after this Rock Creek affair, the secessionists, through shame or chagrin, or with the hope of firing the hearts of all Southern sympathizers, tried to keep alive the impression, and even published it as a fact, that it was the Federal troops who did the firing that killed Colonel Holloway and his comrades. Colonel Holloway had sufficient timely notice of the approach of the Federal detachment to get his men out and in position, in the event of finding it necessary to assume the offensive or defensive. Through sympathy and curiosity, quite a number of citizens from Independence and vicinity visited his camp daily. When the near approach of the Federal detachment was announced, and the secession companies were ordered out, and formed in line on each side of the road, the secession citizens retired a short distance to the rear, so that they could watch the movements of the hostile forces. But these citizens were not in a position to see the Federal detachment, nor all the men of the secession companies, after they had been placed in their proper positions. When, therefore, the citizens heard the firing, they supposed that both parties were engaged in the conflict. Even some of Colonel Holloway's own men probably at first thought that the Federal detachment participated in the firing. The secession leaders, having committed the blunder of killing and wounding their comrades, showed no disposition to correct the false impression that had gone out in the excitement of the moment. They seemed to think that the false account of the affair would help their cause more than the truth, and it was a pretext from which the editors of the secession newspapers drew inspiration to fire the Southern heart. They characterized it as an outrageous attack by the Federal power upon the peaceable citizens of the State, and passionately appealed to all Southern men to rally to arms and fight for Southern independence. For several days after the affair those who knew that the secessionists had fired upon themselves by mistake were very cautious in making any statement about it not in accord with the popular view. The distorted account having been published far and wide over the State had the effect of arousing many to take up arms against the Government, who, had they been correctly informed, would probably have awaited further developments of the issue.

CHAPTER IV.

CAPTURE OF JEFFERSON CITY AND ACTION AT BOONVILLE.

WE may now leave St. Louis, as the military operations of most exciting interest were, immediately after the conference between General Lyon and Governor Jackson, transferred to the interior of the State, to that romantic region known as the Ozark Range. Even before General Harney relinquished command the last time, he had received information that Confederate troops were being organized and equipped in Northwestern Arkansas for service in Missouri. And when General Lyon resumed command of the Department on the 1st of June, he also received information which plainly indicated that extensive preparations were being made for an early invasion of Missouri by Confederate troops from Northwestern Arkansas. Brigadier-General Ben. McCulloch, who had recently been promoted by the Confederate Government from the colonelcy of a Texas regiment on account of the conspicuous part he took in the capture of the United States Arsenal and arms at San Antonio, Texas, early in the spring, was assigned to the command of the Indian Territory, south of Kansas. He had arrived at Fort Smith, Arkansas, and commenced organizing his forces, preparatory to moving them north towards Missouri, a short time before General Lyon assumed command of the Department of the West. The presence of hostile forces near the southwestern border of the State, and the proclamation of Governor Jackson calling out fifty thousand State militia to drive the Federal forces out of Missouri, convinced General Lyon that no time should be lost in putting his troops in motion to occupy the Capitol at Jefferson City, and to attack and disperse such bodies of State troops as were collecting at different points in the interior for the purpose of opposing the United States authority. Having made such arrangements as were possible for supplies, on the 13th of June he put his troops, consisting of Captain Totten's light battery, Second Artillery; one company of the Second Infantry; two companies of recruits for the Regular service, under Lieutenant W. L. Lothrop, Fourth Artillery; Colonel F. P. Blair's First Regiment, Missouri Volunteers; and nine companies of Colonel Henry Boernstein's Second Regiment, Missouri Volunteers, on several steamboats, and proceeded up the Missouri River to Jefferson City, where he arrived on the 15th, and occupied the place without opposition. Governor Jackson and the State officers having precipitately left the capital on the 13th, General Lyon, after leaving Colonel Boernstein with three companies of his regiment in command of the place, re-embarked on the boats on the 16th with about seventeen hundred troops, artillery and infantry, and continued up the river to Boonville, forty-eight miles northwest, where he was informed that Governor Jackson had collected about three thousand State troops, with the intention of making a stand.

The boats were stopped for the night a mile below Providence, about fifteen miles below Boonville, and early the next morning, the 17th, steamed up to Rockport, about seven miles up the river, where it was reported that a small force of State troops were stationed some four miles below Boonville with the view of making a vigorous defence. General Lyon landed his troops on the south bank of the river about seven o'clock, a mile or so above Rockport and about seven miles below Boonville, and immediately took up the line of march to meet the enemy. The troops having been brought up on boats were in fine condition, and having unbounded confidence in their commander, moved forward with a firm, steady step. On landing, General Lyon left Captain Richardson's company, First Missouri Volunteers, and one eight-inch siege howitzer and an artillery party, to guard the boats. He instructed Captain Richardson to advance to a position up the river which would be within range for the siege howitzer, and then open upon the rebel camp. He next made the disposition of his troops for attack or defence while on the march. Two companies of the Second Missouri Volunteers, under Major Osterhaus, were thrown forward as skirmishers. They were followed at the proper distance by one company of the Second Regular Infantry, Captain Totten's battery, two companies of Regular recruits under Lieutenant Lothrop, Colonel Blair's regiment of Missouri Volunteers, and four companies of the Second Missouri Volunteers under Lieutenant-Colonel Schaefer. The boats moved up the river to keep even with the troops marching in the order described. The column, after having marched about two miles, met the advance pickets of the enemy, which opened fire and then fell back. To develop the strength and intentions of the enemy, Major Osterhaus' two companies were deployed to the right of the road, and Company "B," Second Infantry, to the left of the road, and two pieces of Totten's battery were brought into position and fired several shots at a party of secessionists within range. It was soon discovered, however, that the main force of the enemy had not yet been reached.

General Lyon continued to advance, but with caution, for the enemy were now near at hand. From what he could see and ascertain of the enemy's position, he deemed it advisable to throw forward an additional force to the right of the road to march in line with the advance of his column. Lieutenant Lothrop, with a company of artillery recruits, Captain Yates' Company "H," First Missouri Volunteers, and one company from the Third Missouri Volunteers, were detached for this service, and after moving forward about a mile the enemy were discovered in force. The company of the Second Regular Infantry which had already been thrown out to the left of the road was now supported by one company under Captain Maurice, First Missouri Volunteers. General Lyon now steadily advanced both his flanks, and in a few moments the two opposing forces were warmly engaged. It was soon observed that a considerable force of secessionists, having the shelter of a house with a thicket of woods behind it, held their position with a good deal of determination. But Captain Totten's battery was quickly brought into position, and after a few rounds of shell rendered effective service in dislodging them. It was while driving the enemy from this position that most of the Federal casualties occurred, for in approaching them so as to be in gun-shot range, General Lyon's troops were obliged to pass over open ground, exposed to a galling fire. But he extended and strengthened his right and left flanks and pushed steadily forward, not allowing the enemy a moment's time to rally or strengthen any of their positions as they fell back. The rebels were now soon driven beyond their camp, which was on the Federal right near the river, and which was taken possession of by Captain Nelson Cole, First Missouri Volunteers, who had been sent to the right to extend the Federal front. In the meantime the boats moved up the river to a point within range of the siege howitzer, which at once commenced to shell the rebel camp with good effect. The retreat of the rebels soon became a stampede, and in their flight they left two pieces of artillery, six-pounders, most of their camp equipage, and about five hundred stand of arms of all sorts. Gen eral Lyon also captured some sixty prisoners, most of whom were young men under the military age, and who represented that they had been misled by the statements of their leaders to take up arms against the United States. He liberated these misguided youths on each taking an oath not to take up arms or serve against the United States during the impending hostilities.

The casualities of the Federal troops during the day were two killed, one missing, and nine wounded. The loss of the rebels, as near as could be ascertained, was ten men killed and some twenty wounded. The wounded were mostly carried off in their retreat.

The engagement and rout of the rebel forces produced intense excitement in Boonville, and as General Lyon was approaching the city, which he entered about two o'clock, he was met by a deputation of citizens, who came, as they said, on behalf of the people to ask security from violence and plunder by his troops. Governor Jackson in his inflammatory proclamation of the 13th had represented the Federal troops as having committed a series of such unprovoked outrages, that many of the citizens of Boonville were in great consternation for fear of violence to their persons or property by General Lyon's forces. On condition that no opposition should be made to his entrance into the city and to his occupying the town, General Lyon informed the deputation that the citizens should not be disturbed in any manner, and that they could pursue their usual avocations. The deputation promised that, so far as was in their power, no opposition should be made to his entrance and occupation of the city, but on reaching its suburbs he required the mayor and city council to accompany him on his entrance. A portion of his troops he quartered in the city, and the remainder he directed to return to the boats stationed opposite the Fair grounds just below the city. He at once set himself to work to correct the erroneous impressions the secessionists had endeavored to create in regard to the intentions of the Federal commander, and in a few days order and a feeling of security were re-established.

The commendable conduct of his officers and men did much to place the Government's policy in the proper light at that point, but it would not correct the false impressions which had spread to other localities throughout the State by the publication of Governor Jackson's proclamation and by impassioned editorials in secession journals. He therefore deemed it necessary to issue a proclamation to the people of the State, in which he briefly set forth the causes which had brought on the conflict between the United States and State authorities. He also stated that he conceived it his duty as an officer of the General Government to maintain its paramount authority with such force as he had at his command, and that it was his wish and purpose to visit any unavoidable rigor arising in the issue upon those only who provoked it. Referring to the fact that the leaders of the rebellion had long experienced the mildness of the General Government, and also to the fact that the clemency which he had shown to those captured at Camp Jackson under General Frost had been misconstrued, he thought it proper to give warning that the Government could not always be expected to indulge in such clemency and mildness, for by so doing it would compromise its own safety and interests.

Colonel Boernstein, who had been left in command at Jefferson City by General Lyon, in a few days by firmness and moderation, restored order at that point and in the adjoining counties. Under his instructions the Union Home Guards of the capital were furnished with arms and instructed in the military drill, and fortifications were constructed to defend the place against attack. He issued a proclamation to the citizens of Cole and adjoining counties, setting forth that he had been appointed by the Commanding General as Commanding Officer of the Post at

Jefferson City, with the view of extending his authority over that section, "in order to preserve the peace and tranquillity of the citizens, and to assist the authorities in the maintenance of the Government and of the Union and the constitutional laws of the country." He also stated that the flight of Governor Jackson from the capital had made it necessary for the Commanding General to appoint a commander for that place, having surveillance over the city and the vicinity, to prevent lawlessness, anarchy, and their consequent evils. Peaceable citizens were to be respected in their persons and property. Slave property would not be interfered with by his command; nor were slaves allowed to enter his lines without written authority from their masters. In about a week after Colonel Boernstein occupied the capital, several officers of the State Government returned, took the oath of allegiance to the United States, and entered upon the discharge of their duties.

Shortly before leaving St. Louis, General Lyon sent out a force consisting of the regiments of Colonels Sigel, Salomon, and B. Gratz Brown, Missouri Volunteers, under the command of Acting Brigadier-General T. W. Sweeney, to the Southwest, to break up any rebel organizations in that direction that might be in process of forming. This force was transported over the southwest branch of the Pacific Railroad to Rolla, which was the terminus of the road. As it was regarded highly important to keep this road open to St. Louis, it was deemed advisable to station Colonel Brown's regiment at Rolla, and to establish a depot of supplies at that point. General Lyon saw that the moment the secessionists found that he was transporting troops and supplies over this road to the Southwest, they would make an effort to destroy it and burn his depot at its terminus. On the arrival of Colonels Sigel and Salomon at Rolla, a train of wagons was at once fitted out to accompany it with supplies, and then they took up the line of march with their regiments for the Southwest, *via* Lebanon, Springfield, and Mount Vernon, to Neosho, where they arrived on the 1st of July. General Sweeney, the commanding officer of the expedition, did not accompany this force. He was detained in St. Louis several days, making arrangements for having the necessary supplies forwarded to his command. On the 23d of June he arrived at Rolla with several companies of Regular infantry, and after establishing a depot at that place proceeded to Springfield, arriving there on the 1st of July, having in the meantime established several posts between that point and Rolla to keep his communication open. He also occupied himself in organizing the Home Guards, as the Union element in the Southwest was largely in the preponderance. But the demands for arms and supplies were so pressing at many other points that he found it impossible to effectively arm and equip the large numbers of loyal men who were anxious to enlist into the service of the Government for the preservation of the Union.

CHAPTER V.

ACTION AT COLE CAMP, MISSOURI.

In the spring of 1861 the secession movement was exciting the attention of all classes throughout the State, but in no section was greater earnestness shown than in Benton County, where the county officers and a majority of the people were on the side of the secessionists. But the leaders of the minority were not to be intimidated, and warmly advocated the cause of the Union in public and private discussions. The secessionists, knowing their strength and being generally of intolerant and domineering dispositions on questions connected with the current political issues, were not inclined to tolerate in their midst those who openly advocated the Union cause, and as early as March ordered A. H. W. Cook and Alexander Mackey, two prominent Union men, who lived near Cole Camp in the northern part of the county, to leave the State. Mr. Cook left immediately and went directly to Springfield, Illinois, and from there to Washington, where he saw Mr. Lincoln and laid before him the exciting state of affairs in Central Missouri. With words of encouragement and advice from Mr. Lincoln, he returned home about the 1st of June with a commission from the President to enroll and organize troops for the Union. He returned home *via* St. Louis, and arrived there in time to participate with General Lyon in the capture of General Frost's brigade of the State Guard at Camp Jackson.

On Colonel Cook's return to Benton County he made his headquarters at Squire John Brill's, about seven miles a little northeast of Cole Camp village, in the midst of a Union German settlement, and commenced at once to enroll and swear into service men for the Union Army. On the 11th of June he gave Captain Henry L. Mitchell a commission from General N. Lyon to act as quartermaster for the troops raised in Benton County. The first week in June he went around quietly to see as many of the Germans and Union Americans as he could on the subject of organizing for their own defence, and got other parties to go around on the same mission, and appointed the 11th of June as the day, and Henry Harm's barn, about four miles north of Cole Camp, as the place, where those friendly to the Union cause were requested to meet for the purpose of perfecting an organization for their own protection and for the defence of the Government.

On the day and at the place appointed, there were not less than six hundred men and a large number of women and children, full of enthusiasm for the Union cause, and five full companies of men were enrolled and sworn into service that day. The next day there was a still larger crowd present, and four more companies of men were enrolled and sworn into service. Company officers were also elected and sworn into service at this place. In his brief address to those present, Colonel Cook informed them that they were not going to be abandoned by the Government, but that it was the duty of all good citizens to assist the Government in the present crisis. As an earnest of their patriotism, the national flag, the Stars and Stripes, was hoisted in their midst, and as its folds were softly wafted with the summer breeze it brought many a tear from the eyes of the older people of the assemblage. About five o'clock that evening the nine companies thus organized left Harm's barn and marched about three miles southeast to the farms of two Germans whose places joined, and encamped in their barns until the 19th of June. The day after arriving at these barns a regimental organization was perfected. Mr. Brill was elected Colonel and Henry Emheiser Lieutenant-Colonel. Colonel Cook, who was acting under orders from General Lyon, directed the movements of the new regiment, and also the movements of some independent companies in the neighborhood. Every spare moment of the new companies was spent in drilling and preparing them for efficient service.

The barns in which the new soldiers were temporarily quartered, were on the north and south sides of the Cole Camp and Duroc road, about three hundred yards apart, and about one hundred yards west of the dwelling-houses near the west end of the lane that divided the farms of the two German farmers, who were staunch Unionists. The Jefferson City and Versailles road, from a northeast direction, intersected the Cole Camp and Duroc road about half-way between Colonel Cook's camp at the two barns and Cole Camp village, which was nearly three miles west. With a perfect understanding between their occupants, the barns were near enough together for the men in them to support each other effectively, in the event of attack. They were framed bullet-proof against an attack made with small-arms, and the one north of the road had a few port-holes to fire from. The nine companies thus organized and also some fragments of other companies not fully organized, were busily employed in drilling and arming and accumulating ammunition and arms until June 16th, when their hostile movements alarmed the secessionists of that section. On the 16th the sheriff of Benton County came alone to Colonel Cook's camp, with a warrant for his arrest and one for the arrest of Captain Mitchell. The sheriff served the warrant on Colonel Cook, but the Colonel of course declined to go along with the officer under the circumstances. He stated to the sheriff, however, that he would make no hostile movements until further orders, unless the secessionists should assume a threatening attitude. After this conference with the sheriff, Colonel Cook allowed his men to go home for three days unless sooner required, except about four hundred men who were kept quartered in the two barns described. In the meanwhile the secessionists were rapidly organizing at Warsaw and other neighboring towns. Six companies of secessionists had been organized in the spring, and had been encamped at Jefferson City for a month or more, and returned to Warsaw about the 1st of June under Colonel Walter S. O'Kane.

On the evening of the 19th of June, a Mr. Tyra, who resided between Warsaw and Cole Camp, and Porter Mitchell, son of Captain Mitchell, came to Colonel Cook's camp and informed him and his officers that the secessionists were marching from Warsaw, under Colonel O'Kane, fully a thousand strong, and would attack him by midnight. There was but little time to prepare to meet the attack. That evening, however, Colonel Cook and his officers held a council to decide what should be done to meet the threatened attack. After careful deliberation, it was decided that the force already stationed at the barns should remain, and couriers were immediately sent out with orders directing the men who had been permitted to go home on the 16th, to return to the camp at the earliest practicable moment—that night if possible. It was thought that as many as three companies could be got in by two o'clock the next morning, which would be as early as it was calculated that the secessionists would arrive from Warsaw to make the attack. To be as well prepared for the threatened attack as possible, Colonel Cook had three pickets put out on the Cole Camp road, two pickets on the Jefferson City and Versailles road, and two pickets on the Duroc road. He also had about half a dozen mounted patrol pickets that passed to and fro from camp to the outside picket stands. With this disposition of guards it was thought that a surprise would be prevented. But not so. About three o'clock on the morning of the 20th, the cavalry and infantry of the secessionists advancing killed one of the pickets on the outside picket stand on the Cole Camp road, and came on and killed both of the pickets at the second station, and approached unobserved to the third picket near the north barn, who fled without discharging his gun, and rushed into the barn leaving the double door wide open.

Meeting with no opposition, the secessionists followed close on at his heels to within a few yards of the barn. When the alarmed picket rushed into the barn, much excited, and waked his comrades from their slumbers and informed them of the presence of the enemy, the secessionists came right up to the door and fired several volleys into them as they were getting up, and the several volleys killed in the barn twenty-one men. The few men in the barn not wounded rallied and returned the fire, and killed six of the leaders of the secessionists, and wounded a number of their men in the ranks. Captain Elsinger, of Colonel Cook's command, who was stationed behind a fence and three corn-cribs with twenty-four men, fired volley after volley into the ranks of the secessionists at short range with good effect. When his ammunition had nearly run out and he saw that all the men not captured and killed had got out of the barn, the captain then retreated towards the timber, and in the direction of the men who had been stationed in the south barn. During the fight he was protected by the fence and cribs, and did not lose any of his men. The 215 men stationed in the south barn did not do any fighting, but were fired into by the secessionists, and had four men killed and two wounded. This loss was due to the Unionists being deceived by the secessionists carrying the national flag at the head of their column and in line. One of the outside Union pickets was captured and killed by this deception, but his comrade, who was expecting the enemy, managed to make his escape. Those killed by the enemy were not shot, but bayoneted. The secession leaders were said to have excused themselves by saying that the discharge of their guns would have aroused the Unionists stationed at the barns to be in readiness. But the killing of the man captured on the picket stand was clearly unjustifiable. About three hundred of the men that Colonel Cook had sent his couriers after the evening before the fight, were marching to his assistance, and had got within two miles of his camp when the attack opened, but they did not understand the situation well enough to come on and attack the enemy from the rear or flank, as they could have done effectively.

At the time that the secessionists came up and killed Colonel Cook's outside picket, the mounted patrols of the Unionists were between that station and the Jefferson City road, and were therefore cut off from the main command. Colonels Cook and Brill and Lieut.-Colonel Emheiser were in the barn north of the Cole Camp road with 170 men, and Captains Henry Miller and Henry Groteheier were in the barn south of the road with 215 men. Just before the close of the fight Captains Miller and Groteheier came out between the two barns with their companies, and formed them in line, but seeing the secessionists in line near the barn north of the road, with the national flag flying, hesitated to fire upon them. It was while they were standing hesitating what to do that the secessionists fired into them, killing and wounding six men, including Captain Miller, who was badly wounded in the neck.

It was now getting daylight, and all Colonel Cook's men not killed and captured retreated east through the lane on the Cole Camp and Duroc road, and when they got through the lane, turned south and entered the wood, a growth of underbrush and young timber, and there rallied and re-formed in line and drove back the cavalry of the secessionists who had undertaken to pursue them. In the fight in the timber the Unionists had one man killed and the secessionists had two or three men killed and wounded.

In the entire operations of the day the Unionists had 36 men and officers killed and 61 men and officers wounded. Captain Mitchell reported that the secessionists lost not less than 100 men and officers in killed and wounded. On the side of the Unionists Colonel Brill was killed and Lieut.-Colonel Emheiser was shot through the neck, and Captain Mitchell had four slight wounds. On the side of the secessionists, Mr. Leach, editor of the *Southwestern Democrat*, at Warsaw, and also five other prominent men from that place, were killed. Captain Mitchell, who returned to the barn that day under a flag of truce, to look after the Union killed and wounded, reported that he saw three wagon-loads of dead secessionists that had been gathered up from the field for interment. Mr. Tyra, who had from patriotic motives hastened to Colonel Cook's camp, and informed him of the approach of the enemy, on his return home that evening met Colonel O'Kane's command on Cole Camp Creek near his house, and they took him and got all the information they could out of him, and then tied him to a tree and shot him to death.

After Colonel Cook left St. Louis he was kept advised of the movements of General Lyon as much as possible, with the view of co-operating with him. There was an understanding between them that, as soon as General Lyon moved up the Missouri River, cautiously feeling his way, Colonel Cook should co-operate with him as far as practicable. General Lyon was to bring arms and equipments for Colonel Cook's men, which he did. About the time of the action of Colonel Cook's force with the enemy near Cole Camp, General Lyon landed his little army a few miles below Boonville, and attacked and drove out of that place Governor Jackson with his State Guard forces. The second day after the action of Cole Camp, Governor Jackson passed through the village in his flight from Boonville to Warsaw, at which place he expected to get reinforcements. Colonel Cook left his men near Cole Camp the evening after the fight, and started out to reach General Lyon, and found him at Boonville, just after he had routed Jackson's forces. He also found that General Lyon was unable to make immediate pursuit of the Governor's demoralized forces for want of transportation. In a few days, however, he hired a sufficient number of citizens' teams to haul his baggage and supplies. Instructions were sent to Captain Mitchell, at Cole Camp, to send to Boonville, as early as practicable, ten teams, for the purpose of bringing along, with General Lyon's army, ammunition, tents, and equipments for Colonel Cook's men, who were acting on the defensive in small detachments in the timbered section around Cole Camp.

As soon as General Lyon collected up sufficient transportation, he started south in pursuit of Governor Jackson, *via* Smithton and Leesville on Grand River, and crossed the Osage River at Osceola, and then continued his march south *via* Humansville to Grand Prairie, twenty miles west of Springfield. At Smithton, two companies of Colonel Cook's force met him to receive supplies and instructions. The General halted his troops at that place a day or two to await reports from his scouts, who, he hoped, would bring him information that would enable him to formulate a definite plan of operations. With the two companies that met him at Smithton, he sent Colonel Cook's arms and equipments to Cole Camp, sixteen miles south. He then resumed the march southwest from Smithton, and Colonel Cook, with his two companies of recruits and train of arms, ammunition, and equipments, marched due south twelve miles, where he was met by Captain Mitchell at the Mackey farm with six hundred men, who were delighted to witness the return of their comrades with substantial assistance. The whole command of eight hundred men marched that evening to Cole Camp, four miles south, where the arms, ammunition, equipments, and tents were issued to the several companies that night. After issuing the arms and supplies to his men, Colonel Cook was instructed by General Lyon to proceed to Warsaw and take possession, if possible, of a large quantity of powder, tent-cloth, arms, and commissary and quartermaster stores that the secessionists had stored there for arming and equipping the State Guard.

In a day or two after arming and equipping his men, Colonel Cook moved out of Cole Camp with about one thousand men, and took up the march for Warsaw, a distance of twenty miles. There were 270 mounted men, and the balance of his command were infantry. A short time before sundown the command reached Mr. Bird's place on Duran's Creek, five miles north of Warsaw, and encamped for the night. The next morning at daybreak the entire command took up the march again for Warsaw. Captain Mitchell and Lieutenant Bacon Montgomery were sent in advance with the 270 mounted men, and entered town just after daylight, and temporarily made prisoners about one hundred men, mostly citizens of Warsaw, but Southern sympathizers. In this movement Colonel Cook captured fifteen hundred one-pound cans of fine rifle powder, fifteen hundred kegs of fine rifle powder, a good many tons of pig- and bar-lead from the Granby mines, seventy stand of small-arms, a steamboat-load of sail- or tent-cloth, a lot of State Guard clothing, four rebel flags, and twelve hundred "false faces" that had been used by the "Border Ruffians" when they went into Kansas to vote to make it a slave State before the War of the Rebellion commenced.

The day after his arrival at Warsaw, the Colonel got instructions from General Lyon at Osceola, to march north to Sedalia and Georgetown for the purpose of breaking up several secession camps in the vicinity of those places. After breaking up the secession camp near Georgetown Colonel Cook received further instructions from General Lyon to proceed to Colonel McGuffin's farm in Johnson County and break up a secession camp there. His expedition into that section was successful beyond his expectations. He captured at McGuffin's farm one thousand secessionists and paroled them on the ground. A lot of stock was also captured, but under instructions from General Lyon it was returned to the owners. Colonel Cook had altogether now, in infantry and mounted troops, not less than seventeen hundred men. Having been informed of the position of the enemy, he came up within three quarters of a mile of Colonel McGuffin's farm, formed his infantry in line in the prairie, on an elevation in plain view of the secession camp, and then sent his cavalry under Captain Mitchell and Lieutenant Bacon Montgomery unobserved around to the rear of the camp. When the cavalry reached the rear of the camp, a dash was made on Colonel McGuffin's house, which was being used as headquarters for recruiting and organizing, and the Colonel and several of his officers were captured, and they surrendered the men, who were encamped about two hundred yards from the house. The secessionists were completely surprised, and this important capture was made without the firing of a gun on either side. All the inferior arms were broken up and those worth any thing were taken off by Colonel Cook to Georgetown and distributed to his men. Immediately after returning to that place he received instructions from General Lyon to join him at Springfield, which he did, taking with him three hundred men, infantry and cavalry. The balance of his command, under Colonel Emheiser, was ordered to Jefferson City. Central Missouri was now almost free of any organized forces of secessionists, and the operations of supreme importance were rapidly shifting to the southwestern part of the State. In that section the storm was gathering and it was evident that in a short time the opposing forces must become engaged in a violent struggle.

CHAPTER VI.

BATTLE OF CARTHAGE.

LEAVING Springfield, the scenes of exciting interest are shifted to the southwest border counties of the State, to the section occupied by Colonel Sigel's forces. On his arrival at Sarcoxie, twenty-two miles northeast of Neosho, on the 28th of June, Colonel Sigel received information that a force of about eight hundred secessionists, under command of Major-General Sterling Price, of the State Guard, were encamped on Pool's Prairie, six miles south of Neosho. He also received information that Governor Jackson, with several divisions of the State Guard under Generals Rains, Parsons, Slack, and Clark, was encamped a few days before at several points between Papinsville and Lamar, some sixty to seventy-five miles north of him, and that the Governor was endeavoring to join his forces with those of Price, with the view of turning upon the Federal forces of General Lyon that had routed him at Boonville, and that were reported to be in pursuit. Finding himself between the secession forces, Colonel Sigel determined to march against the force under General Price, encamped on Pool's Prairie, and if successful, turn and attack the northern forces under Jackson, but before he arrived at Neosho he ascertained that the force encamped on Pool's Prairie had heard of his advance and fled in the direction of Camp Walker, near Maysville, Arkansas, a small town on the

State line and only a few miles from the southwest corner of Missouri. At Granby and Neosho the Unionists turned out and received the Federal troops with much enthusiasm, and marched with them through the streets of those towns. These loyal demonstrations of the Unionists were noted with gall by the secessionists. Those who participated in them enjoyed the triumph of their cause for a very brief season.

On arriving at Neosho, Colonel Sigel despatched a courier to Colonel Salomon, commanding a battalion of the Fifth Regiment Missouri Volunteers *en route* from Mount Vernon, to join him by forced marches. Colonel Salomon arrived at Neosho on the 3d, and on the morning of the 4th of July Colonel Sigel set out with his command to meet the secession forces under Governor Jackson, approaching from the north. Before leaving, however, he detached Captain Joseph Conrad with his company of ninety men of the Third Missouri Volunteers to remain at Neosho, posted in the brick court-house, to watch the movements of the enemy from the south, and to afford protection to the Union citizens of the vicinity. Three miles north of Neosho the State road forks, the right-hand road leading to Carthage, twenty miles north, and the left-hand road leading to Grand Falls, sixteen miles northwest. At the forks of this road Colonel Sigel detached Captain John F. Cramer, with two companies of the Third Missouri Volunteers and with a section of artillery, to proceed to Cedar Creek and Grand Falls for the purpose of intercepting any flying detachments of the enemy that might be marching down the State line road. Colonel Sigel, with his main command proceeded on the direct road towards Carthage, first having instructed Captain Cramer to join him at Dimond Grove, fifteen miles north of Neosho. At Cedar Creek Captain Cramer received orders to rejoin the main column by the nearest practicable route, which he did near Carthage that evening. Captain Joseph Indest's company, however, which had taken the advance, and which marched to Grand Falls, was unable to rejoin Colonel Sigel until the morning of the 5th.

After a hard day's march Colonel Sigel pitched his camp, on the evening of the 4th of July, about a mile southeast of Carthage on the south side of Spring River. A march of twenty-two miles during the day, and the very warm weather had taxed the physical endurance of his troops to such an extent that they were much worn in body and spirits, so that a night's rest was needed to prepare them for another day's severe exertion. The sudden appearance of so large a force of Federal troops as Colonel Sigel had in Southwest Missouri was quite a surprise to the secessionists, and many of those who had taken an active part in the secession movement, and who had advocated the driving out of all Union men, fled in great consternation, and did not stop in their flight until they had reached the command of General Ben. McCulloch at Camp Walker, Arkansas. Since the Government mails had stopped, the people of this section could get no reliable information of recent army operations or of movements of troops. On his arrival at Carthage, Colonel Sigel was informed that Governor Jackson's forces were directly in his front, not more than ten to fifteen miles distant, and that a detachment of secessionists had that day been at the mills near Carthage procuring flour. It was also ascertained that most of this detachment had remained at the mills until the Federal troops came in sight. Several Union citizens visited the Federal camp that evening and gave Colonel Sigel valuable information in regard to the movements and position of the secessionists. The Colonel ordered every thing put in readiness so that he could march out the next morning and attack the Governor's forces. The Federal command was composed of nine companies of the Third Regiment Missouri Volunteers under Lieutenant-Colonel Hassendeubel, 550 men; seven companies of the Fifth Regiment Missouri Volunteers under Colonel Charles E. Salomon, 400 men; and two batteries of light artillery, of four guns each, under Major Frank Backof.

In his flight from Boonville Governor Jackson expected to be pursued by General Lyon, but he had no idea of meeting a Federal force in Southwest Missouri. He had not heard of Colonel Sigel's command in the southwest until he heard of it on the night of the 4th of July directly in his front. His forces consisted of four divisions of the State Guard, with seven pieces of artillery. Most of his men were armed with shot-guns and rifles, and very few wore uniforms. His second division was commanded by Brigadier-General James S. Rains, and had present on the morning of the 5th, 1,203 infantry and artillerymen, 608 cavalry, and three pieces of artillery. Brigadier-General John B. Clark, commanding the third division, reported 365 men and officers present. The fourth division, commanded by Brigadier-General William Y. Slack, consisted of 500 cavalry under Colonel B. A. Rives, and 700 infantry under Colonel John T. Hughes and Major J. C. Thornton. The sixth division, commanded by Brigadier-General Monroe M. Parsons, consisted of Colonel Kelley's regiment and Major Dill's battalion of infantry, Colonel Brown's regiment of cavalry, and a battery of four guns under Captain Guibor; in all about 1,000 men. From official sources it appears that Governor Jackson had, to oppose the Federal force of Colonel Sigel, not less than 4,375 men.

On the evening of the 4th, Colonel Monroe, who had been sent forward by General Parsons with a detachment of ninety-five men to take possession of the mills near Carthage, discovered the Federal encampment near town. He immediately despatched a courier to General Parsons with this information, and after some reconnoitring to obtain more definite information of the strength and intentions of the Federal force, fell back to the main command on Coon Creek, some ten miles north. General Parsons ordered his division out under arms, and had his wagons loaded with baggage with the intention of moving on Carthage that night, but Governor Jackson countermanded the order, and his troops rested until morning. Early on the morning of the 5th, Colonel Sigel marched out of his camp near Carthage, crossed Spring River about a mile north of town, and soon came upon the open prairie. He then advanced slowly and cautiously on the Lamar road in the direction of the position the secessionists were reported to have occupied the evening of the 4th. His baggage trains, under a small escort, followed in his rear at a distance of a mile or so. After marching nine miles north of Carthage and about three miles north of Coon Creek, he came in sight of Governor Jackson's forces drawn up in line of battle on an elevated position gradually rising from the north side of Coon Creek, perhaps one and a half miles distant.

His advance guard, with one piece of artillery, soon became engaged with the advance of the secessionists, which had been thrown forward under Captain J. O. Shelby. Descending the slope on the south side of Coon Creek, in columns of companies and with skirmish line thrown out, Colonel Sigel drove back the Governor's advance, and crossed to the north side of the creek with his whole force, except one company of the Third Missouri Infantry and one piece of artillery, which he posted south of the creek to guard against a movement of the enemy's cavalry toward his rear and baggage. There was only a narrow strip of timber along the creek, perhaps less than one half mile wide, and emerging from it on either side the troops came upon a smooth prairie covered with a luxuriant growth of wild grass. The meadow grounds of a large estate were not more suitable for manœuvring troops than the gentle slopes of this beautiful prairie section. It had, however, the disadvantage of exposing the weakness of a small force, for a scout or spy posted on a given ridge could, by careful observation, estimate very closely the number of troops passing over the next ridge, a distance of two or three miles off.

On coming into the prairie on the north side of Coon Creek, Colonel Sigel formed his troops in line of battle within about half a mile of Governor Jackson's position. Major Henry Bischoff, with a battalion of the Third Regiment, took a position on the extreme left in close column, and next to him on the right there was a battery of four guns. The Fifth Regiment, in two separate battalions, under Colonel Salomon and Lieutenant-Colonel Wolff respectively, formed the Federal centre. On the right of the battalion of the right centre three guns were posted under Captain Essig. And the first battalion of the Third Regiment, under Lieutenant-Colonel Hassendeubel, was posted on the extreme right of the line. After making this disposition of his troops, Colonel Sigel advanced his line some two hundred yards, and then ordered Major Backof to open fire with his seven pieces of artillery against the line of the enemy.

In the line of battle formed by Governor Jackson's forces, General Rains' division occupied the extreme right, General Slack's division the right centre, General Clark's division the left centre, and General Parsons' division the extreme left. Three pieces of artillery came into battery in the centre of Colonel Weightman's brigade, which formed the left of General Rains' division. Four guns of General Parsons' division were also thrown into battery on his right near Colonel Weightman's left. The rebel generals having thus formed their line of battle, promptly responded to the fire of the Federal guns with the four pieces of Parsons' division under Captain Guibor, and in a moment thereafter, with the three guns of General Rains' division under Captain Bledsoe. The batteries of both sides kept up a brisk fire for half an hour. In this artillery contest the Federal guns threw grape and shell a distance of seven hundred yards into the ranks of the secessionists, killing and wounding several men and horses. Seeing that Colonel Sigel had no cavalry, the rebel generals determined to surround him, and for this purpose General Rains led a large mounted force against the Federal left, but beyond the range of small-arms, and Colonel Brown, commanding General Parsons' cavalry, was directed to turn the Federal right.

While these movements were in progress, Colonel Sigel directed the fire of his seven guns against the enemy's right centre, causing the fire from Jackson's artillery to slacken at that point. The flanking movements of the enemy, however, soon made it necessary for the Federal commander to fall back to the south side of the creek and make a new disposition of his troops. His force was too small to extend his line to meet the flank movements of the Southern forces. On retiring to the south side of the creek he directed Lieutenant-Colonel Hassendeubel to take the first battalion of the Third Regiment, a battalion of the Fifth Regiment, and a battery of four guns under Captain Wilkins, and return to the baggage train some distance back, and defend it against the threatened attack of the rebel cavalry. With the other two battalions of the Third and Fifth regiments, and Captain Essig's battery, Colonel Sigel formed a new line south of the creek, and fought and held the Southern infantry and artillery for about two hours, inflicting upon them their heaviest losses. In the meantime the mounted troops of Generals Rains, Parsons, and Slack had gained Colonel Sigel's rear and formed in line at the crossing of Buck Branch, or Bear Creek, thus cutting off his line of retreat.

The situation was now becoming extremely serious, and he found it necessary to turn his attention to this force in his rear, as he would shortly want to cross with his troops and baggage train the creek behind which the enemy were posted. He therefore left his position on Dry Fork and ordered a battalion of infantry and two guns to the left, and a battalion of infantry and two guns to the right of his reserve and baggage train, and directed Colonel Hassendeubel to take three companies of the Third Regiment and form in line in front of the baggage train, which had now turned and was moving south on the road to Carthage. In the retrograde movement from Dry Fork two companies of infantry and a section of artillery formed the Federal rear-guard, and effectually kept the enemy back. Frequent efforts, however, were made by Governor Jackson's forces to overpower this small force, but every time the secessionists came up within range a round or so of grape-shot from the Federal guns, and a volley from the two companies of infantry, checked them and threw them into more or less disorder. By the time the secessionists had rallied and were ready to renew the conflict with strengthened front the Federal guns were limbered up and moving off, supported by the infantry companies.

Having formed the main body of his troops in line in front of the baggage train, Colonel Sigel directed that after firing one volley on coming within easy range, they should charge the enemy and break his line. The movement was executed in a gallant manner, and in a few moments the secessionists were routed, their flight being accompanied by the victorious shouts of the Federal troops. In this conflict the Federal artillery rendered effective service. A storm of grape and canister from each of the pieces engaged swept through the ranks of the secessionists, knocking men and horses headlong and stirring up the greatest confusion. Major Backof directed his officers to keep up the fire from their guns until the enemy passed out of range on the Federal flanks. Now that his front was clear of the enemy, Colonel Sigel crossed the creek with his troops and baggage and retreated unmolested across a four-mile prairie to the heights on the north side of Spring River, which are about a mile and a half north of Carthage. He was closely followed by the secessionists, some of their troops now and then approaching within range of the Federal artillery. In marching over the broad prairie the opposing forces were most of the time in plain view of each other. After crossing to the south side of Buck Branch Colonel Sigel held the ford for some time with his artillery, thus forcing the rebel generals to seek crossings of the stream above and below the regular ford.

It was a very warm day, and the almost continuous right and left oblique marching to cross a stream or gain a position, fatigued the rebel infantry very much, so that their pursuit of the Federal column was not as spirited as it might have been under more favorable conditions. Before reaching the heights of Spring River, General Rains, with the cavalry of his own division and Colonel Rives' regiment of cavalry from General Slack's division, endeavored to flank the retreating Federal troops on the right. Failing in this movement General Rains next attempted to intercept the Federal troops in crossing Spring River. He took up a position in the timber on each side of the Carthage road and waited for the advance of Colonel Sigel. The Federal commander saw the rebel mounted troops making a wide circuitous march through the prairie to gain his front, and hastened to make preparations to break through their line. On nearing the timber he brought up his artillery, supported by two battalions of infantry, and at once opened a brisk fire against the enemy with grape and shell. In less than half an hour he had cleared his front, so that his troops and trains crossed Spring River and marched on to Carthage with little annoyance. He had no sooner driven the rebel mounted troops from his front and flanks by the vigorous use of his artillery and by several rounds of musketry from his infantry than the rebel infantry and artillery began to press upon his rear. To hold this force in check for a short time, he took up a strong position on the north side of Spring River with two battalions of infantry and four pieces of artillery, and the moment the secessionists came within range opened upon them with shell with good effect.

Governor Jackson's forces, however, continued to advance until Colonel Sigel directed his artillery officers to use grape and canister liberally. A sharp conflict now took place between the opposing forces, in which the infantry and artillery of both sides became engaged. The volleys of musketry and the roar of artillery was heard for miles around, and the wounded and dying, men and horses, showed the havoc made by the volleys of musketry and by the storm of shot and shell and grape and canister. Colonel Sigel succeeded in holding the enemy back until his force crossed Spring River and took up the march for Carthage. He had some anxiety about keeping his communication open with Mount Vernon and Springfield, and to this end ordered Lieutenant-Colonel Wolff to take two companies of infantry and a section of artillery under Lieutenant Shaffer and pass Carthage and occupy the heights east of town on the Sarcoxie road. He also ordered Captain Cramer to take two companies of infantry forward and post them so as to guard against a movement of the enemy from the west of town. In the meantime the mounted troops of General Rains, Colonel Rives, and Colonel Brown crossed Spring River at points above and below the ford at which the Federal force crossed, and spreading themselves through the woods, moved forward to surround the Federal troops in town.

It was nearly five o'clock when Colonel Sigel reached Carthage, and he was desirous of giving his troops a little rest, as they had already marched eighteen miles that day, and had been almost constantly engaged with the enemy since nine o'clock in the morning without food, and exposed to the burning rays of a midsummer sun. His tired men had scarcely thrown themselves upon the ground to snatch a few moments' rest, when the secessionists approached from several points and opened fire upon his outposts. The Federal troops sprang to arms, and taking shelter behind buildings and fences, returned the fire with vigor and destructive effects. When he came to a halt, Colonel Sigel had taken the precaution to have his batteries posted to bear upon the approaches to town, and the moment after the rebels renewed the attack the Federal guns were pouring a stream of grape and canister into their exposed ranks from every quarter. In a short time the rapid and well-directed fire of the Federal infantry and artillery drove the rebels back into the woods that came near town on the north and west.

During the short respite that followed this sharp conflict in town, Colonel Sigel resumed the march on the road to Sarcoxie and Mount Vernon. His rear-guard was attacked just as it was leaving town, by the rebel forces that came pouring in from different directions, intending to surround the Federal troops. On the heights a mile southeast of town he got another good position, from which he used his artillery to good advantage in throwing grape-shot and shells into the ranks of the enemy, checking their advance. But his guns had fired only a few rounds from this position, when the batteries of General Parsons' divisions and Colonel Weightman's brigade were brought forward, posted on a ridge, and responded energetically for a short time. While the batteries of both sides were thus engaged, the infantry of the divisions of Generals Slack, Parsons, and Clark, and of Weightman's brigade of Rains' division, were pushed forward under shelter of a skirt of woods with the intention of flanking the Federal troops. At the same time part of the rebel cavalry moved forward and engaged the skirmishers on the Federal flanks, but were effectually kept back by the Federal infantry and artillery.

Night was now drawing near, and knowing that he had not a sufficient force to fight a pitched battle with the rebel forces with a probability of success, Colonel Sigel again retreated in the direction of Mount Vernon, pursued by the cavalry of Generals Parsons' and Slack's divisions. To free his rear-guard from the annoyance of this pursuing force, he halted again and took up a position about two and a half miles southeast of Carthage, where the Sarcoxie road passes into the woods, and directed his artillerists to unlimber their guns and throw a few rounds of shot and shells at such bodies of the enemy as were still in sight. It was now getting dark; he saw no more of the secessionists, and his troops moved on unmolested to Sarcoxie, a distance of twelve miles, that night. Night was probably as welcome to the rebel as to the Federal troops, for most of them, including even most of those of the mounted force, made no effort to continue the fight after Colonel Sigel passed Carthage. In the several artillery contests of the day, and in the manœuvring of troops, the secessionists were placed to some disadvantage. They were obliged in every instance to bring their guns into battery in the face of a destructive fire from the Federal guns. While engaging the enemy with one battery, Colonel Sigel had his other battery take up a position on his line of retreat, ready to open fire the moment his engaged battery commenced to withdraw from action. He also used his batteries with equal advantage in protecting his flanks, rear, and front, whereas the secessionists could bring their batteries into action only when the Federal troops made a stand. Several times during the day the Federal batteries were masked, and every time the secessionists came within easy range threw into their ranks a terrific shower of grape and canister, killing and wounding men and horses on every hand.

The casualties on the Federal side during the day were thirteen men killed and thirty-one wounded. In the four divisions of Governor Jackson's forces the casualties were seventy-four men killed and wounded.

This battle of Carthage, as it was called, created intense excitement throughout Western Missouri. All day long the sound of the thundering artillery was heard by people living within a radius of twenty to twenty-five miles. From the exaggerated accounts of the battle, it was generally believed in that section that the casualties on both sides were much greater than they actually were.

Colonel Sigel arrived at Sarcoxie about midnight, and encamped until the next morning to rest his men, and then he resumed the march to Mount Vernon and from thence to Springfield. After giving up the pursuit, Governor Jackson's forces went into camp in and around Carthage, and the next day marched to Neosho, where they met General Ben. McCulloch's command, and seventeen hundred State Guard troops under General Sterling Price. There was great rejoicing among the secessionists because they had successfully cut their way through the Federal line and joined their friends coming up from the south. Before leaving Fort Smith on the last of June, General McCulloch had heard of Governor Jackson's flight from Jefferson City, his defeat at Boonville by General Lyon, and sent a messenger to him advising him to retreat south with his forces, and offering to form a junction with him near the State line in Southwest Missouri for the purpose of checking the Federal advance. On his arrival at Camp Walker, seven miles south of the southwest corner of Missouri, General McCulloch was informed that there was great danger of Governor Jackson being cut off by a Federal column that had marched into Southwest Missouri *via* Rolla and Springfield. He had already ordered the concentration of upwards of five thousand Confederate troops in Northwestern Arkansas in anticipation of the advance of the Federal troops. He saw that if he rendered Governor Jackson assistance, no time could be lost in moving forward to join him. He saw Generals Pearce and Price who were encamped in the vicinity of Camp Walker and Cowskin Prairie with the Arkansas and Missouri State troops, and arranged to march at once to the relief of Governor Jackson. He took three thousand mounted men of his own command, and on crossing the line into Missouri was joined by General Price with seventeen hundred mounted men. With this force he pushed forward on a forced march, and on the night of the 4th of July encamped on Buffalo Creek twelve miles southwest of Neosho. He ascertained that night from secessionists who had fled from Neosho in the morning, that Colonel Sigel had been there and marched north that day, leaving there a detachment of about one hundred men as a garrison. Secessionists who had fled from Neosho, and who were perfectly familiar with the roads leading into town, were at hand ready to act as guides.

On the morning of the 5th of July, having given his troops needed rest, General McCulloch despatched two columns on different roads to capture the Federal detachment at Neosho. Major McIntosh, with five companies of cavalry, led one column, and Colonel Churchill, with six companies of his own regiment of Arkansas Mounted Riflemen, led the other. It was arranged that the two columns should reach Neosho at the same time. Soon after Colonel Sigel marched out with his main command, Captain Conrad, commanding the Federal detachment left at Neosho, noticed that the secessionists who remained there carried in their expressions signs of suppressed satisfaction, and acted as if some mysterious movement with which they sympathized was on foot. They showed in their general demeanor that they had confidence in the near approach of the Confederate forces. Captain Conrad, being without cavalry, had no means of sending out a scout to ascertain if the enemy were in the vicinity. He could easily enough, in a short time, have pressed a sufficient number of horses into the service from the secessionists to have mounted his company, but as there had not up to that time been a precedent of the kind by Federal officers serving in Missouri, he did not feel like taking upon himself the responsibility of adopting such a measure. To guard against a surprise, however, he sent out patrols every half hour, day and night, and stationed extra sentinels at different points about town.

Every thing passed off quietly enough on the 4th and also on the 5th up to about one o'clock, when the enemy came pouring into town from the south and west, upwards of a thousand strong, under Major McIntosh and Colonel Churchill, of the Arkansas Mounted Riflemen. Major McIntosh, with his column, arrived near town a short time before Colonel Churchill, and fearing that the Federal troops would get notice of his presence and endeavor to escape, determined to make the attack without waiting for Colonel Churchill. He ordered Captain Carroll to take his company of cavalry and make a detour and come into town on the road the Federal troops would probably take if they found an opportunity to retreat. He dismounted the four companies of Mounted Riflemen about a quarter of a mile from town, and marched them by platoons at double-quick time to within two hundred yards of the court-house, where the Federal company were posted, and halting, sent forward an *aide* to demand of the Federal commander the surrender of his force, giving him ten minutes to decide. Finding that he was surrounded by an overwhelming force, and that he could not probably hold his position more than a few hours, Captain Conrad, after a few moments' consultation with his officers, surrendered to Major McIntosh. While the terms of surrender were being arranged, Colonel

Churchill came up with his six companies of well-equipped men.

After the Federal company surrendered and were disarmed, they were placed in the court-house, where they remained until the 8th. They were then released, the officers on their parole of honor, and the enlisted men on their oaths, not to serve any more against the Southern Confederacy during the war. The captain and his men were treated in a friendly way and with proper consideration by the officers of both the Missouri and Arkansas troops, but by their enlisted men and the secession citizens in the most insulting and brutal manner. The Federal company were all Germans from St. Louis, and as the Germans throughout the State had espoused the Union cause almost to a man, and were among the first to enlist into the Union regiments organized, the secession papers were unsparing in their abuse of them, and had aroused among the secessionists an intensely bitter feeling against them. This bitter feeling was aroused to such a pitch in the secessionists of Neosho and vicinity, that they threatened to kill Captain Conrad and his men in the streets, in consequence of which, when they left town on the evening of the 8th, they were furnished with an escort of thirty men, under Captain Boone, to accompany them four or five miles from camp. They now marched day and night, with short intervals for rest, and reached Springfield, a distance of eighty miles, in less than two days and a half, suffering much from fatigue, heat and thirst, and want of food. Their canteens and haversacks had been taken from them by the rebel troops, and they were not allowed to take any rations from the commissary supplies they had on hand when captured.

After General McCulloch had effected a junction with Governor Jackson, and had had a conference with him and his generals in regard to the line of action to be pursued in the immediate future, he returned with his command to Camp Jackson, near Maysville, Arkansas, and employed his time in drilling his troops and preparing them to take the field against the Federal forces concentrating at Springfield under General Lyon. As the Missouri forces were in no condition to take the field immediately, Governor Jackson marched them, except part of General Rains' division, to Cowskin Prairie, in the southwest corner of the State, a few miles from General McCulloch's camp, for the purpose of effecting a better organization of them. Though McCulloch and Jackson had with their forces combined upwards of twelve thousand men, they were convinced, since the engagement with Colonel Sigel, that their troops could not be made very effective for active operations against well-disciplined troops until a more thorough organization took place. The fact that Colonel Sigel had been able with one thousand men to cut his way through and keep at bay a force nearly five times as large as his own, had the effect of damping the military ardor of many of those who had been thirsting for the blood of Northern soldiers.

Now that the rebel forces occupied Southwest Missouri, the Union men deemed it safest to fly to the woods and hills for concealment. Instead of respecting the rights of property of all classes, as Colonel Sigel's troops had done, the rebel troops took all the serviceable horses they could find belonging to Union citizens. In many cases secessionists accompanied the rebel soldiers to point out their Union neighbors whose property was to be taken. Here and there a wife or mother, in the absence of husband or sons, stood at the gate to plead with armed and hostile men to spare the property of which the family had become possessed after many years of toil, hardships, and sacrifices. Thus was introduced a phase of war of which few, if any, had ever dreamed. But now that its desolating effects were beginning to be felt, the property of Union citizens was seized and appropriated for the use of the rebel army, in spite of the tears of women and children. Men who, a few days before, were pursuing their peaceful occupations on the farm, at the carpenter's bench, or in the blacksmith's shop, fled from their fields and shops and concealed themselves as well as they could in the woods and hills, and were fed clandestinely by their families. The bloody threats of the secessionists, and their acting as informers against Unionists, produced a feeling of insecurity among Union men, so that, in seeking their safety, they left their scythes in half-cut swaths, their ploughs in mid-furrows, and their work in unfinished condition.

CHAPTER VII.

BATTLE OF WILSON CREEK.

WHEN we turned to notice the operations of the Southwest Expedition under General Sweeney, General Lyon was still at Boonville preparing to move south with his command towards Springfield. He had intended to leave Boonville on the 26th of June, but, owing to the difficulty of procuring transportation for his necessary supplies and baggage, he was detained until July 3d. He was also busily engaged in designating troops and officers to occupy the most important towns along the Missouri River, and in getting boats properly armed to patrol that river to prevent the boats navigating it being used for transporting supplies and hostile troops to the secessionists. It was no small task to provide the necessary supplies and equipments for his little army which was about to take the field, and as he had no regular quartermasters or commissaries, nor any officers in his command familiar with the duties of the officers of those departments, he was obliged to give his personal attention to a great many small things which should have been looked after by staff officers, had proper ones been detailed and assigned to duty with him. Intelligent men taken from civil life, without any military experience, required some instructions before they could make out proper requisitions for supplies, and before they could issue the supplies obtained, according to the prescribed forms of the Army Regulations.

General Lyon was informed of the arrival at Fort Smith, Arkansas, of General Ben McCulloch on the 25th of May, 1861, with instructions from the Confederate authorities to organize a strong force at that point of troops from Louisiana, Texas, and Arkansas, for the purpose of marching into Southwest Missouri to co-operate with the secession forces under Governor Jackson. The Federal general also heard of the encampment of a body of rebel troops in Northwestern Arkansas, near Maysville, under General Pearce, and he knew, from current reports, that it was the intention of the rebel leaders, after a junction of their forces, to march to Springfield, and, if practicable, from thence to the Missouri River. Knowing that the rebel leaders were doing every thing possible towards organizing and concentrating their forces for the purpose of assuming the offensive, he saw that, if the cause of the Government was to be sustained in the Southwest, and Union citizens protected, that he should be at Springfield at the earliest practicable moment. He directed Colonel Harding, commanding the St. Louis Arsenal, to forward to Springfield, *via* Rolla, the terminus of the southwest branch of the Pacific Railroad, the necessary supplies for the troops to be concentrated at Springfield. And, having given further instructions in regard to keeping his communication open between St. Louis and Springfield, he took up the line of march for the Southwest on the morning of the 3d of July. On leaving Boonville his command consisted of three hundred Regular troops, infantry and artillery, the First Regiment Missouri Volunteers, two companies of the Second Regiment Missouri Volunteers, the First Regiment Iowa Volunteers—in all, aggregating about two thousand four hundred men. He had also ordered Major Sturgis, at Fort Leavenworth, Kansas, to join him at Osceola, Missouri, with his command of four companies of the First United States Cavalry, and the First and

Second Regiments Kansas Volunteers, amounting to two thousand two hundred men.

At Smithton, eight miles east of Sedalia, he made a brief halt to turn over to Colonel Cook's command, that had been recently organized near Cole Camp, such arms and ammunition as could be spared. He then resumed the march to the Southwest, to Leesville, and from thence to Osceola, where he crossed the Osage River. On account of high waters in the Grand and Osage rivers, he was obliged to ferry his troops and trains across them, thus causing a delay of four days. The column under Major Sturgis, marching down the western border counties of Missouri from Fort Leavenworth, experienced the same difficulty in crossing the Osage River, thus preventing it from co-operating with Colonel Sigel in the engagements near Carthage on July 5th. Colonel Sigel had endeavored to communicate with the column of Major Sturgis before attacking Governor Jackson's forces, but of the several scouts which he sent out for that purpose, only one returned, and he brought no reliable information of the whereabouts or movements of General Lyon or Major Sturgis.

From Osceola General Lyon marched *via* Humansville to Grand Prairie, about fifteen miles west of Springfield, where his troops went into camp for a few days. In his anxiety to learn the situation of affairs in the Southwest, he left his command and with his escort rode into Springfield. He realized that the enemy, with forces vastly superior to his own, were directly in his front, and he was grievously disappointed to find that the supplies which he had ordered from St. Louis to Springfield, before leaving Boonville, had not arrived. It was his intention to move against the enemy at once, but now he could not undertake an advance immediately with a reasonable prospect of success. His troops had made long marches, done much effective service, and suffered much from heat and fatigue. Some of his soldiers were without shoes, and their clothing was getting dilapidated. They were poorly fed and incompletely supplied with tents. They had been in service several months and had not yet received any pay. The terms of service of many of the three months' volunteers would soon expire, and but few of them could be induced to re-enlist until they received their pay and clothing from the Government. This state of things in the face of the enemy caused General Lyon painful anxiety. A considerable majority of the people of that section were in favor of the Union, and he thought that the Government should furnish him troops and supplies to enable him to maintain his position. Colonel Chester Harding, who had been charged with forwarding his supplies from St. Louis, saw his requisitions filled and the supplies shipped from St. Louis. But on account of the incompetency of the receiving and forwarding officer at Rolla, the terminus of the railroad, and the difficulty of hiring sufficient transportation at that point, the supplies lay there a week or so, instead of being promptly sent on to Springfield. Thus it seemed that every thing conspired against him, and to add to his already numerous embarrassments, General Scott ordered five companies of his Regular troops to Washington. He thought that the West was being needlessly sacrificed by the Washington authorities, and he repeatedly urged that reinforcements be sent to him with the least possible delay, as the forces of Generals Price and McCulloch were collecting directly in his front, estimated at twenty-five thousand strong.

By the 11th of July the column under Major Sturgis had arrived, and all General Lyon's troops, numbering about seven thousand men, were encamped in the vicinity of Springfield. General Sweeney, who had been at Springfield and Mount Vernon for several weeks, was unable to make effective reconnoissances to the south and southwest, on account of having no mounted troops in his command. He kept himself informed, however, of the most important movements of the enemy by individual scouts and by the reports brought in by Union people fleeing before the rebel forces. The Federal commander having no cavalry at his disposal for scouting purposes, was placed at a serious disadvantage, for mounted detachments of rebel troops came almost in sight of his camp and committed depredations on the property of Union citizens without the fear of punishment. On his arrival at Springfield General Lyon saw that he could not get along without cavalry, and at once set to work and soon organized several battalions of Home Guards for scouting purposes and to act in conjunction with the Regular cavalry under Major Sturgis in protecting his flanks. The scarcity of arms and clothing alone prevented him from calling into active service several thousand Home Guards, for large numbers of Union men were anxious to enlist to stay the rebel advance, which was daily becoming more threatening.

On the 19th of July, General Lyon received information which he deemed reliable, that a rebel force of five hundred men were at Forsyth, forty-five miles south of Springfield, collecting stock, supplies, clothing, provision, etc., for the rebel army. He determined to break up the rebel encampment and if possible capture the supplies which had been collected, and for this purpose, directed General Sweeney to take one thousand five hundred men, consisting of the Second Kansas Volunteers, under Colonels Mitchell and Blair, a battalion of five hundred men of the First Iowa under Lieutenant-Colonel Merritt, one section of Totten's battery and two companies of Regular cavalry under Captain Stanley, and proceed to Forsyth with as little delay as practicable and attack the enemy. General Sweeney pushed forward with his command on a forced march, and reached Forsyth on the evening of the 22d of July. The latter half of his line of march was over a rough and broken region of the White River Mountains and Bald Knobs, so that the enemy were not likely to receive sufficient timely notice of his advance to make much preparations to meet it. The enemy had posted a mounted picket guard of three men about three miles north of town. Two of the men were captured by a company of Kansas mounted Rangers which General Sweeney had placed in the advance of his column. One of the rebel pickets, however, escaped and reached town and gave the alarm of the Federal approach in time to enable the enemy to form in line. But the dust had scarcely fallen to the ground, which was upraised by his horses feet, before Captain Stanley with his Regular cavalry came dashing along in rapid pursuit. One of the rebel prisoners having stated that there were one thousand men in the rebel encampment, General Sweeney felt some anxiety for Captain Stanley, and sent to him an order to hold the enemy in check until the artillery and infantry could come up. The infantry moved forward for several miles at double quick time. In the meantime Captain Stanley had engaged the enemy who had formed to receive him. After a few moments of sharp conflict between the opposing forces, the rebels fled to the hills and surrounding thickets, keeping up a scattering fire as they retreated. They soon commenced, however, to collect in considerable numbers under cover of the woods and bushes on the hills to the left of town, with the apparent intention of making a stand. By the time they had rallied, and were about to resume the fight, General Sweeney came up with his infantry and artillery.

The little town of Forsyth was on the east side of Swan Creek and on the north bank of White River, about half a mile from the junction of those streams. It was also at the foot of a high hill or mountain that lay to the north and east. To get into town on the Springfield road, Swan Creek had first to be crossed, and as there was only one crossing near town the rebels made an effort to hold it. But when General Sweeney came up he deployed his infantry through the woods and ordered his section of artillery to take up a position from which, after throwing a few rounds of shells and canister into the rebel ranks, the enemy were dislodged and sent flying over the hills and through the woods in much confusion, leaving their supplies of provisions, clothing, arms, and ammunition, which were stored in the Court house, to fall into the hands of the Federal troops.

On the Federal side, there were two men wounded, and four horses killed, one of them from under Captain Stanley. On the rebel side eight to ten men were reported killed and wounded, and among them Captain Jackson, who had taken an active part in the skirmish. The captured arms and ammunition were distributed among the Union Home Guards of the county, and the clothing and provisions among the Federal troops of the expedition. General Sweeney remained in Forsyth until noon of the 23d, looking after the captured property, and then returned to Springfield, arriving there in the afternoon of the 25th. Though the expedition accomplished its purpose, it entailed severe hardships upon the infantry who marched ninety miles in less than five days, over a rough, broken, hilly country. This action at Forsyth was the first skirmish in which the volunteer soldiers had participated, and they displayed commendable coolness and courage.

Military operations were progressing rapidly, and Southwest Missouri was getting to be a vast military camp. To the observer of current events it was evident that the opposing armies could not long occupy that section without a great conflict taking place between them. In the midst of continued embarrassments, General Lyon endeavored to conduct the movements of his troops so as not to needlessly waste their strength. His subsistence supplies were running short, and he found it necessary to draw on the resources of the country he was occupying. The Home Guards, which he had organized, were usefully employed in procuring supplies for his troops, and scouting the country and watching the movements of the enemy. Captain Clark Wright, commanding a company of Dade County Mounted Home Guards, was stationed at Greenfield, forty-five miles northwest of Springfield. The Union citizens were willing to sell their grain to the Government, and Captain Wright took his men into the fields and with thrashing machines thrashed out large quantities of wheat, conveyed it to the mills in the vicinity, and had it ground into flour. He then procured material and made sacks and sacked the flour and sent it in a train to General Lyon. He also kept out scouting parties to the southwest as far in the direction of the rebel camp as practicable; sent a man into General Rains' camp, and by his earnestness and activity in reporting to General Lyon the movements of the enemy, rendered invaluable service to the Federal cause. The moment that General McCulloch changed his position from Bentonville, Arkansas, to Cassville, Missouri, information was conveyed to Captain Wright, who in turn immediately advised General Lyon. About the same time Captain Wright's scouting parties returned and reported to him that the forces of General Price, which had been encamped for several weeks on Cowskin Prairie, in the southwest corner of Missouri, had broken camp and were moving in a northeast direction, and that advance detachments of cavalry had already reached Neosho, Sarcoxie, and Carthage. As this movement of the enemy threatened to cut him off from the main army at Springfield, Captain Wright sent a dispatch by a special courier to General Lyon setting forth that if the position at Greenfield was to be maintained and the supplies which he had accumulated secured for the army,

Yours truly
N. Lyon

reinforcements should be sent to him immediately. General Lyon at once directed Major Sturgis, commanding First Brigade, to send five companies of the First Missouri Volunteers and two companies of the Regular cavalry, to the support of Captain Wright at Greenfield. Colonel Deitzler, commanding First Kansas Volunteers, was also directed to send four companies of his regiment to Greenfield to co-operate with the force detached from the First Brigade. The commanding officers of the detachments were instructed to attack the enemy vigorously if they had advanced to the vicinity of Greenfield and were not found in too strong force. But if found too strong, then the Federal force should retire to Springfield *via* Chesapeake, bringing along Captain Wright's command and the supplies which he had collected.

The closing days of July found General Lyon filled with anxiety for the safety of his little army and the success of the Union cause in the Southwest. He was still obliged to issue to his troops less than half the regular allowance of several substantial articles of the army ration; a considerable number of his soldiers were yet without shoes; others, whose terms of service had just expired, were claiming their discharges, and the defeat of the Union army at the battle of Bull Run, Virginia, had a depressing effect upon the minds of his men and upon the zeal of the Union citizens of that section; while on the other hand, the news of the rebel victory strengthened the cause of the secessionists, and made many of those who had hitherto been quiet and undemonstrative, assume attitudes of boldness and defiance towards the Government. The reinforcements which the Federal general was expecting, were sent from St. Louis to other threatened points; the rebel generals were concentrating their available forces at Cassville, fifty-five miles southwest of Springfield, and preparing to attack him in a few days, and the prospects of the immediate future were gloomy enough.

General Lyon, having obtained reliable information that Generals Price and McCulloch had planned as soon as their forces formed a junction to move against him in two columns, one under McCulloch to advance upon the Cassville road from the southwest, and the other under Price upon the Neosho and Springfield road from the west, determined not to await the combined attack of the rebel forces, but to march at once against the stronger column under McCulloch, advancing on the Cassville road, and strike it about twenty-five miles southwest of Springfield; and if successful in routing it, turn and attack the force advancing from the west under Price. He knew that Price and McCulloch had upwards of eight thousand mounted troops, and he was averse to the idea of being surrounded by them, as they could cut off such subsistence supplies and forage as he had been getting from the surrounding country, and upon which his army was almost entirely dependent.

His scouts having reported that the main column of the rebel army was advancing upon the Cassville road, General Lyon ordered that every thing be put in readiness for battle, and marched out of Springfield on the morning of the first of August, with all the troops that could be spared from that point, and encamped that evening on Wilson Creek, ten miles southwest of Springfield on the Cassville road, where he was joined by Major Sturgis' brigade, which had been occupying a position near Little York, about four miles west of the crossing of Wilson Creek, for some ten days. He also ordered the detachments which had been sent to Greenfield for flour, and to support Captain Wright's command, to join him at the earliest practicable moment. On the 2d he marched about six miles southwest on the Cassville road. His advance was composed of four companies of Regular infantry, under Captain Frederick Steele, Second infantry, and Captain Totten's battery. His command marched along leisurely until nine o'clock, when his advance guard met a detachment of the enemy's cavalry, which had been thrown forward by General Rains, whose position was about three miles back, at McCulla's store, where there was an excellent spring and good grounds for camping purposes. Captain Steele immediately deployed two companies of his battalion as skirmishers, one to the left of the road and one to the right, while a section of Totten's battery came into position in the road and threw a shell towards the rebel cavalry, after which they rapidly fell back on the main road. Captain Steele's skirmishers were called in, and the Federal forces moved forward again a distance of about two miles, when the rebel scouts fired several shots at the Federal cavalry flankers on the left of the road. General Lyon directed Captain Steele to again deploy two companies of his battalion to the right and left of the road as skirmishers and flankers as before. It was now deemed advisable to move cautiously, as it was not known but that the rebel generals were endeavoring to draw the Federal commander into an ambuscade. The rough and broken condition of the country seemed to favor such a scheme. A forward movement of the Federal column was again ordered, and after advancing about a mile and a half the rebel cavalry in considerable force were discovered some distance in front, where the road ascended the hill, and it was evident that they intended to contest the further advance of the Federal army. At the point now reached by the Federal advance, and for nearly a mile beyond, the road passed through a narrow valley, the low hills on the south side of which, instead of being continuous, were broken, forming a succession of spurs, which were clothed with a meagre growth of scrubby oaks with heavy foliage. A company of Regular infantry was deployed as skirmishers along the ridge of the spur nearest the enemy's position. In the rear of this company, and on the next spur behind the foremost one occupied, was posted another company of infantry to act as a reserve. To the right of the road a company of mounted rifles was deployed to skirmish through a cornfield, with a company of infantry posted a short distance in the rear as a reserve.

A troop of Regular cavalry under Captain D. S. Stanley was also formed on the right of the road some forty yards in the rear of the reserve. Captain Steele was directed to hold his position, if practicable, until the intentions of the enemy were more fully developed. In the event, however, of being too hotly pressed, he was ordered to retire, keeping the enemy in check. It was now getting late in the afternoon, and General Lyon, with the remainder of his army, fell back about one mile and a half to Hayden's farm, so as to encamp near water. General Rains, who commanded the advance division of Price's wing of the rebel army, as soon as he received information of the Federal advance, moved out with six hundred cavalry to meet it. Shortly after arriving at the front he reconnoitred the Federal position, and, observing the retrograde movement of the main body of General Lyon's troops, concluded that they were retreating. He therefore dismounted part of his command to act as sharp-shooters, and about five o'clock commenced an attack on the left of Captain Steele's position above described. His force was repulsed in the first attack upon the Federal left, but strengthening his right and centre he advanced again to the attack, and with such vigor that the Federal skirmishers, occupying the ridge of the spur nearest his position, were obliged to retreat upon the reserve, after which skirmishers and reserve fell back into the road, where Captain Steele came to their support with two companies of Regular infantry. Captain Stanley, who had up to this time occupied a position on the right of the road, was now directed to move his troop of cavalry to a position on a commanding spur on the Federal left and front, to prevent the enemy from turning Captain Steele's left flank. Captain Steele, having formed his infantry in line, advanced upon and drove back the enemy, while Captain Stanley charged down from the heights on the left with his cavalry, and cut through the rebel lines. The conflict at this point was quite severe and exciting, and for a few moments hand to hand, when the rebels were forced to retreat, leaving about two hundred horses tied in a ravine. Just as Captain Steele was on the point of bringing away these horses he received an order from General Lyon to retire. Supposing that a strong force of the enemy were concealed from his view by heavy foliage and an intervening ridge, and were threatening to cut him off, the order to retire was immediately obeyed, thus yielding up a trophy which had been fairly won.

General Rains, having rallied his men, and observing the retreat of Captain Steele, followed him up with a brigade of cavalry to within a quarter of a mile of General Lyon's line of battle. Captain Totten's battery was quickly brought forward, and opened fire upon them with shells, and after a few rounds dispersed them. When the shells came tearing through their ranks, and exploding in rapid succession, the greater portion of General Rains' force became panic-stricken, and fled in the greatest confusion, and continued their flight until they came near the outposts of the main army encamped on Crane Creek, some ten miles back. This ended the skirmish known as Dug Springs, and as the enemy retreated out of sight, General Lyon went into camp for the night, taking the precaution to post strong picket-guards on all the roads and paths leading to his camp.

The casualties on the Federal side were four killed and six wounded. On the Confederate side the losses were reported to be somewhat greater.

On the next day, August 3d, General Lyon advanced to McCulla's store, where General Rains had had his headquarters on the 2d. This place is twenty-four miles southwest of Springfield, on the Cassville road, in a rather narrow hollow in the midst of thick timber. Captain Samuel McCulla, one of the owners of the property, was an officer in the Union Home Guards with General Lyon, and knew every by-road and path in that section. General Lyon was now within six or seven miles of McCulloch's division, encamped on Crane Creek. Knowing the nearness of General Lyon, and supposing that he intended to attack the rebel army at Crane Creek, the rebel generals immediately commenced to concentrate their troops and artillery at that point. For convenience of camping and obtaining subsistence and forage, the several divisions of the rebel army were encamped within ten to fifteen miles of each other when the concentration commenced.

On the 3d of August the combined forces from Missouri, Louisiana, Arkansas, and Texas were concentrated near Crane Creek, under Generals Price, McCulloch, and Pearce, and preparations made to advance at once against General Lyon. General McCulloch did not impress the Missouri generals as being very zealous in his co-operation. It was thought by them that his actions suggested a bid for supreme command of the combined forces. He was a brigadier-general in the Confederate service, while Price was a major-general of the Missouri State forces, an older man of wider experience. Price was a brigadier-general in the Mexican war, when McCulloch was only a captain. But, that there might be no conflict of authority, or want of co-operation between the different forces, General Price, on Sunday, August 4th, on his own motion, turned over the Missouri forces, for the time being, to General McCulloch, who at once assumed command of the combined armies, and issued an order of march.

General Lyon remained at McCulla's farm until the 4th, when, after a council of the principal officers of his command, in which the situation was fully discussed, he decided to return to Springfield with his army. It was deemed impracticable to advance further for want of supplies; besides, by doing so, he thought that he would expose the small force left at Springfield to capture by the enemy, who were at that moment throwing forward a mounted force on the Neosho and Springfield road, a few miles to the north of him, and threatening to cut him off. An order was therefore given to fall back, and on the evening of the 5th the troops arrived at Springfield, except a force of about two thousand men under Major Sturgis, commanding First Brigade, and Lieutenant-Colonel Andrews, First Missouri Volunteers, which encamped four miles southwest of the city.

The rebel generals, having made preparations to attack General Lyon at McCulla's farm, did not throw forward their cavalry to annoy him in his retreat, as was anticipated. But, the day after his arrival at Springfield, the advance guard of the rebel cavalry encamped at Wilson Creek, and, the day following, the main army, consisting of infantry and artillery, came up. General Lyon made some preparations to attack this advance cavalry division the first night after its arrival at Wilson Creek, and orders were issued for the advance of a portion of the troops under Major Sturgis and Colonel Andrews, which were still encamped four miles southwest of the city, but owing to the difficulty of getting definite and reliable information in regard to the strength and position of the enemy until the night was far spent, the order was countermanded, and Major Sturgis and Colonel Andrews were directed to march their commands to Springfield next day and take position in the line of defences. The combined rebel armies were now at Wilson Creek, only ten miles distant; General Lyon knew that he was on the verge of a great conflict, and he did not take a very hopeful view of the situation. His appeals for assistance had not been responded to. He thought, however, that he might extricate his little army by retreating towards Rolla. But the thought pressed upon his mind: should he give up the Southwest without a desperate struggle? Hundreds of Union people, fleeing before the rebel army, were daily arriving in Springfield, greatly excited, and bringing along their household effects, cattle, horses, etc. These people gave exciting accounts of the vastness of the rebel army. Some of those who had seen the Southern troops pass certain points, declared that it took them nearly all day, and that they claimed to have from thirty to forty thousand men. The Southern soldiers, as they marched along, probably with the view of producing an overawing effect, gave to the citizens an exaggerated account of the strength of the combined Southern forces.

The time had now arrived when General Lyon saw that he must either fight or retreat at once, and, if he decided to fight, the further question was presented to him: should he await the attack of the enemy, or should he march out and attack the enemy in their position? After debating the matter in his mind, with some conflicting thoughts, he determined to march against the enemy. But on the evening of the 8th of August, before issuing orders for the movement of his troops, he called a council of war, composed of the principal officers of his command, and in the presence of the council he said: "Gentlemen, there is no prospect of our being reinforced at this point; our supply of provisions is running short; there is a superior force of the enemy in front, and it is reported that Hardee is marching with nine thousand men to cut our line of communication. It is evident that we must retreat. The question arises, what is the best method of doing it? Shall we endeavor to retreat without giving the enemy battle beforehand, and running the risk of having to fight every inch along our line of retreat? Or, shall we attack him in his position and endeavor to hurt him so that he cannot follow? I am decidedly in favor of the latter plan. I propose to march this evening with all our available force, leaving only a small guard to protect the property which will be left behind, and, marching by the Fayetteville road, throw our whole force upon him at once, and endeavor to rout him before he recovers from his surprise." None of the officers present offered any objections to this plan, though its execution was deferred until the night of the 9th, on account of a large portion of his troops who had just returned from a reconnoissance on the Little York road, and who had been without food since morning, being too much exhausted to march immediately. Even the troops who remained at their stations about the city obtained but little rest, having been kept upon their arms during the day by the frequent reports that the enemy were advancing, and that an attack was looked for at any moment. A supply train having just arrived from Rolla, that night and the next day were spent in issuing shoes and clothing to his troops, of which many stood in great need, and in making preparations for the impending conflict. Detachments of Regular cavalry and Mounted Home Guards were kept out in the direction of the enemy's position to watch his movements, and to guard against surprise. But, as the enemy made no demonstration in force during the day, by evening the Federal troops were well rested and in good condition to go into battle.

The rebel generals allowed their troops also to remain in camp on the 9th for the purpose of resting and recruiting their strength. They had brought forward their infantry from Cassville and Crane Creek on a forced march, and as the weather was very warm, and the roads very dusty, the infantry had suffered much from fatigue and heat.

CHAPTER VIII.

BATTLE OF WILSON CREEK.—CONCLUDED.

ON the morning of the 9th, General Lyon and Colonel Sigel had a conference in regard to the plan of attack upon the enemy in his position at Wilson Creek. The conference had the effect of causing the General to change his original plan of throwing his whole force against the enemy, to dividing his command into two columns, which should be in position, and commence the attack at two points simultaneously at daylight the next morning.

On marching out of Springfield on the evening of the 9th, the Federal army was organized into four brigades. The First Brigade, commanded by Major S. D. Sturgis, consisted of one battalion of four companies of Regular infantry, under Captain J. B. Plummer; a battalion of two companies Second Missouri Volunteers, under Major P. J. Osterhaus; Captain Wood's mounted company, Second Kansas Volunteers; one company of Regular cavalry, under Lieutenant Canfield; and Captain James Totten's light battery of six pieces, Second United States Artillery.

The Second Brigade, commanded by Lieutenant-Colonel George L. Andrews, was composed of his own regiment, the First Missouri Volunteers; one battalion of four companies of Regular infantry, under Captain Frederick Steele; and one light battery of four guns under Lieutenant John V. DuBois.

The Third Brigade, commanded by Colonel George W. Deitzler, was composed of his own regiment, the First Kansas Volunteers; Colonel Robert B. Mitchell's Second Kansas Volunteers; and the First Iowa Volunteers, under Lieutenant-Colonel William H. Merritt.

And the Fourth Brigade, commanded by Colonel F. Sigel, was composed of his own regiment, the Third Missouri Volunteers; Colonel C. E. Salomon's Fifth Missouri Volunteers; two companies of Regular cavalry, under Captain E. A. Carr and Lieutenant Charles E. Farrand; and one battery of six guns under Lieutenant Shaffer.

A force of two hundred and fifty Home Guards was left at Springfield, with two pieces of artillery, to guard the trains and public property. The column under Colonel Sigel left camp, on the south side of Springfield, at half-past six o'clock in the evening, and moved down on the left or south of the Cassville road, and arrived at daybreak on the 10th within about a mile of the extreme right and rear of the enemy's camp. The Colonel now advanced slowly towards their camp, and with the two companies of Regular cavalry, cut off and captured about forty rebel soldiers who claimed that they were out searching for food. Having cut off all stragglers and parties coming from the Confederate camp, Colonel Sigel then advanced unperceived to a position within sight of the rebel tents, formed his line of battle, and waited for the signal, which was to be the firing from General Lyon's column before opening fire upon the enemy.

General Lyon, with the First, Second, and Third Brigades, amounting to four thousand men, and about two hundred and fifty mounted Home Guards, under Major Clark Wright, left Springfield at the same hour in the evening as Colonel Sigel's column, and marched out on the Little York road about six miles; then taking a road that led him nearly due south, advanced until the head of his column came in sight of the enemy's camp-fires. It was now about one o'clock in the morning, and the command was halted and the troops rested on their arms until early dawn, when they were wakened from their dewy slumbers with as little noise as possible, and resumed the march southward. The column moved only a short distance, when the advance came upon the enemy's pickets, who at once fled towards the rebel camp, and gave the alarm of the near approach of the Federal troops. General Lyon at once directed Captain Plummer to take his battalion of Regular infantry, which had formed the advance of the army during the night, and deploy them to the left as skirmishers. And Major Osterhaus, commanding a battalion of the Second Missouri Infantry, who had marched next to Captain Plummer, was directed to deploy to the right and form a skirmish line. Colonel Andrews next brought forward his regiment, the First Missouri Volunteers, in columns of companies to support Captain Totten's battery, and then the column advanced about a mile and a half, when the skirmish lines of the opposing armies became warmly engaged. It was now five o'clock.

The Southern troops having rested on their arms during the night were quickly brought into position after the point from which the attack was being made was ascertained. From the position now reached by Totten's battery, which was immediately in the rear of the centre of the line of skirmishers, the enemy could be seen in considerable force formed in line of battle on the crest of a high ridge running nearly parallel to the Federal line of march, and also to the valley of Wilson Creek. General Lyon now commenced to form his line of battle. Colonel Andrews was directed to form his regiment, the First Missouri, to the right, which he did, and deploying one company as skirmishers, advanced up the hill in column of companies. At ten minutes past five o'clock, just as his skirmishers were nearing the summit of the hill, they came in plain view of and opened a well-directed fire upon the enemy, consisting of two brigades of General Rains' division of Missourians, who were only a short distance in front. Riding forward a few yards, and seeing the enemy in force, Colonel Andrews immediately reinforced his line of skirmishers and ordered his regiment forward into line of battle. He had just formed it in line when a heavy fire was opened upon his left flank by a hitherto unobserved force of the enemy from a thick undergrowth of woods. The regiment, the First Missouri, promptly and effectively returned the fire, and the companies which had been deployed as skirmishers assembled on the right to prevent his flank being turned. The battle had now fairly opened, and the firing along Colonel Andrews' front was very severe for a short time, after which the enemy retired to rally and re-form their line. The First Kansas Volunteers, under Colonel Dietzler, which had also been ordered into line on the left of the First Missouri, and which was separated from that regiment by an interval of about sixty yards on account of a ravine, moved forward at a double-quick, engaged the enemy, and after a sharp conflict of about twenty minutes, compelled them to retire. The First Missouri and First Kansas Volunteers, having gained the summit of the hill, Captain Totten, who had assisted with his battery in driving the enemy from the first position, brought forward his guns in the centre. Captain Plummer's battalion of Regular infantry and Captain Clark Wright's mounted Home Guards were still operating on General Lyon's extreme left, while Major Osterhaus' battalion, Second Missouri Volunteers, occupied a position on the extreme right flank, with his right resting on a ravine, which turned abruptly to the right of the Federal rear. The First Iowa and Second Kansas Regiments, and Captain Steele's battalion of Regular infantry, General Lyon held as a reserve.

After the Confederates were driven from their first positions along his front and the firing had slackened and almost ceased, General Lyon looked over the field to his front, and left and right flanks, and had just commenced to make some slight changes in the disposition of his troops and batteries for the purpose of vigorously renewing the attack, when the enemy, whom General Price had rallied under Generals Rains, Slack, McBride, Parsons, and Clark, were observed advancing from the foot of the slope against his centre, and left and right wings, and the moment they came within range, opened a heavy fire against his entire front. The First Missouri and First Kansas Regiments replied vigorously, and the next moment advanced against the enemy, delivering volley after volley into their ranks with such disastrous effects that they were again obliged to give way. In the meantime the First Iowa Volunteers had been ordered into line on the left of the First Kansas to support Captain DuBois' battery which had come into position on its right and opened fire on a battery occupying a position near the enemy's extreme right. On the extreme Federal left, Captain Plummer moved his battalion of Regular infantry in a line along a ridge until it terminated in the valley through which Wilson Creek runs. The creek runs along near the foot of the ridge, forming a kind of lacuna, which was impassable at that point and for thirty or forty yards above and below. Along the banks of the stream too, directly in his front, there was an almost impenetrable thicket. These obstacles, however, were soon overcome, and Captain Plummer with his battalion emerged in good order into the cornfield beyond, when the enemy were discovered a short distance in front. A sharp conflict of small-arms at once ensued, but the fire of the enemy soon slackened. Captain Plummer continued to advance in the direction of a battery of the enemy, which was posted on a hill some two hundred yards in front, with the intention of charging it if practicable.

Colonel McIntosh, Adjutant-General of McCulloch's division, seeing that the Confederate battery was in imminent danger of capture, at once massed two regiments, Hebert's Third Louisiana and his own regiment, the Second Arkansas Mounted Rifles, dismounted, and hurled them against Captain Plummer's left and front and checked his further progress. A severe struggle now took place, and the number of men on both sides who fell upon that part of the field attested the courage with which they fought. The Louisiana and Arkansas regiments, under Colonel McIntosh, advanced through a thicket to the fence surrounding the cornfield and opened such a hot fire upon Captain Plummer at thirty to forty yards' range, that he was obliged to fall back through the field in the direction of Totten's battery, which still occupied a position near General Lyon's centre. The enemy crossed over the fence and pushed on through the corn- and oat-field almost at a double quick, and were making considerable havoc in Captain Plummer's little command, when Captain DuBois, whose battery was about one hundred yards to the left of Totten's battery, turned his guns upon the enemy and enfiladed their line with grape-shot, shell, and canister, with such disastrous effect that they were quickly thrown into confusion. The Confederate officers soon commenced rallying their broken troops behind a house on the right of their line, when Captain DuBois observing them, threw twelve-pound shot at the house and struck it twice. They then displayed a hospital flag and fell back, after which Captain DuBois directed his guns to another part of the field, throwing shot and shell into the Confederate lines and at the Confederate battery. The several sections of Totten's battery had up to this time been paying attention mainly to the Confederate battery in front, but played upon the enemy's lines when they advanced within range with good effect.

The battle had now raged fiercely along the Federal

front for upwards of two hours with alternating results. General Lyon's left flank had been pressed back, but as the enemy had also been driven from that quarter by the destructive fire of DuBois' battery, that part of the field was at this stage of the battle almost neutral ground. The roar of small-arms and of the thundering artillery, which had just extended all along the front, now gradually died away for a few moments, except on the extreme right of the Federal line, where the First Missouri Volunteers were contending against a superior force of fresh troops of the enemy who were endeavoring to turn the Federal right. When General Lyon, who had been closely watching the movements of the enemy on every part of the field, saw this desperate effort to turn his right flank, he directed Captain Totten to move a section of his battery to the support of the First Missouri. In a few moments the captain had his guns in position at the right of the regiment, and just as he was about to open upon the enemy his attention was called to a regiment of Southern troops in line within two hundred yards of his position, displaying a Federal and a Confederate flag together. Not understanding the meaning of this strange action, he was for a moment undecided in opening fire upon them, fearing that by some accident they were Federal troops who had moved to that position. In a moment more, however, the fire from these troops revealed their true character, and in an instant Captain Totten opened upon them with canister from both pieces, and drove them back with great slaughter. This piece of audacity and attempted deception on the part of the enemy had also been noticed by Captain Cary Gratz, First Missouri Volunteers, while advancing at the head of his company. But the mounted rebel officer who was carrying the Federal flag and leading on his men soon yielded up his life for his bravado and attempted fraud, for the moment he approached within range, Captain

Gratz drew his revolver, fired, and he fell from his horse. Not being struck in a vital part, however, he quickly arose to his feet and attempted to escape into the lines of his comrades, when Captain Gratz fired a second shot, which hit him, pitching him headlong into the shades of darkness. To avenge the death of their leader, the Southern soldiers at once levelled their muskets, and before the breeze had wafted away the smoke that arose from the volley, Captain Gratz fell, pierced by five balls.

The moment that Colonel Sigel, from the position he had taken up on the extreme right and in the rear of the Confederate camp, heard the firing by General Lyon's division to the northwest, he opened his battery upon a large force of Arkansas, Texas, and Missouri troops under command of Colonels Churchill, Greer, and Brown. The men of Colonel Churchill's regiment were preparing their breakfast, when suddenly they heard the booming of artillery in their rear, and in another instant saw exploding shells dropping in their midst, while a perfect shower of grape-shot came rattling through their camp, knocking over men, horses, and mules, and camp kettles, and creating the greatest excitement and consternation. After falling back some distance to the woods, Colonel Churchill rallied his regiment and was moving down the road in the direction of Springfield, when he was met by an aide from General Price asking for reinforcements for the support of General Slack, whose division was formed on the right of the Confederate line, and hotly engaged with the First Iowa Regiment, then occupying the left of the Federal line. In the meantime the effective fire of Colonel Sigel's infantry and artillery had so broken up and demoralized Colonel Greer's Texas regiment that it did very little fighting during the further progress of the battle. Colonel Sigel moved forward, crossed to the west side of Wilson Creek and planted his battery, supported by his infantry, near the centre of General McCulloch's camp. The Confederate killed and wounded and their arms and equipments lay scattered on every side. In a short time, however, General McCulloch collected together some two thousand men, infantry and cavalry, from the different regiments of his division, and Reid's battery of General Pearce's Arkansas division, and advanced to attack Colonel Sigel's force. When the Confederates approached within range, Colonel Sigel opened fire upon them with his artillery, using grape and canister with good effect. His infantry, the Third and Fifth Regiments Missouri Volunteers, were also brought into action, and with their long-range muskets made considerable havoc in the Confederate ranks. The Confederate officers raved a good deal in endeavoring to get their men to charge, but Colonel Sigel's fire was so effective that McCulloch's troops did not come nearer than forty to fifty yards of the Federal line, and were then, after about half an hour's conflict, obliged to fall back in no little confusion to the woods and hills to the northeast.

The roar of battle some two miles northwest, between the forces of General Lyon and General Price, was now becoming more distinct. Colonel Sigel was desirous of co-operating with General Lyon as effectively as possible, and left the position he had taken in the enemy's camp, and moved to the northwest until he came to the Fayetteville road, with the intention of attacking the Southern army in the rear. But when he arrived at Sharp's farm near the point where he intended crossing the Fayetteville road, he saw detachments of the enemy coming from the direction of the heavy firing, and as the firing at that moment seemed to be slackening, he supposed that the enemy directly in his front were broken detachments and were retreating. But their movements showed that they were preparing to attack him, and he immediately ordered his battery into position on an elevated plateau, and formed his infantry in line across the road, with the Regular cavalry under

Captain Carr and Lieutenant Farrand on each of his flanks. After skirmishing a short time with the enemy, and after the firing to the northwest had almost entirely ceased, he noticed a regiment of Confederate cavalry moving along a ridge several hundred yards on his right towards the south, from which movement he concluded that the attack made by General Lyon had been successful, and that he was in pursuit of the Southern forces. In another moment one of his skirmishers and one of his staff reported to him that General Lyon's command was advancing up the road from the direction of Springfield. Colonels Albert and Salomon at once notified their men not to fire upon troops coming from the direction of the recent heavy firing, while Colonel Sigel cautioned the commanding officer of his artillery to the same effect.

While the Federal troops were thus awaiting the approach of their comrades as they supposed, the Confederates advanced to within two hundred yards of their position and opened fire upon them from two batteries, one being posted near the Fayetteville road and the other to the right on the hill along which the Southern troops were at first thought to be retreating. At the same time the Confederate infantry moved forward against Sigel's right, firing as they advanced. The report quickly spread among Colonel Sigel's men that General Lyon's troops were firing upon them, which caused the greatest consternation and confusion. Even after Colonel Sigel ordered his artillery officer to open fire, the gunners reluctantly came forward to serve their pieces, and the infantry hesitated in levelling their muskets until the Confederates had advanced within ten paces. It was now too late to turn back the avalanche of Southern troops, for in advancing and keeping up a steady fire they soon killed and wounded a number of artillery horses, drove the gunners from their pieces, and turned the flanks of the infantry, so that they were obliged to fall back. A portion of Colonel Hebert's Third Louisiana Volunteers led the Confederate advance and captured four guns of Sigel's battery before they were moved twenty yards from where they were posted. Colonel Sigel endeavored to rally and keep his men together, but the Confederates encouraged by their success and overwhelming numbers, pressed him so closely that his command was soon broken up, and some two hundred and fifty of his troops captured. Though he had two companies of regular cavalry to skirmish, feel the strength of the enemy, and to operate on his flanks, they were of little use after the tide of disaster set in against him. There was an unpleasant suggestion involved in the fact that the commanding officers of these companies brought their men off the field without the loss of a single man killed or wounded.

Immediately after the breaking up and demoralization of Colonel Sigel's command, and the capture of all his artillery except one gun, the Confederate generals directed their combined forces against the corps of General Lyon. A considerable number of their troops had also become demoralized from the first shock of the battle, and were moving from the field in a southwest direction as rapidly as possible. The Union flag which the Confederate regiment displayed on General Lyon's right in front of the First Missouri, and which embarrassed to some extent the operations of the Federal troops, had just been captured from Colonel Sigel's command, and the Confederate officer displayed it as a trophy.

At this stage of the battle no decisive advantage had been gained on either side, between the forces of Generals Lyon and Price. The First Missouri, First Kansas, and First Iowa Regiments had repeatedly driven, with the assistance of Totten's and DuBois' batteries, the masses of Southern infantry to the foot of the slope, but were in every instance compelled to retire to the summit of the ridge near the batteries, which was the key to the Federal position. A short time after the Confederates were repulsed in the attack in which they carried the Union flag, they made a desperate effort to force their way in large numbers along the Springfield road with the view of turning the Federal left flank. The progress of this movement brought them within range of four pieces of Totten's battery, and four pieces of DuBois' battery, and several regiments of Federal infantry. As soon as they emerged from behind the thick woods into open ground, Plummer's battalion of Regulars, the First Kansas and First Iowa Regiments, and Totten's and DuBois' batteries opened a hot fire upon them, and after a short conflict compelled them to retire, and they made no further demonstration on the Federal left during the battle. They were met by a perfect storm of grape-shot and musket-balls, and suffered a heavy loss in killed and wounded. It was now nearly nine o'clock. The battle had raged with great fury for upward of three hours with only a few short intervals in the firing. The casualties in officers and men in General Lyon's centre, composed of the First Missouri and First Kansas Regiments, had been heavy. The colonels of both these regiments, Andrews and Deitzler, had had their horses shot under them, and had also each received a wound and been borne to the rear. General Lyon, therefore, desired to relieve these regiments by ordering his reserves to the front. The First Kansas having been thrown into some disorder, was relieved by the First Iowa under Colonel Merritt. About this time, while leading his horse along his left centre endeavoring to rally his troops, which had just been forced to fall back in considerable confusion before an overwhelming force of the enemy, he had his horse killed, and received himself two wounds, one in the ankle and one in the head. He had noticed that every time the Southern troops advanced, their line of battle was unbroken and stronger than in the preceding assault. He saw that General Price had fresh troops to fill up the gaps made by the destructive fire of the Federal small-arms and artillery, while nearly all his own troops had been called into action, leaving him no reserves to fill up his decimated ranks.

The roar of the artillery, the screaming of shot and shell, and the whizzing of musket-balls showed with what earnestness the antagonist forces were engaged. Realizing the great odds against which he was contending, and the desperate valor of the enemy, General Lyon retired a few paces to the rear and remarked to one of his aides: "I fear the day is lost." In a few moments, however, Major Sturgis rode up, dismounted one of his orderlies, and tendered the horse to the General, who soon mounted it, and riding toward the right, saw the line of the First Missouri giving way. At this critical moment Lieutenant-Colonel C. W. Blair, of the Second Kansas Volunteers, rode up and in a few words explained to the General the position of his regiment, and requested that it be ordered to the front. General Lyon at once gave the order, and Colonel Blair galloped back and informed Colonel Mitchell, who brought forward his regiment promptly. When he arrived near the right of Totten's battery, he was joined by General Lyon. To encourage the men the General rode at the head of the column with Colonel Mitchell, swinging his hat in the air, and just as they had raised the crest of a ridge in front of Totten's battery, and while the regiment was still marching in column by the flank, they were fired upon by the enemy from a concealed position, and both fell, General Lyon being instantly killed and Colonel Mitchell severely wounded. Colonel Blair now took command of his regiment and had Colonel Mitchell removed to the rear. He also directed Lieutenant Schreyer to take two men and carry back the body of their brave leader, General Lyon. As no time could be lost, he immediately formed his regiment in line of battle, and after a sharp conflict of about twenty-five minutes forced the enemy to retire down the slope to seek the shelter of their artillery. A short time before this conflict took place, General Price had ordered Captain Guibor's battery into position near the centre of his line of battle, after which it threw grape-shot and shell vigorously for probably twenty minutes, doing considerable damage. Totten's battery, however, soon got its range, and after throwing shells into it for a while, silenced it. Majors Sturgis and Schofield having rallied the troops on the Federal left, and strengthened the line with Captain Steele's battalion of Regular infantry, the battle was renewed with desperate courage, and raged with an incessant din of arms for perhaps half an hour on that part of the field after the fall of General Lyon. Several times during this conflict volleys of musketry would break out along the contending lines and increase to a continuous roar, which, blending with the thundering tones of artillery, produced an awful and indescribable volume of sound.

After the volleys of musketry had gradually died away, and the Confederates had retired from the field and out of sight, almost complete silence prevailed for about thirty minutes. Indeed some of the Federal officers thought that the battle was over, and that the Southern forces had retreated from the field to return no more. During this temporary cessation of hostilities, Major Schofield, Assistant Adjutant-General and Chief-of-Staff to the Commanding General, informed the principal officers of the command of the death of General Lyon, and Major Sturgis, being the ranking officer of the Regular army present, assumed command of the Federal troops on the field. The officers highest in rank in the different regiments and battalions still fit for duty were hastily called together for the purpose of determining the course that should be adopted at once. It was evident that one of two movements must be commenced with the least possible delay. The army must either retreat or move forward in pursuit of the enemy. In this brief conference it was the opinion of the officers present that it would be unsafe to commence pursuit of the enemy without first hearing from Colonel Sigel and whether his operations had been successful or unsuccessful. The army was already badly crippled, for nearly one third of the men and about one half of the officers of two regiments, the First Kansas and First Missouri, had been killed and wounded, besides the troops were running short of ammunition. They had marched all night, and had been fighting since early in the morning, and were suffering much from heat, thirst, and exhaustion. Major Sturgis saw that, should he attempt to withdraw from the field, the enemy, still about fifteen thousand strong in his front, would pursue him, and with their numerous cavalry overwhelm and annihilate his little army.

While still undecided as to what should be the next movement, the conference was suddenly terminated by the approach of a large body of Confederate infantry from over the hill, directly in the Federal front. The fragments of the First Missouri and Major Osterhaus' battalion of the Second Missouri Volunteers had been rallied and withdrawn from the right and sent to support DuBois' battery on the left. The fragments of the First Kansas Regiment were formed in the rear of the First Iowa to support Totten's battery. Captain Steele's battalion of Regular infantry, strengthened by Captain C. C. Gilbert's company from Plummer's battalion, formed on the left of the First Iowa. As soon as it was known that the enemy were advancing in force, Major Sturgis directed Captain Steele to send out a company of skirmishers to the left and front as far as the brow of the hill. The company sent out under Captain Lothrop had scarcely reached the point designated when the enemy opened such a hot fire upon him that he was obliged to retire. Still farther to the right, and about the same time, Colonel Blair sent forward several small detachments of his regiment, the Second Kansas, to examine the enemy's position, but as none of these parties returned, he shortly rode some twenty yards to the right of his position himself, when a company of Confederates, partially concealed from his view, discharged a volley at him, killing his horse, but from which he escaped uninjured.

In the meantime, General Price had established a battery under the crest of a hill somewhat to the left of the Federal front. It immediately opened a terrific fire on the Federal line, using grape and canister and shrapnel, with the view of covering the advance of a strong force of infantry which had been brought up for the purpose of capturing Totten's battery. A terrible conflict now took place along the entire Federal front. The two opposing lines approached within a few yards of each other, so that the smoke from the heavy volleys of musketry ascended as one dense volume. Several times the Confederate infantry advanced within ten paces of Totten's guns. But at every advance Captain Totten threw a perfect shower of grape and canister into their ranks, and they were literally mowed down. The First Iowa Regiment and Captain Steele's battalion also poured an effective fire of musketry into their flanks. General Price threw forward fresh regiments to fill up the gaps caused by casualties, and for a time it looked as if the Federal centre would be overwhelmed. Captain Gordon Granger, Major Sturgis' Assistant Adjutant-General, realizing the critical situation, rushed to the rear for the supports of DuBois' battery, consisting of three companies of the First Missouri, three companies of the First Kansas, and two companies of the First Iowa Regiments, and brought them forward in double-quick time, and throwing them against the right flank of the enemy, poured into it such effective volleys of musketry that it was quickly forced back. At no time during the day had the Federal line maintained its position with greater firmness. Officers and men were animated with extraordinary courage and determination. They realized that should the Confederates break through their line at a single point it would probably result in the complete rout and destruction of the Federal army. As the reserves had all been called into action, any indication of yielding or breaking would encourage the enemy to press forward and overwhelm the Federal flanks and centre.

While Major Sturgis' left and centre were fiercely engaged, his right, under Colonel Blair, was holding the enemy in check in that quarter, and pouring volley after volley into their ranks with disastrous effect. Shortly, however, the Confederates commenced pressing him so closely with superior forces, that he felt the need of artillery to enable him to hold his position. At his request, Major Sturgis directed Captain Totten to send him a section of his battery. It came up in time to save his regiment from being overwhelmed, for, under the direction of Lieutenant Sokalski, the pieces threw a perfect shower of iron hail into the ranks of the Southern troops. In order to shield his men as much as possible from the galling fire of the enemy, Colonel Blair ordered them to lie down and load and fire. The fire of his troops in this position was effective, and it served to reduce his casualties to a minimum.

The battle had now raged, like a consuming fire, for six hours, and the Confederates, after repeated charges, had failed to dislodge the Federal troops from their position on the summit of the ridge. After the defeat and demoralization of Colonel Sigel's force, Generals

Price and McCulloch concentrated their combined forces and hurled them against the corps of General Lyon, with the hope of crushing it by one furious charge. But, in their desperate assaults, they failed to break the Federal centre, to turn either of the Federal flanks, or to capture any of the guns of Totten's or DuBois' battery. The southern slope of the hill was thickly strewn with their dead and wounded. Every charge had cost them a fearful loss of life, for the Federal troops were armed with muskets of the latest improved models, and the officers and men of Totten's and DuBois' batteries belonged to the artillery corps of the Regular Army, and thoroughly understood their duties. Generals Price, Slack, and Clark, of the Missouri Southern forces, had been wounded; Colonels Weightman and Brown, brigade commanders of Price's army, had been killed; and a number of colonels of regiments had been seriously wounded. When therefore Captain Granger brought forward the fragments of the decimated Federal regiments which had been supporting DuBois' battery, and directed them against the Confederate right flank, it soon gave way, and in a moment later their centre, and then their entire line retired from the field, down through the valley covered with thick woods towards their camp on Wilson Creek, somewhat to the right of the Federal centre.

Just before the close of the last fierce struggle along the front of the two armies, about eight hundred Confederate cavalry appeared on the right and in rear of the Federal position, and had formed in line below the crest of the hills with the apparent intention of charging Totten's battery. When they approached within easy range, Captain Totten suddenly turned several guns of his battery upon them, and after throwing a few rounds of grape and canister and shell into their ranks, succeeded, with the assistance of several companies of the First Missouri and First Kansas Regiments, in driving them from that part of the field in the greatest confusion. The guns were served with such precision that each discharge was terribly effective, for the enemy were at the time advancing obliquely to the line of fire. As grape-shot and shell came crashing among them, men and horses in heaps were overthrown in wild confusion. This was the only demonstration made by the Confederate cavalry against the Federal flanks or rear during the battle. The Confederate forces having been repulsed all along the Federal front, Major Sturgis, about half-past eleven o'clock, gave the order for his troops to retire. Captain DuBois' battery was sent with its support, consisting mainly of Major Osterhaus' battalion of Second Missouri Volunteers, to occupy a hill in the rear, to hold the enemy in check while the Federal troops were being withdrawn from the field. Very soon after Major Sturgis commenced to retreat a considerable force of the enemy made a demonstration on his right flank, which, however, was quickly repulsed by Captain Steele's battalion of Regular infantry. The Federal troops now moved slowly and unmolested to the open prairie, about two miles northeast of the battle-ground, and made a short halt, to enable the surgeons to gather up the wounded and put them in ambulances and bring them along.

No tidings having been received from Colonel Sigel, and no firing having been heard from that part of the field which he had at first occupied since about half-past eight o'clock, Major Sturgis was undecided whether to continue his retreat to Springfield, or whether he should take up a stronger position in the vicinity and await intelligence from Sigel. In a short time, however, one of Sigel's men arrived, and reported to Major Sturgis that Sigel's command had been completely broken up, his artillery captured, many of his men taken prisoners, and that the Colonel himself was either killed or taken prisoner. Most of the troops under Major Sturgis had not only used up nearly all the ammunition with which they had been supplied, but also the greater part of that which had been obtained from the cartridge-boxes of the killed and wounded. In view of the failure of Colonel Sigel's column, of the heavy casualties in his own command, and of the limited supply of ammunition on hand, Major Sturgis directed the troops to continue the retreat to Springfield. When his command reached Little York it was joined by Lieutenant Farrand, with his company of Regular cavalry, one gun of Sigel's artillery, and a considerable portion of the troops of Sigel's brigade.

After Colonel Sigel's command had been broken up and five pieces of his battery captured, Lieutenant Farrand marched in a southerly direction with his company, with the view of circling around the Confederate camp and reaching Springfield with as little opposition as possible. He had marched only a short distance from the battle-field when he fell in with some of Colonel Sigel's retreating troops, who were much scattered and apparently lost. He halted his company long enough to get quite a number of the infantry-men together. He also met and detained one of the guides who had guided Colonel Sigel's column from Springfield to the battle-field. Lieutenant Farrand directed the man to guide him back to Springfield *via* Little York, as this would likely be the route by which General Lyon's command would return to Springfield. The party at once moved on, but had marched only a short distance when it came to one of the guns of Sigel's battery, which had been abandoned. The tongue of the limber was broken, one of the horses taken out, and one of the three remaining ones was badly wounded. With some perseverance, the lieutenant succeeded in bringing the gun along, and shortly came to the caisson, which was full of ammunition. He determined to bring it along also. As it was necessary to take out the wounded horses and replace them by sound animals, he was detained with three men until his company and the infantry-men had got some distance in advance. He was obliged, however, to abandon the caisson after overtaking the retreating troops, in order to hitch the animals which were drawing it to the gun. He also, with the assistance of Lieutenant Morris, Colonel Sigel's Adjutant, procured a number of wagons from the citizens of the neighborhood and sent them back on the road to pick up and fetch along the wounded. Major Sturgis arrived at Springfield with the troops of his own command and most of those of Colonel Sigel's brigade who had escaped from the scene of conflict, about five o'clock in the afternoon. His ambulances were crowded with the wounded, but by some inadvertence the body of General Lyon was left on the field. General McCulloch, however, sent it to Major Sturgis that evening.

The casualties of the Federal army under General Lyon on this hard contested field, according to official reports, were as follows:

Command.	Officers.			Enlisted men.			Aggregate.
	Killed.	Wounded.	Missing.	Killed.	Wounded.	Missing.	
Staff	1						1
First Missouri Vols., Col. Andrews	1	12	2	76	210	8	309
First Kansas Vols., Col. Deitzler	4	8		73	187	20	292
First Iowa Vols., Col. Merritt	1	5		11	133	4	154
Second Kansas Vols., Col. Mitchell		1		4	59	6	70
Sigel's Brigade, Third and Fifth Mo. Vols		3	2	15	31	231	282
Second Missouri Vols., Osterhaus' Battalion				2	24		26
Plummer's Battalion Regular Infy.		1		19	51	9	80
Steele's Battalion Regular Infantry		1		15	43	2	61
Totten's Battery				4	7		11
DuBois' Battery				2	2	1	5
First U. S. Cavalry, Co. D					1	3	4
Carr's Squadron Regular Cavalry						4	4
Major Clark Wright's Home Guards					2	0	2
Kansas Rangers					1		1
Total	7	31	4	221	751	288	1,302

The casualties of the combined Southern armies, according to official reports, were as follows:

Command.	Officers.			Enlisted men.			Aggregate.
	Killed.	Wounded.	Missing.	Killed.	Wounded.	Missing.	
Army of Missouri under General Price:							
General Price's Staff		1					1
General Slack's Division	5	1		35	84	30	155
General John B. Clark's Division	3	2		23	75		103
General McBrides' Division		5		22	119		146
General Parsons' Division	1	1		15	47		64
General Rains' Division	3	2		59	195	11	270
Confederate Army under General McCulloch:							
First Regt. Arkansas Mtd. Rifles	3	11		39	144		197
Second Regt. " " "		3		10	51		64
McRae's Battalion Ark. Vols				2	7		9
Third Louisiana Vols	1	3		8	45	3	60
Reid's Battery					1		1
First Arkansas Cavalry	1	1		5	22	19	48
Third Arkansas Vols	2			23	84	1	110
Fifth Arkansas Infantry				3	11		14
Fourth Arkansas Infantry	—	—	—	—	—	—	—
Total	19	30		244	885	64	1,242

As already stated, General Lyon marched out of Springfield with about four thousand men and ten pieces of artillery in his division to make the attack. Colonel Sigel had in his separate brigade one thousand two hundred men and one battery of six guns. Generals McCulloch and Price had, according to official reports, five thousand three hundred infantry, six thousand mounted troops, and fifteen pieces of artillery. They also had several thousand irregular horsemen armed with shotguns and ordinary hunting rifles, such as most of the men of that section used. This irregular force, however, did very little fighting, and McCulloch claimed that it even embarrassed the operations of the organized troops.

CHAPTER IX.

RETREAT FROM SPRINGFIELD TO ROLLA, AND RETROSPECT.

WHEN Major Sturgis reached Springfield with his command, he found that Colonels Sigel and Salomon had arrived there an hour or so before him. A consultation of the principal officers of the command fit for duty was soon held at the quarters of Major Schofield, Chief of Staff, for the purpose of deciding the movement that should next be made. Major Sturgis resigned his command to Colonel Sigel, and stated his conviction of the necessity of the army retreating towards Rolla before the Confederate forces could organize for pursuit. There was no opposition to this plan, and it was soon decided that the troops should leave Springfield the next morning at two o'clock. No time could be lost. Colonel Sigel arranged the order of march, and Major Schofield commenced immediately to get the troops and trains in readiness to move. There were some three hundred and seventy wagons in the baggage and supply trains of the army. These and the troops would stretch out upon the road several miles, even when moving in the closest order possible.

As soon as it was known that the Federal army was going to retreat, a great many Union families, in fact all who could leave, commenced making preparations to move with the troops. A large number of Union families had moved into Springfield from the Southwest during the last two weeks for Federal protection, and when the news spread among them that the army was about to retreat, some of them became almost wild with excitement. They were, in most cases, unprepared to take their stock and personal effects, that they had brought there, any farther from their homes. Many believed, too, that they would be able to return to their homes in a few days, instead of being compelled by the hard necessities of the situation to move farther away.

The troops, having partaken of food and a few hours of much-needed rest, commenced moving out at the hour designated. But the rear-guard did not leave the city until after daylight. The Federal officers were apprehensive that the Confederate forces would reach town early next morning to renew hostilities; but they made no demonstration whatever, and the Federal army was permitted to retire unmolested. General Price did not arrive with his troops at Springfield until late in the afternoon of the 11th, and no effort was then made to annoy the retreating Federal troops. The combined Southern forces were really defeated on the field, and were not at all anxious to renew the conflict. After the third day's retreat, Major Sturgis assumed command of the Federal troops, and on the 17th arrived at Rolla, about one hundred and twenty-five miles northeast of Springfield. The warm weather made the march very fatiguing to the troops and animals. On account of the rough and broken condition of the country over most of the route, the long trains were obliged to move very slowly, and to make frequent halts to repair or remove from the road a broken-down wagon. In passing over this rough section, the breaking down of a single wagon on several occasions detained most of the long train and rear-guard for several hours. The troops were fatigued standing in column in the hot sun, by such accidents, almost as much as by constant marching. The wagons of the trains were not the Regular Army pattern, but such as could be hired of citizens where the trains were made up.

In the first reports of the battle and of the retreat of the army, Colonel Sigel got credit for more glory than was justly due him. These reports were calculated to impress those not familiar with the facts, that he saved the army from destruction by the great skill which he displayed in conducting the retreat. His retreating fight with Governor Jackson's forces at Dry Fork and Carthage had no doubt made him a reputation disproportionate to the results accomplished. As the Confederate generals were not prepared to make a vigorous pursuit, the Federal army simply retreated to Rolla at its leisure. Colonel Sigel was severely criticised by the officers of General Lyon's division for losing his artillery and colors and permitting his command to be broken up. Though he neglected to take certain precautions, which a skilful and vigilant officer would have taken at such a time, yet perhaps the failure of his column should not be attributed wholly to gross carelessness and incapacity on his part. The positive statements of his officers and men showed that they thought the advancing column of Confederates under General McCulloch, who broke his line, were the troops of General Lyon's division. Colonel Greer, of the Texas regiment, who occupied a position on the right of General McCulloch's line in the attack on Sigel's force, stated that part of Colonel Sigel's men appeared embarrassed and at a loss what to do. In a divided attack on an enemy, such an accident as that to which Colonel Sigel attributed his misfortune might easily occur. The probability of it occurring, however, would of course be much diminished if every body of soldiers of the opposing forces carried their national flag and wore their national uniform. The term of service of the men of the Fifth Regiment Missouri Volunteers of

Colonel Sigel's brigade had expired on the 1st of August. A battle was imminent, and he induced them, company by company, to remain in service eight days longer. This second term expired on the 9th, the day before the battle. The efficiency of the Third Regiment had also been greatly impaired by the discharge of about four hundred three months' volunteers, whose terms of service had recently expired. The recruits by whom they were replaced had received very little instruction in the drill, and could not, therefore, be handled on the field like troops familiar with their duties, and who had seen active service. His artillery-men, too, consisted of infantry taken from the Third Regiment, and were mostly recruits who had not yet become familiar with their duties, having had only a few days' instruction in the artillery drill. Nearly two thirds of his officers had left him, on account of their commissions having expired, and some companies had no commissioned officers at all. Under the circumstances, perhaps few officers would have sustained the cause of their country more honorably. That he made a good deal of havoc in the ranks of the Confederates, until he mistook them for General Lyon's troops, is shown in the official reports of General McCulloch's officers.

It was after dark when the remains of General Lyon arrived at Springfield from the battle-field of Wilson's Creek. The surgeons endeavored to preserve the body by injecting arsenic into it, but were unsuccessful, owing to the fact that, having been exposed to the rays of the sun nearly all that hot summer day, decomposition had already commenced. Had the remains been brought along when the army retreated from the field, the dead hero might have been buried that evening, with proper military honors. But when the army retreated from Springfield, the body was left behind again, and not a soldier discharged his farewell shot over the grave of his revered and fallen leader. Shortly after the army left, Mrs. Phelps, wife of Hon. John S. Phelps, Member of Congress from the District of Southwest Missouri, and a true Union woman of Springfield, hearing that the body was still in the city and unburied, requested and obtained permission to take possession of it, for the purpose of having it decently interred. She had the body placed in a wooden coffin, and the wooden coffin enclosed in a zinc case, which was hermetically sealed. Thinking it possible that the remains might be molested by the Southern troops when they marched into the city, Mrs. Phelps had the coffin placed in an out-door cellar, near her residence, and covered over with straw. After the Confederate forces moved into Springfield, General Parsons' division of Price's army encamped on the Phelps' farm, in the suburbs of the city. As Mrs. Phelps was still apprehensive that the coffin might be discovered and the remains disturbed, through the curiosity of the soldiers, she had it removed and buried after nightfall. Immediately after the Federal army returned to Springfield from the battlefield, a special messenger was sent with a despatch to Rolla, and from thence to St. Louis, to announce the result to General Fremont. On the 13th, General Fremont telegraphed the Secretary of War that General Lyon had been killed on the field, and that his army, under Colonel Sigel, was retreating towards Rolla.

The news of the death of General Lyon, and the brave spirits who fell with him on that bloody field, quickly spread all over the North, and created profound expressions of sorrow. As soon as the relatives of General Lyon received definite information of his death, they determined to have his remains brought to his native home in Connecticut for interment. Mr. Danford Knowlton, of New York City, a cousin, and Mr. John. B. Hasler, of Webster, Mass., a brother-in-law, of the deceased, left New York City on the 15th of August for St. Louis to get the body. When they arrived at St. Louis they were disappointed to find that it had not been brought forward, although General Fremont had been requested by telegraph to send for it. After getting letters from General Fremont to insure their admission into the Confederate lines, and for protection on the route, Messrs. Knowlton and Hasler proceeded *via* Rolla to Springfield. They stopped at the camp of Major Sturgis, near Rolla, one night, and, while there, met Captain Emmet McDonald, of General Price's army, who had just arrived, under a flag of truce, from Springfield, on a mission in regard to an exchange of prisoners. As he was about to return to the headquarters of the Southern army at Springfield, his courteous offer to accompany Messrs. Knowlton and Hasler to that point was accepted. An ambulance, drawn by four fine mules, was furnished by Colonel Wyman, commanding the post of Rolla, and, with Captain McDonald as guide, the party passed the Confederate outposts and pickets and drove into Springfield on the afternoon of the 22d, without any kind of interruption.

Messrs. Knowlton and Hasler at once repaired to the headquarters of General Price and made known their business, and presented the letter of General Fremont. When General Price glanced at the address, "To whom it may concern," he threw the paper contemptuously aside, with the remark that he could read no document thus directed. In other respects, however, he displayed no lack of civility, but, on the contrary, was very courteous and obliging to the strangers. He offered to grant them every facility to enable them to accomplish the object of their journey. Having ascertained that Mrs. Phelps had taken charge of the General's body, they were at once driven to her place, and had it disinterred and placed in a metallic coffin weighing three hundred pounds. Information of the arrival of the party, and of their mission, was conveyed to General Parsons, who was still encamped on the Phelps' farm with his brigade. He at once introduced himself to the relatives of the distinguished dead, and extended to them numerous civilities. He also tendered to them a guard for the body and a team during the night, which were accepted. The next morning the party, after visiting the general hospital to obtain a list of the Federal wounded and their condition, started back to St. Louis and the East. When they were ready to return, General Price tendered them a military escort for the body, but it was declined. The party arrived in St. Louis on Monday evening, the 26th, "and, at the solicitation of General Fremont, remained over Tuesday, in order to give time for a suitable demonstration" of respect to the memory of the dead soldier. The city put on deep mourning, and the manifestations of profound sorrow were seen upon the expressions of the people on every hand.

On Wednesday, the 28th, the remains were attended by a military and civic procession, from General Fremont's headquarters to the depot of the Ohio and Mississippi Railroad, and delivered to Adams Express Company, to be conveyed East under an escort of officers and a detachment of enlisted men. Crowds of people assembled at nearly all the railroad stations between St. Louis and Cincinnati to show their respect and affectionate regard for the memory of the distinguished officer who had offered up his life in defence of his country. At Cincinnati, on the morning of the 29th, the funeral cortege was received by the military of the city, and the coffin, after being transferred from the cars to the hearse, and wrapped in the United States flag, was borne in solemn procession to one of the largest halls in the city, where it lay in state during the day, and was visited by multitudes of all classes. The escort left Cincinnati at ten o'clock, the night of the 29th, with the remains, and arrived in New York City, Saturday the 31st, where distinguished honors were also paid to the memory of the deceased. The Governor's Room had been fitted up for the reception of the corpse, where it lay in state for three days. Flags were displayed at half-mast on all the public buildings in the city, and on a portion of the shipping in the harbor. It was estimated that fifteen thousand people visited the remains on Saturday and Monday, as a token of respect to the gallant officer who died as a true soldier of the Republic in full discharge of his duty.

The remains and St. Louis escort left New York Monday evening, September 2d, and were conveyed by the New Haven Railroad to Hartford, Connecticut, arriving there Tuesday afternoon, September 3d. On Wednesday, the 4th, the body was conveyed from Hartford to Eastford, the native home of the General. As the remains did not reach Eastford until after dark, the coffin was placed in the Congregational Church of the village overnight, in charge of the City Guard of Hartford. Here, on Thursday, September 5th, the last funeral rites were performed over all that was mortal of General Nathaniel Lyon. After the memorial exercises and orations were concluded, the body was conveyed from the church in a hearse, drawn by four magnificent black horses, to the cemetery at Phœnixville, two miles distant, and deposited in a grave beside his honored parents, in accordance with a desire which he had expressed while living. When the pit was partly filled, the City Guard of Hartford fired three volleys over the grave, and the band performed a solemn dirge. The solemn occasion drew together a large assemblage. Not only did the people of the neighboring villages and hamlets turn out to honor the memory of the deceased, who had gone forth from among them to fight for the perpetuity of free institutions, but there were also present distinguished officers and citizens of the State and from other sections of the country.

Having followed the remains of General Lyon from the bloody field of Wilson Creek to their last resting-place in the valley and among the hills where his early life was passed, it will be well to return briefly to the scene of his late operations in Southwest Missouri. His military operations from Camp Jackson to Wilson Creek were brilliant almost beyond comparison, and had attracted the attention of the whole country. Throughout the North, the feeling was becoming universal that the interests of the Government in the Southwest could not be entrusted to safer hands. In three months he organized an army, and drove the secessionists from St. Louis, Jefferson City, and Boonville into the southwest corner of the State. And in the sections over which his operations extended, he constantly made friends for the Union cause, instead of alienating the people by rash acts, as had been done in another part of the State by another Federal commander. About two weeks after he arrived at Springfield, he was informed that members of his command had been guilty of seizing, and appropriating to private use, the property of Union citizens of the vicinity, and of arresting citizens who were pursuing their peaceful avocations. He immediately issued an order setting forth that the property and persons of all law-abiding citizens, no matter what their private opinions might be, so long as they did not take, or excite others to take, an attitude of hostility to the Government, should not be molested. He stated that the cases of plundering, wanton destruction of property, and the disregard of personal rights, of which he had heard with pain, were disgraceful to his troops, a violation of his own orders, and contrary to the policy of the General Government. And he declared his determination to use all possible means to suppress such unscrupulous conduct.

The Confederate leaders had published statements, and endeavored to make it appear that the Federal troops were committing all sorts of outrages upon the persons and property of the citizens, and thus alienated many who, had they been better informed, would not likely have thrown off their allegiance to the Government. General Lyon not only wished to show to the people that the Government was not only desirous of protecting its loyal citizens, but he also saw that to permit a spirit of lawlessness among his troops would soon result in such demoralization that they could not be relied upon for effective operations in the field. He was thoroughly impressed with the idea that an army without discipline was merely a mob, and would be next to worthless in contending with the well organized troops of a bold and defiant enemy,—an enemy, too, who was fond of boasting of his prowess and superior fighting qualities. The conduct of the Border Ruffians during the troubles between the Free-State and Proslavery parties in Kansas before the war, had given the people of Missouri a bad name throughout the North, so that, when the Rebellion came on, there was a marked tendency among the officers and soldiers from the free States on entering Missouri to treat all classes as secessionists. The feelings of the Unionists were often deeply wounded by such ill-conceived conduct. Nor did it always come with good grace from the citizen soldiers of States that furnished fewer soldiers for the Union than Missouri. But in General Lyon the Union people found a staunch and steadfast friend, who appreciated their condition, and who would not permit reckless violations of their persons and property. He recognized the loyal element of the State, and saw that a large army of Union troops could be raised for the purpose of sustaining the cause of the Government.

Within two days after the battle, most of the Southern troops moved forward and encamped about Springfield, but they were in no condition to follow the retreating Federal force. General Price at once published his official report of the battle in one of the Springfield papers, and as it did not bestow as much praise upon General

McCulloch's troops as they claimed they were entitled to, the effect was to alienate them and chill their enthusiasm for the success of the Confederate cause in Missouri. Holding his appointment from the Confederate Government, and being at the head of a well organized and well armed and equipped division of Confederate troops, General McCulloch regarded the poorly organized and poorly armed and equipped troops of General Price with great contempt; and the generals of the Missouri secession forces he characterized as mere politicians, utterly unfit to organize and command troops, and from whom no important achievement need be expected. To guard his troops against the demoralization which he affected to believe contact with the Missouri forces would bring about, he encamped apart from General Price's army. With all his contempt for Price's army, he never mentioned the fact that it did most of the fighting on the Confederate side at Wilson Creek. The report of casualties for the Southern armies shows that General McCulloch had one regiment,—Colonel Churchill's Arkansas Mounted Rifles, that suffered in killed and wounded in about the same proportion as the Missouri troops. But this regiment joined General Price immediately after they were driven from their camp by Colonel Sigel early in the morning. It was no doubt irritating to General McCulloch to have constantly thrust upon his attention the fact that troops, which he had contemptuouly regarded as a miserable rabble, had fought with more determination and execution and sustained far heavier losses than his own well drilled and finely armed and equipped troops. The casualty reports showed what troops had done the fighting, and did not need any words of comment from the commanding generals.

During the two weeks the Southern armies were encamped in the vicinity of Springfield, there was no exchange of courtesies between Generals Price and Mc-

Culloch and their generals, and very little visiting between their subordinate officers and men. General McCulloch was not received as a conquering hero in Southwest Missouri, and altogether he was considerably disappointed, for in a letter to General Hardee, in which he made several uncomplimentary allusions to General Price's army, he remarked: "And from all I can see, we had as well be in Boston, as far as the friendly feelings of the inhabitants are concerned." In that section the Union element predominated, so that most of the people showed by their actions that they regarded the Southern armies as invaders and enemies, rather than friends and deliverers. It was noted by the Confederate officers that, after the Federal troops withdrew from Springfield, the place seemed to be almost deserted.

General McCulloch, who had been encamped at Pond Springs, near Wilson Creek, since the 13th, left there on the 25th with his division for Fayetteville, Arkansas, where he arrived on the 31st of August. General Pearce's division of Arkansas State troops, that had been encamped near General McCulloch since the battle, left their camp August 21st for Bentonville, Arkansas, where they were mustered out of service, their terms of service having expired. Before General McCulloch set out on his retrograde movement, he was invited by General Price to join him with his men and artillery on a march to the Missouri River. But, to use his own expression, the Texas General dared not join General Price, for fear of having his troops demoralized. His declining to further co-operate with the Missouri forces did not cause General Price to change his plans in regard to his expedition to the Missouri River. The two weeks he was encamped at Springfield had enabled him to do much towards perfecting the organization of his forces, so that, on the 26th of August, he set out for Lexington, *via* Fort Scott, Kansas.

CHAPTER X.

ACTION AT DRY WOOD.

AFTER General Lyon's army was withdrawn from Springfield and Southwest Missouri, General Price saw that if the State became one of the Confederate States, the Confederate forces should at once commence aggressive operations, and, if possible, unfurl their victorious banners in the heart of the State. He saw, too, that his army would increase in numbers from active operations, and decrease from inactivity. He proposed to march to the Missouri River and establish himself, and then to invade and lay waste Kansas, and invited General McCulloch to join him in the enterprise, with his division of Texas, Louisiana, and Arkansas troops. The Texas General, however, declined to move his troops any farther north. In the first place, he had little faith in the ultimate success of the expedition, and, in the next place, his ruffled pride had not been sufficiently appeased to co-operate with the Missouri General in a hearty spirit. He knew, too, that the terms of service of the most of the Arkansas troops would expire in a few weeks, and that unless they re-enlisted, the strength of his division would be materially decreased. General Price was inclined to be conciliatory, for the sake of advancing the Confederate cause in the State; but it was all to no purpose, General McCulloch was immovable.

Finding that General McCulloch would not join forces with him, General Price determined to accomplish such results as were possible with his own army,—the State Guard. He left Springfield about two weeks after the battle of Wilson Creek with some ten thousand men, with the intention of taking Fort Scott, Kansas, and then marching through Kansas to the Missouri River, striking it at Kansas City. He knew that the secession element was much stronger in North and in Central Missouri, than in all the region south of the Missouri River, and he was constantly in receipt of information that if he could march to the river in the neighborhood of Lexington, he would be joined by General Martin Green from North Missouri with some four thousand men. He knew that there were no Federal troops between Springfield and Lexington; that there was only a small force of about two thousand men, composed of Missouri Home Guards and a regiment of Illinois volunteers under Colonel Mulligan, at the latter place, and that he could march directly there without opposition. The Union Home Guard organizations that had come into existence in many of the counties south of the river, under authority of General Lyon, were disbanded after the battle of Wilson Creek, so that after the retreat of the Federal army from Springfield, the western half of Missouri south of the river was completely in possession of the secessionists.

After the defeat of the Union army at Wilson Creek, the prominent men of Kansas expected that Generals Price and McCulloch would lead their victorious legions to the invasion of the newly admitted free State. The Territory had suffered the year before from an unprecedented drought, and the people had become greatly impoverished, yet it was thought that as many of Price's army were men who had belonged to the Border Ruffian bands, who had invaded the Territory in behalf of the Proslavery party and had committed many outrages upon the Free-State people, they would again eagerly engage in an enterprise that promised them an opportunity of further satiating their revenge upon their old opponents, the Free-State men of Kansas. General James H. Lane, the recently elected Senator from Kansas, saw, the moment hostilities commenced, that his State would very soon require a considerable force of troops stationed along her eastern border to protect his people against the depredations of the Missouri secessionists. The State had already put into the field two regiments, who had gallantly maintained her honor on the bloody field of Wilson Creek. These two regiments were ordered out of the State directly after they were organized, thus leaving the people of the border counties of Kansas at the mercy of the companies of secessionists that were organized in all the border counties of Missouri. On the earnest solicitation of General Lane, authority was obtained from the War Department for raising five additional regiments from Kansas. But when the battle of Wilson Creek was fought, scarcely a battalion had been recruited for each, the Third, Fourth, Fifth, Sixth, and Seventh Regiments. The defeat of the Union army at Bull Run, followed closely by the defeat of General Lyon's army at Wilson Creek, aroused the people to a realization of the situation that war flamed at their very doors.

In almost every locality there were a few men who had had some experience in war on a small scale during the Kansas troubles between the Proslavery and Free-State men, but men familiar with regular military organization and discipline were not easily found. Fathers with their sons visited their nearest towns to hear the latest news of the movements of the armies, and the war excitement increased. Those who aspired to military honors and had obtained authority to raise companies were zealous in drumming up recruits. Every day of the week, at intervals of an hour or so, at the different recruiting stations in the border counties of Kansas, the fife and drum might have been heard calling the citizens to arms. Those just in from the country to hear the latest news of army operations were soon attracted in groups around the fife and drum corps. Here the situation was discussed, and here the patriotism and martial pride of the young men were aroused, and they accompanied the recruiting officer to his office, where each signed an agreement to serve the United States three years or during the war to put down the rebellion, and were then sworn into the service.

Companies were rapidly recruited, but in many cases the officers were totally unacquainted with military instruction. Very few of them, perhaps, had ever seen Scott's or Hardee's Tactics, or witnessed a soldier go through the manual of arms. Good drill-masters were much in demand. Companies organized in the neighborhood of Forts Scott, Leavenworth, or Riley, were generally fortunate enough to have some one to instruct them in their respective arms of the service. Around each of these military posts a number of sergeants, corporals and intelligent private soldiers, who had served one or more terms in the Regular Army and who had been honorably discharged therefrom, had settled, and finding their knowledge of militarv instruction much in demand, joined some of the companies being raised in their midst. In most cases they were soon promoted to commissioned officers. In nearly every town too, there were perhaps several men who had served in the Mexican War and who knew something of military discipline. Hence raw as the people were in the art of war, they were not slow in finding instructors in discipline and organization.

The companies organized in Southern Kansas were ordered to Fort Scott to rendezvous and to receive their clothing, arms, and equipments, and most of the companies organized in the northern part of the States received their outfits at Fort Leavenworth. Many a rustic youth after leaving aside his citizen garb and putting on the bright new Federal uniform surprised his friends by his improved appearance. Each recruit thus taken into the service was rapidly put through the course of instruction prescribed for soldiers of the Regular Army when it was practicable. In nearly every infantry company there were one or two soldiers more awkward than the rest, and noted for their slowness in learning how to catch and keep the step. But a few weeks daily drilling in the squad, company, and battalion improved these most awkward men in soldierly bearing in a wonderful degree.

Most of the officers were as green in regard to making out requisitions for the necessary supplies for their companies as they were in regard to the school of the soldier, for the Army Regulations had been a sealed book to them. But at Fort Scott there were several volunteer officers of fine business qualifications, who had had some experience in Government matters, and among them was Major W. C. Ransom, who, with much labor and patience instructed and assisted many of the officers in making out their requisitions for supplies in proper form. Fort Leavenworth was the depot from which supplies of the various kinds were drawn, and the chiefs of the several departments there were Regular Army officers, and each promptly filled all proper requisitions made upon his department, if the supplies were on hand. The demand for arms had been so great all over the country that the ordnance officers could not furnish all the troops raised in Kansas with the newest and most improved models of muskets and carbines. Some companies, however, were furnished with Springfield muskets and Sharp's carbines, the best infantry and cavalry arms then in use.

A week or so after the battle of Wilson Creek the rumor became current that General Price was preparing to invade Kansas. General Lane and other prominent men addressed the people, appealing to them to rally to the defence of their homes and firesides. Every effort was made to raise as large a force of Kansas volunteers to meet and check the invader as possible.

In Southwest Missouri the people were nearly equally divided on the issues of the war; but after the withdrawal of the Federal troops from that section, the outspoken Union men either followed Lyon's army to Rolla, fled to Kansas, or concealed themselves in the woods and hills, for they were hunted down, and when found, captured and sometimes shot by mounted parties of secessionists, who rode over the country, appropriating the property of Union people, and committing other lawless acts without any restraint except such as they voluntarily imposed upon themselves. Under these circumstances hundreds of Union men living in the border counties of Missouri fled to Kansas. Many of them suffered great hardships to escape from the rebels, often travelling on foot at night on dim roads, guided only by the light of the stars. The country south of Fort Scott, for a distance of seventy miles, is almost continuous prairie, and was covered with wild grass, in some places high as a man's head, and in travelling upon the dim paths over that section the Union refugees were generally drenched from head to feet by the dew on the grass, so that when they reached Fort Scott they were so exhausted from fatigue and hunger that they were almost helpless for several days. In many instances the men before leaving their homes arranged for their families to join them at a given place in Kansas in a short time, with their horses and cattle and such household effects as could be brought along. But in nearly every case in which a family started to Kansas with their live-stock they were obliged to turn back with the loss of most of their property. Those who expressed themselves in regard to going to Kansas as an asylum were looked upon with greater disfavor than if they were simply Union men.

The Unionists might, and many of them did, oppose the freedom of the slaves, but a man desiring to go to Kansas was supposed to be in sympathy with the abolitionists, and was therefore regarded by the hot-headed secessionist with much bitterness. The Union men of Southwest Missouri, being unable to organize companies for their own protection at home, enlisted into Kansas regiments soon after their arrival in that State. In a good many of the companies of the Kansas regiments raised during this exciting time, probably two thirds of the men were from Missouri.

Fort Scott, Mound City, Paola, and Olathe were the principal points along the Kansas border at which the newly organized companies and battalions were stationed. Detachments of cavalry were sent out from these points every few days into Missouri to ascertain the movements of the secessionists in the border counties of that State. Reports of intended attacks upon the troops at these stations, and of depredations upon Unionists in Missouri, were almost daily brought in by Union refugees. Many a night, upon the strength of a report of some excited citizen or scout, were the troops aroused by the long roll, or call to arms, beat upon the snare-drum. In at least one instance the alarm arose from the excited person seeing a herd of cattle so far off upon the distant prairie that he could not distinguish them from men. At first the recruit thus aroused felt sure that a battle was imminent, and his heart beat almost audibly, but after a few weeks the beating of the long roll at night had a less exciting effect upon the recruits.

By the middle of August the five new regiments which General Lane had been authorized to raise, could muster an effective force of twenty-five hundred men. Having received information that General Price was preparing to invade Kansas, General Lane at once commenced collecting all the available troops in the State at Fort Scott, the point which would likely be the first attacked. Colonel William Weer, Fourth Kansas Volunteers, was placed in the immediate command of the troops at that post on his arrival there about the 20th of August. General Lane had not yet arrived from Fort Leavenworth, where he was detained looking after the organization of the troops and the forwarding of supplies for them. Having made arrangements for obtaining and transporting the necessary supplies for his command, he proceeded to Fort Scott, arriving there on the last of August.

In the meantime General Price, who left Springfield on the 26th at the head of his army, arrived at Dry Wood, a point twelve miles east of Fort Scott, on the night of the 1st of September. General Rains' division, which was made up of troops from Southwest Missouri, was given the advance. Arriving at Dry Wood, the General sent forward some three hundred mounted men under Captain Rector Johnson to make a reconnoissance. Captain Johnson moved forward on the Greenfield and Fort Scott road until he came in sight of Fort Scott on Sunday evening, September 1st. About a mile and a half east of Fort Scott he came upon, captured, and drove off eighty Government mules, that had been sent out to graze upon the prairie. Several herders and the picket stationed near the point where the stock were captured, came into the post as quickly as possible and reported what had taken place. The troops were at once called to arms and several companies of cavalry sent out to skirmish with the enemy. But after capturing the mules and several prisoners, the rebel force returned to their main command at Dry Wood, being closely pursued by the cavalry companies of Captains L. R. Jewell and H. S. Greeno of the Sixth Kansas Volunteers as far as the State line. Not knowing the strength of the enemy and night having fallen, Captains Jewell and Greeno posted a strong picket near the State line and then returned to Fort Scott. They ascertained that the rebel detachment, after crossing the line into Kansas, had taken off as prisoners all the able-bodied men found at home. These citizen prisoners, however, were subsequently released or escaped.

General Lane, who had just arrived from Fort Leavenworth, assumed command of all the troops at the post and in Southern Kansas. He had received information which satisfied him that Price's main army was in the neighborhood of Dry Wood, and he thought it likely that the rebel general might endeavor to move up during the night so as to be in readiness to attack the next morning. To guard against a possible surprise, he ordered pickets posted out two to three miles on all the roads leading into Fort Scott from the south, east, and north. He also despatched a courier to Colonel C. R. Jennison, commanding the Seventh Kansas Volunteer Cavalry, then encamped near Barnesville, twelve miles north on the Little Osage, to bring forward his regiment on a forced march. The Colonel moved promptly and reached Fort Scott about three o'clock the next morning. Colonel James Montgomery's battalion Third Kansas Infantry and Colonel Hamilton P. Johnson's battalion, Fifth Kansas Volunteer Cavalry, also arrived during the night and the next morning. On the morning of the 2d, General Lane ordered Colonels Johnson and Jennison to take the available mounted force of their regiments, together with two or three cavalry companies of the Sixth Kansas Volunteers, in all about twelve hundred men, and move out in the direction of Dry Wood, and reconnoitre the position of the enemy, ascertain something of his strength, and, if possible, develop his intentions. These troops left Fort Scott about ten o'clock and encountered the enemy in force at Dry Wood about two o'clock in the afternoon. A lively skirmish ensued in which several men were killed and wounded on each side. General Rains declined to be drawn out of the timber, where he had his troops posted to good advantage for receiving an attack, and the Federal officers were too cautious to attack a masked force which they believed to be superior in numbers to their own.

Though the opposing forces were unable to join in close combat, they continued to fight at long range until about five o'clock, when the Federal officers withdrew their forces from the field and fell back to Fort Scott. Just at sundown two or three ambulances returned to Fort Scott from Dry Wood with the Federal wounded, and in a short time afterward the head of the cavalry column appeared in sight. About this time a report came to General Lane that the enemy in strong force were pursuing his cavalry, and that the rebel generals intended to attack Fort Scott that night. The Kansas Commander at once ordered out all his infantry, about one thousand men, and marched them out on the road nearly two miles east of town, and formed them in line in the open prairie, and waited an hour or so for the enemy to advance. In the meantime a violent thunder-storm was gathering in the northwest, and being unable to ascertain any thing concerning the movements of the enemy, since his cavalry had left the field, General Lane returned to Fort Scott with his infantry about ten o'clock in the midst of a terrific rain and thunder-storm. He was satisfied that the rebel forces would advance early the next morning and attack the post, and believing that his force was insufficient to meet them, he ordered all his troops to withdraw from Fort Scott that night and fall back to the north side of the Little Osage, fourteen miles northwest. A rumor was current that the town was to be burned as soon as the enemy came in sight. The soldiers therefore packed their knapsacks to the utmost capacity, and no doubt in many cases with useless articles that they had brought with them into the service.

At eleven o'clock General Lane's infantry filed out of town and took up the line of march for the Little Osage.

They had all scarcely crossed the Marmiton River just north of the town, when the storm burst again and the rain poured down in torrents. The vivid flashes of lightning and the loud peals of thunder impressed the soldiers with the fact that they were obliged to expose themselves to the fierce rage of the elements as well as to man's inventions of destruction.

As soon as it was known that General Lane had ordered his troops to fall back from Fort Scott, most of the citizens commenced getting ready to leave with the army. When the next morning dawned the town was almost deserted by the male citizens. Some four hundred of Jennison's cavalry, however, stayed all night, having been ordered to remain until the enemy appeared in sight, and they destroyed and damaged the property of the citizens in a disgraceful manner. Early on the morning of the 3d, all General Lane's trains and troops, except the outpost left at Fort Scott, arrived on the north side of the Little Osage, where it was decided to make a stand should General Price determine to follow up and give battle.

Large details were at once made from the troops and set to work throwing up fortifications to command the approaches to the position. The troops worked industriously, and by the evening of the 4th had constructed perhaps a quarter of a mile of breastworks. General Lane named the place Fort Lincoln in honor of the President. On account of the steep banks on each side of the Marmiton and Osage rivers, there were very few good crossings over them. The recent heavy rains had slightly raised these streams so that they were rendered impassable for trains and artillery for several days. To guard against a flank movement, General Lane ordered three hundred cavalry to guard the Barnesville ford of the Osage, one and a half miles west of the State line, and five miles east of Fort Lincoln. He also kept his cavalry scouting the country between the Marmiton and Osage rivers, as far east as the State line, and officers commanding detachments were instructed to give immediate notice of the advance of the enemy.

The presence of a large rebel army encamped within four or five miles of the Kansas line created great excitement among the people of the border counties. It was generally believed that if not checked in their progress the country they marched over would be laid waste. At any rate the situation was such that General Lane called out all the able-bodied men of Bourbon and adjoining counties, to serve for a period of fourteen days in defending Kansas against the rebel invasion. In this emergency call he got out in two or three days upward of one thousand men. Though such an irregular force would not be very effective against well-organized troops, they would be of some service in keeping up a bold front. After despatching a courier to Major Prince, the commanding officer at Fort Leavenworth, to send forward all the reinforcements he could spare with as little delay as possible, and after making all possible preparations for resisting the further advance of the enemy, General Lane received information that General Price had broken up his camp at Dry Wood, and had taken up the line of march for Lexington.

The rebel general saw that if he invaded Kansas his advance would be contested at every point, and that his progress would likely be so much delayed that by the time he arrived at the Missouri River General Fremont would probably have thrown forward from St. Louis and North Missouri a large force to meet him.

The Federal troops thus collected for opposing the rebel invasion of Kansas were subsequently known as "Lane's Brigade." As soon as General Lane received definite information through his scouts and escaped Union prisoners that the enemy had abandoned the plan, temporarily at least, of invading Kansas, and were marching toward Lexington, he at once commenced moving most of his troops north along the State line, where they could watch the movements of the rebel forces. The battalion of the Sixth Kansas Volunteers under Colonel W. R. Judson was ordered to return to Fort Scott to garrison the post and to scout the country south of that post. General Lane's little army was isolated from any other Federal force, and serious apprehensions were felt lest the enemy should attempt to enter the State at some point north of Fort Scott. In several despatches General Lane laid before General Fremont the condition of affairs along the Kansas border and urgently appealed for reinforcements. In a few days, however, the danger of invasion was felt to be passed, and the attention of General Fremont and his brigadiers was directed to Lexington, to the reinforcing of Colonels Mulligan and Peabody, who were holding that place with about three thousand men.

The officials reports showed that the casualties on the Federal side in the action at Dry Wood were five killed and twelve wounded, and on the Confederate side four killed and sixteen wounded.

Even after Price had moved north to attack Lexington, there were still fears that General McCulloch would make an effort to take Fort Scott. In reply to his communication, the Confederate Secretary of War had authorized him, if he thought proper, to take position at that place with his command. For the next month and a half the protection of all Southern Kansas was left to the battalion of infantry and cavalry of the Sixth Kansas Volunteers stationed at Fort Scott under Colonel W. R. Judson.

CHAPTER XI.

THE SIEGE AND FALL OF LEXINGTON.

THE secessionists magnified the action at Dry Wood on the 2d, claimed that they had gained an important victory over General Lane's forces, and boldly declared that General Price would march to the Missouri River, and take possession of all the towns on that river west of Boonville. To the Union men in Southern Missouri the situation looked gloomy in the extreme. The rebel army marched northward without resistance, and the Unionists could not hear of success crowning the Union arms in any quarter. On the contrary, slight reverses on the Federal side they heard of through secession sources as great disasters. The numbers of Federal killed and wounded in any given action were magnified ten to twenty times, and the rebel losses were stated as insignificant.

That the Federal officers highest in command in Missouri displayed an utter lack of aggressiveness and concert of action after the death of General Lyon was apparent to the intelligent men of both sides. General Pope, with an army of nearly five thousand men, was employed in North Missouri in chasing bands of rebel guerillas, while Colonel Mulligan, with a regiment of Illinois volunteers, and Colonel Peabody, with fragments of three or four regiments of Missouri Home Guards, was stationed at Lexington and Warrensburg, south of the Missouri River, to confront the rebel army under Price. A large Federal force of perhaps ten thousand men was also encamped around Jefferson City.

A few days after the action at Dry Wood reports reached Colonels Peabody and Mulligan that Price was advancing upon Lexington with a large army. These Federal officers at once notified General Fremont, and appealed to him for reinforcements. In the meantime detachments of secessionists from Central and Western Missouri were daily joining Price and giving him accurate information of the numbers and position of the Federal troops at Warrensburg and Lexington. The rebel general also ascertained that the Government had large quantities of quartermasters' and commissary supplies stored at Lexington, and that the Federal troops had a battery of light artillery and several mortars,—all of which would make a prize worth making a zealous effort to seize. Colonels Peabody and Mulligan, hearing of the advance of the rebel forces, at once commenced fortifying Lexington, with the view of holding out until reinforcements arrived. Colonel Everett Peabody had under his command Majors Van Horn's and Berry's battalions of Missouri cavalry, the Thirteenth and Fourteenth Regiments Missouri Home Guards, and the Twenty-fifth and Twenty-seventh Regiments Missouri Mounted Infantry. Part of this force was posted at Warrensburg, thirty miles south of Lexington, to look after the secession organizations in that section, and to give notice of any advance of the rebel army from the South.

On the 10th of September the cavalry advance of General Price's army arrived at Warrensburg, but the Federal commander, not deeming his force strong enough to check the enemy more than a few hours, evacuated the place about midnight, and fell back to Lexington, burning several bridges behind him to retard the movements of the rebels.

In the meantime General Parsons, with a division of three thousand secessionists, had marched north parallel with the columns of Price and Rains, but about twenty-five miles east of their line of march, and taken possession of Georgetown, some four miles northwest of Sedalia, the terminus of the Missouri Pacific Railroad. General Fremont was promptly advised of these movements of the enemy. He saw now that the troops of Peabody and Mulligan were isolated, and he knew that they could not hold out long against the converging columns of the combined rebel forces. He therefore immediately telegraphed orders to Colonel Jeff. C. Davis, commanding the Federal forces around Jefferson City, to move forward with reinforcements to the relief of Lexington at once. The troops could be transported over the Pacific Railroad to Sedalia, within fifty miles of Lexington, in a few hours. It would then have taken only two days' easy marching to have reached the besieged troops, or to have come up with and attacked the enemy in the rear. But Colonel Davis found abundant excuses for not complying with his instructions to move forward until it was too late. He first complained that he had not sufficient wagon transportation to convey his supplies when his troops were transported to the end of the railroad. In the next place, two days' supplies would not be sufficient to start out with to attack the enemy. Instead of putting himself at the head of a strong column and marching to the relief of the Federal garrison at Lexington, he frittered away a whole week in preparing to meet imaginary contingencies. His troops were perhaps better equipped with the necessary appointments of an army taking the field than most of the rebel forces. The country between Sedalia and Lexington was the richest agricultural section of the State, and would have afforded ample supplies for subsisting his troops and animals. He knew that the rebel generals improvised means of transportation by impressing teams from citizens of the country through which they marched. The emergency was great, and he could have adopted a similar course without casting an unfavorable reflection upon the Government. Then again, the river was open, and Lexington could have been reinforced by sending up troops by steamboats.

But while General Fremont and his lieutenants were thus wasting precious time, General Price was daily drawing his lines tighter around the beleaguered garrison at Lexington. He was also being steadily reinforced by the State Guard forces from the different districts of North Missouri. The divisions of Generals Thomas A. Harris and Martin E. Green and Colonel J. P. Saunders crossed the Missouri River from North Missouri, and joined him in time to participate in the siege of Lexington. From Warrensburg he resumed the march toward Lexington as soon as his infantry and artillery came up. He also despatched orders to General Parsons, at Georgetown, to join him near Lexington.

On leaving Warrensburg, General Price, at the head of a large cavalry force, again pushed forward to overtake the retreating Federal detachment, but he was unable to do it. He continued the pursuit to within two and a half miles of the Federal fortifications, when he again halted, bivouacked for the night, and waited for his infantry and artillery. At daybreak, on the morning of the 13th, a skirmish took place between his pickets and the Federal outposts. He ordered his main force at hand to the support of his pickets, and Colonels Mulligan and Peabody reinforced their outpost. The Federal troops at once opened a brisk fire upon the rebels, when General Price, not wishing to be drawn into a general engagement, fell back two or three miles, until he met his infantry and artillery. He then moved forward again with his army, and driving in the Federal outposts, found the Federal troops drawn up in line near the city. A sharp skirmish ensued, but the Federal commanders were not willing to hazard a battle, and withdrew their forces to the intrenchments. General Price at once moved up his forces, and took positions within artillery range of the Federal fortifications, and opened fire upon them with shot and shell from Bledsoe's and Guibor's batteries. The Federal battery responded with much energy, and Federal sharpshooters were posted so as to annoy the rebels as much as possible.

Thus the booming of artillery, from early in the afternoon until the shades of night had fallen, announced to the citizens of the city and the surrounding country that the opposing forces had commenced the struggle for the possession of that important place. General Price became satisfied that the Federal garrison were determined to resist his attacks to the last extremity, and, feeling that his force was not strong enough to make a successful assault, and being short of ammunition, withdrew his army to the Fair Grounds, near the city, and encamped there until the 18th.

Colonels Peabody and Mulligan daily looked for reinforcements, under Colonel Davis, from Jefferson City, and under General Sturgis, from Mexico, Missouri. During the respite allowed them by General Price, waiting for his ammunition train, the Federal commanders at Lexington were busy in strengthening their position. They were advised of the intentions of the enemy of renewing the attack in a day or so, with augmented forces and more extensive preparations.

In the meantime, his ammunition train having arrived from Springfield, and having also received large reinforcements, General Price again moved his army into the city, and surrounded the Federal troops in their fortified position. He ordered General Rains to occupy, with his division of upward of three thousand men and two three-gun batteries, a strong position north and east of the Masonic College, around which the Federal troops had thrown up intrenchments. General Parsons was directed to occupy with his division a position southwest of the Federal works, and to open upon them with Captain Guibor's battery. The Confederate divisions of General Steele and Colonel Jackson were posted near the divisions of Generals Rains and Parsons as reserves, but as the Federal force was not strong enough to fight in the open field to advantage, the rebel general was not obliged to bring his reserves into action. Colonel Rives, who commanded General Price's fourth division in the absence of General Slack, was ordered to lead it along the river bank to a point immediately beneath and west of the Federal fortifications. He was soon reinforced by portions of the divisions of Generals McBride and Harris.

The different divisions of the rebel army having taken the positions assigned to them, General Price, at ten o'clock on the morning of the 18th, ordered his batteries to open fire upon the besieged Federal garrison, and in a short time thereafter pushed forward his skirmish lines within range of the Federal small-arms. A few moments after this, the conflict with small-arms also became quite animated on both sides, but without either side gaining any decided advantage. The Confederate officers were anxious to gain protected positions for posting part of their men to fire upon the Federal troops when they exposed themselves above their works. But the moment the rebels showed any intention of making an assault by exposing themselves in unprotected positions within range, Colonel Mulligan ordered his battery to use grape and canister generously. The Federal sharpshooters, too, with unerring aim brought down promptly many a Southron while peering around at a distance deemed safe yet not beyond rifle range. Gradually General Price's forces secured protected positions, from which sharpshooters and skirmishers were thrown out to annoy the Federal troops.

Colonel Mulligan made several sorties during the day to dislodge the rebels from the positions thus gained, and was, in a measure, successful. A Federal force of three or four hundred men occupied a strong position around Anderson's house, on the summit of a bluff overlooking the Missouri River, and about one hundred and twenty-five yards from the Federal intrenchments. This position General Price determined to carry by assault, and ordered up for the purpose the divisions of Generals Harris and McBride and Colonel Rives. In a short time the rebel forces were on the ground, and under the eyes of their leaders moved forward, and, after a short struggle, captured the position. Knowing its importance as a part of his defences, Colonel Mulligan ordered out a strong force to retake it, which he did in the evening, after making a gallant charge. But as he was pressed at other points, the Federal commander could not spare a sufficient number of troops to hold this important position. He had reoccupied it but a short time when the rebel generals rallied their forces in overwhelming numbers and, after a severe conflict, retook it, and held it during the remainder of the siege. At the end of the struggle the ground was strewn over with the dead and wounded of both sides, and the pools of blood here and there attested with what earnestness men will fight for fancied wrongs, as well as for a Government that guarantees the freedom of all, limited only by the like liberty of each. While this conflict for the possession of the heights near Anderson's house was going on, part of the rebel force, under Colonel Rives, moved down the bank of the river and captured a steamboat partly freighted with Government supplies. The possession of the heights near Anderson's house was of great advantage to the rebel forces, for, besides being a position from which they could more effectually use their artillery against the Federal works, it also enabled them to command the river and to obstruct Colonel Mulligan's water supply.

When the sun descended and darkness covered all, the soldiers of the opposing forces rejoiced, for they had suffered much from fatigue, thirst, and excessive heat during the day's operations. From morning until the dusk of evening the roar of artillery was almost incessant, while with small-arms the skirmish and volley firing were well-nigh continuous. General Price's forces occupied during the night the positions they had gained during the day. Strong guards were posted in front of his several divisions, with instructions to give instant notice should they discover the Federal forces preparing to make a night assault upon the Confederate lines. But the night passed without general alarm, and when the morning of the 19th dawned, General Price's forces had strengthened their positions at different points by temporary field-works, and were prepared to draw their lines tighter around the Federal garrison. The day was consumed in skirmishing and desultory firing on both sides. General Price could not advance his lines beyond the field-works constructed, without exposing his men to a sweeping fire of the Federal artillery. He was extremely anxious to bring his operations to a successful conclusion as speedily as possible, lest he should also have to fight Federal reinforcements which were reported to be marching to Lexington.

The situation with the Federal garrison was also becoming serious, for their water supply had been cut off by General Price's army. In constructing the fortifications, the Federal officers had not made ample provision for supplying the troops with water in the event of a siege. By holding certain defensive positions the supply of water could have been maintained, but if these should be taken no provision was made for supplying the troops with water after they fell back behind their second line of defences.

Several hundred bales of hemp found in the warehouses of Lexington suggested to the Confederate leaders a new plan of constructing defensive works for approaching the Federal fortifications. In making a reconnoissance of the hospital position on the bluff, General Harris came to the conclusion that his operations would be much facilitated and attended with less loss of life by the construction of flank defences, and for this purpose requested of General Price permission to take about one hundred and fifty bales of the hemp thus found. The request was granted and the morning of the 20th dawned with brighter hopes for the success of the Confederate arms.

Colonels Marshall and Mulligan could have escaped with their troops and with the public property to the north side of the Missouri River any time between the 13th and 18th, for two steamboats were lying at the wharf subject to their orders. But having received instructions from General Fremont to hold the place to the last extremity, they did so, and then it was too late to retreat.

General Harris having obtained the bales of hemp required, had them transported to the points designated and saturated with water to prevent them from taking fire from the exploding shells of the Federal guns or from the discharge of small-arms in the hands of the rebel infantry posted behind them. They were then arranged in a line and pushed forward by the rebel soldiers toward the Federal position in parallel approaches. This new movement was vigorously met by the Federal commander. Under his direction the captain of the Federal battery turned his guns upon the movable works of the enemy, and in a short time was throwing shot and shell and grape and canister against and around them with such tremendous energy that the rebels were temporarily checked in their advance. The earth trembled from the shock of the thundering artillery and from exploding shells, and nearly every pane of glass in the windows of the nearest buildings was broken to pieces. Finding that his movable breastworks were going to afford such satisfactory protection to his troops in approaching the Federal works, General Price renewed the attack with the utmost vehemence from every quarter. His four batteries, under Captains McDonald, Clark, Guibor, and Kelley, were posted so as to cross-fire the Federal position, and the shot and shell from them were very destructive among Colonel Mulligan's horses and mules. A few of the Federal soldiers were also killed and wounded by pieces of exploding shells.

In spite of every effort of the Federal commander, the enemy continued to advance under cover of their movable breastworks. From early in the morning until two o'clock in the afternoon the roar of battle was continuous. The cross-fire of the rebel batteries was beginning to tell with considerable effect upon the Federal troops, and they were much exhausted and suffering from intolerable thirst for want of water. Colonel Mulligan and his principal officers met in council, and the situation was briefly discussed. Even should they hold out another day there was no prospect of the arrival of reinforcements, and they were not strong enough to cut their way through the rebel lines and escape. They were deeply sensible that through the blunder or incompetency of the Department commander or his subordinates, they had been placed in a most humiliating position. Seeing no way by which they could escape, they resolved to open negotiations with General Price with a proposition to surrender the Federal forces under their command upon certain terms. A white flag was displayed from the Federal works, and the firing soon ceased on both sides. General Price sent forward one of his staff to ascertain the object of the flag. After some discussion it was agreed by the Federal officers that the Federal forces should lay down their arms and surrender themselves prisoners of war. To the soldiers of Colonel Peabody's command, who had recently left their homes in different parts of Missouri to defend the honor and integrity of the Government, it was a moment of grief and anguish almost insupportable, when they saw the Stars and Stripes, the emblem of national unity and of equal rights among men, hauled down and replaced by the rebel flag. They knew that they would soon hear the bitter taunts and insulting remarks of their secession neighbors who had espoused the Southern cause and joined the rebel army.

When the Federal troops stacked their arms and surrendered, General Price at once took possession of the Federal fortifications and public property captured. In his official report he stated that his entire loss during the siege was 25 killed and 72 wounded. The casualties on the Federal side were 39 killed and 120 wounded, and 3,000 prisoners. Among the prisoners were Colonels Mulligan, Marshall, Peabody, White, Grover, Major Van Horn, and 118 other Commissioned Officers. The Government also lost upwards of 1,000 head of horses and mules, about 100 wagons, large quantities of quartermaster's and commissary supplies, together with 5 pieces of artillery, 2 mortars, and 3,000 stands of arms. Lieutenant-Colonel B. W. Grover, Twenty-seventh Missouri Volunteers, was mortally wounded.

The fall of Lexington was a severe blow to the Union cause in Missouri. It was a disaster that was due to a series of unpardonable blunders and want of concert of action among subordinate Federal commanders, and came near producing a panic of such magnitude as would have left Kansas at the mercy of the rebel armies of Generals Price and McCulloch. Had General Fremont shown an aptitude for coördinating the movements of troops to accomplish a given purpose, he could have thrown forward to Lexington, in four or five days, not less than 25,000 men, and this, too, without withdrawing troops from threatened points in Southeast Missouri. The fall of Lexington was not only felt in Missouri, but it startled the loyal section of the country, and President Lincoln, becoming impatient of the barren results of General Fremont's operations, directed General Scott to telegraph him: "The President is glad you are hastening to the scene of action. His words are: 'He expects you to repair the disaster at Lexington without loss of time.'" General Fremont had fully ten days' notice of the advance of Price upon Lexington, and in which to either withdraw the troops from that point or to reinforce them. On the 5th of September, General Lane sent a dispatch from Fort Lincoln by special courier to Major Prince, the commanding officer at Fort Leavenworth, that Generals Price and Rains had the day before broken up camp at Dry Wood, near Fort Scott, and were reported to be marching on Lexington with ten thousand men and seven pieces of artillery. Major Prince received this dispatch on the 7th, and immediately telegraphed it to General Fremont in St. Louis, which was then the headquarters of the Western Department.

General Fremont ordered Generals Pope and Sturgis to reinforce Mulligan at Lexington with the troops of their respective commands operating in North Missouri. General Sturgis marched from Mexico with four thousand men, and arrived on the north bank of the Missouri River, opposite Lexington, shortly after the rebels captured the ferryboat, and, having no means of crossing the river, was obliged to become an idle spectator to the unequal conflict. When he found it impossible to cross the river, and saw that Lexington must certainly fall in a day or so, he marched his column to Kansas City, the next point it was supposed the enemy would attack. It was a point of great importance, and one that the Government was unwilling to give up without a hard struggle, for its possession by General Price would give him easy access to the border counties of Kansas, which he had threatened with devastation.

While on the march to Lexington, General Price sent orders to Generals Thomas A. Harris and Martin E. Green, commanding the secession forces in North Missouri, to join him, by forced marches, in the neighborhood of Lexington at the earliest practicable moment. They hastily collected their forces together, and in a few days were on the march to join their chief, thus leaving North Missouri almost free from armed secessionists.

The movement described left General Pope free to throw forward into Lexington at least four thousand troops, but for some unexplained reason it was not done, although the men could have been transported by railroad to Chillicothe or Hamilton, within fifty miles of Lexington. But his indifference to the fate of the Federal forces at Lexington was not the only charge the Union men of North Missouri laid against him. They were mortified and annoyed at his conduct in the administration of affairs in his district. In their prayers and petitions to the Department commander, protesting against his conduct they characterized him as a tyrant and madman. He proposed to hold the Union citizens as well as the secessionists responsible for the depredations and warlike acts committed by the armed bodies of secessionists. A train on the Hannibal and St. Joseph Railroad was fired into by a force of armed secessionists a few miles west of Palmyra in Marion County. For this act of the enemy he proposed to hold the law-abiding citizens of Marion County responsible—Unionists as well as secessionists. He issued an order requiring the County Court to pay all the expenses of quartering the Federal troops in their midst. On the failure of the County Court to provide for quartering and subsisting the troops in the county, he notified the City Council of Palmyra to do so, and on their refusal to comply with his order the troops were to take the supplies wherever they could get them.

That section was soon in a state of anarchy. The drunken and lawless acts of the Federal soldiers were believed to have been countenanced from headquarters, instead of being corrected. Union men were insulted, and robbed, and plundered of their property, and his policy was regarded as a license for such acts. In one instance it was asserted and not denied that the members of a regiment shipped over sixty head of horses and mules, taken from citizens, to Chicago, to be sold, the proceeds of which went to the men's private accounts. In numerous other cases the Federal soldiers appropriated to their private use the property of the citizens of the localities through which they marched or where they were stationed. The Federal soldiers also in several cases fired at the citizens from the railroad trains with as little concern as they would fire at a flock of birds. Such abuses tended to alienate all classes instead of making them fast friends of the Government. Bands of secessionists were allowed to organize and commit depredations within less than a day's march of the idle Federal troops, and weeks passed without efforts being made to disperse them.

General Pope took such a peculiar view of the situation that he tried to persuade General Fremont that the disturbances in that section were purely local, and that the people were "merely fighting with each other . . . to satisfy feelings of personal hostility of long standing." And of the Union citizens who protested against his actions, he charged them with wanting to raise Home Guards for self-protection, so that the United States would be obliged to distribute a large amount of money among them in payment for services, supplies, and equipments, which would benefit the people of that section. With a finely equipped army of fully five thousand men he did scarcely any thing to chastise the organized bodies of bridge-burners and train-wreckers, who continued to increase in numbers and boldness until they marched south to join General Price near Lexington.

But in spite of the strange conduct of the Federal

commander of the district, Colonel David Moore organized a force of Union Home Guards in Northeast Missouri, and continually attacked and harassed General Green, then commanding the secession forces in that section, and compelled him to hasten his departure therefrom.

General Lyon had won the affection of the Union men in Southern Missouri by giving them protection and by encouraging them to organize for their own protection, a policy more rational than that which General Pope adopted.

General Pope was not alone in the short-sighted policy of punishing the citizens indiscriminately for the war-like acts of the secessionists. He had a rival in General Lane, commanding the Kansas Brigade, then operating in the western counties of Missouri, between Fort Scott and Kansas City. General Lane had acted with commendable energy and zeal in raising and organizing troops to defend Kansas from invasion. As Generals Price and Rains marched north towards Lexington after the action at Dry Wood, General Lane continually threatened the left flank of the Southern forces, and no doubt did much good in preventing detachments of secessionists from making raids into Kansas. Hearing that a considerable force of secessionists had been left at Osceola to guard Price's ammunition train and other supplies collected at that point for his army, General Lane made a rapid march with his command to that place for the purpose of capturing or distroying the train and supplies. When he arrived near town he met with some resistance by a small force of the enemy. He then ordered up his battery of four guns and commenced to shell the woods and town. After a little skirmishing the secessionists retreated, and General Lane moved into town, and not only destroyed the stores which had been collected for the Southern forces, but burned the place to ashes. It was the county-seat of St.

Claire County, was at the head of navigation on the Osage, and contained much substantial wealth for a town of its size.

Many of the merchants of Western and Southwestern Missouri and the Indian Territory, had their goods shipped from the East to Osceola by steamboats, and from thence hauled in wagons to their destination. As it was the nearest shipping point to the lead mines of the Southwest, hundreds of tons of lead turned out by the Granby Mines were hauled there annually and shipped to St. Louis.

In destroying the town General Lane seemed to be unconscious of the fact that his conduct would be just excuse for retaliation, and that it might possibly come with interest. And he did not seem to realize that he was making a name for his command that should not attach to troops engaged in honorable war. Perhaps upwards of one third of the people of St. Claire County were Unionists, and many of the men were in the Federal army; some, too, in Kansas regiments. General Lane destroyed and appropriated their property with the same recklessness that he did the property of the secessionists. He was incapable of seeing that the loyal people of Missouri were entitled to the protection of the Federal Government, even if they were fighting its battles.

CHAPTER XII.

SPRINGFIELD RETAKEN AND ABANDONED.

AFTER the fall of Lexington, General Fremont commenced to concentrate his forces for an active campaign against General Price's army. On the 27th of September he left St. Louis for Jefferson City to take command of the troops in the field in person. He had collected, at different points in Central and Western Missouri, for the campaign, about forty thousand troops, organized into five divisions.

General David Hunter, commanding the First Division, of 9,750 men, was directed to take position at Versailles, about forty miles southwest of Jefferson City. This division formed the left wing of the army.

General John Pope was assigned to the command of the Second Division, of 9,220 men, and was directed to move to Boonville, fifty miles northwest of Jefferson City. His division formed the right wing of the army and occupied positions at Boonville, Glasgow, and Brunswick, and points on a line between those places.

The Third Division, 7,980 strong, under General Franz Sigel, forming the advance of the army, was posted at Sedalia and Georgetown, sixty-four miles west of Jefferson City, with instructions from the General to keep in communication with the troops stationed at Marshall, in Saline County.

General Asboth, commanding the Fourth Division, of 6,451 men, constituting the reserve, was directed to take position at Tipton, on the line of the northern branch of the Pacific Railroad, thirty-eight miles west of Jefferson City.

The Fifth Division, of 5,388 men, under General McKinstry, formed the centre of the army, and was posted at Syracuse, five miles west of Tipton.

The last week in September, General S. D. Sturgis had 3,000 men holding Kansas City, and General J. H. Lane had 2,500 men near the State line between Fort Scott and Kansas City to protect Kansas from invasion by the secessionists. At this time there was no certain communication between the forces of Sturgis and Lane and General Fremont's other divisions, for General Price's army occupied the territory between them.

On the 3d of October General Fremont ordered a forward movement of the five divisions, constituting the *Army of the West*. The general movement of the several divisions was in the direction of Sedalia, which threatened to cut Price's army off from the South. Finding that General Fremont was concentrating a large force at Sedalia, the terminus of the Pacific Railroad about fifty miles distant, and had taken the field in person, General Price left Lexington about the 1st of October with his army and commenced to retreat south with an immense train of plunder. He marched leisurely, crossed the Osage River at Osceola, and on October 16th encamped near Greenfield, one hundred and fifty miles south of Lexington. General Fremont, as was generally claimed, had ample time to have concentrated his forces in the neighborhood of Warrensburg, thirty miles west of Sedalia, the terminus of the railroad, and about the same distance south of Lexington, for the purpose of cutting off Price from the south. Such a movement, it was held by those criticising General Fremont's operations, would have compelled Price to fight, disperse, or surrender his forces. But as he was permitted to retreat from Lexington and cross to the south side of the Osage without molestation, the Federal troops were obliged to turn their faces to the south, and in a tedious pursuit endeavor to overtake their wily foe.

General Fremont moved up from Jefferson City to Tipton, and on October 11th ordered another movement of the several divisions of the Army of the West towards the southwest in pursuit of Price's army.

General Pope, commanding the right wing, was directed to march the troops of his division, including those of Colonel Jeff. C. Davis' Brigade, posted at Georgetown, by way of Sedalia to Leesville on Grand River, thirty miles southwest of Sedalia.

General Sigel, commanding the Third Division, was directed to start from Sedalia on the 13th of October, and by three marches, by way of Spring Rock and Cole Camp, occupy Warsaw on the north bank of the Osage, about forty miles south, and immediately commence preparations to cross the river at that point.

General McKinstry was directed to march with the Fifth Division from Syracuse *via* Cole Camp to Warsaw, and coöperate with General Sigel if necessary. The river was not fordable, so that the army was detained at Warsaw several days constructing a bridge over the Osage for crossing the troops, trains, and artillery.

No enemy appeared on the south bank to dispute the crossing of the troops or offer opposition to the construction of a bridge, so that the batteries under protection of which the pioneers were set to work were not obliged to fire a single shot.

General Hunter was directed to move with the left wing from Tipton on the 13th of October, and in four marches proceed by way of Versailles and Minerva to Duroc Ferry on the Osage, about fifteen miles below Warsaw.

General Asboth was directed to start from Tipton on the 14th of October and march the Fourth Division by way of Cole Camp to Warsaw.

The retreat of Price's army from Lexington, left Generals Sturgis and Lane at Kansas City and along the Kansas border, free to use their forces in co-operation with General Fremont's main army. They were, therefore, ordered to move south by way of Clinton in Henry County, and to keep within supporting distance of General Pope's division on the extreme right of the army.

The several division commanders moved forward with their troops as directed, and on the 16th of October a detachment of cavalry and four companies of Missouri infantry, of General Sigel's advance, commenced crossing the Osage in a flat boat. In addition to the pioneer corps, details of men from the infantry regiments were made to get out timber and work on the bridge. By the troops working incessantly day and night, the bridge was finished in a few days, and by the 22d the divisions of Generals Sigel, McKinstry, and Asboth had crossed to the south side of the Osage and were on the march to Springfield. General Pope's division, which had marched to Leesville, on the right of the army, not finding the Osage fordable directly in front, were obliged to change their line of march to the southeast by way of Warsaw, and also crossed the Osage on the improvised bridge at that point on the 25th of October.

The first division under General Hunter crossed the Osage at Duroc Ferry, and in the general advance kept within supporting distance of the other divisions.

The commands of Generals Sturgis and Lane crossed the Osage above Osceola, and marching southeast came in communication with General Sigel's division near Cornersville in Hickory County.

General Fremont arrived at Warsaw on the 16th, and remained there until the 22d, when most of his troops having crossed the Osage, he moved forward to Cornersville on the road to Bolivar and Springfield. For some eight to ten miles on both sides of the Osage the country is rough and hilly, so that he was obliged to have his sappers and miners do much work on the main road leading south, to make it passable for his heavy trains of artillery, baggage, and supplies. The rapid movement of his cavalry south saved the bridge over the Pomme de Terre River at Fairfield, eight miles south of Warsaw, from being destroyed by the enemy. From Cornersville to Bolivar and Springfield the State road ran over smooth, open prairies, except where it crossed creek or river bottoms and the breaks of the creeks and rivers. The several divisions of the army having struck a more open country, could now move forward with greater facility. They were within easy supporting distance of each other, and could perhaps in case of an emergency be concentrated at a given point within twenty-four hours.

This fine army of upwards of forty thousand men moved forward as if hourly anticipating an attack; yet as a matter of fact there was no danger whatever, for Price's army was one hundred miles away, retreating rapidly south. From the conflicting reports brought in by scouts, spies, and Union refugees, General Fremont was unable to decide whether the enemy were retreating towards Arkansas or had come to a stand and were determined to fight on ground of their own choosing.

The moment General Price found that General Fremont's army had advanced to Warsaw and had commenced crossing the Osage, he broke up camp near Greenfield and retreated southwest to Neosho. The country directly south of this place is rough and broken, and well adapted for defensive operations. The Granby lead mines, seven miles northeast of Neosho, were furnishing the Confederacy about two hundred thousand pounds of lead per month, a quantity sufficient to supply the small-arms of the Confederate army.

The fugitive secession governor, Jackson, called the Legislature together at Neosho. Of course the Union members, who constituted a majority of those legally elected, were not present. After a session of about two weeks, the rump Legislature thus convened passed an ordinance of secession and elected delegates to the Confederate Congress. The reported advance of General Fremont's army south of the Osage hastened the adjournment of the Legislature at Neosho and the retreat of Price's army towards the southern line of the State, for the purpose of forming a junction with the Confederate forces under General McCulloch, then posted at Cross Hollow in Benton County, Arkansas.

After a brief halt near Cornersville, about twenty-five miles south of Warsaw on the west side of the Pomme de Terre River, to allow the several divisions of his army to cross the Osage and take their proper positions in the general advance, General Fremont resumed the march towards Springfield *via* Bolivar with the advance division under General Sigel. Shortly after dark, on the evening of the 24th, he sent forward Major Chas. Zagoni with 150 men of his body-guard, and Major F. J. White with 180 mounted men detailed from the First Missouri cavalry to make a reconnoissance in the direction of Springfield. Majors Zagoni and White marched all that night, and the next day about twelve o'clock captured five men of the rebel picket guard and of a foraging party, eight miles north of Springfield, from whom information was obtained that a force of at least 1,500 Confederate troops were in town that day. One of the rebel pickets not captured hastened to camp and gave the alarm of the Federal advance, so that the Confederate officers immediately got their men out in line ready to receive an attack.

It was decided by the Federal officers after some deliberation to move forward and attack the enemy, even though it appeared from reports that they outnumbered the Federal detachments five to one. Feeling sure that the secessionists would be informed of their approach in time to make some preparations to receive them, Majors Zagoni and White determined to make a detour of five miles to the southward and to approach the Confederate camp from the west on the Mount Vernon road. Emerging from the woods near this road, just west of Springfield, the Federal cavalry came unexpectedly upon the secessionists drawn up in line of battle. On first coming in full view of the enemy, Major Zagoni did not find the ground suitable for forming his men in line. He was therefore obliged to march several hundred yards through a lane, and at the end of it take down a rail fence and form in full view of the Confederate camp. In a moment his troops were in line, and he ordered them to charge the enemy. His men dashed forward in gallant style, and in a few moments broke the line of Confederate infantry and cavalry in several places, dispersing their cavalry and compelling their infantry to retire to the woods. Part of the Confederate cavalry fled through town. Major Zagoni rallied his men and pursued them, and charging through the streets in every direction soon cleared the town of armed secessionists. He then returned to the court-house and raised the Union flag over it, and liberated the Union prisoners who had been confined by the secessionists. It was now getting dark, and having suffered a heavy loss of men and horses, he decided to retire until he met the advance of the army. His men were exposed to a hot fire from the time they entered the lane until they passed through it and formed in line.

The casualties on the Federal side were sixteen men killed and twenty-six wounded. Major Zagoni reported that his men buried twenty-three Confederate dead on the field.

In the meantime General Fremont had been pushing forward with General Sigel's division, and arrived at and occupied Springfield on the evening of the 27th of

October. The divisions of Generals Pope and Hunter, and the commands of Generals Lane and Sturgis were back some three or four days' march. On his arrival at Springfield General Fremont sent out his cavalry in every direction to ascertain the position and movements of the enemy. After some four days, his scouts brought him information that Generals Price and McCulloch had united their forces in the southwest corner of the State, and were advancing rapidly to attack him. Believing the reports of the Confederate advance, he despatched orders to Generals Pope and Hunter to push forward with their divisions as rapidly as possible.

The reported advance of the Confederate armies originated from General Price's movement of his forces from the neighborhood of Neosho to Cassville, about thirty-five miles southeast, on the Springfield and Fayetteville road, for purposes of observation. This movement was an advance towards Springfield, but General Price had no notion of marching to attack the Federal army at that place. He did not believe that General Fremont's army was much more than half as large as it really was, until the Federal divisions had crossed the Osage and commenced to advance rapidly towards the south and southwest part of the State. A few days after the Federal troops commenced arriving at Springfield, intelligent secessionists left that place and went directly to Price's headquarters and reported to him what they had seen and heard, and gave him something approaching a correct statement of the strength of the Federal army that was moving against him.

An officer sent out by General McCulloch with a detachment of Texas cavalry to make a reconnoissance in the vicinity of Springfield returned and reported that General Fremont had 48,000 to 50,000 men and 120 pieces of artillery, and was preparing for an immediate forward movement. This report, which was corroborated by information from other sources, alarmed Generals Price and McCulloch, and General Price immediately retreated from Cassville to Pineville, twenty-five miles west. Around Pineville the country is hilly and rough, and he considered that point the best in Southwest Missouri for taking up a defensive position, for with the heavy timber that covered the hills and hill-sides, it would be easy to obstruct the roads and approaches by felled trees.

General McCulloch occupied a position with his cavalry near the Springfield and Fayetteville road and near where that road crosses the State line from Missouri into Arkansas. He kept his infantry and artillery back to the rear some fifteen miles at Cross Hollow, and immediately commenced to obstruct the roads and approaches to his main camp by felling timber across them. On an examination of the country around his position, he came to the conclusion that it could be turned to the east, and that it would not be prudent to risk a battle there with the superior Federal forces. He thought that it would be better to fall back to the Boston Mountains, about fifty miles south, to make a stand, and so informed General Price.

To embarrass and delay the advance of the Federal army as much as possible, General McCulloch destroyed all the mills, forage, and grain, as far in the direction of Springfield as his detachments of Texas cavalry could go with safety, and advised General Price to pursue a similar course. The Missouri general was strongly and decidedly opposed to such a policy, for he saw that it imposed upon many of his own people, and upon the families of his own soldiers, a punishment severer than any that had been proposed by the Federal commanders. He saw, too, that such a policy would alienate many who had warmly espoused the cause of the South and in return expected protection, and would make positive and open enemies of those who had not yet taken a decided stand with either party.

Detachments of General McCulloch's cavalry visited the farms on each side of the Springfield and Fayetteville road, for a distance of ten to fifteen miles, and along the fertile valleys of Crane Creek, Clear Creek, and Flat Creek, and set fire to the stacks of hay, oats, and wheat, and to the cribs of corn and other grain that had been thrashed out and stored away by the farmers. Thus the people were obliged to witness the destruction of their property, and to find themselves reduced to the verge of starvation by the arbitary will of a man who had little regard for their rights and feelings or even for their sufferings.

On the 12th of November Generals Price and McCulloch had a conference near Pineville, and agreed upon a plan of defensive operations to be adopted as soon as the Federal army advanced from Springfield. General Price stated that their combined forces amounted to 25,000 men, and he thought that by taking advantage of good defensive positions they could check the advance of the Federal troops. His troops belonged to the State Guard and were opposed to being taken out of the State, and if taken out his army would gradually melt away and lose its efficiency.

While the Confederate generals were thus preparing for a defensive campaign, the different Federal divisions of the Army of the West arrived at Springfield, and some of the brigades advanced to the southwest as far as the battle-field of Wilson Creek. General Fremont had now retaken Springfield, and driven the Southern armies out of the State or into the extreme southwestern corner of the State, and was ready to commence further offensive operations. A great many Union men who had fled to Rolla and Sedalia during the latter part of the summer returned with the army and were daily arriving, to be reinstated in their homes, confidently hoping that the Federal troops would permanently hold the country. But their hopes were not then to be realized.

On the 2d of November General Fremont received an order from the War Department relieving him from the command of the Department of the West, and instructing him to turn it over to Major-General David Hunter, commanding the first division. The failure to reinforce General Lyon, the fall of Lexington, and the enormous expenses incurred in organizing the Army of the West, with perhaps some intriguing, created the impression at Washington that General Fremont was not the proper officer to command the department. The result of it all was that Hon. Simon Cameron, Secretary of War, and General Lorenzo Thomas, Adjutant-General of the Army, made a tour west and visited St. Louis and Tipton, where General Fremont was on the eve of moving south, for the purpose of making an investigation of the administration of affairs connected with the Army of the West. In the investigation it appeared that the methods of obtaining supplies for the army were not in conformity with the methods provided in the Army regulations and in the acts of Congress, and that proper economy was not observed and enforced by the commanding general in the administration of the public service. The result of the investigation was laid before the President, and it was decided to remove General Fremont.

When the order was issued relieving him from command, Mr. Lincoln wrote a letter to the new commander of the Department of the West, in which he proposed to offer a few suggestions. He suggested that, as Price's army had probably retreated into Northwestern Arkansas, leaving the southwestern part of the State of Missouri free from the enemy, the Army of the West should give up the pursuit, and halt and divide into two corps of observation and retire to Rolla and Sedalia, the termini of the railroads. It was also suggested that General Lane should retire to the Kansas border with his command, and that by judicious co-operation of the Federal forces the enemy would not likely attempt to return to Missouri before or during the approaching cold weather. General Hunter, who had perhaps intrigued for the removal of General Fremont, coincided with the President's views, and in a few days issued orders for the retrograde movement of the army.

On the 8th of November the troops commenced to fall back from Springfield and vicinity. A corps of about nine thousand men, under General Sigel, retired in the direction of Rolla. General Pope, with the balance of the army except General Lane's command, retired in the direction of Sedalia *via* Warsaw. General Lane fell back to Fort Scott, Kansas, and distributed his troops along the border to protect the people of Kansas from incursions by the Missouri secessionists. In a short time the troops under Generals Pope and Sigel reached their destinations and went into camp.

The retreat of the army from Springfield was a severe disappointment to the Union people of Southwest Missouri. It was estimated by intelligent Union men of that section that the laying waste of the country by the Southern troops and the falling back of the Federal army from Springfield, was the cause of upwards of four thousand men, women, and children leaving their homes without money or means for providing for the necessaries of life during the approaching winter. Nearly everybody who sympathized with the Union cause in Missouri regarded the withdrawal of the Federal troops from Springfield as the greatest military blunder which had up to that time been made in the West. It had cost the Government some millions of dollars to occupy that section by General Fremont's army, and now it was surrendered, without a struggle, to a demoralized and retreating foe. The utter rout of the Federal forces would not have had, it was generally asserted, a more reviving effect upon the waning cause of the secessionists in Missouri, than the retreat of General Fremont's army from Springfield.

On the morning of the 16th of November, a few hours after having received information that the Federal forces had commenced to retreat, General McCulloch started from his camp, some seventy miles southwest of Springfield, with his whole available mounted force, in pursuit, hoping to overtake and capture some of the Federal trains and detachments. But when he arrived at Springfield on the evening of the 18th, he found that the Federal troops had been gone a week, and that it was useless to pursue them farther. He returned in a few days with his troops to Northwestern Arkansas, and requested and obtained permission to visit Richmond for the purpose of giving the Confederate authorities correct information in regard to military and civil affairs in the section in which he had been serving during the past summer and autumn.

General Price received information of the retreat of the Federal troops from Springfield about the same time as General McCulloch, and issued an order for his army to take up the line of march north in the direction of Newtonia and Osceola on the morning of the 16th of November. In a few days his divisions spread over the country between Fort Scott and Springfield, and were engaged in plundering and robbing the Union people of their property with unpitying recklessness. The advance of General Fremont's army forced hundreds of violent secessionists to leave the State with the Southern army as it fell back. When it became known that the Federal troops had retreated, and that Price was marching towards the interior of the State, most of the secessionists returned to their homes with much bitterness of feeling, and were generally unsparing in their denunciations of the Unionists.

General Price's proclamation calling for fifty thousand men encouraged and licensed the confiscation of the property of the Union people. He said that there was two hundred million dollars' worth of property belonging to the Union men of Missouri which could not be removed, and that if the Federal authorities took the property of the secessionists, they should have its value with interest out of the property of the Unionists. In the sudden withdrawal of the Federal army from Springfield and the sudden return and reoccupation of the country by Price's troops, a good many Union men who had ventured home were cut off and captured by the latter and held as political prisoners. These prisoners were subject to the threats and abuse of the Southern soldiers and camp followers, and no consideration was shown them or attention paid to their comfort, and as the cold weather of winter came on they suffered the severest hardships from cold and hunger.

On his march towards the Osage General Price announced his intention of taking his army to the Missouri River again, and urged General McCulloch to join his forces with him in the enterprise. General McCulloch had left for Richmond when General Price's request for co-operation reached his headquarters; but Colonel McIntosh, who was left in command of his division, declined to co-operate for the reason that his Southern troops were not furnished with warm enough clothing to engage in a winter campaign in the rigorous climate of Missouri, and for the further reason that he was satisfied that no good would come out of the enterprise.

General Price advanced with his army to Osceola on the Osage, but did not venture to go north of that place towards the Missouri River, for he probably saw that if he attempted to do so his army would likely be captured or destroyed. Though the Union cause in Missouri suffered much by the withdrawal of the Federal army from Springfield, there was now a prospect that a more vigorous and rational policy would henceforth be pursued.

If General Hunter had intrigued for the removal of General Fremont, his triumph was of short duration, for on the 9th of November, before he got back to St. Louis, General H. W. Halleck was assigned to the command of the Department of the West. The new commander soon had his energies taxed to the utmost in looking after the affairs of his extensive department. General Price, having been permitted to return to the interior of the State with his army, had organized extensive uprisings of the secessionists in many of the counties north of the Missouri River. It was considered essential by the Federal commander that these uprisings should be put down before making a forward movement in the direction of the recently evacuated territory of the southwest.

CHAPTER XIII.

BATTLES OF CHUSTO-TALASAH AND CHUSTENAHLAH, CREEK NATION, INDIAN TERRITORY.

In the summer and fall of 1861 the Confederate authorities sent agents to the different Indian tribes of the Indian Territory for the purpose of endeavoring to win them over to the Confederate cause, or to stir up strife among them on the issues of the war. A few Indians, mostly half-breeds, in the Chickasaw, Choctaw, Cherokee, and Creek tribes owned slave property; but as a general rule very few of the Indians of any of these tribes manifested any interest in the question of slavery. When the Confederate commissioners first approached the full-blood leaders of the Creek and Cherokee tribes on the subject of severing their relations with the United States, the Indians expressed themselves cautiously but decidedly as preferring to remain neutral in the great conflict that was plunging the country into blood and strife.

Conspicuous among the leaders of the Indians who took a positive and decided stand against organizing the Indians to oppose the Federal Government, was Hopoeithleyohola, the old chief of the Creek tribe. The Confederate commissioners had succeeded in winning over ex-Chief McIntosh by appointing him Colonel, but perhaps upwards of two thirds of the people preferred to be guided by the counsels of their venerable old chief, Hopoeithleyohola. In the fall of 1861, Colonel Douglas

H. Cooper, commanding Department of Indian Operations under authority from the Confederate Government, made several ineffectual efforts to have a conference with the old chief, for the purpose of effecting a peaceful settlement of the difficulties that were dividing the nation into two hostile camps. Hopoeithleyohola suspected that forcible and arbitrary measures were about to be taken against him. He had no confidence in the promises of Colonel Cooper, and paid no attention to his overtures made through some of the leading men of the nation. Finding that the secessionists were going to make war on him unless he joined them, he determined to make such resistance as was in his power, and at once commenced organizing his warriors for the conflict which he saw was near at hand. He knew that more than one half of his own people were with him ; that many of the Seminoles and Cherokees would join him rather than the Confederates, and through the United States Indian Department he had received some encouragement that the Federal Government would send him assistance from Kansas. Of Indians and negroes he estimated that he could, perhaps, bring into the field about fifteen hundred men, armed mostly with rifles and shot-guns ; but he knew that the Indians were all fine marksmen. He was satisfied that he could hold his own against the disaffected Indians of his tribe who had espoused the Confederate cause. If they should be reinforced by white troops, then he knew that the issue would be doubtful ; but he thought that he would be able to give the combined forces a good deal of trouble, for he was thoroughly acquainted with the trails and defensive positions of his country. If driven from one position he could retire to another, and if driven from all, he could retire to Kansas, where he expected to meet his friends and allies.

Failing to get Hopoeithleyohola into conference for the purpose of discussing the question of his bringing his followers over to the Confederate side, Colonel Cooper determined to collect all the troops at his disposal, attack the old chief, and force him into submission or drive him from his country. For this purpose he took with him from Fort Gibson, on the 15th of November, fourteen hundred white and Indian troops, consisting of a detachment of the Fourth Texas Cavalry, under Lieutenant-Colonel Quayle; six companies First Regiment Chickasaw and Choctaw Mounted Rifles, under D. N. McIntosh, the Creek war chief, and the Creek and Seminole battalion, under Major John Jumper, Seminole chief. He moved up the Deep Fork of the Canadian River in search of Hopoeithleyohola's camp. Toward the end of the first day's march the abandoned camp of the Union Indians was found, and the trail from it followed until about four o'clock in the afternoon of the 19th, when the smoke from his new camp was discovered near the Red Fork of the Arkansas River. Colonel Quayle charged this camp with his Texas cavalry, but found on entering it that it had been recently deserted. It was only an outpost. Colonel Quayle pursued the retreating Indians some few miles until they entered the timber skirting a creek, upon which the main body of Hopoeithleyohola's forces were encamped.

As soon as the Texas troops came within rifle-range of the timber, Hopoeithleyohola's warriors poured a well-aimed volley into them, suddenly checking their advance, throwing them into confusion and causing their immediate retreat. Seeing the effect of the volley, the Union Indians quickly advanced, keeping up a hot fire as they moved forward, and in less than half an hour drove their assailants from the field with the loss of upward of twenty men killed and wounded. It was getting dark as the Texas troops and Choctaw Indians approached the timber, and for a short time the flashes from the rifles of the Union Indians came from the dark recesses of the forest with great rapidity and telling effect. After the Confederate attacking party had fallen back to the main command, Colonel Cooper decided to move forward and renew the fight, but as it had become very dark when he arrived on the ground of the recent skirmish, no engagement took place that night. Hopoeithleyohola, finding that he could not hold out against the combined forces of white troops and Indians, retreated north during the night in the direction of Kansas. The Confederate forces did not follow him, but marched into his camp the next morning, and found a few old ponies and broken wagons, which were useless.

About this time General Fremont had arrived at Springfield, Mo., with a large Federal army, and was daily expecting to move south for the purpose of attacking Generals McCulloch and Price, whose forces were encamped in Southwest Missouri and around Cross Hollows and other points in Northwestern Arkansas. As General McCulloch expected that he would soon need all the white and Indian troops operating in the Indian country to check General Fremont's advance, he ordered Colonel Cooper to march with all his troops to a point near Maysville, on the Arkansas line, so as to be within easy co-operating distance. The colonel promptly complied with this order, thus leaving Hopoeithleyohola undisturbed and master of the field for several weeks. In this interval he was busy in making preparations to resist the forces of those leaders who had made war upon his people without any just cause.

In the meantime General Fremont was relieved and the command of the Federal forces at Springfield turned over to General Hunter. This general ordered his army to fall back from Springfield to Syracuse, Sedalia, and Rolla, for the purpose of going into winter quarters.

On receipt of the information of the retreat of Fremont's army from Springfield, General Price, commanding the Missouri State Guard, co-operating with the Confederate troops, at once moved north to Osceola, on the Osage River, and General McCulloch moved most of his army, composed of Texas, Louisiana, and Arkansas troops, into Northwest Arkansas and Southwest Missouri, and directed Colonel Cooper to return with his command to the Indian country and prosecute the war against Hopoeithleyohola. The Confederate general then left for Richmond, leaving Colonel James McIntosh in command of the troops of his district. As the Cherokees were almost as much divided on the issues of the war as the Creeks, the old Union chief, Hopoeithleyohola, was kept informed of every movement of the secessionists, and determined to give them blow for blow.

Having made the necessary preparations, Colonel Cooper left Spring Hill, near Concharta, on the 29th of November, with some one thousand one hundred mounted men, composed mainly of the troops who were in the first expedition, and marched in the direction of Tulsey Town, in the neighborhood of which place he was informed by escaped prisoners that Hopoeithleyohola was encamped with all the warriors of his nation. After some skirmishing Colonel Cooper's command came in sight of the Union Indians, strongly posted at Chusto-Talasah, or Little High Shoals, on Bird Creek, on the 9th of December. Colonel Drew, commanding the Cherokee regiment of five hundred men, and Colonel Sims, with three hundred men of the Fourth Texas Cavalry, encamped at different stations in the Nation, were ordered by Colonel Cooper to join him on the march to Tulsey Town. Colonel Drew arrived in the neighborhood of Hopoeithleyohola's camp on Bird Creek one day in advance of the main command under Colonel Cooper, and received information that the old chief of the Creeks was desirous of making peace. This information was communicated to Colonel Cooper on his arrival on the 8th of

December, and he at once authorized and directed Colonel Drew to send an officer to Hopoeithleyohola with instructions to propose a conference with him the next day, and to assure him that he (Colonel Cooper) did not desire the shedding of blood among the Indians. Major Pegg, of the Cherokee regiment, was sent to present the propositions of Colonel Cooper. When he reached Hopoeithleyohola's camp he found him surrounded by his warriors, all painted for the fight and ready to make the attack upon the Confederate forces that night. Colonels Cooper and Drew were encamped with their forces about two miles apart that night on Bird Creek, and as soon as the information reached Colonel Drew's camp that Hopoeithleyohola was preparing to make an attack his Indians became panic-striken and fled, leaving their camps with their tents standing. It turned out, however, that the Union Indians did not make the anticipated attack, and the next morning Colonel Cooper sent down a detachment of his command and brought in the tents, horses, wagons, and equipage which had been abandoned in Colonel Drew's camp.

The Confederate officers were now satisfied that Hopoeithleyohola meant to fight, and Colonel Cooper at once commenced preparations to attack him with his whole force. He sent out Captain Foster with two companies of cavalry on the morning of December 9th to make a reconnoissance. After marching down Bird Creek about five miles with his main command Colonel Cooper met Captain Foster returning, who reported that he had found the enemy in large force lower down the creek. In a few moments now Hopoeithleyohola's warriors were seen at different points along the timber skirting Bird Creek, and Colonel Cooper ordered his train parked in the prairie, leaving a guard of one hundred men with it, and then proceeded to form his troops in three columns to commence the engagement. The Choctaws and Chickasaws were formed on the right, the Texas troops and Cherokees in the centre, and the Creeks on the left. Colonel Cooper moved forward his three columns at a quick gallop, and in a short time drove the Union Indians from their advanced position to the stronger and well chosen position at Chusto-Talasah. While Colonel Cooper was thus engaged, his rear-guard, which had not yet come up, was attacked by about a hundred of Hopoeithleyohola's warriors, who, suddenly emerging from the timber, advanced whooping and firing. The Confederates were in the way of being put to flight when they were reinforced by a squadron under Captain Young from the Choctaw and Chickasaw regiment, who in turn forced the Union Indians to retire to the timber on Bird Creek.

The position chosen by Hopoeithleyohola at Chusto-Talasah, where he determined to make a stand and fight the rebel forces, was naturally a very strong one to resist an attack made with small-arms. It was at a gorge of a bend of Bird Creek, the bend being in the form of a horseshoe and 400 or 500 yards in length. The creek made up to the prairie on the side approached by the Confederate forces in an abrupt and precipitous bank about thirty feet high. On the opposite side of this bank was the inside of the horseshoe or bend, which was densely covered with heavy timber, cane, and tangled thickets. The position was also strengthened by felled trees and by the creek forming the horseshoe, which was deep and only fordable at certain places known only to the Union Indians. In this bend Hopoeithleyohola's forces were posted after they were obliged to fall back in the preliminary skirmish. A house and crib at the mouth of the bend served as a shelter for a while, from which his sharp-shooters kept back the Confederates. The Union Indians, however, were finally driven from this position back into the bend, contesting with much obstinacy the ground fought over.

The Confederate troops made repeated efforts to dislodge them from the bend, but without success. Every time a detachment of Hopoeithleyohola's warriors showed themselves in an opening or in the prairie, the Confederates charged them to the timber, when a volley from the concealed Indians threw the charging column into confusion, and sent it back in a hasty retreat. Thus the fight was kept up for about four hours, each party alternately advancing and retreating, when the Confederates withdrew from the field and retreated to their camp, some five miles back. At times the firing was quite spirited on both sides. On the Confederate side Colonel Cooper reported a loss of fifteen men killed and thirty-seven wounded. Hopoeithleyohola's loss was not known exactly, but was much less than that of the Confederates, from the fact that his warriors fought nearly all the time from protected positions of their own choosing. Colonel Cooper was so badly crippled in the engagement that he retreated to Fort Gibson to await supplies and ammunition from Fort Smith. Hopoeithleyohola fell fack in a northwesterly direction to Shoal Creek, a tributary of the Verdigris, took up a strong position, and awaited the further movements of the Confederate forces.

Colonel Cooper had been so severely punished in the engagement with Hopoeithleyohola, on the 9th of December, that he felt obliged to call upon Colonel James McIntosh commanding the Confederate forces at Van Buren, Arkansas, for reinforcements. Colonel McIntosh agreed to furnish the troops and to lead the column in person, to subdue or drive from the country the obstinate old chief of the Creeks; and for this purpose he took a force of sixteen hundred mounted men composed of five companies of Colonel Lane's South Kansas-Texas Regiment, the available strength of Colonel Griffith's Sixth

Texas Cavalry, seven companies of Colonel Young's Third Texas Cavalry, Captain Bennett's company of Texas cavalry attached to division headquarters, and four companies of the Second Arkansas Mounted Riflemen, under Captain Gibson. He marched to Fort Gibson, and had an interview with Colonel Cooper, and entered into arrangements for mutual co-operation in the campaign against Hopoeithleyohola. He was to march up the Verdigris River with his column, according to the proposed plan, while Colonel Cooper's column should move up the north side of the Arkansas River and get in the rear of the Union Indians. With the troops described, at noon, on the 22d of December, Colonel McIntosh left Fort Gibson and marched in search of the enemy. After going into camp, on the evening of the 25th, part of Hopoeithleyohola's force appeared in sight, but the Confederate commander declined to be drawn into a fight. He sent out a regiment of cavalry, however, to observe the movements of the Union Indians, and to guard against a surprise. Early on the morning of the 26th he left camp, and moved cautiously in the direction of the mountains, which extended back into the Big Bend of the Arkansas River, where it was reported that Hopoeithleyohola was encamped with his forces. Before noon the advance of the Confederate force reached Shoal Creek, a tributary of the Verdigris, and as soon as Captain Short had crossed the stream a heavy fire was opened upon him by the Union Indians from a position partly concealed. The Confederates recoiled from the volley, but Colonel McIntosh coming up with the main body, quickly ordered the troops into line. Colonel Griffith was ordered into position with his regiment on the right, and Colonel Young on the left. Colonel Lane, with his regiment, and Captain Bennett's company and the four companies of the Second Arkansas Mounted Infantry, were posted in the centre. The Union Indians were posted along the brow of a wooded hill, along the base of which flowed Shoal Creek. Part of them were mounted and part, under Halek Tustenuggee, the Seminole chief, were dismounted, and fought from behind trees and rocks. They kept up a continuous fire upon the Confederate troops until they crossed the creek that separated the opposing forces.

After skirmishing for a short time, Colonel McIntosh ordered his troops to cross Shoal Creek, and then charge the Indians on the hill. The right wing, under Colonel Griffith, had been dismounted to attack the Indians on the flank. About twelve o'clock the bugles sounded the charge, and the Confederate forces dashed forward, and in a moment more were climbing the hill amid a shower of bullets that came from the rifles of Hopoeithleyohola's warriors posted behind trees and rocks along the crest of the hill. The Indians held their position for some time with remarkable stubbornness, but were finally obliged to fall back before superior numbers of the well-equipped Confederate troops. Hopoeithleyohola and Halek Tustenuggee frequently rallied their forces, and bravely resisted every step of the advance of the Confederates. After the Indians were finally driven back through their camp, they lost a good deal of their property, which in the hurry and excitement of the moment could not be collected and sent forward with the women and children. The battle lasted until four o'clock in the afternoon, when the Indians retreated into the rocky gorges and deep recesses of the mountain, where they could not be pursued to advantage. In his command Colonel McIntosh reported a loss of nine men killed and forty wounded. The loss on the side of the Union Indians is not definitely known. Through Confederate sources it was stated at two hundred and fifty killed. This estimate is too large, unless the Confederates killed the women and children they captured. The Confederate loss was probably heavier than Hopoeithleyohola's in the battle, but the Confederates were charged with killing a good many Indians and negroes who were cut off from their command during the engagement. The number thus killed is not known. Near Hopoeithleyohola's camp the Confederate troops captured one hundred and sixty women and children and some ponies and sheep, but no warriors are reported to have been taken.

Immediately after the engagement Hopoeithleyohola set out for Kansas with all the warriors, women and children of his nation, together with such property as his people could collect. In his retreat he was joined by large numbers of Cherokees and Seminoles, who sympathized with him, and were willing to share with him the hardships incident to exile rather than be forced to submit to Confederate dictation. Fate dealt hard with the old Union chief and his devoted followers. They were driven from their homes in midwinter and obliged to face the pitiless storms and chilly blasts of the North for many days before reaching the land of their friends and deliverers. In the last battle many of them had lost most of their live-stock, property, and personal effects, and their sufferings on the retreat through snow, sleet, mud, and ice, pursued by a relentless foe, were indescribable. Many a brave warrior who, through fatigue or through efforts to take his family and personal effects along with a poor or almost broken-down team, had fallen behind, was cut down by the swift Texas cavalry or murdered by Stand Watie's Indians, who were unable to find the foe until he was on the retreat. The weather was so severe that Colonel Cooper reported that one of his soldiers froze to death while on the expedition against Hopoeithleyohola.

CHAPTER XIV.

RAID ON INDEPENDENCE AND INCIDENTS OF THE WAR ON THE BORDER.

AT the commencement of the war there was much bitterness of feeling between the Proslavery men of Missouri and the Free-State men of Kansas. For several years prior to the war a man from Kansas, if known to be a Free-State man from that Territory, could not with safety travel through some of the western border counties of Missouri. He was liable to be abused or injured and his property injured or destroyed. In some instances, Free-State men, or supposed Free-State men, had their wagon-covers cut up, their wagon spokes cut out, and their horses shot. In ordinary conversations a Free-State man dared not assert the dignity of his manhood in maintaining his own side of a question, particularly if it were a political question, without danger of personal injury or insult.

In Border-Ruffian times organized bands of Proslavery men from Missouri went into Kansas and robbed and plundered the Free-State men of their property, and were thought none the less of at home for doing so. A man sold a horse on the Public Square at Independence at auction, was asked in regard to the title, and replied that he had a Kansas title, which was regarded as good, for the reason that a citizen of Kansas dared not come into the county and contest the title or claim his property.

When the war commenced and the Kansas volunteers were organized, they remembered the domineering spirit of the Proslavery men, the indignities to which the Free-State men had been subjected when they crossed the line into Missouri, and how they had been robbed and plundered of their property in Kansas.

In the latter part of September, 1861, Colonel C. R. Jennison, of the Seventh Kansas Cavalry, was temporarily stationed at Kansas City, with his regiment, which was recently organized. In the contests between the Free-State and Proslavery men he had been shot and wounded near to death by them in Southern Kansas. His name had figured prominently in the newspapers for several years before the war as a leader of the Free-State men in Southern Kansas. His regiment was therefore made up of men who participated or sympathized with him and Montgomery in their contests with the Proslavery men during the Kansas troubles, and were anxious to get even on old scores. Up to the latter part of September, 1861, no Federal troops had been stationed at Independence, and none had been there except Major Prince's command of Regular cavalry and infantry that marched down there the day after the Rock Creek affair, and marched back to Kansas City the next day. The domineering spirit of the secessionists had been intensified during the summer, for the rebel armies had been successful in several engagements in Virginia; Price's and McCulloch's armies had compelled General Lyon's army to withdraw from Springfield after the battle of Wilson Creek; and General Price had marched almost without resistance from Springfield to Lexington, and laid siege to and captured that place. While these important events had been taking place mainly in favor of the secessionists, the Unionists of Jackson County, largely in the minority, were persecuted, spotted, and several killed, among them Rev. Samuel Stewart, a minister of the Old Methodist Church.

The Union men looked around for relief against these outrages, and one William Miles, City Marshal of Independence, and other Union men of the county, went to Kansas City and reported the situation to Colonel Jennison. After some preparation the colonel made a rapid march from Kansas City, and arrived at Independence, and had the town surrounded by seven o'clock in the morning. Very few of the citizens knew any thing of his approach until they saw his soldiers marching in on nearly every street. The secessionists, who had long been in the habit of acting in an overbearing manner towards Union men, were greatly surprised, and quickly commenced hunting hiding-places. It has been said, and perhaps truly, that the man, backed by numerous sympathizers, who will mistreat a stranger from another State, is invariably a coward.

Colonel Jennison's men searched the town thoroughly and brought out from their hiding-places in cellars, barns, garrets, etc., men who had never tolerated in their presence those who advocated free speech, equal rights, and Free-State doctrines. All classes of men, Unionists as well as secessionists, were gathered up by the troopers to the number of three or four hundred, and marched to the Court-House Square and corraled there, as the citizens called it. It was nearly twelve o'clock before the citizens were all gathered up and brought into the square.

In the meantime part of the troops had been busy gathering up plunder, such as horses, carriages, guns, fine furniture, etc. This property was all brought to the Public Square. The carriages, buggies, and wagons were strung out around the Public Square, and the furniture and household goods were piled up on the stone sidewalk around the court-house iron fence, and extended nearly around the square.

After the citizens had been corraled and the plundered property had been brought to the Public Square, Colonel

Jennison read from his seat in his saddle a list of Union men who could come out of the crowd corraled. When he had finished reading off the list he then directed Mr. Miles to pick out of the crowd all the remaining Union men, cautioning him that for every secessionist he picked out he, Colonel Jennison, would give him a cut over the face with his sabre. Directly after Mr. Miles commenced picking out the Union men, the mounted soldiers surrounding the Public Square, with their carbines resting on their right legs, talking among themselves, remarked that, if they commenced shooting at exactly one o'clock, at the rate the men were being picked out, they would not have a shot apiece. This conversation of the soldiers was heard by most of the secessionists, and some of them were deeply affected, and it was reported that many of them imagined that they could feel the blood trickling from their wounds.

After the Union men had been separated from the secessionists, they were directed to the south side of the square, where Colonel Jennison addressed to them a few words of apology, to the effect that he regretted to cause them the inconvenience; that his men were strangers among them, but that they could now go and hunt out their property that had been gathered up, and take it home. He then gave the assembled secessionists a lecture. He talked to them nearly half an hour, reminding them of the wrongs that they had committed against Union men, and what they might expect if they persisted in committing such wrongs; that for every Union man killed, ten of the most prominent secessionists of Jackson County should suffer death. The property of the secessionists was loaded into twelve to fifteen wagons, and taken to Kansas City, and afterwards carried off into Kansas. As the loaded wagons were getting ready to leave, and as Colonel Jennison had finished his lecture to the secessionists, they were permitted, after the soldiers had been withdrawn from around the square, to return to their homes.

There was a rather comical side to this serious affair. When the train started out on Lexington Street, nearly all the wagons, carriages, and buggies were loaded with every description of household goods and furniture, and with colored women and children. This was the first opportunity the colored people of this section had to taste of their freedom, with United States soldiers standing between them and their masters. The wagon-train going out of town, with household goods and furniture and colored children thrown into the wagons in a promiscuous manner, made an amusing picture. There were some instances in which colored people who had been well treated by their masters, and who had promised solemnly to stay with them and await the result of the war, were carried away by the excitement of the moment and went off with their deliverers willingly. Some few, however, showed, from their expressions, that they had some doubts about their newly acquired freedom being permanent. For some time before this, a good many secessionists of this section had been sending their slaves off south to Arkansas and Texas. They saw that such property would not be very secure near the Kansas border.

After Colonel Jennison left, the secessionists of Independence and vicinity were more guarded and cautious in their actions towards the Union men, and the latter could meet at their headquarters, without being molested or insulted. About twice a week some twelve to fifteen Union men would meet at this place to read the St. Louis *Democrat*, a staunch Republican paper, and to discuss the news from the seat of war. So much of the news, during the summer and autumn, had been adverse to the Union cause that its friends at these meetings often departed from the room with expressions of disappointment and sorrow. They knew that they had staked all in placing themselves on the side of the Union, and that ultimate defeat of the Union cause meant their ultimate ruin.

In another of Colonel Jennison's raids into Missouri about the time of his raid on Independence, an incident occurred that is worth relating, as showing some of his traits of character. He had captured or taken from a store in Harrisonville a lot of ready-made clothing, and in his march towards the Kansas line a number of colored people left their masters and went along with his command, either on their own motion or by persuasion of the soldiers.

When he pitched his camp near the Kansas line, he took from the colored men who had come along one whose coat and pants were old, greasy, tattered, and torn; whose hat looked as if it had been worn out, cast away, and picked up and used again; and whose shoes were of the coarsest kind, and so nearly worn out as to show his toes, and ordered him to get upon a dry-goods box that had been brought along with clothing in it. The colored man probably thought that he was going to be sold to the highest bidder, and of course dared not disobey the Colonel's order, and mounted the box, looking about as dilapitated as his clothing, or as troubled in mind as those who had been put on the block to be sold and carried to some Southern plantation to wear their lives away under hard-hearted overseers. When he had mounted the box, Colonel Jennison ordered him to pull off his old shoes, and next his pants, and handed him an elegant new pair of broadcloth pants and told him to put them on. He did so, and their good fit showed that the Colonel had measured him almost as accurately by inspection as the merchant tailor would have done with his tape. The colored man looked down at his new pants, cast a glance at the soldiers and all around, and seeing no contracted brows, no indications of threatened harm, commenced losing his distressed expression, to grow younger, and to straighten up.

Colonel Jennison walked around him, and after viewing him carefully declared that he looked like a man, and not a chattel, and told him to pull off his shirt, which was patched and ragged, and handed him a new white shirt with starched linen bosom to put on. He also handed him a pair each of shoes and stockings to put on, which he did. By this time the colored man had a good deal of sunshine in his expression; he had become more erect, and the colonel, still walking around him and inspecting him from head to foot, declared that he believed he was a man and not a chattel.

The colonel next gave him a collar, a black satin vest and black cloth coat, all new and of the right size, and a new hat to put on, which he did with an expression beaming with happiness and delight. The expression of fear had left him, and straightening up he looked a good many years' younger than a few moments before, and continuing to observe him closely from head to foot from different positions, Colonel Jennison declared that he was a man; that the idea entertained by many in Missouri that he was a chattel was all a mistake.

While nearly all Federal officers in command of troops at this early period in the war were returning slaves to their masters, the camps of Kansas regiments were safe asylums for colored people who sought them for their freedom. There were some officers and men of Kansas regiments who would have been willing to return colored refugees to their masters, but there was from the very beginning a feeling of opposition—and an opposition strong enough in numbers to have raised a mutiny had an officer attempted to return colored refugees to their masters. A man who came about camp looking for his slaves, or who was endeavoring to get an order to take them home, would perhaps be told that there was a good deal of careless shooting around camp, and that perhaps it would hardly be safe to linger too long. A hint of this kind was generally sufficient to satisfy the most persistent searcher for his property that he had better leave.

CHAPTER XV.

MILITARY OPERATIONS IN WESTERN AND CENTRAL MISSOURI.

AFTER General Fremont's army fell back from Springfield in the early part of November, Fort Scott, Kansas, was a Federal station right on the border of the territory occupied by the Southern troops. General Price's army was encamped from the neighborhood of Stockton to Osceola on the east, and part of General Ben. McCulloch's troops was stationed at Carthage in Southwest Missouri, scarcely more than a day and night's march from Fort Scott. Scouting parties were frequently sent out in the direction of the Kansas border to observe the movements of General Lane's command. Many of Price's men had returned to their homes temporarily, and Captain Henry Taylor's company of guerillas or rangers were operating in Vernon and Barton counties, and plundering and driving out the Union people of that section. As the rebel forces on the east and southeast were in positions to make a concerted movement against Fort Scott, the Sixth Kansas Volunteers stationed at that post under Colonel W. R. Judson were kept out scouting almost constantly to guard against surprise and capture. The secessionists had threatened to burn the town in retaliation for the burning of Osceola in the fall by General Lane. In fact they had to some extent retaliated by advancing up the Neosho River and burning Humboldt, a small town forty miles west of Fort Scott.

Union refugees were almost daily coming into Fort Scott and reporting to the post commander of the depredations committed by bands of secessionists in the border counties of Missouri, and he realized that his isolated position required the greatest vigilance on his part. On the morning of the 6th of December he sent out Lieutenant R. J. Lewis, Sixth Kansas Volunteers, with ten picked men, mounted, and three citizen scouts, James and William Norris, and Pratt Breeden, to the Horse Creek section of Vernon County, Missouri, to obtain, if possible, information of the movements of Price's army on Sac River, south of Osceola, and of McCulloch's forces on Spring River in Southwest Missouri. The first day Lieutenant Lewis' detachment marched about thirty miles in a southeast direction, and reached a point in the southeast part of Vernon County, where they ascertained from citizens that Captain Taylor's band of secessionists was in that section and might be met at any moment. During the day several small detachments of rebels were seen and chased on Horse Creek, and one prisoner captured, from whom information was obtained that part of Taylor's company was in the immediate neighborhood. As it appeared that Taylor's force was much stronger than the Federal scout, Lieutenant Lewis, about ten o'clock that night, after he had stopped at the house of Ewell Riggs, a Union man, about one mile west of a place called Shanghai, for the night, sent one of his men back to Fort Scott for reinforcements. He did not think that his movements had been so closely watched by the secessionists in the evening as to disclose to them where he stopped for the night, and he did not take the precaution to put out pickets to guard the approaches to the house, and give the alarm should the enemy advance to surprise and attack him.

On retiring that night, however, he directed his men to dispose their arms so that they could lay their hands on them at a moment's warning, for he was mindful of being in the enemy's country.

The secessionists had watched the movements of the Federal detachment in the afternoon, and having ascertained where it stopped, collected some twenty-five men of Taylor's band to attack it early the next morning. Mr. Riggs' house was a frame of half-inch siding, and would afford but little protection against Minie-balls fired into it at short range. But if the men in it were not surprised, it would give them some advantage in fighting a superior force. The night had nearly passed without alarm, so that just before daylight, on the morning of the 8th, privates L. H. Mylius and Ben. Yelton of Lieutenant Lewis' detachment arose and went out and fed their horses and returned and were waking up their comrades, when Mr. Riggs' little son twelve years old came running into the room where the soldiers were, and told them excitedly that a "whole lot" of men were coming up towards the house. The soldiers and scouts instantly seized their guns and were about to open fire, when private Mylius thinking that the men coming up were the reinforcements from Fort Scott, stepped out of the door to see who they were. Just at this moment the rebels, who had approached within twenty feet, for it was yet quite dark, saw Mylius come out of the house, and called to him to surrender. He replied that he had not come there for that purpose, and started back into the house, when the rebels fired a volley into the door and through the siding, wounding Mylius and eight others of the party. The moment Mylius discovered that the men coming up were rebels, he called out to his comrades to open fire upon them, which they did, wounding several, one or two mortally, as was afterwards ascertained.

The moment the Federal detachment opened fire, the secessionists fell back about two hundred yards to obtain shelter. Most of Lieutenant Lewis' party were armed with Sharp's carbines, which threw balls a greater distance than shot-guns and hunting rifles, and they used them effectively against the enemy until they passed behind a hill out of sight. The secessionists had calculated on surprising and killing most of the Federal detachment, and of capturing their horses, but now that they were discovered and exposed to a hot fire, they were anxious to retire as quickly as possible beyond the reach of Federal bullets.

Thinking that the enemy might shortly return with reinforcements to renew the attack or to besiege him, Lieutenant Lewis decided to return to Fort Scott with such of his men as were able to ride, and at sunrise they were all in their saddles and on the march except Mr. Mylius, who was so badly wounded in the shoulder with five buckshot that he was obliged to be left. H. M. Mayberry, B. Yelton, Ben. White, and William Norris were all severely wounded, but with much suffering were able to return with the rest of the detachment.

Lieutenant Lewis ascertained from the prisoner taken, that the main rebel army under General Price, some fourteen thousand strong, was encamped the day before on Sac River about thirty miles east and a few miles southwest of Osceola ; that it was the understanding that General Price was on the march to the Missouri River, and intended to again attack and capture Lexington if it was occupied by Federal troops, and that he had again requested General McCulloch commanding the division of Texas, Louisiana, and Arkansas troops stationed in Northwestern Arkansas and in Southwest Missouri, to join him in the proposed expedition to the Missouri River and in the invasion of Kansas.

In spite of the efforts of the Post Commander at Fort Scott, Confederate scouting parties gradually became bolder. The evening of the 5th of January, 1862, was bitter cold and there was about six inches of snow on the ground.

A picket guard of six men of the Sixth Kansas was posted at a house on the road leading to Nevada near the State line, five miles east of Fort Scott. The weather was so severe that the men relaxed their vigilance to enjoy the comforts of a good fire in the house. While they were thus absent from their station a few yards distant, some forty men of Captain Taylor's company of secessionists rode up, and before the Federal picket could prepare to fight, demanded their surrender. Finding that they were cut off from their horses and exposed to the fire of the secessionists at short range, the corporal of the Federal picket surrendered. The men were paroled and returned to Fort Scott about dark. A detachment of about one hundred and fifty cavalry was at once sent out under Captain Greeno to endeavor to overtake the secessionists, but they had got so much the start that they could not be overtaken that night.

General Price's position near Osceola, on the Osage, gave him control of Western Missouri from the south line of the State to the Missouri River. He could now send out his recruiting parties into North and Central Missouri to enroll and organize those desiring to fight for the Confederacy under his leadership. To assume as bold a front as was considered expedient, he threw General Rains' division north of the Osage. Having advanced so far north, a great many secessionists were encouraged to believe that he would retake and occupy Lexington during the winter. He had been on the Osage only a short time when he received information that several large detachments of recruits from north of the Missouri River were desirous of joining him, but that there was some danger of their being intercepted by the Federal troops stationed at Sedalia. As some of the recruits were unarmed, and others poorly armed, he lost no time in sending a mounted force of eleven hundred men to Lexington to escort them through to his army. The mounted force thus sent out, after remaining in Lexington part of a day, was joined by two thousand five hundred recruits, and then the united forces marched towards Osceola.

General Pope, commanding the Federal troops at Sedalia, had been keeping out strong reconnoitering detachments in the directions of Osceola and of Lexington, and heard of the movements of the secessionists, and determined to intercept them if possible on their march south. He was satisfied that the movements of the Federal troops were watched by Southern sympathizers, and reported to the rebel officers operating in Central and Western Missouri with as little delay as possible. He detached for the expedition two brigades under Colonels Steele and Davis of about four thousand men, infantry, cavalry, and artillery, and in order to deceive the secessionists of Sedalia as to his destination, he marched eleven miles southwest of the city and encamped for the night. It was given out that the destination of the expedition was Warsaw. On the morning of the 16th of December, General Pope directed his column nearly due west, and by making a forced march of thirty miles reached a position at sunset west of the Warrensburg and Clinton road, about half-way between those places and about two miles east of Chilhowee. His advance guard, consisting of four companies of Iowa cavalry under Major Torrence, pushed forward and captured the rebel picket at Chilhowee, from whom it was ascertained that a force of two thousand two hundred secessionists was encamped six miles north of town.

After resting his command for an hour or so, he threw forward ten companies of cavalry and a section of artillery, under Lieutenant-Colonel E. B. Brown, Seventh Missouri Volunteers, to attack the Confederate camp, and to pursue the secessionists if they declined to fight. He also reinforced Major Hubbard with two companies of Merrill's

Horse, Second Missouri Cavalry. In the morning he had sent forward, on the road to Clinton, Major Hubbard with four companies of the First Missouri Cavalry, to watch the movements of the enemy from the direction of Osceola, and to intercept any couriers to the Southern army at that place. Having made these dispositions of his troops, he followed Colonel Brown, with his main command in two columns. One column moved north on the Chilhowee and Warrensburg road, and the other moved around to the northwest and advanced on the Rose Hill and Warrensburg road. The secessionists did not wait for Colonel Brown to get his troops into line, but fled westward and passed around General Pope's left flank, and then moved south. Colonel Brown at once commenced pursuit, and kept it up all that night, the next day, and the next night up to midnight, as far south as Johnstown, near the eastern line of Bates County. He pressed the rebels so closely that they broke up into several detachments; but the main force continued their flight in the direction of Osceola. They were obliged to abandon their wagon trains, but, in their rapid flight, the teamsters had driven their teams off on to by-roads and into farm-yards, and as the wagons and teams had been pressed from the citizens of the country, they could not all be identified and picked up by the Federal troops.

From Johnstown Colonel Brown turned east towards Clinton, to scour the country and to intercept and pick up detachments of the enemy who had left the main command during the hot pursuit. Having completely dispersed the rebel force, he returned and joined General Pope near Warrensburg, on the morning of the 18th. In the expedition he took one hundred and fifty prisoners, and captured sixteen wagons loaded with tents and supplies. These rapid movements of General Pope spread alarm among the secessionists of that section, and many left their homes and moved south within General Price's lines.

On the return of Colonel Brown's command, General Pope at once commenced another important movement. He had ascertained that there was another large force of secessionists north of him, and, on the morning of the 18th, marched leisurely on the road to Warrensburg. Before arriving there, however, the spies and scouts, which he had sent out in the direction of Lexington and Waverly before leaving Sedalia, reported to him that two large forces of secessionists were marching south from Arrow Rock and Waverly, and would probably form a junction and encamp that night at the mouth of Clear Creek, about a mile south of Milford and about ten miles northeast of Warrensburg. To close all outlet to the south, he took up two positions with his troops between Warrensburg and Knobnoster. The two towns are ten miles apart, and about the same distance from Blackwater, where Clear Creek empties into it. General Pope's next movement was to direct Colonel Jeff. C. Davis, Indiana Volunteers, to take five companies of the First Iowa Cavalry under Major Torrence, two companies of the Fourth Regular Cavalry under Lieutenant Copley Amory, and a section of artillery, and march to Milford by a route east of the road the enemy was marching on, and endeavor to turn his left flank and rear. At the same time, Major Marshall, with Merrill's Horse, Missouri volunteers, was directed to march from Warrensburg and form a junction with Colonel Davis, at Milford, by taking a route west of the road the enemy was marching on, and thus turn his right and rear. While these dispositions of the Federal troops were being made, the Confederate force of thirteen hundred men, consisting of parts of two regiments of infantry and three companies of cavalry, under Colonel Robinson, marching south from Waverly and Arrow Rock, on the Missouri River, were going into camp in the timber, on the west side of Blackwater, opposite the mouth of Clear Creek, that flows down from the south. General Pope had taken the precaution of not allowing any citizens to pass through his lines to carry information of his movements to the secessionists. There was a bridge over the Blackwater, just below the mouth of Clear Creek, and only a short distance from the village of Milford. Colonel Robinson had thrown out pickets southeast of the bridge, on the road leading to Knobnoster, and his camp was not perhaps more than a quarter of a mile back of the bridge, so that he could in a few moments, if threatened with attack, put his main force in a position to command it.

Late in the afternoon the command of Colonel Davis, which had been sent out by General Pope from Knobnoster, drove in the enemy's pickets over the bridge across the Blackwater. The stream was deep and impassable, except by the bridge over it, which was held by a strong Confederate force on the arrival of the Federal advance, under Lieutenant Amory, Fourth Regular Cavalry. On arriving at the river, and finding that the enemy were defending the bridge, Lieutenant Amory dismounted his three companies of Regular cavalry and gave the Confederates two volleys, after which they commenced to give way. Lieutenant Amory then mounted his men, and gave the order to charge, and carried the bridge by assault. The secessionists retreated in confusion to their camp, closely pursued by the Federal cavalry. On arriving in sight of the Confederate camp, one company of Regular cavalry, under Lieutenant Gordon, dismounted and fired two volleys into the line of the secessionists, which they returned, killing two and wounding eight Federal soldiers. In a few moments Colonel Davis had his troops in position, ready to make an assault on the Confederate camp, but, before giving the order to charge, a flag of truce appeared. Finding that there was no chance of escape, Colonel Robinson surrendered his entire command of thirteen hundred men just at dark.

Immediately after they surrendered and were disarmed,

the prisoners were marched to General Pope's camp three miles west of Knobnoster, where they arrived about midnight. It was a bitter cold night and the Federal soldiers and prisoners suffered the severest hardships. Of the prisoners captured there were three colonels, Robinson, Alexander, and Magoffin; one lieutenant-colonel, Robinson; and one major, Harris, and fifty-one captains and lieutenants. Colonel Magoffin had been captured in that section the latter part of June by Colonel Cook's command from Cole Camp, and paroled, and he was in arms again in violation of his parole. About 1,000 horses and mules, 73 wagons loaded with powder, lead, and subsistence supplies, and 1,000 stands of arms fell into the hands of the Federal troops.

While these operations were going on under the immediate direction of General Pope, Major Hubbard of the First Missouri Cavalry, who had been sent to Clinton in Henry County from Sedalia, with four companies of his regiment, to watch the movements of the secessionists from the direction of Osceola, was also successful in clearing the section through which he marched of armed bodies of rebels. He pursued a scouting party from General Rains' command into his camp, which was north of the Osage, and captured one entire company of secessionists, with tents, baggage, and wagons. These successful operations of General Pope not only had the effect of stopping General Price's progress north from Osceola to the Missouri River, but of turning him south, for immediately after receiving information of the capture of Colonel Robinson's command with supply train, he withdrew General Rains' division from the north side of the Osage, and took up the line of march for Springfield. Failing to reach the Missouri River as he had given out, disappointed the rebel forces that organized north of the river in anticipation of joining him at Lexington by Christmas. His proclamation had not brought him the recruits he had calculated it would. He was actually losing more men who were returning to their homes at the expiration of their terms of service, than he was gaining in recruits.

Having forced Price to fall back south from the Osage, General Halleck, the Department Commander, next turned his attention to clearing North Missouri of rebel forces and organized bands of bridge burners. He had received information which led him to believe that the disturbances and uprisings in North Missouri were due to predetermined plans of the rebel leaders. He therefore directed General Prentiss, commanding the district of North Missouri to commence at once a vigorous campaign against the Southern forces of that section. In many of the counties of that section, organized bodies of secessionists, from a few hundred men up to two or three thousand, had appeared and were causing the greatest disquietude. Bridge burners, too, acting under instructions from General Price, were endangering the lives of peaceable citizens and giving the Federal authorities much annoyance. They were disguised as citizens of the country, were well armed, rode good horses, and in small detachments of half a dozen or so, were generally able to overpower the guards and set fire to the bridges and escape before a sufficient force of troops could be collected to pursue and take them.

General Halleck issued an order on the 22d of December, that men disguised as peaceable citizens and caught in the act of burning bridges, or destroying railroads or telegraph wires, should be immediately shot. A good many such offenders were pursued by the troops, overtaken and shot, and others were captured and tried by a military commission and condemned. About the 20th of December the several secession forces operating in Howard, Boone, and Callaway counties, were reported to be upwards of 3,000 strong. They were destroying railroad property and even threatening to attack Jefferson City. General Prentiss determined to check their operations, and break up their organization as speedily as possible. Generals Schofield and Henderson, commanding the Missouri State troops in that section, were directed to co-operate with him. He left Palmyra, Mo., on the morning of December 24th and arrived at Sturgeon, Boone County, on the evening of the 26th, with five companies of the Third Missouri Cavalry under Colonel John M. Glover, and five companies of sharpshooters under Colonel John W. Birge. On his arrival at Sturgeon he soon ascertained that a considerable force of secessionists were concentrating near Hallsville in Boone County, about twelve miles south, under Colonel Dorsey. He at once sent forward one company of cavalry under Captain Howland, Third Missouri Cavalry with instructions to make a reconnoissance as near the enemy's position as practicable and then return and report his observations. The captain moved forward to Hallsville, but found no secessionists. He then resumed the march and when about two miles south of town, encountered the enemy in force and captured nine prisoners, but in endeavoring to withdraw his company, the secessionists discovered his weakness, and Colonel Dorsey threw forward a superior force to attack him. In the skirmish that followed, Captain Howland was wounded and taken prisoner with one soldier.

On the return of the rest of Captain Howland's company to Sturgeon, General Prentiss moved out at two o'clock on the morning of the 28th to attack the enemy. His whole force numbered four hundred and seventy men. He pushed forward and at eight o'clock came upon one company of the enemy in position on the left of the road leading from Hallsville to Mount Zion Church, about sixteen miles south of Sturgeon. He quickly made preparations to go into action. Part of Colonel Glover's cavalry were dismounted to engage the secessionists in front, while two companies of sharpshooters were directed to gain their rear, if practicable. On observing this movement, which threatened to flank them, the secessionists commenced to fall back toward their main command. At this moment Colonel Glover moved forward rapidly and opened fire upon them, killing five men and capturing seven prisoners. From the prisoners taken, General Prentiss ascertained that the secessionists were nine hundred strong, and that their main force was posted at Mount Zion Church, one and a half miles in his front. He now moved forward his command, and on arriving near the position of the enemy, dismounted one company of the Third Missouri Cavalry, to engage them, and sent three companies of sharpshooters through a field on his right to skirmish with, and, if practicable, drive them out of the woods. The sharpshooters being unable to dislodge the secessionists from the woods, Colonel Glover was directed to take his available force and move to their assistance, which he did at a double-quick. A severe conflict now took place, and for half an hour the rattle of musketry was incessant, and the opposing forces joined in a hand-to-hand fight. With desperate courage and resolution, the Federal troops held every inch of ground gained, and finally got into the midst of the rebel camp. Seeing that the enemy were beginning to yield, though with much stubbornness, General Prentiss brought forward his two companies of sharpshooters, which had been held in reserve, and put them into action, and in a few moments more the secessionists were driven from the field in the greatest disorder, leaving their dead and wounded on the ground.

The casualties on the Federal side as reported by General Prentiss were 3 killed, 17 severely wounded, and 46 slightly wounded. He reported the casualties on the side of the secessionists at 25 killed, 150 wounded, and 30 prisoners. He also captured 90 horses and 105 stands of arms. The Confederate wounded were collected and put in the church, and farmers and friends in the neighborhood notified to come in and render them assistance.

Thus the year closed with the secession forces broken and dispersed in small detachments north of the Missouri River, and Price's army on the retreat south from the Osage to Springfield. And General Halleck, commanding the department, had gathered sufficient information to satisfy himself that he could at once adopt a more aggressive policy in regard to military operations in Missouri.

CHAPTER XVI.

THE SOUTHERN ARMY DRIVEN OUT OF MISSOURI.

BY direction of General Halleck, on the 28th of December, 1861, General Samuel R. Curtis was assigned to the command of the district of Southwestern Missouri, with headquarters at Rolla. The new commander of the district at once directed Generals Asboth and Sigel to put their divisions in readiness for an immediate forward movement against the Southern army in the southwest part of the State.

General Halleck had received conflicting reports of the movements and strength of General Price's army at Springfield. But after carefully considering the situation, he decided to send General Curtis against him with a force deemed sufficient to engage him, defeat him, and drive him out of the State. The two divisions of Generals Asboth and Sigel encamped at Rolla, about nine thousand strong, could be put in motion in the direction of Springfield at once, and, if found necessary, they could be reinforced by one or more divisions from Sedalia, La Mine, or Jefferson City.

On assuming command of his district, General Curtis directed Colonel E. A. Carr, Third Illinois Cavalry, to take a brigade of seventeen hundred cavalry, and march in the direction of Springfield with the view of feeling the strength of the enemy, and of attacking and cutting to pieces any outposts if not found in superior numbers. Just before this cavalry expedition left Rolla, however, information had been received from Springfield, which led General Curtis to believe that not more than two thousand men of Price's army were at that place. A few days after this, however, a number of Union refugees from the neighborhood of Springfield and southwest of there arrived at Rolla, and reported that Price's army at that point was not less than twelve thousand men.

In his march to the southwest, Colonel Carr's scouting parties captured several rebel soldiers, and from them he ascertained that Price intended making a stand at Springfield, and that McCulloch's forces then in winter quarters at Fayetteville and Cross Hollows, Arkansas, would march to his assistance if the Federal forces threatened to attack him from the direction of either Sedalia or Rolla. The sleet and snow and bad roads delayed Colonel Carr's cavalry expedition at the Gasconade River a few days. He sent out scouting parties every day, who returned and reported that they could hear of no large force of the enemy east of Springfield.

General Curtis was desirous of moving the main body of his army from Rolla to Lebanon the first week in January, but he was obliged to await orders from General Halleck, who was embarrassed with orders from Washington requiring him to send at once to Cairo and Paducah, twenty-four thousand men. To comply with these orders he saw would strip the Department of the Missouri of troops and necessitate abandoning the proposed expedition against Price. He therefore urged the Washington authorities to allow him to send forward General Curtis to attack and, if possible, drive Price out of the State. In the meantime reports of the aggressive movements of the enemy reached General Halleck, and he decided to order General Curtis to advance from Rolla without awaiting advices from Washington. In view of the reported aggressive movement of the enemy, Colonel Carr was ordered to fall back until he met the infantry and artillery, which were at the same time ordered forward from Rolla.

When the army was on the point of leaving Rolla to open up the campaign against Price, General Curtis invited his division commanders, Generals Sigel and Asboth, to his quarters, to give an expression of their views as to whether the troops about to march were sufficient to make success reasonably certain. Information from spies just in from Price's camp, and the statements of rebel prisoners recently captured and examined, convinced the Federal generals that they would have to fight, when the forces of Price and McCulloch were united, an army of not less than twenty-five thousand men. The Federal force at Rolla and vicinity was about twelve thousand men. As the army moved forward, Rolla, the base of operations, would require a garrison of two thousand troops. A force of perhaps nearly two thousand troops would also be required to escort supply trains from Rolla to the army and return. It was reported that Price had been fortifying Springfield, and under all the circumstances the council of generals decided that six regiments were required, in addition to the troops already furnished, before the army could with safety move against the enemy. General Halleck was notified of the decision of the council, and he at once directed General Pope, commanding the divisions at Otterville and Sedalia, to send a division of four thousand men with two batteries, to report to General Curtis. General Pope sent General Jeff. C. Davis' division, and instructed General Davis to march *via* Linn Creek and join General Curtis at Lebanon, fifty-six miles northeast of Springfield. As soon as he was advised that he would be reinforced by General Davis' division from Otterville, General Curtis directed Colonels Carr and Osterhaus to move forward their brigades from near Waynesville to Lebanon.

Colonel Clark Wright, commanding a battalion of Missouri cavalry, had, however, on the 22d of January, advanced and taken possession of the town after a short skirmish, two days before the arrival of the brigades of Colonels Carr and Osterhaus. In the running fight that took place, Colonel Wright's force killed Captain Tom Craig, a notorious Confederate officer, and captured one prisoner.

General Curtis now determined to make Lebanon a depot of supplies and to concentrate his forces there as rapidly as practicable. On the arrival of the different divisions he would be required to subsist upwards of twelve thousand troops, and forage about half as many cavalry, artillery, and transportation animals away from his base of operations. In an army just organized he saw that this was a matter requiring careful consideration. It was desirable that the troops and animals should subsist off the country as far as practicable. The Union people along the line of march would be willing to sell the army such supplies of forage, flour, meal, hogs, and cattle as they could spare, and if the needs of the troops were pressing, the secessionists might be made to contribute something towards maintaining the army. During the past fall and winter Price's army had subsisted off the Union people of Southwest Missouri, and many families, whose male members had sought refuge in the Union lines, were reduced to the verge of starvation. No other argument was needed tô convince the Union officers and soldiers, that the secessionists should be made to feel the effects of the war which they had provoked.

Colonel Carr was instructed, on occupying Lebanon, to collect in the section tributary to it such supplies of forage, flour, meal, beef, and pork as could be obtained without inconvenience to the citizens for the other divisions of the army that would move forward in a few days. Colonel John S. Phelps, member of Congress for Southwest Missouri, who had raised a regiment in his district for the Federal service, accompanied Colonel Carr's advance to Lebanon, and did good service in collecting supplies by going among the people and talking to them, to encourage them in their devotion to the Union.

On the 31st of January General Curtis arrived at Lebanon, leaving Generals Sigel and Asboth at Rolla to move forward as soon as other forces, which had been ordered from St. Louis and were *en route*, should arrive. The storms of sleet and snow during the month had been hard on the troops and animals. And now that the army had commenced to move, the roads were getting in terrible condition. When a few warm days came the snow and ice melted, the ground thawed, and the heavy trains cut the roads up so that the progress made was with much difficulty. On the 7th of February, Colonel J. C. Davis' division from Otterville, and the balance of the troops from Rolla, under Generals Sigel and Asboth, arrived at Lebanon.

The Army of the Southwest was now concentrated; the enemy were only fifty-five miles distant, and now the Federal troops, who had the last few weeks courageously and with great fortitude contended with sleet and snow and frost and mud, were ready and eager to strip for the fight.

When the troops had all arrived at Lebanon, General Curtis reorganized his forces by dividing them into four divisions, and called the combined forces the Army of the Southwest. General F. Sigel was assigned to the command of the first and second divisions, which were under General Asboth and Colonel P. J. Osterhaus.

Colonel J. C. Davis was assigned to the command of the third division, and Colonel E. A. Carr to the command of the fourth division. Colonel Phelps' regiment Missouri Volunteers and Bowen's battalion Missouri Cavalry were unassigned, but under the direct orders of the general commanding.

Turning to the movements of the commanding general of the Confederate forces in Missouri, we find General Price at Springfield actively engaged in transferring as many of his State Guard troops into the Regular Confederate service as possible. Missouri had recently been admitted as a State of the Southern Confederacy; she had been called upon through her governor to furnish her quota of troops, and General Price had been promised a commission as major-general in the Confederate army, as soon as he raised and offered a division of troops for the Confederate service. He was disappointed in General McCulloch's refusal to co-operate with him in certain aggressive movements, but now, about the middle of January, 1862, that he was informed that the Federal army at Rolla, under General Curtis, was preparing to advance against him immediately, he renewed his request to the commanding officer of McCulloch's division, at Fayetteville, Arkansas, for assistance. In December, 1861, General McCulloch put his troops in winter quarters at Cross Hollows and Fayetteville, and started for Richmond to confer with the Confederate authorities on the subject of military affairs west of the Mississippi, leaving Colonel James McIntosh in command, with headquarters at Fort Smith. Colonel McIntosh informed General Price that he had ordered Colonel Hebert, commanding at Fayetteville, to put his brigade in immediate preparation to move as soon as advised of the advance of the Federal force from Rolla; that, if the General was in danger of immediate attack, he (McIntosh) would join him in advance of the troops from Fayetteville and Cross Hollows.

While preparations were thus being made for McCulloch's division to march to the assistance of Price at Springfield, Major-General Earl Van Dorn was assigned by the Confederate authorities to the command of the Trans-Mississippi District, embracing Arkansas and Missouri, with headquarters at Jacksonport, Arkansas. From information he had obtained up to the 10th of February, he did not believe that General Price's position at Springfield was seriously threatened, for, on the 7th, he ordered the available part of McCulloch's division to Jacksonport, from which point he designed a movement against St. Louis, and suggested to General Price that he should strike the Federals a blow at Rolla, and then hold himself in readiness to join forces between Salem and Potosi in the grand march on St. Louis. His plan of operations would no doubt have looked well to an ideal conquering hero, but he clearly did not show the sagacity of his antagonists, Generals Halleck and Curtis, who had calculated in their aggressive movement to receive blow for blow given.

Thus failing to receive the promised assistance of the Confederate troops in Northwestern Arkansas, and being in constant receipt of information of the concentration of Federal troops at Lebanon, General Price hastily called in such of his forces as were stationed at different points in Southwest Missouri. At the request of the Confederate authorities he had sent a detachment of about one thousand men to Granby, in Newton County, to guard the lead-mines at that place while being worked. These mines had been supplying the Confederacy with large quantities of lead for making small-arms ammunition, but these troops, too, were now obliged to be withdrawn from that important station, which might at any moment be visited by a raiding force from Kansas. When his different detachments arrived, General Price had an army at Springfield of upwards of 12,000 men and 42 pieces of artillery. The returns of McCulloch's division showed that, on the 31st of January, 1862, of troops of all arms there were 10,677 men and 18 pieces of artillery.

Having detached a sufficient force to hold Lebanon and

to secure his line of communication, General Curtis, on the 9th of February, issued an order for his troops to resume the march to Springfield on the morning of the 10th, in three columns. A special train was provided to take along six days' light rations and the necessary covering for the troops. The commanders of divisions were directed to arrange their marches so as to arrive in the vicinity of Marshfield by four o'clock in the afternoon of the 11th. The several divisions marched on parallel roads as far as practicable, and all arrived in the vicinity of Marshfield, twenty-five miles northeast of Springfield, on the evening of the 11th. Resuming the march from this point, the army encamped on the evening of the 12th on Pearson's Creek, nine miles north of east of Springfield. As it was not known but that General Price would march out and give battle, General Curtis in approaching the enemy kept out a sufficient force of cavalry on his flanks to guard against a surprise.

Shortly before arriving at Pearson's Creek, the Federal advance encountered the rebel scouts, and in the skirmish and running fight that ensued one man on each side was mortally wounded. That evening at dusk, after the Federal troops had gone into camp, at the end of a weary day's march, General Curtis' outer picket, consisting of four companies of the Third Illinois Cavalry, was attacked by a regiment of Confederate cavalry that had been sent out from Springfield that afternoon. The Federal picket was quickly reinforced, and after Major Bowen, with his howitzers, sent a few shots into the enemy's lines, they retired to Springfield, and that night General Price commenced to evacuate the city. The country around the city for several miles is mostly prairie and large fields, and was favorable for manœuvring troops, but the decision of General Price to retreat made it unnecessary for the Federal general to do any manœuvring or to expend much ammunition to capture the place.

At ten o'clock on the morning of the 13th, General Curtis entered the city with his army, and at once hoisted the national flag over the court-house. Most of the people rejoiced to see the Stars and Stripes again floating over the chief city of the Southwest. General Price had made no calculation of the determination of General Curtis, and in consequence of having made no preparation for retreat until the last moment, was obliged to leave large quantities of forage, flour, and other stores collected for his army, to fall into the possession of the Federal forces.

The main body of Price's army retreated southwest on the Springfield and Fayetteville road *via* Wilson Creek, and his rear-guard was scarcely out of sight of the city when the Federal advance entered it. General Curtis, therefore, sent forward his cavalry at once to attack and harass the rebel rear, and if possible capture a part of their train. After stopping in the city a few hours and detaching a sufficient force for a garrison, he pushed on with his army in pursuit of the retreating rebel hosts, attacking them vigorously wherever they made a stand. A detachment of his cavalry, pursuing a division of the enemy on the Little York road, overtook their rear-guard at that place, and killed three rebels and captured fifteen wagon-loads of supplies and a number of prisoners. After passing McCulla's store, twenty-four miles southwest of Springfield, on the military or wire road, the country becomes more broken, is heavily timbered, and cut up with deep rocky ravines or hollows, and is impassable for artillery and trains except along the established roads. In pursuing the enemy over this rough region of the Ozark range, General Curtis saw the necessity of advancing with caution and of keeping his army well in hand, for if General Price should determine to make a stand at any one of the several strong defiles along the road, it might require a desperate struggle to dislodge him. The Federal advance, consisting of Major W. D. Bowen's battalion Missouri Cavalry, came upon the enemy encamped at Crane Creek in the afternoon of the 14th, and at once attacked them, throwing ten shells from his howitzers into their camp, killing fifteen and wounding nine men. In this affair he also captured thirty prisoners, including one colonel. Finding that the enemy were endeavoring to outflank him, he fell back on the main column.

The next morning General Curtis moved forward to Crane Creek, but when his troops commenced forming in line the enemy retreated. The precipitate flight of the enemy from this point determined General Curtis to order forward his cavalry to overtake and charge them. The Federal cavalry overtook them at Flat Creek, where General Price made a stand, taking a strong position supported by artillery. The howitzers, with the cavalry, returned the fire of the rebel guns, and held the enemy at a distance until General Curtis arrived with heavier batteries and infantry, and got them into position and opened fire. After a short cannonade the enemy were again put to flight, and closely pursued by the Federal forces in the direction of Cassville. By abandoning this strong position it was evident that General Price was determined not to hazard a general engagement until he met in his retreat the troops of McCulloch's division.

After the Federal army left Springfield, General Sigel's two divisions marched out on the Neosho road, which was north of the Springfield and Fayetteville road, but ran nearly parallel with it for about twenty-five miles. By pursuing the enemy on parallel roads to the southwest, the several divisions of the Federal army could support each other to better advantage than if they marched in open order upon a single road.

The rapid movement of General Curtis' army had the effect of cutting off a number of Confederate recruiting parties, some of which were captured by the Federal forces operating in Missouri. General Edwin M. Price, son of General Price, was among those captured while on his return to the army from North Missouri with recruits.

From Flat Creek to the Sugar Creek crossing of the Fayetteville road in Arkansas, General Curtis pushed General Price so closely that it was with the utmost difficulty that he saved his trains and artillery. Every time the rebel rear-guard formed across the road or behind the projecting spurs of the hills adjacent to the road, the Federal cavalry charged and drove them forward. After the vigorous attack at Flat Creek, General Price became satisfied that General Curtis was not content with simply capturing Springfield, but that he was pursuing with his main army with a determination to fight. The Confederate general therefore sent despatches to the commanding officer of McCulloch's forces at Fayetteville, stating that he had been fighting the Federal army for several days, and urging him to move to his assistance at the earliest practicable moment.

On the morning of the 16th, when the booming of the Federal artillery was echoing from hill to hill in Northwestern Arkansas, Colonel Hebert left Fayetteville for Cross Hollow, where most of his command were in winter quarters, and he ordered his troops forward from that place to a point ten miles north on the telegraph road, where they were to meet General Price's forces. This position at Sugar Creek was a strong one, and Price determined to make a stand at it when McCulloch's troops reinforced him. He placed his heavy batteries, supported by infantry, in position to command the approaches of the defile.

General Curtis' advance came up and opened fire upon the enemy with mountain howitzers, but soon found it advisable to wait for heavier field-batteries and infantry before pressing the attack. In a short time the heavy Federal field-batteries came up, and also opened fire.

After a few rounds of shot and shell, General Curtis ordered a cavalry charge, and drove the enemy from their chosen position with the loss of many killed and wounded. On account of the steep hollows and rocky hill-sides it was an unfavorable locality for manœuvring cavalry, but the Federal troops moved irresistibly forward, completely routing the enemy. In this gallant action General Curtis reported a loss of thirteen killed and fifteen to twenty wounded.

Cross Hollow, the boasted stronghold of the Confederates, was now only twelve miles south of the Federal advance. It was an extensive cantonment, and had many good substantial buildings for barracks and quarters and for storing army supplies. About four thousand men of McCulloch's division were in winter quarters there, until aroused by the sound of the advancing Federal artillery and the arrival of Price's messengers with despatches earnestly appealing for assistance. When General Fremont's army was at Springfield in November, 1861, preparing to pursue the combined rebel forces into Northwestern Arkansas, General McCulloch boasted that he had prepared and made Cross Hollow a trap to take from the Federal general all his artillery, if he ventured into that region. His only fear was that he would be unable to draw the Federal general into the trap set for him.

So much had been said about the strength of the place, and now that the Confederate armies were united, General Curtis expected that the rebel generals would make a desperate fight rather than yield it. He therefore waited at Sugar Creek until his divisions had all arrived, and then he determined to send forward heavy reconnoissances and explore the country around Cross Hollows, and ascertain as far as practicable the most available approaches to it. On the morning of the 18th he sent General Asboth with a cavalry force of about twelve hundred men, consisting of the Benton and Fremont Hussars,

Missouri Volunteer Cavalry, and two pieces Captain Elbert's battery, Missouri Light Artillery, to take Bentonville, if practicable. After marching down Sugar Creek some four miles, General Asboth struck the Cassville and Bentonville road, and soon came upon and surprised a dismounted rebel cavalry picket, and captured some of their horses and all their saddles and bridles. He then proceeded to Bentonville and occupied the place a few minutes after twelve o'clock, and took down the secession flag that was floating from the court-house, and collected from the bushes around town sixty men who had endeavored to escape on the approach of the Federal cavalry. As thirty-two of the prisoners were rebel soldiers taken with arms, the general brought them back to camp; the balance, being citizens, he released on taking the oath of allegiance. He also captured a number of wagons and teams hauling supplies to the rebel army, a rebel mail-bag from the post-office with letters containing valuable information, and the Post quartermaster's office and papers. He was so much embarrassed with the care of the prisoners and public property captured that he was unable to make as thorough an examination of the topography of the country west of Cross Hollow as was desirable. It was ascertained, however, by careful inquiries that the section in question was intersected by roads in all directions, and adapted to cavalry and artillery manœuvres in flank of the enemy's position.

In the meantime the Confederate generals were busily engaged in strengthening their position at Cross Hollow by felling trees and obstructing the approaches by the wire road, the road on which General Curtis had been pursuing them. But after his reconnoissances had returned and reported, General Curtis decided not to be so obliging to the enemy as to attack them from the quarter which they had prepared for him. Instead of attacking them in front, he moved his army from Sugar Creek to Osage

Springs, six miles west of Cross Hollow, and commenced preparations for attack from that quarter. This bold flank movement compelled the enemy to evacuate their strong position without a struggle. And in evacuating it they burned most of the buildings, with the stores, provisions, and arms, which they were unable to take away in their haste. Besides the rebel sick and wounded, a considerable part of the supplies collected for the rebel army, fell into the hands of the Federal forces.

The left wing of General Curtis' army now rested on Cross Hollow and his right on Osage Springs. Immediately after the evacuation of Cross Hollow by the enemy, General Curtis despatched General Asboth with a brigade of cavalry and a battery of light artillery, to make a reconnoissance in force against the enemy in the direction of Fayetteville, and to take Fayetteville if possible. General Asboth moved forward on the direct road, from Mudtown on the morning of the 23d, skirmished with the enemy's rear-guard, killing and wounding several men, and entered Fayettville at eleven o'clock without encountering any serious resistance. On entering the town he directed that the Union flag be hoisted over the court-house, and he issued a proclamation setting forth that peaceable citizens should be protected in their persons and property. He ascertained that the main body of the rebel army were retreating into the Boston Mountains, where Generals Price and McCulloch expected to meet heavy reinforcements from the south, and where General Van Dorn was daily expected to arrive to take command of the combined Confederate forces. Many of the principal buildings around the court-house square were burning when the Federal forces arrived, having been fired by the Confederates to destroy the army supplies which were stored in them and which could not be carried away in the hasty evacuation of the town.

On the approach of the Federal troops, a cavalry force

of some three hundred men of the rebel rear-guard formed in line a short distance south of town. Observing them, General Asboth ordered his cavalry to charge them, and in a few moments put them to flight. The Federal general captured several prisoners, some supplies, and thirty wagon-loads of lead which the Confederate authorities had recently brought from the Granby lead-mines in Southwest Missouri. Fayetteville was the most important town in Northwestern Arkansas, and is situated in the midst of a picturesque region, the bold outlines of the Boston Mountains to the south and southwest, being plainly in view. It was also surrounded by a fine agricultural section.

General Asboth thought that he could hold the place if his force could be strengthened by two infantry regiments, but General Curtis directed him to return, for he considered Fayetteville too far in advance of his main command to be held as an outpost. He was also satisfied from information obtained from different sources that it was the intention of the enemy to return on him as soon as they met the reinforcements under General McCulloch from Fort Smith and General Pike from the Indian country, and as soon as General Van Dorn arrived to take command.

After the Confederate forces had been driven into the Boston Mountains, and had felled trees across the roads to obstruct the Federal advance, Major L. S. Ross, of Colonel Stone's Sixth Texas Cavalry, was detailed to take a scout of five hundred men and move east of the Springfield and Fayetteville road to the rear of General Curtis' position at Cross Hollow and Osage Springs, and endeavor to cut off and destroy his supply trains *en route* from Springfield. About eleven o'clock on the night of the 25th of February, Major Ross struck the wire road at Keetsville, some twenty miles in the rear of General Curtis, and attacked Captain Montgomery's company of

Missouri cavalry, encamped at that place, and killed two men and cut loose and stampeded his horses. Captain Montgomery soon rallied his men, and a general fight ensued, lasting nearly half an hour. The Confederates were three times repulsed, but Captain Montgomery was finally obliged to fall back under cover of the brush, where he maintained his position until he had driven the enemy out of town. The Federal train at the time of the attack was within half a mile of Keetsville, but Captain Montgomery very prudently turned it back to Cassville and covered it in his retreat to that place. The Confederate force burned five sutler wagons, sustained a loss of three killed and ten wounded in the action, and then retreated and rejoined the Confederate army in the Boston Mountains. Colonel C. A. Ellis, First Missouri, and Colonel Clark Wright, Sixth Missouri Cavalry, were sent back by General Curtis with detachments of their commands to meet the supply trains and escort them through to the army, and missed the Confederate force under Major Ross by only a few hours.

Finding that General Curtis was not going to pursue them beyond Fayetteville, the Confederate generals, at their camps in the Boston Mountains, at once commenced reorganizing and concentrating their forces for the final struggle. They kept their cavalry well employed in annoying the flanks of the Federal army, in attacking Federal foraging parties, and in burning the mills in that section to prevent the Federal forces from using them in making flour and meal.

After General Curtis had forced the rebel armies to evacuate Cross Hollow, he directed the third division of his army, under Colonel Jefferson C. Davis, and the fourth division, under Colonel E. A. Carr, to move forward and occupy the place. The first and second divisions, under Generals Sigel and Asboth, were directed to take position at McKissick's and Cooper's farms, three and a half miles a little west of south of Bentonville. General Curtis found it necessary to thus spread his army out over the country, to obtain forage for his animals and subsistence for his troops, to observe the movements of the enemy, and to keep detachments of rebel cavalry from passing around his flanks. His front, with the foraging and scouting parties sent out every day from the two main camps, covered a distance of upward of twenty miles.

From an examination of the topographical features of the country about Sugar Creek Crossing, while encamped there after the action of the 17th, General Curtis became satisfied that it afforded a stronger position for defensive operations, if attacked by a superior force, than Cross Hollow. Information was reaching him daily through his scouts, spies, and Union refugees, that the Confederate generals were making extensive preparations to return immediately and give battle. Having selected Sugar Creek as the place where he would make a stand against the combined rebel forces, on the morning of the 1st of March General Curtis directed Colonel Davis to march with his division and take position on the heights of Pea Ridge on the north side of Sugar Creek, a short distance on the west side of the Springfield and Fayetteville road, and to make preparations to receive the enemy in the approaching conflict. A position having now been selected for the Federal forces to rally upon on the approach of the combined rebel armies, the division of Colonel Carr at Cross Hollow, where General Curtis had his headquarters, and the divisions of Generals Sigel and Asboth, at McKissick's farm, continued to send out every day scouting parties to the front and on the flanks, to observe the movements of the enemy and to protect the Federal foraging parties. A detachment of about one thousand men, consisting of details from the Ninth Iowa Infantry, Colonel Phelps' Missouri regiment, one battalion

Third Illinois Cavalry, one section of the Dubuque, Iowa Light Artillery, and one section of Major Bowen's mountain howitzers, were sent out on the morning of the 4th from Cross Hollow, under Colonel Vandever, Ninth Iowa Volunteers, commanding Second Brigade, Fourth Division, to make a reconnoissance to Huntsville, some thirty miles to the southeast. Colonel Vandever arrived at Huntsville at noon on the 5th, and ascertained that a Confederate force of some three hundred men were encamped three miles beyond the town. He pressed on and captured a portion of the enemy's stores in their camp and several prisoners. From the prisoners thus captured he obtained information that the enemy were advancing in force from the Boston Mountains to attack the Federal forces at Cross Hollow and near Bentonville; that General Van Dorn arrived on the 3d and had assumed command of the combined Confederate forces. The Colonel at once countermarched his command and encamped that evening three miles northwest of Huntsville. At two o'clock on the morning of the 6th he received a despatch from General Curtis to return as rapidly as practicable and rejoin the main command at Sugar Creek. His command resumed the march at half-past three o'clock in the morning, and marched steadily all that day in the direction of Sugar Creek, and reached there that evening.

CHAPTER XVII.

BATTLE OF PEA RIDGE.

ON the arrival of General Van Dorn at the camp of the combined Confederate forces in the Boston Mountains, on the 3d, a major-general's salute of forty guns was fired in his honor, which was heard by General Curtis at his headquarters at Cross Hollow. Having heard of General Price's precipitate retreat from Springfield, General Van Dorn hastened from Pocahontas to assume command of the Confederate forces in Western Arkansas, to turn them upon the Federal Army of the Southwest. His arrival afforded the other Confederate leaders an opportunity to harangue their troops and explain away to them the recent disastrous retreat. They appealed to them passionately and with burning zeal to rise up in their might and drive the insolent invader from their sacred soil, assuring them of their superior numbers and of the certainty of winning a glorious victory.

A council of the Confederate generals was held on the 3d, at General Van Dorn's headquarters, and the order of march made out. The army was to move north in the direction of Bentonville, on the morning of March 4th, with three days' cooked rations, and General Price's army of Missouri troops was to take the advance. Instructions were sent to General Albert Pike to march with his division of Texas and Indian troops, about six thousand strong, along the State line road until he struck a road leading to the northeast, to Elm Springs, eight miles north of Fayetteville, where he would join the main army. When he arrived at this point he was to march to the attack of the Federal forces in the rear of McCulloch's division. On the morning of the 4th the numerous divisions of the Confederate army turned their faces to their foe, and were in motion northward, the advance arriving that evening at Fayetteville. That night a number of Union citizens in and about Fayetteville, having found that the advance of the Confederate army had arrived, escaped between the rebel pickets on by-roads, and rode to the Federal camp at Cross Hollow, arriving there about two o'clock in the afternoon, and reported to General Curtis of the rapid approach of the enemy. Several of the General's scouts also came in about the same time, and reported that the enemy were advancing in force, and that their advance would reach Elm Springs, twelve miles distant, that evening.

It was a cold, blustery day, and snow had fallen so as to cover the ground, and General Curtis did not apprehend an immediate attack. He sent couriers at once to General Sigel at McKissick's farm, and to Colonel Vandever *en route* to Huntsville, with instructions to move immediately with their commands to Sugar Creek. Colonel Carr, commanding the fourth division at Cross Hollow, was directed to break up camp that evening at six o'clock, and march to Sugar Creek. A foraging party, sent out that morning with several wagons and teams in the direction of Fayetteville, were captured by Colonel Stone's Sixth Texas Cavalry advancing on the Fayetteville and Springfield road. When his troops were in readiness to march, Colonel Carr was obliged to destroy some stores and camp equipage, in consequence of the loss of his forage teams captured. General Curtis accompanied Colonel Carr's division, and arrived at Sugar Creek at two o'clock on the morning of the 6th. From the two divisions of Colonels Davis and Carr, now on the ground selected for making a stand, he ordered details made and set to work felling trees to obstruct certain roads to prevent the enemy having too many approaches. Other parties were employed in constructing temporary breastworks to strengthen his position. All the obstructions to the roads and the temporary field-works thrown up were made with the view of repelling attack from the front and flanks. And when Colonels Davis and Carr took their positions early in the morning of the 6th on the projecting hills commanding the valley of Sugar Creek, their troops faced to the south.

Late in the evening of the 5th, General Sigel received General Curtis' despatch to march immediately with the first and second divisions to Sugar Creek; that the enemy had already passed Fayetteville. That night, shortly before ten o'clock, he also received information from Colonel Schaefer, Second Missouri Volunteers, stationed at Osage Mills, that the enemy had fired on his picket in the direction of Elm Springs. He quickly realized the dangerous position of his two divisions and despatched orders to Colonel Schaefer to break up camp at Osage Mills immediately and march with his regiment directly to Bentonville, first having sent his cavalry company to Osage Springs to cover his right flank. He also despatched couriers with instructions to Major Conrad, Third Missouri Volunteers, who had been sent out on a scout the day before with a detachment of three hundred men and one piece of artillery in the direction of Maysville, and to Major Meszaros who had been sent out with eighty cavalry in the direction of Pineville, to rejoin the army at Sugar Creek at the earliest moment practicable. He next issued orders for his two divisions to march at two o'clock in the morning of the 6th *via* Bentonville to Sugar Creek. The second division under General Asboth arrived at Bentonville about four o'clock, halted for a short time to allow the division train to come up, and then marched undisturbed to Sugar Creek, arriving there at half-past ten o'clock. He was closely followed by the first division under Colonel P. J. Osterhaus, who arrived at Sugar Creek perhaps an hour later. All General Sigel's trains had passed through Bentonville by eight o'clock, on the road to Sugar Creek. The General remained at Bentonville with his rear-guard until ten o'clock, awaiting the arrival of Lieutenant John Schipper, Benton Hussars, Missouri Cavalry, whom he had sent with twenty men the night before to Osage Springs to communicate with Colonel Schaefer, and to act as a mounted picket on the Bentonville and Fayetteville road, with instructions to report the moment he discovered that the enemy were advancing in force.

General Sigel had kept back as rear-guard only about six hundred men and five pieces of artillery, consisting of three hundred and twenty-five men of the Twelfth Missouri Volunteers under Major Hugo Wangelin, five companies of the Benton Hussars, Missouri Cavalry, under Colonel Joseph Nemett, and two mounted companies of the Thirty-sixth Illinois Volunteers under Captains Albert Jenks and Henry A. Smith respectively. The Twelfth Missouri Infantry had stacked their arms and were resting at ease, and the troops had been in town upward of half an hour, when suddenly, without alarm, large bodies of the rebel cavalry were discovered approaching from the rear and flanks to surround the town and Federal troops. General Sigel immediately ordered his bugler to call his troops to arms, marched them out of town, and formed them in line in the heavy woods and underbrush a short distance north of the town. Having now checked the enemy who were also forming in line of battle in town, he directed his artillery to proceed on the road to Sugar Creek. He soon discovered, however, that another body of rebel cavalry had moved around to the southeast and formed near the Sugar Creek road, thus cutting him off. He informed his officers that his troops would be obliged to cut their way through the rebel lines. The artillery, supported by the Twelfth Missouri Infantry, was brought forward, and after throwing a few rounds of shell into the line of the rebel cavalry, they dispersed in every direction. The Federal column then moved forward again, not however without the cavalry and infantry, marching on the flanks and in the front and rear, continually skirmishing with the enemy who were pressing them from all sides. Colonel Nemett, who marched in rear of the artillery with one hundred men of the Benton Hussars, was pressed so closely by the enemy for several miles after leaving Bentonville, that he was obliged to turn, face and charge the enemy every ten or fifteen minutes, to keep them back.

To guard against the enemy dashing up and shooting down the artillery horses, General Sigel directed one company of the Twelfth Missouri Infantry to march by the flank on the right of the pieces, and another company of that regiment to march by the flank on the left of the pieces, each prepared to fire by ranks to the right and left, and each supported by a company of cavalry. After passing a few miles to the east of Bentonville, the country was broken and brushy, and not adapted to manœuvring cavalry or operating artillery effectively except up or down the road to the front or rear. On each side of the road along the ridges there was a thick growth of low scrubby black-jack which no mounted force could pass through, keeping their alignment. From the ridge the road passed into a deep hollow, the steep, rocky hill-sides of which also presented serious difficulties to the movement of cavalry.

Colonel Gates of General Price's division, commanding the Confederate Cavalry advance, was quite persevering and attacked the retreating Federal force from every accessible point. In moving forward through the woods and over the hills, in their efforts to gain positions near the head of the Federal column, the Confederate cavalry became very much scattered, so that General Sigel most of the time, for five or six miles on the retreat, was nearly surrounded by the enemy. The firing between the skirmishers in the rear and on the flanks was incessant until General Sigel met reinforcements from Sugar Creek at half-past three o'clock in the afternoon. His artillery was well handled and effectively used every time the enemy endeavored to rally in the road in front or rear.

As soon as the information reached General Asboth and Colonel Osterhaus, who had joined General Curtis at Pea Ridge and were preparing their encampment on the extreme right of the army, of the perilous situation of General Sigel and his small detachment, they hastened back on the double-quick with the first and second divisions, to the assistance and rescue of their comrades. When they met the General, he had just broken through the rebel cavalry, but they were still in hot pursuit and endeavoring to cut him off. General Asboth and Colonel Osterhaus commenced to form their troops in line of battle immediately along the crests of the hills commanding the Bentonville and Sugar Creek road, and quickly checked the farther advance of the rebel cavalry. Two pieces of Captain Hoffmann's Fourth Independent Battery, Ohio Light Artillery, were placed in position on a bend in the narrow defile formed by Sugar Creek Hollow, supported by the Fifteenth Missouri Volunteers. The Seventeenth Missouri Volunteers, under Major Poten, were deployed as skirmishers. In a short time the enemy had collected in considerable force, and commenced to advance with skirmishers on the hills and artillery in the valley. After an artillery duel lasting half an hour, and a few shots between the skirmishers, the enemy ceased firing and the Federal forces marched back to camp to bivouac on the northern ridges skirting Sugar Creek Hollow, west of and on the right of the third and fourth divisions.

In General Sigel's retreat from Bentonville and in the final repulse of the enemy on the evening of the 6th, General Curtis reported the Federal loss at twenty-five killed and wounded. Colonel Vandever's command from Huntsville, having made a forced march of forty miles, also arrived at the Federal encampment as the light of day was fading into darkness.

The Federal divisions had now all united without any serious loss. General Curtis felt much solicitude on this day of the 6th, for fear some of his detachments marching to rally on the position at Sugar Creek might be cut off by the rapid approach of the enemy. Immediately on the arrival of the first and second divisions, large details from them were set to work fortifying their position in anticipation of a night attack.

After all the detachments had got in on the evening of the 6th, General Curtis posted General Asboth's second division on the extreme right of his line, facing south by southwest; Colonel Osterhaus' first division was posted on the left of the second division, forming the right centre; Colonel Davis' third division was posted on the left of the first division, forming the left centre; and Colonel Carr's fourth division formed the extreme left of the Federal line near the telegraph road, facing south.

The troops thus posted for the night occupied the high ground and ridges formed by hollows running out from Sugar Creek Valley, and their encampment extended for about two miles northwest of the telegraph road on the north side of Sugar Creek. In the rear of the Federal position was a high rocky hill, perhaps upward of one hundred feet high, known as Pea Ridge. From northwest to southeast it was several miles long. Its sides were rather steep and covered mostly with scrub timber. Its eastern end arose a short distance west of Elkhorn Tavern, which is situated on the west side of the telegraph or main Springfield and Fayetteville road. The north side of Pea Ridge is rough and broken by defiles or hollows that run off into Big Sugar Creek. The Bentonville and Keetsville road runs up Sugar Creek on the north side of Pea Ridge, and enters the telegraph road about three miles north of Elkhorn Tavern. A quarter of a mile north of the tavern was the head of Sugar Creek, a rough gorge, known as Cross Timber Hollow, through which the telegraph road runs north to Keetsville, seven miles. East and west of the road around Cross Timber Hollow there was much heavy timber, with here and there thick growths of scrub oak. About the tavern on the west side of the telegraph road, there was an apple orchard and field of ten acres. East of the telegraph road in front of the tavern there was a level ridge, along which ran a road to the east. This ridge was covered with timber, some places with large timber and some places with thick growths of thrifty young oaks. For some distance on the south side of it the ground was comparatively smooth. A short distance on the north side of it were the heads of the rough, rocky gorges that run off into Cross Timber Hollow. South of the ten-acre field and orchard around the tavern on the west side of the telegraph road, was a woods pasture of perhaps one hundred acres. This woods pasture contained a fine growth of heavy oak timber. South of it, extending for more than a mile on the west side of the road, were several large open fields. On the east side of the telegraph road between Elkhorn and the south fork of Sugar Creek, there were also several fields. In the large field west of the telegraph road and south of the woods pasture and in the rear of the Federal position, the Federal trains were parked. The Bentonville and Sugar Creek road intersected the telegraph road a short distance south of Elkhorn Tavern. A great many trees had been felled by the troops to obstruct all the roads and approaches from the south and southwest, and the Federal divisions under the ever watchful eye of General Curtis were now in their positions to receive the attack of the combined forces of General Van Dorn.

On his arrival at the Confederate camps in the Boston Mountains, General Van Dorn was informed of the positions occupied by the Federal divisions, as well as the points held by detachments from them at the mills in the surrounding country. He therefore determined to march rapidly by the Fayetteville and Bentonville road, capture as many of the Federal detachments as possible, cut off General Sigel at Bentonville, and crush his two divisions, and throw his combined and victorious forces against General Curtis at Sugar Creek. When he arrived at Bentonville at eleven o'clock, he was disappointed in seeing the rear-guard of General Sigel's divisions leaving town as the Confederate advance entered it. The pursuit of the detachment of the Federal rear-guard, brought the Confederate army some seven miles northeast of Bentonville and within a mile or so of the extreme right of the Federal position at Sugar Creek. General Van Dorn had been advised that the Federal forces had strengthened their position by intrenchments, and his officers in charge of reconnoitring parties reported to him that evening that all the roads and approaches to the Federal position on the south and southwest had been obstructed by felled trees. He was in the presence of the Federal army, and the point of attack must be decided at once. The Confederate army was halted on the Bentonville and Keetsville road as if to bivouac for the night, the advance resting near where the road forks, the right-hand road leading to the Federal position on Sugar Creek and the left-hand road to Keetsville and Cassville.

When darkness had fallen a council of the Confederate

generals was held to determine the plan and point of attack. In the discussion it appeared that Generals McCulloch and McIntosh were thoroughly acquainted with all the roads and topographical features of that section, having had their troops stationed in that neighborhood and at Cross Hollow at different times since July, 1861. In the fall of 1861 they had thoroughly examined the country about Sugar Creek and Cross Timber Hollow, with the intention of making a stand when General Fremont was preparing to march from Springfield to attack them and General Price. They pointed out to General Van Dorn that by making a detour of eight miles he could get directly in the rear of the Federal position on the telegraph road leading from Springfield to Fayetteville. To reach the point desired, the army would move forward northeast on the Bentonville and Keetsville road until it intersected the telegraph road, and then turn and march south on the latter road until the troops came near enough to the Federal position to form line of battle and open the attack.

General Van Dorn decided to adopt this route, and then gave the necessary orders to his generals to have every thing in complete readiness. He also decided to accompany General Price with his army in the movement around to the rear of the Federal position on the telegraph road. General Price's army resumed the march at eight o'clock that evening. It was calculated that the movement could easily be accomplished by daylight on the morning of the 7th, but on account of the obstructions in the road which the Federal troops under Colonels Davis and Dodge had made by felled trees, the march was impeded, and General Price's troops did not reach the telegraph road until near ten o'clock. After marching some two miles south on this road, along the deep valley of Cross Timber Hollow, his advance encountered the Federal pickets a short distance north of Elkhorn Tavern.

On resuming the march on the night of the 6th, General

Van Dorn instructed Generals McCulloch, McIntosh, and Pike to bring forward their divisions on the Bentonville road to a point nearly north of Leetown, and then to move south through the woods and attack the left of the Federal position near that place, assuming that General Curtis had changed front. The tedious work of removing the obstructions from the road, so that General Price's artillery and trains could pass, not only retarded the movement of his troops, but also the troops of McCulloch's and Pike's divisions. The troops were kept moving all night at short intervals, yet they marched only three to six miles, and it was sunrise when the divisions of Generals McCulloch and Pike reached a point where they were directed to leave the Bentonville road and march southeast through the woods and fields in the direction of Leetown to attack the left of the Federal position.

In this final preparation for attacking the Federal forces General McCulloch commanded the right wing of the Confederate army, composed of Louisiana, Texas, and Arkansas troops, and General Albert Pike the Indians and Texans. The white troops of McCulloch's division belonged to the regular Confederate service, and were the best drilled and disciplined troops in the Southern army in the west. After leaving the Bentonville road, General McCulloch marched his troops in several columns on by-roads and through fields southeast in the direction of Leetown, and on approaching that place formed his infantry in line on his left under Colonel Hebert; and his cavalry division, under General McIntosh, formed on the right of the infantry. General Pike formed his Indians and Texans in line directly in the rear of General McIntosh's cavalry. The troops thus formed were about one and a half miles nearly west of Elkhorn Tavern and the telegraph road.

Somewhat to the northeast of them, but west of the telegraph road, was Pea Ridge, or Sugar Mountain. South and southwest of this mountain the country was comparatively level, with here and there small prairies, fields, and thick growths of woods.

The Confederate line of battle is now formed facing south, in the rear of the Federal position. General Price's army has formed across the telegraph road a short distance north of Elkhorn Tavern, and McCulloch's army has formed in the fields and woods a short distance north and northwest of Leetown. Between the two Confederate corps thus formed there is a gap of nearly two miles.

General Curtis had all along recognized the important fact, that to make his army efficient the troops should be furnished with proper subsistence and covering. He was ever solicitous for their comfort. After partaking of a supper of good substantial army rations, his troops were allowed an unbroken rest on the night of the 6th. They also got their breakfasts on the morning of the 7th. To compensate for his inferiority in numbers, the Federal general had caused trees to be felled to obstruct the roads, so that the Confederate army was kept in motion all night to march a few miles, and when the morning of the 7th dawned the rebel troops were tired, hungry, and worn in body and spirit.

Early in the morning of the 7th, reports came to General Curtis that the troops and trains of the Confederate forces were moving all night northeast on the Bentonville road, in the direction of the telegraph road, to gain the rear of the Federal army. The reports were corroborated by scouts that were sent out to ascertain the facts. General Curtis immediately called his division commanders together at General Asboth's tent, and directed a change of front to the rear of his entire line. In this change the troops held their respective positions, but their order in the line was reversed, the extreme right becoming the extreme left. When he had accomplished the change of front that had become necessary, General

Curtis' new right was to rest on Elkhorn Tavern, and his new left on Sugar Creek where his right had recently rested, so that his new line would face north and northwest.

Without waiting for the completion of this movement, he directed Colonel Osterhaus to take a detachment of cavalry and light artillery, supported by infantry, and open the battle by an attack from his centre on the probable centre of the enemy in the direction of Leetown. On the evening of the 6th, Major Eli Weston, Twenty-fourth Missouri Volunteers, stationed at Elkhorn Tavern, had placed a cavalry picket, supported by infantry, on the Huntsville road, and on a cross-road leading into the Bentonville and Springfield road. About three o'clock in the morning of the 7th, one of his pickets was captured near the Bentonville road by a party of rebel cavalry, but the picket escaped in the darkness. Directly after daylight other pickets reported to him that a force of the enemy was moving around on his left flank. He immediately ordered Captain Barbour Lewis, First Missouri Cavalry, and Captain James H. O'Connor, Third Illinois Cavalry, to take their companies, which had been attached to his command, and move forward, supported by Captain S. P. Barris' company of the Twenty-fourth Missouri Volunteers, in the direction of the cross-roads, and reconnoitre the enemy and ascertain their strength and intentions as far as practicable. On arriving at a point about three quarters of a mile a little west of north of Elkhorn, near where the picket had been stationed, the Federal detachment saw, at a short distance in front, a small force of rebel cavalry. The detachment at once commenced to deploy on each side of the road, with the cavalry in the centre, and to move forward, seeing which the Confederate force fell back through a field into the timber and brush. Continuing to move forward in line, the Federal detachment drove the enemy from their position in the brush, and pursued them about a mile, when they rallied to the number of one hundred and fifty. They were, however, soon driven from this position by a few volleys from the infantry under Captain Barris and Lieutenant Hart. Finding that they were near the main rebel army, the officers commanding the several Federal detachments fell back to Elkhorn Tavern, and Captain Barbour Lewis rode immediately to General Curtis' headquarters and reported the situation in front.

Colonel Osterhaus' column was just moving out in the direction of Leetown when Captain Lewis arrived. General Curtis immediately directed Colonel Carr, who was present, to move his division, which was now on the extreme right in the changed front, into position to support Major Weston as soon as possible. In a few moments, after Captain Barris and the two cavalry companies returned to Elkhorn, a report came in that the enemy were advancing in large force from the north on the telegraph road. Major Weston then sent Captain R. W. Fyan down that road with his company of the Twenty-fourth Missouri Volunteers, to ascertain if the enemy were advancing from the direction of Cassville. Captain Fyan had not proceeded down the telegraph road more than three-quarters of a mile when he came in sight of the rebel cavalry. He then threw out a few skirmishers on each side of the road, and advanced some two hundred yards farther, when the enemy opened a cross-fire upon him from both sides of the road, wounding one of his men. He returned the fire, and then ordered his company to fall back about two hundred yards to keep the enemy from flanking him. Having discovered the enemy in force, he despatched a messenger back to Elkhorn for reinforcements. Major Weston sent to his assistance companies H and I of the Twenty-fourth Missouri, under command of Lieutenant James J. Lyon.

On the arrival of Lieutenant Lyon, Captain Fyan observed the enemy moving around on his right towards the Huntsville road. He then marched his company across to the Huntsville road through the woods, and, after reaching that road, deployed his men as skirmishers on both sides of it, and advanced until he came to a field, where he took position along the fence to await the further movements of the enemy. He was not held long in suspense, for, in a few moments, the enemy commenced to make their appearance in heavy masses in the edge of the woods directly in his front. While Captain Fyan moved to the right, Lieutenant Lyon, Captain Thomas A. Reed, and Captain S. P. Barris, of Major Weston's command, deployed their companies as skirmishers to the left or west of the telegraph road, to hold the enemy in check until reinforcements arrived, or until ordered to fall back. The firing between the opposing skirmish lines was quite spirited at times, but the losses were not heavy, for each party took advantage of the covering of trees, stumps, and logs as much as possible.

Captain Fyan held his position along the fence of the field on the Huntsville road, about half a mile nearly east of Elkhorn Tavern, until nearly eleven o'clock, when Colonel Dodge's brigade of the fourth division, consisting of the Thirty-fifth Illinois Volunteers, under Colonel Smith; the Fourth Iowa Volunteers, under Lieutenant-Colonel John Galligan; Major McConnell, with two battalions of Third Illinois Cavalry; and Captain J. A. Jones' First Iowa Battery, came up and formed in line of battle. The Thirty-fifth Illinois formed on the left, the Fourth Iowa in the centre, and the Third Illinois Cavalry on the right. Four pieces of the First Iowa Battery were placed in position near Elkhorn Tavern, and the other two pieces east of the tavern near the right centre of the brigade. On the arrival of Colonel Dodge's brigade, Captain Fyan withdrew his company from the skirmish line, and marched to join his regiment on the left of Colonel Carr's division resting on Pea Ridge.

In the meantime, Generals Van Dorn and Price had been busy in posting their troops and batteries on the hills and ridges in the most advantageous positions to open the battle. The divisions of Brigadier-Generals Price and A. E. Steen, John B. Clark's third division, Colonel James P. Saunder's fifth division, General D. M. Frost's seventh and ninth divisions, and General James S. Rains' eighth division of the Missouri State Guard of Price's army, and Colonel Colton Greene's Third Brigade Missouri Confederate Volunteers were posted on the left of the Confederate line east of the telegraph road, and faced Colonel Dodge's Federal brigade.

Colonel Henry Little's First Brigade, and General William Y. Slack's Second Brigade, Missouri Confederate Volunteers, were posted on the right or west side of the telegraph road, the extreme right of the line resting on the eastern slope of Pea Ridge or Sugar Mountain. The Confederate cavalry on the right of the Confederate line was commanded by Colonel John T. Hughes, and on the left by Colonel Elijah Gates. The eight batteries of artillery of General Price's army were posted at several commanding positions along his line thus formed.

Colonel Carr, who had accompanied his leading brigade under Colonel Dodge, found, when he arrived at Elkhorn Tavern, that the Confederate forces were endeavoring to flank the Federal position at the tavern on the east near Clemens' house. Colonel Dodge extended his line to meet the threatened movement, and directed Lieutenant David, commanding the right section of the First Iowa Battery, to open fire upon the enemy. At the same time, a company of the Fourth Iowa Infantry was thrown forward as skirmishers, who soon became warmly engaged with the rebel skirmish line. The enemy now opened vigorously upon Colonel Dodge with shell, solid and grape-shot, from Captain Emmet McDonald's battery. In a short time, however, the rebel skirmishers were driven back by Colonel Dodge's right and centre.

While Colonel Dodge was thus looking after his right flank, Colonel Carr had taken the left section of the First Iowa Battery under Lieutenant Gambell, and the Thirty-fifth Illinois under Colonel G. A. Smith, and moved down the telegraph road near the head of Cross Timber Hollow, and opened fire on a rebel battery on a bluff to his right front. The enemy immediately replied, and were soon pouring such a storm of shot, shell, and grape around the Federal battery, that Colonel Carr deemed it advisable for it to change position. He also sent to Captain Jones, who had been posted at Elkhorn Tavern with the centre section of his battery as reserve, to bring it forward to the assistance of the left section in playing upon the rebel position. Captain Jones moved at once and took position on the right of Lieutenant Gambell, commanding the left section, and commenced shelling the rebel battery.

On the Confederate side General Price had ordered into position, near McDonald's battery, three additional batteries—the batteries of Captains Guibor, Clark, and Wade—to work upon the Federal position. The rebel artillerists having got the range of the Federal guns, bursting shells and solid and grape-shot fell thick and fast around them with destructive effects. Captain Jones and Lieutenant Gambell were wounded; several men of the battery were killed and wounded; several artillery horses were killed and disabled; two caissons were struck by rebel shells and exploded, and three out of the four pieces were disabled and obliged to retire. While this furious fire of the rebel artillery was going on, Colonel Smith advanced with the Thirty-fifth Illinois Volunteers, and engaged the rebel infantry and drove them back some distance, but was soon wounded in the head by a shell and in the shoulder by a bullet and compelled to retire.

Becoming satisfied that there was a heavy force of the enemy in his front, Colonel Carr sent back to General Curtis requesting him to send forward Colonel Vandever's second brigade of the fourth division, which consisted of the Ninth Iowa Volunteers under Lieutenant-Colonel Frank J. Herron, Colonel John S. Phelps' regiment of Missouri volunteers, one battalion Third Illinois Cavalry, and Captain M. M. Hayden's Dubuque battery, Iowa light artillery. Colonel Vandever marched his brigade from near Sugar Creek to Elkhorn Tavern, a distance of about one and a half miles, as quickly as practicable, and formed in line in advance of the tavern on the left of Colonel Dodge. The Dubuque battery at once opened a brisk fire on the enemy, from its position in the telegraph road, east of Elkhorn Tavern, and soon after Colonel Vandever's whole line of infantry became hotly engaged with the rebel infantry. The roar of artillery and the heavy volleys of small-arms told of the earnestness with which the opposing forces had joined in the struggle which was to decide whether the Union or Confederacy should control Missouri and the country south and southwest of her, and in a wider sense the destinies of the peoples of North America. Colonel Carr's left and centre under Colonel Vandever were now opposed on the Confederate side by the brigades of General Slack and Colonel Little with four batteries.

After consuming upwards of an hour in throwing shot and shell into the woods west of the telegraph road, occupied by the Federal left, and in playing upon the Dubuque battery in the telegraph road, and compelling it to retire, General Price ordered General Slack and Colonel Little, aided by Colonel Gates' cavalry, to charge the Federal position. Encouraged by the success of their batteries, the rebel line moved forward gallantly over the rough ground, until they approached within easy range of the Federal line, when Colonel Vandever's brigade poured a terribly destructive fire into their ranks, causing them to recoil and fall back precipitately without returning an effective fire. Colonel Vandever immediately advanced his brigade, driving the enemy before him until they had fallen back on their reserves. He then retired to his former position near the telegraph road, a few hundred yards in advance of Elkhorn Tavern, at the same time keeping his skirmish line well to the front.

In this conflict General Slack, commanding the brigade on the extreme right of Price's army, was mortally wounded and Lieutenant-Colonel Cearnall severely wounded. For an hour or so after this an incessant firing was kept up by the skirmish lines on both sides along the entire front, extending from near the summit of Pea Ridge to Colonel Dodge's right, resting near Clemens' house.

About two o'clock there was a lull in the battle and the firing had almost ceased. Colonel Carr rode over to the right of his line under Colonel Dodge, east of Clemens' house and north of the road running east from Elkhorn Tavern, to see how well his troops in that quarter were maintaining their position. In his absence General Van Dorn ordered an advance of the brigades of Slack and Little and Burbridge against the Federal left wing under Colonel Vandever. The Confederates advanced up a hollow just west of the telegraph road and through the bushes on both sides of the road, followed closely with their batteries. Colonel Vandever ordered forward his infantry to meet the enemy, when a desperate conflict with small-arms ensued along the crest of the hill just west of the telegraph road and about three hundred yards north of Elkhorn Tavern. Upwards of one hundred men and officers of the Ninth Iowa Infantry, and some seventy-five men and officers of Colonel Phelps' Missouri regiment, were killed and wounded in this action. Major William H. Coyle, Ninth Iowa, was wounded in the shoulder; Colonel Phelps had three horses shot under him and received a contusion from a shell; and Major W. F. Geiger, of Colonel Phelps' regiment, also had a horse shot under him. The Confederates were finally driven back to the foot of the hill north of Elkhorn Tavern, when their batteries opened fire on the Federal line. Colonel Vandever again retired and formed his line just in advance of Elkhorn Tavern, leaving the enemy in possession of the ground which the Federal line had occupied early in the day.

Seeing that he was pressed by greatly superior numbers of the enemy on his right, left, and centre, Colonel Carr sent to General Curtis requesting reinforcements. The General sent him Major Wm. D. Bowen, with a company of Missouri cavalry under Captain F. W. Benteen, and two pieces of artillery under Lieutenant Madison. On his arrival, Major Bowen was directed to take position on the road between the Ninth Iowa and Twenty-fourth Missouri, well towards Colonel Carr's extreme left, on the eastern slope of Pea Ridge or Sugar Mountain. Colonel Vandever's line had just retired from the range of the rebel artillery, and the firing had almost died away along the front.

The ominous stillness of the field was soon broken, however, for the Confederate forces advanced again and renewed the assault along the entire Federal line with infantry and artillery. Slack's and Little's brigades had now been strengthened by Frost's division from the Confederate left. The Confederate right being thus strengthened furiously assaulted the Federal left, under Colonel Vandever, but failed to dislodge the Federal infantry from their position in the edge of the timber. It was at this point that Major Bowen, with his two howitzers and cavalry, did good service in repulsing the enemy. In this conflict he fired twenty-four rounds from each of his guns. At this time, too, Captain Hayden, commanding the Dubuque battery, while endeavoring to place his guns in position on a commanding elevation, lost one piece by going near a large body of the enemy, who were concealed in the brush, and who rushed out and charged upon it and, by shooting down the horses, captured it. Colonel Dodge was directed to draw his forces near, so as to fill up the gap between the left of his brigade and the right of Colonel Vandever's, occasioned by extending his line to the right to prevent the enemy from flanking him. While Colonel Carr's left and centre had been obliged to retire on a line with Elkhorn Tavern, Colonel Dodge had also been forced to yield some ground. He formed the right of his line west and south of the field that lay south of the road in front of Clemens' house, thus covering his men with a rail fence and forcing the enemy to cross an open field to reach him. He directed Lieutenant David to open fire upon the enemy with his right section of the First Iowa Battery. The enemy replied with eight guns, slowly advancing. Colonel Dodge's section of artillery soon exhausted their ammunition, and retired. He brought up his skirmishers and placed them on the left, to fill the gap next to Colonel Vandever's brigade. The enemy had kept up a hot fire from their batteries for perhaps upwards of an hour, and they were now beginning to use canister.

Colonel Dodge could see the Confederate officers through the open woods placing their batteries in position and arranging their troops for a charge. The Federal infantry lay behind the rail fence, so as not to attract attention, with instructions not to fire a shot until the enemy had advanced to within fifty yards of the fence. The rebel artillery ceased firing, and Colonel Dodge's men knew what it meant. In a few moments a long line of infantry, in butternut and gray, was seen to emerge from the woods and to enter the field from the east and southeast. It was General Clark's division, reinforced by detachments from other divisions of Price's army. As soon as they entered the open field and perfected their alignment, they were ordered to double-quick. The Federal soldiers now quietly awaited their approach, and when within fifty to seventy-five yards of the fence, poured a terrific volley of musketry into their line, killing and wounding one hundred and seventeen men and officers on the ground. The Confederate line recoiled before this terrible shock, and fell back to the woods east of the field in confusion, where the officers rallied and re-formed their men. In their retreat from their exposed position, the Confederates suffered some casualties from the continuous fire of musketry kept up by the Federal soldiers. The fire of the Confederate line produced few casualties on the Federal side. Colonel Dodge had a horse killed under him, and received a slight wound in the hand. He also had several men wounded. It was now nearly three o'clock.

The fortune of the Federal arms was waning with the day on the right of the army. The Federal troops had fought against great odds, and held on to the positions, from which they were gradually forced, with heroic fortitude. But Colonel Carr became satisfied that the enemy were too strong for him, and again sent to General Curtis for reinforcements. The General sent him from Colonel Davis' third division a battalion of five companies of the Eighth Indiana Infantry, under Lieutenant-Colonel David Shunk, and three rifled field-pieces of Captain Klauss' First Indiana Battery, with instructions to "persevere." On this force reporting to him, Colonel Carr temporarily attached it to Colonel Vandever's brigade, and placed it in position at Elkhorn Tavern, but shortly afterward directed Colonel Shunk to report to Colonel Dodge on the right.

The roar of the battle again subsided. In the several assaults made during the day, Generals Van Dorn and Price had been able to advance their line nearly a quarter of a mile. They now determined, before the shades of night should fall, to make another desperate effort to crush the Federal division in their front. During the interval of calm they were busy in gathering their forces and posting them for the final struggle of the day, which they hoped would crown their arms with success. It was arranged that General Price, with the Confederate left wing, should open the assault against the Federal right. The heavy firing on the Confederate left was to be the signal for the advance of the entire Confederate line. To avoid the great loss of life it would probably require to dislodge Colonel Dodge's Federal infantry from their position behind the fence of the field south of Clemens' house, it was decided to make the position untenable by flanking it on the right.

General Curtis had not been idle. He had been over different parts of the field during the day, and directed the general movements of his army, and knew when he could afford to take troops from one part of his line to strengthen it at another point. He regretted the disproportionate sacrifice of his right, but it became a necessity to prevent a possible disaster to his army.

It was between three and four o'clock when the Confederate left renewed the battle by a heavy fire which was the signal for the general advance of the Confederate line. Under the eyes and direction of Generals Van Dorn and Price, the Confederate army now moved forward in an unbroken line to the assault. In a few moments the Federal line was encountered, when the storm of battle burst forth with tremendous fury along the entire front of the contending forces. The sharp volleys of small-arms and the almost continuous roar of the deep-toned artillery, told that Death was on the wing. The Federal line had been greatly thinned by casualties during the day, and it was a severe test of their courage and devotion to require the troops to meet another assault made mostly by fresh forces, supported by upwards of forty pieces of artillery. After the battle had raged with great fury for perhaps upwards of half an hour, Colonel Dodge discovered that the enemy were about to turn his right flank. He checked their first movement by ordering his men to fire a volley into them when they had advanced within one hundred feet of his line. Finding that his force was insufficient to extend his line to meet another threatened flank movement of the enemy on his right, he sent for reinforcements, and Colonel Carr sent him the battalion of the Eighth Indiana Infantry under Colonel Shunk, and the three pieces of Klauss' First Indiana Battery. He formed the Indiana infantry on the right of the Fourth Iowa Infantry, and directed the officer commanding the three rifled pieces to go into battery on his left. After firing three or four rounds, however, the guns were obliged to retire from the field to avoid being flanked by a regiment of rebel infantry.

About this time General Van Dorn placed his batteries in favorable positions and concentrated a tremendous artillery fire on the Federal position around Elkhorn Tavern. The few Federal guns that remained on the field made feeble reply to this terrible storm of shot and shell and grape. Towards evening the air became more resonant, so that the rapid succession of echoes and re-echoes of the sound of the thundering artillery produced a profound impression upon the minds of those favorably situated among the hills and hollows of that section for hearing them. The heavy artillery fire on the Federal centre at the tavern again ceased and the Confederate infantry advanced to the assault in heavy masses. In a few moments after Colonel Carr had sent Colonel Shunk's battalion of infantry to the support of Colonel Dodge on the right, and before Colonel Vandever could close up the gap thus caused, the rebel infantry were seen swarming up the telegraph road, up the hollow west of it, and from the brush into the open space directly in front of the Federal position in front of the tavern. The opposing lines were now within a few paces of each other, and the conflict with small-arms that ensued became terrific for a short time. In this desperate struggle Colonel Vandever's brigade was forced by overpowering numbers of Little's brigade and Frost's division to retreat across the field south of the tavern and west of the telegraph road; but the troops soon rallied behind a rail fence in the edge of the timber. The Thirty-fifth Illinois, on the left of Colonel Dodge's brigade and near Colonel Vandever's right, was also forced to give way at this time.

General Frost and Colonel Little now brought up their batteries and placed them in position in front of the tavern. One of the rebel batteries posted near Colonel Dodge's left, after the Thirty-fifth Illinois had fallen back, commenced to enfilade his line with a heavy fire, so that he, too, was obliged to retire. His left having been forced to yield first, he ordered Lieutenant-Colonel Chandler, of the Thirty-fifth Illinois, to rally his men, which he did, driving the enemy back some fifty yards, when he was surrounded and taken prisoner with forty men. Before the rebel batteries had got fairly into position and in operation, in front of the tavern, the Federal guns of the Dubuque battery, the three guns of Klauss' Indiana battery, and the two guns of Major Bowen's Missouri light artillery, posted some three hundred yards south of the tavern on either side of the telegraph road, opened a heavy fire of grape and canister into the advancing line of Confederate infantry, and checked them until Colonel Carr rallied and partly re-formed his line. In a short time, however, the Confederate batteries got into position and commenced playing upon the Federal batteries with shot and shell, and from their superiority in number of guns compelled the Federal guns to leave the field.

In the meantime a large force of rebel infantry of Little's and Frost's divisions advanced through the woods, and, coming upon Hayden's Dubuque battery, captured two pieces, first shooting down several of the artillerymen while endeavoring to attach the guns to their limbers. Here also took place another sharp conflict with small-arms, in which the Federal line under Colonel Carr was again forced to fall back, and in which Lieutenant-Colonel Herron, commanding the Ninth Iowa Volunteers, had his horse shot under him and was wounded and captured. Colonel Carr had been wounded several times; Colonel Smith, one of his regimental commanders, had been wounded and left the field; Colonel Chandler and Colonel Herron, regimental commanders, had been captured; most of his field officers had been wounded and captured; and his line in the seven hours' conflict had been forced back nearly a mile.

Late in the evening, while the battle was thus fiercely raging around Elkhorn Tavern, General Curtis, having satisfied himself that his extreme left was no longer in imminent danger, ordered forward his first and second divisions to the assistance of Colonel Carr. General Asboth immediately took four companies of the Second Missouri Volunteers and four pieces of the Second Ohio Battery, under Lieutenant Chapman, of Colonel Schaefer's first brigade, second division, and moved from his camp by the telegraph road to the aid of Colonel Carr near Elkhorn Tavern. Arriving on the ground near where Colonel Vandever's brigade had made its last stand, some three hundred yards south of the tavern, and from which his men were retiring, hard pressed by the enemy, General Asboth directed Lieutenant Chapman to throw his four guns into battery on the left of the telegraph road as quickly as possible and open fire upon the Confederate infantry with grape and canister. Colonel Carr's battle-worn and bleeding soldiers, retiring in line, met the reinforcements under General Asboth with shouts of joy, and in a few moments the four guns of the Second Ohio Battery, having replaced the three guns of the Dubuque battery, were throwing a perfect storm of iron hail into the line of the exultant foe, instantly checking his advance. Not only was the advance of the rebel infantry checked, but in less than half an hour they were driven out of the heavily timbered woods south of Elkhorn Tavern and west of the telegraph road by the heavy fire from the guns of the Second Ohio Battery, assisted by several guns of the batteries of Colonel Carr's division.

Having thus checked the advance of the Confederate army, General Asboth directed Colonel Schaefer to take the four companies of the Second Missouri Infantry and deploy them as skirmishers to the right and left of the telegraph road, and then advance steadily through the woods in the direction of Elkhorn Tavern. The gallant Colonel formed his skirmish line and moved forward and soon encountered the Confederate line of infantry and drove them back through the woods until he reached the fence, some two hundred yards south of the tavern. General Asboth now directed Lieutenant Chapman to follow him with the four guns of the Second Ohio Battery to a position on the left of the road that commanded the Confederate position around Elkhorn Tavern. Lieutenant Chapman quickly brought his guns into battery and at once commenced playing upon the enemy with shot and shell. His guns were soon replied to by a Confederate battery. A fierce artillery contest now took place, which lasted until dark, when the ammunition of the Second Ohio Battery being nearly exhausted, and the rebel battery having ceased firing, General Asboth withdrew his force to the position he occupied when he first came on the field in the evening.

In the meantime, General Curtis, who had accompanied General Asboth to the field, rode over to the right and met Colonel Dodge retiring, having just checked an advance of the enemy by ordering the Fourth Iowa to halt and turn and fire their last round of ammunition into the

Confederate line. Not realizing fully the situation, and supposing that, with his reinforcements he could readily regain the lost ground, General Curtis ordered the Fourth Iowa to face about, fix bayonets, and charge. Although the regiment had exhausted their ammunition, the men faced about, and moved forward with firmness, but soon discovered that the enemy had retired.

The sun descending behind the western hills, a mantle of darkness was soon drawn over the bloody field, alike welcome to both combatants, which put an end to the terrible strife. Leaving the four companies of the Second Missouri Volunteers as a guard along the line of his most advanced front and centre, General Curtis retired about three hundred yards southwest with the balance of his infantry and artillery, and formed a new line along the edge of the timber with fields in front, where his troops slept upon their arms during the night. The rest of the troops of the first and second divisions, which General Curtis had ordered up, did not arrive on the field in time to participate in the last fierce struggle of the evening.

CHAPTER XVIII.

BATTLE OF PEA RIDGE, NEAR LEETOWN.

WHILE the right wing of the Federal army had been thus fiercely engaged during the day, the first, second, and third divisions, forming the left wing and centre, had not been idle. Indeed, General Curtis had been so closely pressed at all points that he was obliged to put into action his reserves. He regretted the great sacrifice of life in his fourth division, but he saw that it was necessary to save his right wing from disaster. In the morning, a few moments before Colonel Carr started with his division to check the advance of the enemy on the telegraph road in front of Elkhorn Tavern, Colonel Osterhaus, commanding the first division, moved out with a force to open the battle in the direction of Leetown. It was about ten o'clock when he left camp on the heights of Sugar Creek. His cavalry was under the command of the gallant Colonel Cyrus Bussey, Third Iowa Cavalry, and consisted of five companies of that regiment under Lieutenant-Colonel Henry H. Trimble; four companies of the Fifth Missouri Cavalry, Benton Hussars, under Colonel Joseph Nemett; four companies of the First Missouri Cavalry, under Colonel C. A. Ellis; and two companies of the Fourth Missouri Cavalry, Fremont Hussars, under Lieutenant O. P. Howe. Three pieces of Captain Elbert's battery, Missouri light artillery, accompanied the cavalry.

The infantry was commanded by Colonel Nicholas Greusel, Thirty-sixth Illinois Volunteers, consisting of his own regiment, with Captain Hoffman's battery, Ohio light artillery, and the Twelfth Missouri Infantry, under Major Hugo Wangelin, with three pieces of Captain Welfley's battery, Missouri light artillery. Lieutenant-Colonel Hendricks, commanding the Twenty-second Indiana Infantry of Colonel Davis' third division, was also ordered to report to Colonel Osterhaus to support the movement in the direction of Leetown.

Colonel Bussey, commanding the cavalry, proceeded north to Leetown, and from thence to the open fields about one mile north. The artillery and infantry followed close in his rear, and took position in the fields north of Leetown. North and northwest of Leetown there were several fields extending from Pea Ridge to the southwest, a distance of one and a half miles, except that near the middle of this space there was a belt of woods of a thick growth of low, scrubby oaks, that divided the succession of fields. Colonel Osterhaus rode forward and came up with Colonel Bussey just as the head of his column was emerging from the belt of woods between the fields, and was entering a small field that lay directly east of a much larger field. On the west side of the large field there was a thick growth of small oaks and underbrush, and on the northwest end of it there was a small prairie of about one hundred and fifty by three hundred yards. On entering the first field, Colonel Bussey sent forward two companies of the First Missouri Cavalry to reconnoitre the woods west and north of the large field. Advancing across the small field in a northwest course he came to the road going west, and followed it until he came to the small prairie lying north of the large field.

Here the Federal cavalry came in plain view of the Confederate cavalry moving south, about a half-mile distant. Colonel Osterhaus, who was now at the head of the column with Colonel Bussey, ordered up the three pieces of Captain Elbert's battery, and two companies of the First Missouri Cavalry, armed with revolvers and revolving carbines, to form on the right and left of the guns to support them. While the guns were coming into battery, and the companies of the First Missouri Cavalry were forming to support them, Colonel Osterhaus directed Colonel Bussey to form the remainder of the cavalry in line of battle as fast as they came up. Colonel Trimble formed the companies of the Third Iowa Cavalry in the rear of the three guns parallel with the road, facing north. Colonel Nemett was directed to form the four companies of the Benton Hussars on the right of the Third Iowa, which was in the rear and on the right of the guns, facing west.

Directly in front of Colonel Osterhaus' line that faced west, General Pike's division, composed of regiments of Texas and Choctaw and Cherokee Indian cavalry, was formed in line on the Confederate right. The Confederate left and centre, under Generals McCulloch and McIntosh, extended along the west line of fence of the field north of the belt of woods separating the fields. The small prairie, where Colonel Osterhaus formed his cavalry in line and placed his battery in position, extended to the field on his right, behind which the Confederates were forming in heavy masses. But as soon as his guns were in position, the Colonel directed Captain Elbert to open vigorously with grape and shell on the troops in his front to the west. The gunners quickly got the exact range of the Confederate line, and were soon throwing such a destructive shower of shell and grape into the ranks of the Texan and Indian troops as to produce much disorder and wellnigh a stampede. Seeing the disorder produced in the visible part of the Confederate line by his heavy artillery fire, Colonel Osterhaus ordered Colonel Bussey to send two companies of cavalry down the road to charge the enemy before they received reinforcements. Lieutenant-Colonel Trimble took two companies of the Third

Iowa Cavalry and galloped down the road some three hundred yards in columns of fours, and, passing into the timber west of the small prairie, suddenly and unexpectedly came upon the Confederate infantry at short musket range, drawn up in line of battle. After passing from the open ground, Colonel Trimble was unable to advance in line on account of the fence on his immediate left and the thick brush and woods on his right. On approaching the rebel infantry, he wheeled his companies into line facing the foe, and that moment received from him a heavy volley of musketry, killing and wounding a large number of his men and horses. Colonel Trimble himself was wounded in the head. He at once fell back with such of his command as had not been killed and were not too badly wounded to accompany him.

At the same time that he moved forward with his two companies, Colonel Osterhaus ordered Colonel Bussey with the remainder of the cavalry, except the two companies supporting the guns, to charge from the right and attack General McCulloch's left. Before Colonel Bussey had completed the preparations for the charge, General McIntosh at the head of five regiments of Confederate cavalry, charged down upon the Federal line from the north, breaking through it, capturing the guns, and passing into the large open field to the south and in the Federal rear. In conjunction with General McIntosh, General Pike, with three regiments of Indians and two regiments of Texas cavalry, charged from the west with wild yells and war whoops, more hideous than dangerous. There was a general discharge of small-arms on both sides, but the firing was not effective, for the reason that General McIntosh, in making his grand charge with his numerous cavalry, broke the Federal line by weight of numbers, taking little time in the excitement of the moment for deliberate firing. After firing a volley the Federal cavalry were pressed back into the timber and field in their rear, where the Federal infantry were forming in line. Seeing that his cavalry could not at once be rallied and re-formed in sufficient numbers to check the Confederates, Colonel Osterhaus rode back to meet his infantry. Colonel Greusel, commanding the second brigade, first division, was forming his men in line in the field south of the belt of woods that lay between the succession of fields, when Colonel Osterhaus came up, and in a few moments more the infantry and artillery were ready for action.

The Thirty-sixth Illinois Volunteers formed the left of his line; Hoffman's Ohio battery formed next on the right; the Twelfth Missouri Infantry to the right of the battery, and three pieces of Captain Welfley's battery next on the right, supported by one company of the Thirty-sixth Illinois Volunteers on the right, and the Twenty-second Indiana Infantry on his extreme right. Satisfied that the enemy greatly outnumbered his force, Colonel Osterhaus sent to General Curtis for reinforcements. He had scarcely completed the formation of his line described, when his broken line of cavalry came rushing back, pursued by the enemy's cavalry. At this moment he ordered Captains Welfley and Hoffman to turn their guns upon the rapidly advancing lines of Confederate cavalry, which they did with good effect, almost instantly checking them.

Having checked the movement of the enemy and rallied and re-formed the Benton and Fremont Hussars, Colonel Osterhaus ordered his artillery officers to turn their guns upon the enemy in the field west of him, and the prairie north of the field. In less than thirty minutes the batteries had swept the field and open space clear of the enemy. In a short time, however, a large crowd of Indian and other mounted Confederate soldiers and officers, in no sort of order, through mere curiosity, collected around the three Federal guns which had been abandoned by the cavalry in the first attack. These guns, however, were re-taken and brought in by Colonel Pattison that night. The crowd of Indians around the guns having been observed by the officers of the Federal batteries, several shells were thrown into it, dispersing it and sending the Indians hurriedly into the woods near by in great trepidation.

About this time a group of Confederate officers was observed in an elevated open space on the western side of Pea Ridge, perhaps three quarters of a mile off to the right front of the Federal line. Colonel Greusel directed Lieutenant Bencke, commanding a section of Welfley's battery, to throw three shells into the group on the steep hill-side, which he did, instantly dispersing them. Having driven the Confederate cavalry back into the woods and brush by his well sustained artillery fire, Colonel Osterhaus then threw forward as skirmishers one company of the Benton Hussars to the left, two companies of the Thirty-sixth Illinois Infantry to his left front, and two companies of the Twelfth Missouri Infantry to his right front, to protect Captain Welfley in recovering one of his guns which had been left a quarter of a mile back when the Federal cavalry line was broken in the first action. In the charge, the Confederates shot one of the horses drawing the gun, and in its struggles it broke the tongue of the limber. In approaching the woods near where it was left, the enemy opened a heavy fire of musketry upon the two companies of the Twelfth Missouri Infantry, but they continued to move forward, firing as they advanced, until they had driven the Confederates beyond their range. The gun was recovered under these difficulties and subsequently rendered good service on that field.

Several times the Confederate cavalry and mounted Indians attempted to advance, but each time were met by a storm of shell and grape thrown from the nine guns of Welfley's and Hoffman's batteries, and driven back to seek shelter behind the thick woods and brush. Up to this time the Confederate artlilery had taken no important part in the battle, so that until it entered the lists the fire of the Federal guns was directed entirely against the Confederate line the moment it came within range.

With a strong skirmish line, and with the constant play of his artillery, Colonel Osterhaus had been able to keep back the Confederate cavalry and hold his position until the arrival of Colonel Jeff. C. Davis with most of the third division about two o'clock. The Twenty-second Indiana Infantry, that had since morning been on the field as a part of Colonel Osterhaus' command, now rejoined Colonel Davis' division. Colonel Julius White, commanding the second brigade of the third division, consisting of the Thirty-seventh and Fifty-ninth Regiments Illinois Volunteers, and the Peoria battery Illinois light artillery, having arrived on the field in advance, was ordered by Colonel Davis to deploy his men on the right of Colonel Osterhaus, and engage the Confederate infantry, who could plainly be seen rapidly advancing through the woods near the Bentonville and Elkhorn Tavern road along the foot of Pea Ridge. Colonel White formed his brigade in line about one hundred and fifty yards in front of the Confederate line, which was drawn up in a thick growth of low scrubby oaks. Then the opposing lines advanced slowly, and in almost breathless silence, until they had approached within sixty to seventy yards of each other, when both sides opened fire almost at the same moment, which was maintained with great determination for perhaps three quarters of an hour. The guns of the Peoria battery, which had been placed in position in the southeast corner of a field to support the infantry, played upon the Confederate line with shell, grape, and canister with the most disastrous effects. In the meantime General McCulloch brought up reinforcements, and strengthened his line, and extended it to the left so as to flank Colonel Davis' right under Colonel

White. The heavy musketry firing was now resumed along the opposing lines with great fury for a short time, and until Colonel White's Federal brigade was pressed back some two hundred yards. This retiring of the Federal brigade left exposed two guns of the Peoria battery, and before Captain Davidson could attach them to their limbers a fresh regiment of Confederate infantry suddenly charged from the woods and captured them, first shooting and disabling several of the artillery horses. The sharp volleys of musketry and the roar of the artillery indicated the severity of the conflict. And now, just as the Federal line commenced to retire before the overwhelming numbers hurled against it, Colonel Thomas Pattison arrived on the field with the Eighteenth Regiment Indiana Infantry of the first brigade of the third division. He immediately formed the regiment on the right of the Twenty-second Indiana Infantry under Lieutenant-Colonel Hendricks, and then took command of both regiments. Under instructions from Colonel Davis, who was directing the movements of the troops, and who was anxiously watching the progress of the battle, Colonel Pattison now marched the two regiments in double-quick time by the right flank through the timber towards the Federal right, until he met the Fifty-ninth Illinois retiring in some disorder in a direction perpendicular to his line of movement. He therefore halted a moment and opened his lines to allow the Fifty-ninth Illinois to pass through, after which he closed them again and moved forward until he came to a field at the foot of Pea Ridge. Advancing through this field he changed his line of battle by wheeling to the left. His line now faced nearly west, and west of the field he had just entered was another large open field. Pressing forward he found the Confederates rushing upon the Peoria battery, which had been left unsupported by the Thirty-seventh Illinois Infantry when forced to retire. Having captured the two guns the enemy turned them upon Colonel Pattison. But while the Confederates were exultingly following up their temporary success in pursuing Colonel White's brigade, Colonel Pattison had come into line in the rear of the Confederate left, and delivered a full volley into their ranks, throwing them into confusion, and causing them to abandon the captured guns and to retreat from the field.

As soon as the Confederate line was broken by this unexpected assault in the rear, part of the Confederate troops retreated rapidly by Colonel Pattison's right, and part by his left, through the line of the Twenty-second Indiana, which gave way by order of Colonel Hendricks, and retired from the field. Finding that they were flanked, the two wings of the Confederate army saw that it would require a desperate effort to get out of their perilous position. Colonel White had in the meantime rallied the Thirty-seventh Illinois, and was advancing and firing into the right wing of the Confederate force. In the retreat the Confederate left wing forced Colonel Pattison's left wing under Colonel Hendricks to give way by pouring a desperate volley into it at short range. In this sharp conflict, Colonel Hendricks fell, mortally wounded, and some thirty men and officers of the Twenty-second Indiana were also killed and wounded. While the Eighteenth Indiana Infantry, which unflinchingly held their position at this most critical moment, were pouring deadly volleys into the Confederate force passing the Federal right in retreat, the Confederate force that passed on the Federal left poured a heavy volley on the rear of Colonel Pattison's line, which was rendered ineffective by the Colonel ordering his men to fall prone upon the ground. After the Confederates had delivered their fire, Colonel Pattison ordered the left wing of his regiment to face to the rear and return the fire, which they did, with disastrous effect, strewing the ground with the enemy's killed and wounded. In keeping up the fire from his right he gradually threw back the right of his right wing, at the same time advancing his left until his right wing faced the rear, and then advanced to the open ground in front, still maintaining a heavy fire on the broken and disordered lines of the retreating foe. In a short time the Twenty-second Indiana rallied, and returned and formed on the right of the Eighteenth Indiana Infantry, and Colonel White's second brigade re-formed, advanced, and came into position on the left of Colonel Pattison. Towards the last of this struggle the guns of the Peoria battery coming into position increased the demoralization of McCulloch's army by throwing, in quick succession, round after round, of shell and grape-shot into its retreating and broken lines.

While the battle was thus fiercely raging on the Federal right under Colonel Davis, the left, under Colonel Osterhaus, was also hotly engaged with the rebel right wing. The Fifth Missouri Cavalry (Benton Hussars) formed the extreme left of his line, and several companies of the First and Fourth Regiments Missouri Cavalry, were detached as skirmishers on the right of his line, to fill the gap next to Colonel Davis' third division. The Twelfth Missouri Infantry and Thirty-sixth Illinois Infantry, supported by Welfley's and Hoffman's batteries, maintained the positions they took in the morning to the close of the day's operations. In the assault in which the Thirty-seventh Illinois Volunteers were forced to retire, the Confederate right wing, consisting of infantry and cavalry, furiously attacked Colonel Osterhaus' right, driving his cavalry flankers and infantry skirmish line back upon his main line. He quickly moved the Twelfth Missouri Volunteers, supported by the three guns of Welfley's battery, into position on his exposed flank, and opened fire upon the advancing Confederates, and not only checked their movement against his right flank, but drove them from the field.

The Thirty-sixth Illinois Infantry were moved in close columns to the left of the new position to meet an expected attack from the Confederate cavalry. But skirmishers thrown out from this regiment, assisted by Captain Hoffman's battery, frustrated this threatened movement against his left flank.

To guard against further attempts at turning his left flank, Colonel Osterhaus sent four pieces of Hoffman's battery back to Leetown to take up a position commanding the approaches from the west and northwest. A reserve of infantry from Colonel Davis' division had also been placed in position at that point. The Third Iowa Cavalry, which had taken position on another part of the field after the first attack in the morning, had been ordered back to the Federal left by General Curtis, and took position on the left of Colonel Osterhaus, near Leetown. But now the right wing of General Van Dorn's army, composed of troops from Louisiana, Texas, Arkansas, and the Indian Territory, the best drilled in the Confederate service west of the Mississippi River, were routed along the entire front of Colonels Davis and Osterhaus, with the loss of two of their famous generals, McCulloch and McIntosh, killed, and one of their next-best officers, Colonel Hebert, captured.

Death of General McCulloch.

Senator James H. Berry, of Arkansas, who was a lieutenant in the Sixteenth Arkansas Infantry, gives in substance the following account of the death of General Ben. McCulloch near Leetown.

Some time after the Confederate Indians and white troops had taken a Federal battery, the General rode in front of the Sixteenth Arkansas Infantry, and ordered Colonel Hill to deploy two companies of his regiment as skirmishers, to move south through the thick wood and brush towards a field. Colonel Hill was also directed to follow a few yards in the rear of the skirmishers, and, as soon as they became engaged, to charge with his regiment until he came to the field fence, inside of which the Federal infantry were supposed to be posted.

General McCulloch rode a short distance in the rear of the skirmish line and in front of Colonel Hill's regiment. In moving forward through the brush his skirmishers soon became sharply engaged with the Federal skirmishers, who were posted behind the north fence, inside of the field. The Sixteenth Arkansas Infantry charged as ordered, and when within sixty to seventy yards of the fence ran over the lifeless body of General McCulloch, who had just been shot by the Federal skirmishers. The body of the General was found and recognized by Lieutenant Joseph M. Bailey and several other members of Company "D." The General had been shot through the heart, and died instantly. Lieutenant Bailey reported his death to Adjutant Pixley, who was afterwards Lieutenant-Colonel of the Sixteenth Arkansas, and he ordered a detail of men to take the body to an ambulance in the rear. After it was put in the ambulance it was at once driven to Bentonville, and from thence to Fort Smith, where it was buried.

The General wore, when he rode forward in the rear of his skirmish line, a dove-colored coat that looked like corduroy, and sky-blue pants, and had a Maynard rifle slung from his shoulder. When the Sixteenth Arkansas Infantry reached the fence, the Federal skirmishers who had been posted behind it fell back to the south side of the field, except those killed or wounded. The Confederate leader had despatched the members of his staff to other parts of the field with orders in regard to the formation and forward movement of his line of battle, and was therefore alone when struck by the fatal bullet.

Colonel N. Greusel, commanding second brigade of General Osterhaus' division, threw forward, to check the

Confederate advance, Companies "B" and "G," Thirty-sixth Illinois Infantry. The Federal skirmishers advanced across to the north side of the field and took position behind the fence, and in a few moments saw the Confederate line approaching, and when within easy range opened fire upon it. Peter Pelican, of Company "B," Thirty-sixth Illinois Infantry, seeing a mounted officer in the rear of the Confederate line, took aim and shot him from his horse. The Federal soldier's description of the officer leaves no doubt that it was General McCulloch that he shot.

As soon as the Confederate legions had melted away, disappeared in the thick, scrubby woods beyond the fields, and the Stars and Stripes were triumphantly unfurled over the bloody field, the victorious Federal troops sent up prolonged and enthusiastic cheers, which were re-echoed among the far-off hills and hollows of Northwestern Arkansas.

Colonel Davis on the right, and Colonel Osterhaus on the left, at once threw forward their skirmish lines, with cavalry on the flanks, and scoured the woods for a mile or so in front, and until it was ascertained that the Confederate forces had abandoned the field and were in full retreat. A mile or so off to the northwest their trains could be seen moving on the road in the direction of Bentonville.

At two o'clock in the afternoon General Sigel ordered Major Poten to take a force from the camp north of Sugar Creek, consisting of his own regiment, the Seventeenth Missouri Volunteers, two companies of the Fifteenth Missouri Volunteers under Major Landry, two companies of the Third Missouri Volunteers, two companies of the Fifth Missouri Cavalry, and two pieces of the Missouri light artillery under Captain Elbert, and to move forward on the Bentonville road for the purpose of making a demonstration against the rear of the Confederate army and of threatening their trains. Advancing some four miles on the Bentonville road, Major Poten discovered a considerable body of Confederate cavalry on the hills to the right of the road, and opened fire upon them with the two guns of Captain Elbert's battery. He then sent forward the two companies of Benton Hussars under Major Heinrichs to reconnoitre the enemy's position. The force encountered was under Brigadier-General Martin E. Green, commanding the second division of Price's army, guarding the baggage, ammunition, and supply trains of the combined forces under General Van Dorn. Besides his own division, General Green had in his command, posted at the cross-roads northeast of Camp Stevens, and nearly four miles west of the Federal camp on Sugar Creek, Colonels Dawson's and King's regiments of Arkansas troops, and Major Crump's battalion of Texas cavalry, and one battery of artillery. When Major Poten advanced within six hundred yards of the rebel position, and commenced to manœuvre as if threatening a flank movement, General Green opened fire on the Federal line with three pieces of artillery, severely wounding one man. The two guns under Captain Elbert replied by throwing into the rebel position several rounds of shell, and then Major Poten withdrew his command and returned to camp about dark, capturing eight prisoners on the way back.

In his camp north of Sugar Creek, General Curtis held until late in the afternoon a heavy reserve from the first, second, and third divisions, ready to be moved to any point where the need of assistance was most pressing. As the left wing of the army under Colonels Osterhaus and Davis, north of Leetown, was being hard pressed by McCulloch's corps until about four o'clock, General Sigel took the Fifteenth Missouri Volunteers, the Twenty-fifth and Forty-fourth Regiments Illinois Volunteers, and the two twelve-pounder guns of Welfley's battery, and marched to their assistance. When he arrived at Leetown the firing in front of the Federal left wing had ceased. Although the fading light of day was now melting into the dusk of evening, the thundering of the artillery was still heard on the Federal right around Elkhorn Tavern. General Sigel was here overtaken by an aid, Captain McKinny, from General Curtis, requesting that more reinforcements be sent to the right as speedily as possible. The left wing of five companies of the Twenty-fifth Illinois under Major Richard H. Nodine and four pieces of Captain Hoffman's battery, stationed in reserve at Leetown, were detached and sent to General Curtis, and arrived on the field just at dusk, but in time to participate in the closing struggle of the day.

In the meantime the Fifteenth Missouri Volunteers and Forty-fourth Illinois Volunteers and the two heavy guns of Captain Welfley's battery had been sent forward to report to Colonel Davis, and were ordered into position on the right of his third division along the base of Pea Ridge. From Leetown General Sigel proceeded with the right wing of the Twenty-fifth Illinois Infantry under Colonel Wm. N. Coler, together with several companies of cavalry, to the battle-field north of the village and found Colonels Osterhaus and Davis in full possession of it, and soon ascertained that the enemy had disappeared from their front. The General now requested Colonel Davis to protect his left flank with the troops of the third division, four companies of Benton Hussars and two companies of Fremont Hussars under Colonel Nemett, and then proceeded with the battalion of the Twenty-fifth Illinois and four pieces of Welfley's and Hoffman's batteries upon the road to the northeast along the south side of Pea Ridge, passing the enemy's hospitals and dead and wounded, until he came to the Forty-fourth Illinois and Fifteenth Missouri formed in line. Here he halted his command and ordered Colonel Osterhaus to join him with the Thirty-sixth Illinois and Twelfth Missouri Volunteers.

On the arrival of these regiments he moved them and the troops already on the ground, slowly and cautiously on the road along the south slope of Pea Ridge, about half a mile in the direction of Elkhorn Tavern, until he came to the west end of a large field, in close proximity to the right flank of General Price's army, which had ceased firing, except some cannonading between his left and General Curtis' right. General Sigel at once planted his batteries and brought his infantry into line, and then sent a messenger to General Curtis notifying him that he was near at hand on the left and ready to co-operate. But it was now getting quite dark and it was decided to wait until morning to open the battle.

From the high ground where his troops and artillery were posted the camp-fires of the Confederate forces in the open spaces around Elkhorn Tavern were plainly in view. The enemy having been completely routed and driven from the field on his left and centre, General Curtis shortly after dark directed Colonel Davis to move his division to the support of the right wing formed in line across the telegraph road about half a mile south of Elkhorn Tavern. On return of the troops to the battlefield from reconnoitring the woods in front, details from his division were busy the forepart of the night in collecting the dead and wounded. About midnight Colonel Davis marched his division from the battle-field on the left to join General Curtis on the right, leaving Colonel Nemett with the Benton and Fremont Hussars, Missouri Cavalry, to guard the extreme left of the Federal line during the night. On reaching the telegraph road, Colonel Davis marched his troops north about a quarter of a mile to the cleared land, and then deployed the first brigade under Colonel Pattison to the right of the road, and the second brigade under Colonel White to the left of it. The left of the Eighteenth Indiana rested on the telegraph road, and the right of the Twenty-second Indiana rested on the left wing of the Eighth Indiana, under Lieutenant-Colonel Shunk, which had gallantly fought with Colonel Carr's division during the afternoon. The right wing of Klauss' battery was placed in position opposite the centre of this brigade. The right of Colonel White's second brigade rested on the telegraph road, and his left behind a rail fence with open fields in front. The Peoria battery was placed in position on his right near the telegraph road. In this position the troops of the third division rested upon their arms until morning.

At one o'clock on the morning of the 8th, General Sigel, who had taken up a position at dark on the extreme left of General Curtis' right wing, and near General Price's right, marched the troops of the first and second divisions with him, to General Curtis' headquarters in the rear of his line of battle on the telegraph road, intending to take them to camp to give them rest, food, and fire. In preparing for the struggle of the coming day, General Curtis fully realized that when the earliest beams of light streaked the east his troops should be ready to take their places in line of battle. He therefore suggested to General Sigel that his troops bivouac until morning where they had halted near his headquarters, and that details from them be sent to camp for provisions. The suggestion was concurred in and the troops rested on their arms where they halted until daylight, at which time they were joined by other regiments and detachments of the first and second divisions that had been employed in reconnoissances on the left and in guarding the Federal camp.

General Curtis had now brought on the field all his troops, except some detachments of cavalry and infantry and two sections of artillery left to guard his camps and approaches to his rear, to oppose General Van Dorn's army composed of the united forces of Generals Price and McCulloch. The foe in his front was flushed with success. Sleep sat lightly on his eyelids that night, for he was deeply involved in thoughts, solicitous, concerning the approaching struggle, and the safety of his army.

After the right wing of General Van Dorn's army had been routed, with the loss of its three chief officers (Generals McCulloch and McIntosh killed, and acting Brigadier-General Hebert captured), Colonel E. Greer, Third Texas Cavalry, the senior officer present, assumed command of the troops left on the field. He found them much scattered and demoralized. Artillery firing was heard in the rear on the Bentonville road when Major Poten's force attacked General Green near Camp Stevens, and supposing that the Confederate train was attacked, Colonel Stone's Sixth Texas Cavalry, Colonel Drew's Cherokee Indian regiment, and Major Brooks' battalion of Arkansas volunteers marched to join General Green for its protection.

When night had fallen Colonel Greer had succeeded in rallying most of the troops of McCulloch's shattered legions, and ordered them to bivouac some distance north of the battle-field. At ten o'clock that night he called a council of his leading officers, and it was decided, in view of the situation presented, to march at one o'clock, next morning, to join General Price's army on the left. The order of march was made out for one o'clock, and General Van Dorn at once notified so that he would have time to make other disposition of the troops if he desired. He approved the order, however, and sent instructions to Colonel Greer to move as quickly and as rapidly as possible and to take position on the telegraph road near Elkhorn Tavern. The Colonel took up the line of march at half-past one o'clock, on the morning of the 8th, at the head of his division, now consisting of Hebert's Third Louisiana Volunteers,

Colonels McNair's, McRae's, and Mitchell's Regiments of Arkansas infantry; the Third, Fourth, and Eleventh Regiments Texas Cavalry, Colonel W. P. Lane's regiment of South Kansas-Texas Cavalry, Colonel Embrey's Arkansas regiment, and Captain Hart's Battery, and reached the telegraph road in the rear of Price's army at daybreak. Here, under instructions from General Van Dorn, he marched his troops to a position on the left of General Price's army, and formed line of battle.

Late in the afternoon of the 7th, General Albert Pike succeeded in rallying the regiments of Colonels Churchill, Hill, and Rector, Arkansas infantry, Major Whitfield's battalion of Texas infantry, Colonel Stand Watie's Cherokee Indian regiment, Captain Good's battery, and some other detachments of McCulloch's broken army, and marched them, making a detour of several miles to the north, to the telegraph road, and thence to General Van Dorn's headquarters, which he reached before midnight. His troops were hungry and much worn in body and spirit, having been marching and fighting for three days, and the last day without food. On the morning of the 8th he was directed by General Van Dorn to take position with his command, now consisting of only Stand Watie's Cherokee regiment and Captain Welch's company of cavalry on Pea Ridge, on the extreme right of the Confederate army, to prevent the Federal forces from turning that flank. The other troops and battery he brought along were assigned to positions in the right wing of General Price's army. Three regiments of Arkansas infantry, under Colonel Churchill, were placed in line in the rear of General Frost's and Little's divisions.

During the night General Van Dorn had ordered his batteries posted in advantageous positions, and several of them were masked near the Federal line. Early on the morning of the 8th, after the troops of McCulloch's corps joined him, and were placed in their proper positions, his line of battle extended from the summit of Pea Ridge, nearly a mile northwest of Elkhorn Tavern, to a point nearly a mile southeast of the telegraph road. His left centre was about a quarter of a mile south of Elkhorn Tavern, in and near the edge of the heavy growth of large oak timber west of the road, and south of which were large open fields. His left wing east of the telegraph road was formed in woods of young scrubby oaks, but much of the ground was open enough and smooth enough to allow the manœuvring of troops and artillery. Several small fields were also in front of this wing.

General Van Dorn received by aides-de-camp, about three o'clock in the afternoon of the 7th, information of the death of McCulloch, McIntosh, and Hebert, and of the utter rout of their troops. This information he kept from the troops of Price's army, so that they rested upon their arms confident that on the morrow they would achieve an easy victory.

CHAPTER XIX.

BATTLE OF PEA RIDGE.—CONCLUDED.

WHEN Night, swift traveller, had fled before the dawn, an observer on the western heights of Pea Ridge, looking to the south and west, would have seen, in the plain below, lines of men in blue moving into positions through the fields and through the brush woods which now and then partially obscured them from view. Standing on the southern brow of the ridge he would have seen, from that point, extending to the southeast along the slope of the mountain, through the heavy forest timber and into the more open woods beyond, a great throng of men in dingy-colored lines—lines corresponding very nearly in color to the woods and rocks among which they had bivouacked—moving also into positions.

The nearness of the lines of the two armies enabled the troops posted on the skirmish lines of each to discern the movements along the fronts of their opponents in places where the ground was open enough to permit an extended view. Shortly after the sun had risen above the horizon, report came to Colonel Davis, commanding the Federal centre, that the Confederate infantry could be seen forming in line in the timber south of Elkhorn Tavern. Captain Davidson, commanding the Peoria battery posted near the left of the telegraph road, was directed to open fire upon the rebel forces seen in the timber. He advanced with his battery to the open field on the left of the road in front of Colonel White's brigade and in full view of the Confederate forces, and opened a hot fire upon their line. He was quickly replied to by Teel's battery, which had been assigned to a position between Rives' regiment and General Green's division. After these batteries had exchanged a few shots, Wade's battery on the Confederate side and Klauss' battery on the Federal side, entered the lists, and then for nearly half an hour there was an almost continuous roar of artillery, both sides using grape and canister. The Confederate batteries were masked behind a clump of woods east of the telegraph road, opposite the right wing of Colonel Pattison's brigade of the third division, and not perhaps more than two hundred yards distant. Their heavy fire of grape and canister soon forced Klauss' battery and Colonel Pattison's right wing and centre to retire some two hundred yards. His left wing, resting on the telegraph road in ambush, also soon afterwards retired. The fire of the Confederate batteries soon commenced to enfilade Colonel White's line, which was out of musket range, so that he, too, was obliged to retire a short distance.

About this time Colonel Vandever's brigade of Colonel Carr's fourth division, which was formed on the right of the third division, was also obliged to change position to avoid a raking fire of the Confederate batteries. In the meanwhile General Curtis was establishing his left wing, composed of the first and second divisions, under General Sigel. In this movement the first division, under Colonel Osterhaus, consisted of two companies of the Third Missouri Infantry, the Twelfth and Seventeenth Missouri Volunteers; the Twenty-fifth, Thirty-sixth, and Forty-fourth Regiments Illinois Volunteers; Captain Welfley's battery of five pieces, Missouri light artillery, Captain Hoffman's Fourth Ohio Battery, and Captain Jenks' cavalry company Thirty-sixth Illinois Volunteers.

And the second division, under General Asboth, consisted of six companies of the Second Missouri Volunteers, under Colonel Schaefer; the Fifteenth Missouri Volunteers, under Colonel F. J. Joliat; two pieces Second Ohio Battery, under Lieutenant Chapman; four companies of the Fourth Missouri Cavalry (Fremont Hussars) under Major Heinrichs; six companies Fifth Missouri Cavalry (Benton Hussars), and two pieces of Captain Elbert's battery, Missouri light artillery.

Details were sent to the camps for provisions, so that the troops partook of a hasty breakfast before falling into line. Colonel Osterhaus and Lieutenant Asmussen, of General Sigel's staff, who had been sent forward to the left of the third division to reconnoitre and examine the ground for deploying the first and second divisions, returned in a short time, and then the movement of the troops to complete the Federal line commenced. The Forty-fourth Illinois Volunteers, under Colonel Charles Knobelsdorff, had already been sent forward and formed on the left of the third division. The first division, under Colonel Osterhaus, formed the advanced line, and in coming upon the field he posted the Twenty-fifth Illinois Volunteers, under Colonel Coler, on the extreme right of his line, connecting with the left of the third division. To the left and in advance of Colonel Coler the Forty-fourth Illinois was posted, and on the left of this regiment Captain Welfley's battery. On the left of Welfley's battery the Twelfth Missouri Infantry, under Major Hugo Wangelin, were placed in position, and on the left of Major Wangelin Captain Hoffman's battery, and on the left of the battery the Thirty-sixth Illinois Volunteers, under Colonel N. Greusel, in column by division at half distance. The Third and Seventeenth Regiments Missouri Infantry formed the reserve in the rear of the centre of the first division. The second division with all the cavalry, under General Asboth, posted two hundred and fifty yards behind the first division, was the principal reserve from which General Sigel drew troops to deploy to the right or left as the emergency required.

In the order described General Sigel moved forward with his two divisions. His troops had no sooner entered the large open fields south of Pea Ridge than the Confederate batteries opened a terrific fire upon them from the heights of the mountain. Arriving on a high plateau within a half-mile of the Confederate line, Hoffman's and Welfley's Federal batteries returned the fire of the rebel batteries with shot and bursting shells with great precision and with deadly effect. Under the heavy fire of the Confederate batteries from the heights, General Curtis had now established his left wing, and his line of battle was complete, covering very nearly the entire front of General Van Dorn's line of battle. The storm of battle now burst forth with tremendous fury, and the roar of the eighty pieces of the deep-toned artillery along the fronts of the contending armies revealed to each the strength of its antagonist and the greatness of the struggle. On the Federal left the guns of Hoffman's and Welfley's batteries played upon the rebel batteries on the heights of Pea Ridge; Davidson's and Klauss' batteries, posted in the Federal centre, shelled the heavily timbered woods south of Elkhorn Tavern, where large bodies of rebel infantry were massed. The guns of the First and Fourth Iowa Batteries of the fourth division on the Federal right were also now engaged in shelling the rebel position in the timber south of Elkhorn Tavern.

The heavy artillery fire from the Federal left and centre induced General Van Dorn to strengthen his right wing and centre with troops and batteries. Directly after the batteries opened fire, General Sigel ordered Colonel Coler, commanding the Twenty-fifth Illinois, to advance and take position behind a fence and log barn on the opposite side of an open field, and about one hundred yards in front of Welfley's battery. To gain this position he was obliged to pass over the open field exposed to a heavy fire of shot and shell from the Confederate batteries, which were in full view of his men. Having reached the point he ordered his men to drop prone upon the ground, which they did, remaining in that position for nearly an hour and a half, during which time they were exposed to the terrible fire from the guns of the rebel batteries, aimed mainly at the Federal batteries on the rising ground in the rear. Holding with unflinching firmness the ground thus gained, General Sigel next ordered Colonel Schaefer to take the Second Missouri Infantry and two pieces of the Second Ohio Battery from the reserve, and proceed to the extreme left of his line to operate against General Van Dorn's extreme right. Colonel Schaefer moved promptly, and on arriving at the position pointed out to him, deployed his men as skirmishers, and soon became hotly engaged with the enemy. In a short time, however, he succeeded, with the assistance of the cavalry under Colonel Nemett, in driving the rebels from the thicket at the foot of the Ridge, where they had formed. The two pieces of the Second Ohio Battery co-operated effectively in this movement by shelling and driving the rebel infantry from the brow of the ridge, where they had formed, and by dismounting two guns of the rebel battery. General Sigel now ordered the troops of his front line and his batteries to advance about three hundred yards, and for the troops of his reserve to move forward and occupy the position just vacated by his first line. When this movement commenced, General Curtis ordered the third division, under Colonel Davis, and the fourth division, under Colonel Carr, also to advance, so that his line would be continuous.

The Federal line was now formed across fields and upon ground open enough to admit of easy evolutions of the troops and artillery. The opposing batteries were within easy range of each other, so that the artillery conflict burst forth again with extraordinary energy. In a very short time, however, the Federal batteries of the left wing, under General Sigel, got the exact range of the Confederate batteries on the brow of the mountain. On the extreme Federal left the two pieces of the Second Ohio Battery were reinforced by two pieces of Captain Elbert's Missouri light artillery. These four pieces and the batteries of Hoffman, Welfley, and Klauss, extending towards the Federal centre, poured a terrific shower of shot and bursting shells into the rebel batteries and lines on the mountain for perhaps half an hour.

Before ordering his troops to storm the heights General Sigel was desirous of forcing the Confederate batteries and troops to retire from the commanding position which they were occupying and holding on to with great tenacity. General Little, who was holding this position with his division, comprising the best troops in Van Dorn's army, first placed Good's battery on his right and ordered the Captain to open fire upon the Federal batteries, posted on elevations in the plain below. But Captain Good had fired only a few rounds when the Federal artillerists got his range, and commenced throwing shells into his position with such precision and rapidity that it was deemed advisable to order up Wade's battery to his support. But the guns of Wade's battery were hardly detached from their limbers when the shot and shell from the concentrated fire of the Federal batteries commenced falling so thick and fast around Captain Good's guns and caissons, that he ordered his battery to limber up and leave the ground. Hart's battery was ordered to take his place, but after a few rounds it was also obliged to leave the field. Finally, Wade's battery commencing to run short of ammunition, and having lost several horses killed and wounded, was also compelled to retire. The position it occupied was supplied by Clark's battery, which kept up the fire until Captain Clark fell decapitated by a cannon-ball. His battery was then also obliged to retire.

General Sigel, who had been watching with intense interest the effects his batteries were producing on the rebel position, dispatched Colonel Osterhaus to General Curtis to report progress. While the artillery of the left wing, supported by the infantry, was thus sweeping every thing before it, General Curtis was directing in person the movements of his right wing and centre. Under his instructions, Captain Hayden commanding the three remaining guns of the Dubuque battery on the extreme right, Lieutenant David commanding the First Iowa Battery to the left of Hayden, and Captain Davidson commanding the Peoria battery posted in the centre, kept up a hot fire on the rebel lines and batteries directly in front. Nearly all the Confederate batteries having been silenced, General Curtis ordered an advance of his entire line. Generals Van Dorn and Price, apprehending an immediate charge of Federal infantry, put their lines in defensive positions as far as practicable.

The Federal advance commenced with the left wing under General Sigel, the artillery and cavalry co-operating with the infantry. On returning to his command from the right, Colonel Osterhaus directed Colonel Greusel to throw forward four companies from the Twelfth Missouri and four companies from the Thirty-sixth Illinois to form the skirmish line in the general advance. Colonel Knobelsdorff also ordered four companies of the Forty-fourth Illinois to form on the left of the four companies of the Thirty-sixth Illinois in the skirmish line. The skirmish line thus formed moved across the large field in front in double-quick, followed by the regiments of the first division at a proper distance. Entering the timber north of the field, these troops encountered the Confederate infantry in strong force, and opened fire upon them at short range. At the same time Major Poten, with the Seventeenth Missouri Infantry on the extreme left, and the Third Missouri Infantry on his right, joining the left of the Thirty-sixth Illinois Volunteers, and supported by the Second and Fifteenth Regiments Missouri Infantry under Colonel Schaefer, and a section of the Second Ohio Battery under Lieutenant Chapman, ascended the mountain, and, storming the heights, drove the enemy from their position in great confusion. Colonel Nemett, commanding the cavalry on the Federal left, moved forward on the left and abreast of the infantry. This movement turned the right flank of the Confederate army. The Federal left wing having gained possession of the heights of the mountain, General Curtis ordered his centre, under Colonel Davis, and his right, under Colonel Carr, to advance.

The infantry of the left wing, in long lines of blue, ascending the slope of the mountain, had an inspiring effect upon the troops of the right, but a depressing effect upon the Confederate officers and soldiers who were watching it from several points along the brow of the ridge. In the general advance, General Curtis' third division, under Colonel Davis, occupied the ground between the telegraph and Huntsville roads, and Colonel Carr's fourth division was formed on the right of the Huntsville road, which runs north, nearly parallel with the telegraph road, for a distance of about a mile from the point where the Federal line first formed.

Most of the Confederate batteries having been withdrawn from the front of the Federal right wing, Colonel Davis moved forward with the third division, and, crossing the long and narrow field, engaged the rebel infantry in the woods beyond. Colonel Carr's division, on the right of Colonel Davis, and the cavalry on the right of Carr, under Colonel Bussey, also advanced in this general movement. The opposing armies now joined in furious battle with small-arms and artillery. The incessant volleys of musketry and the roar of the deep-toned artillery in belching forth showers of iron hail through volumes of sulphurous smoke, proved with what earnestness both sides were engaged in the deadly struggle. General Curtis rode along his lines and gave orders in person to his division commanders for the movements of their troops.

In this day's battle the troops of the Federal divisions vied with each other in deeds of valor. No sooner had the gallant regiments, the Third and Seventeenth Missouri Infantry and Thirty-sixth and part of the Forty-fourth Illinois Volunteers, carried the heights of Pea Ridge by assault, than the Twelfth Missouri, under Major Wangelin, ambitious of being among the foremost in deeds of heroic conduct, dashed forward in the face of a hot fire, and in the charge captured three cannon and a fine silk flag from the Dallas artillery of General Van Dorn's army. In this charge the Twenty-fifth Illinois, under Colonel Coler, also participated, charging abreast of and on the right of the Twelfth Missouri. General Sigel's troops, having now carried the heights of the mountain and captured a rebel battery, broke forth in enthusiastic cheers.

In the advance of the Federal line, Colonel Pattison's brigade of the third division drew the fire of a rebel masked battery directly in front. As it had opened with canister, and threatened to do much mischief, Colonel Pattison determined to charge it with his brigade and take it. His men received the order to charge with cheers, and, advancing with fixed bayonets, gradually quickened their movements to a double-quick, seeing which the Confederate officers hastily withdrew their battery. The battery having been removed, Colonel Pattison's brigade, in connection with Colonel White's second brigade of the third division, engaged the Confederate infantry in the thick woods. In a short time, however, the heavy volleys of musketry from the Federal infantry, and the storm of grape and canister thrown from Davidson's and Klauss' batteries, forced the Confederate line to yield, when the shouts of the Federal soldiers again rent the air. Retiring a short distance, the Confederate officers partially re-formed their lines several times. But each line thus formed was quickly swept away by the resistless advance of the Federal infantry, who delivered, with great rapidity and precision, volley after volley of leaden missiles into the retreating lines of the Confederate hosts.

The melting away of the Confederate line was immediately followed by the outburst of prolonged cheering of ten thousand Federal soldiers. Some of the Confederates who had zealously guarded the rear of the Southern army during the entire struggle, on hearing the cheering, and supposing it to come from their own troops, rushed towards the front and came near getting into the fight. Before getting within range of the Federal small-arms, however, these men, who were going to be brave in pursuing and slaughtering a defeated foe, met their own troops retreating. Finding that the victorious shouts were on the Federal side, their courage cooled, and they were swift of foot to leave the field. In the closing struggle of the battle, Colonel Rives, of General Price's army, in endeavoring to make a stand with his troops, fell, mortally wounded.

Every moment the victorious shouts of the Federal troops and the destructive fire from their small-arms and artillery increased the confusion in the wavering and disordered Confederate lines. Confederate officers rode hurriedly to and fro in search of Generals Van Dorn and Price for orders. The quarter of the field where they were last seen was occupied by the advancing Federal troops, and a report got out and spread through the army that they were captured. Instead of the expression of victory almost won that had lately sat upon the countenances of the troops of the Confederate host, there now sat an expression of fear, grief, and despair. In the excitement and confusion of leaving the field, artillery carriages and caissons rattled down the steep hills; officers, in urging their men forward, cried out on every hand: "Close up, close up, or you will all be cut to pieces!" "The Federal cavalry are coming!"

When Generals Van Dorn and Price saw that there was no hope of checking the irresistible advance of the Federal troops, whose victorious shouts every moment sounded louder and louder in their ears, they placed themselves on the extreme left of their line near the Huntsville road, and sent orders to their subordinate commanders to withdraw from the field, and fall back on the Huntsville road in a southeast direction. The troops of the left wing of the Confederate army retreated from the field with their commanding generals on the Huntsville road, while those of the right wing, being pressed closely by General Curtis, and cut off from the left wing, were obliged to retreat north for several miles in the direction of Keetsville on the telegraph road, closely pursued by General Sigel's divisions.

General Albert Pike, who had been posted on the extreme right of the Confederate line, started to General Van Dorn's headquarters for orders, and when he got as far as the telegraph road, met the Confederate troops and batteries leaving the field in the utmost confusion. He tried to re-form the troops and post the batteries so as to command the road, but it was impossible in the excitement that prevailed. Thinking that the Confederate troops would retreat south on the Bentonville road, the road by which they had gained the rear of the Federal army, and the road on which their baggage and supply trains were coming up to join them, General Pike rode forward with several officers of his staff, and by a short cut gained the brow of a hill on that road, and halted with the view of making a stand with the troops and batteries as they came up. But he had no sooner stopped and cast his eyes toward the telegraph road than he saw the Confederate troops were continuing their flight on that road instead of turning to the left and gaining the Bentonville road. There was no time for loitering. The Federal cavalry, with the flying batteries, were pursuing the fugitives of the mighty broken host on all the roads. If a group of a half-dozen or more fugitives here and there stood in perplexing doubt as to what course to pursue, or what direction they should fly, a shell from a Federal gun thrown into their midst instantly forced a decision.

When he saw that he was cut off from his army, and when shells from the Federal guns commenced dropping around him, General Pike and his small party rode forward rapidly in a southwest direction on the Bentonville road, but were in a few moments so hotly pursued by the Federal cavalry that they were obliged to leave the road and take to the woods. After wandering in the hills and mountains for several days, over obscure paths and byroads, the General and his party joined part of the demoralized Confederate forces at Cincinnati, a small town about forty miles southwest on the western line of Arkansas. That part of the Confederate army that retreated north on the telegraph road, after passing Keetsville, turned east, taking the Roaring River and Berryville road, and joined General Van Dorn on the march from Huntsville to Van Buren.

General Cooper, commanding the Indians posted on the right of the Confederate line, retreated from the field in a southwest direction and joined General Green in charge of the troops guarding the trains of the Confederate army. In the general breaking up of the Confederate army, it was several hours before General Curtis ascertained that the main force under Generals Van Dorn and Price had retreated south by turning short to the right and following up an obscure hollow that led into the Huntsville road. He held the third and fourth divisions of his army near the battle-field, and despatched his cavalry in all directions against the broken battalions of the flying foe. General Sigel's force and the several detachments thus sent in pursuit of the enemy, captured some five hundred prisoners, upwards of one thousand stands of small-arms, and caissons, limbers, and other munitions of war abandoned in the hurried retreat. The Confederate army was so broken in *esprit de corps* that the troops of the different divisions halted only a few hours at a time for food and rest until they had crossed the Boston Mountains.

General Van Dorn's movement to the rear of the Federal army separated him from his trains, and thinking that they would inevitably fall into the hands of the Federal troops, ordered them burned. But General Green, who was guarding them with a large force, supported by artillery, succeeded in getting over the mountains with them with no great loss. The defeat and demoralized retreat of the numerous detachments of the Southern army soon spread great excitement among the people of Northwestern Arkansas.

On the afternoon of the 7th, after Generals McCulloch and McIntosh were killed, mounted Confederate soldiers who had become separated from their commands, in a charge as they asserted, were seen singly and in squads of two, three, and four, on all the roads leading south from the battle-field, riding under whip and spur. Before dark a number of such excited stragglers passed through Bentonville speeding on their way south. Colonel Rector, commanding an Arkansas regiment, finding himself cut off from the rebel army, disbanded his men, first directing them to conceal their arms in a safe place in the hills.

After finding that the Confederate army was in full retreat and crossing the mountains in the direction of the Arkansas River, General Curtis at once commenced to inter the dead and to provide for the care of the wounded of both sides. On the 9th he received, under a flag of truce from General Van Dorn, a burial party with a note from the General requesting permission to attend to the duty of collecting and interring the Confederate dead who fell during the battle. In granting the request, General Curtis found the occasion opportune for calling General Van Dorn's attention to the fact that many of the Federal dead on the field were found scalped and their bodies otherwise mutilated. These outrages on the Federal dead were committed in that quarter of the field temporarily held by the Confederate Indians under Pike and Cooper. The Federal soldiers burned with indignation on finding their dead comrades thus shamefully treated, and it was with some difficulty that they were restrained from retaliation by giving some captured Indians a taste of their own perfidy.

General Curtis reported the Federal loss during the three-days' battle at 203 killed, 980 wounded, and 201 missing. In endeavoring to make the disaster to his arms appear as small as possible, General Van Dorn estimates his loss at 1,000 killed and wounded and 300 prisoners. The number of Confederate dead interred on the field was larger than the Federal, but the number of Confederate wounded is not known, detailed reports having been made by only part of the commanding officers of regiments, brigades, divisions, and detachments. In this battle General Curtis proved himself an able and competent general. The Federal Army of the Southwest was fortunate in having him at its head. Under his direction its various movements were coördinated with such precision that not a single movement failed of its calculated effect. He, too, was fortunate in having competent officers to carry into effect the plans of his operations.

The following tables, made up from official reports, show the casualties in the several divisions of the Army of the Southwest commanded by Brigadier-General Samuel R. Curtis, United States Army, at the battle of Pea Ridge, Arkansas, March 6–8, 1862:

Command.	Killed.		Wounded.		Missing.		Aggregate.
	Officers.	Enlisted men.	Officers.	Enlisted men.	Officers.	Enlisted men.	
Brig.-Gen. Franz Sigel, Commanding First and Second Divisions:							
Col. Peter J. Osterhaus, First Division:							
First Brigade, Col. W. N. Coler:							
Seventeenth Missouri, Major A. H. Poten				2		8	10
Twenty-fifth Illinois, Major Richard H. Nodine		3	1	17	1	2	24
Forty-fourth Illinois, Col. C. Knobelsdorff		1		2			3
Second Brigade, Col. N. Greusel:							
Twelfth Missouri, Major Hugo Wangelin		3	3	26		2	34
Thirty-sixth Illinois		4		37	1	26	68
Capts. Jenks' and Smith's Cos., Illinois Cavalry						7	7
Welfley's Battery, Missouri Light Artillery				5			5
Capt. Louis Hoffman's Fourth Ohio Battery				1		4	5
Total casualties, First Division		11	4	90	2	49	156
Brig.-Gen. A. Asboth, Second Division Staff			1				1
First Brigade, Col. Fredk. Schaefer:							
Second Missouri, Lieut.-Col. B. Laibold	2	6		34		11	53
Fifteenth Missouri, Col. Francis J. Joliat						11	11
Not Brigaded:							
Fourth Missouri Cavalry, Major G. Heinrichs	1	7		28		11	47
Fifth Missouri Cavalry, Col. Joseph Nemett		4	1	19	1	1	26
Capt. G. M. Elbert's Battery, Missouri Light Artillery		3		8		8	19
Lieut. Chapman's Second Ohio Battery		1	1	1			3
Total casualties, Second Division	3	21	3	90	1	42	160

Command.	Killed. Officers.	Killed. Enlisted men.	Wounded. Officers.	Wounded. Enlisted men.	Missing. Officers.	Missing. Enlisted men.	Aggregate.
Col. Jeff. C. Davis, Third Division:							
First Brigade, Col. Thos. Pattison:							
Eighth Indiana, Col. Wm. P. Benton	1	4	1	26			32
Eighteenth Indiana, Lieut.-Col. Henry D. Washburn		3	1	22			26
Twenty-second Indiana, Lieut.-Col. John A. Hendricks	2	7	1	32			42
Capt. Martin Klauss' First Indiana Battery				5		6	11
Second Brigade, Col. Julius White:							
Thirty-seventh Illinois, Lieut.-Col. Myron S. Barnes		20	9	112		3	144
Fifty-ninth Illinois, Lieut.-Col. C. H. Frederick		9	2	55			66
First Missouri Cavalry, Col. C. A. Ellis				17			17
Capt. Peter Davidson's Battery, Illinois Light Artillery		2		2		2	6
Total casualties, Third Division	3	45	14	271		11	344
Col. Eugene A. Carr, Fourth Division Staff			1				1
First Brigade, Col. G. M. Dodge:							
Fourth Iowa, Lieut.-Col. John Galligan	1	17	4	135		3	160
Thirty-fifth Illinois, Col. G. A. Smith		14	3	44	6	46	113
Capt. J. A. Jones, First Iowa Battery.		3	2	12			17
Second Brigade, Col. William Vandever:							
Ninth Iowa, Lieut.-Col. F. J. Herron	4	34	5	171	1	3	218
Col. John S. Phelps' Missouri Infantry	2	11	6	64	1	9	93
Third Illinois Cavalry, Major John McConnell		9	4	32		13	58
Capt. M. M. Hayden's Third Iowa Battery		2	2	15		3	22
Total casualties, Fourth Division	7	90	27	473	8	77	682
Unassigned:							
Third Iowa Cavalry, Col. Cyrus Bussey		24	1	16		9	50
Major W. D. Bowen's Battalion, Missouri Cavalry		1	1	2		2	6
Twenty-fourth Missouri, Major Eli Weston		3	1	15		7	26
Total casualties, unassigned		28	3	33		18	82

Command.	Killed.		Wounded.		Missing.		Aggregate.
	Officers.	Enlisted men.	Officers.	Enlisted men.	Officers.	Enlisted men.	
Recapitulation :							
First Division, Col. P. J. Osterhaus		11	4	90	2	49	156
Second Division, Gen. A. Asboth..	3	21	3	90	1	42	160
Third Division, Col. Jeff. C. Davis.	3	45	14	271	—	11	344
Fourth Division, Col. E. A. Carr ..	7	90	27	473	8	77	682
Total unassigned.................		28	3	33	—	18	82
Grand total casualties.........	13	195	51	957	11	197	1,424

CHAPTER XX.

SKIRMISHES AT NEOSHO.

In sending the army under General Curtis against General Price at Springfield, General Halleck expected General Hunter, commanding Department of Kansas, to co-operate with him by throwing forward the troops that had been concentrated at Fort Scott. When the several divisions of the Army of the Southwest under General Curtis formed a junction at Lebanon, fifty-six miles northeast of Springfield, on the 6th of February, there were probably not less than five thousand troops in and around Fort Scott that could have moved south down the line of Missouri and Kansas towards Northwestern Arkansas, to threaten Price's rear and flank, or that could have been moved in the direction of Springfield to form a junction with General Curtis, and thus form the right wing of the combined Federal forces to operate against the Confederate army. Fort Scott is one hundred miles northwest of Springfield, and was in no danger of being attacked from the west or southwest, so that with a proper understanding between the Federal commanders and a disposition to co-operate with each other, two converging Federal columns could have met at Springfield to attack the Confederate forces. While General Curtis moved forward from Rolla with a noble and patriotic zeal worthy of the cause, his troops breasting the storms of sleet and snow in mid-winter, and overcoming every obstacle, the troops in the Department of Kansas were held in inactivity until Generals Hunter and Lane should settle the question, which was in command. The President was desirous of obliging General Lane, then a Senator from Kansas, by giving him a command, but the brigadier-general's command given him was not definitely defined, and it finally turned out that he did not accept the commission.

In his forward movement and in his pursuit of Price, General Curtis repeatedly endeavored to ascertain, but without success, whether the troops from Kansas were marching south and were within co-operating distance on his right. He was much embarrassed in not hearing from them, for General Halleck in his despatches had stated that they should be near at hand. The want of a definite plan of operations or of a proper spirit of co-operation on the part of the department commander, prevented the Federal troops in Kansas, from joining with their comrades under General Curtis in overthrowing the combined Confederate forces under Generals Van Dorn, Price, and McCulloch at Pea Ridge. After remaining at Pea Ridge and vicinity until the 5th of April, General Curtis moved eastward with his army along the Southern line of Missouri to meet the threatened raid of General Van Dorn, which had for its object the destruction of the Federal supply depots at Springfield and Rolla.

This movement of the Federal forces from Pea Ridge to the eastward, and the inactivity of the Federal forces at Fort Scott, left all Southwest Missouri and the Indian Territory, exposed to the lawless operations of all the guerilla bands and independent commands that did not go with Price in his march east to Tennessee. Neosho in Newton County, Missouri, was the central point of this unoccupied section. Detachments of Federal mounted troops from Springfield and Fort Scott were sent out now and then to punish the marauding bands of guerillas who were constantly murdering Union citizens and robbing them of their property, even to the extent of taking children's clothing. The notorious Fisher gang, Yancy Richardson and Doctor Lewis Wills, were among those most conspicuous in keeping up the state of anarchy that existed around Neosho after the Southern army was driven from the Southwest. Many a Union man in that vicinity was torn from the arms of his wife and children in the silent hours of night and taken to some lonely spot in the woods and there shot down, and his lifeless corpse left to be devoured by hogs and birds of prey. When the Federal cavalry marched into that region to afford protection to the law-abiding citizens, the authors and instigators of the bloody acts referred to, fled to the hills and thickly timbered bottoms and concealed themselves until the Federal troops left.

The moment General Curtis' army moved away from Pea Ridge, Colonels Coffey, Stand Watie, and other rebel officers of independent commands, returned to Northwestern Arkansas and the northern part of the Indian Territory with their men, and on several occasions came in contact with the Federal cavalry scouting in Southwest Missouri. Major J. M. Hubbard, commanding First Battalion First Missouri Cavalry, stationed at Cassville, hearing of the presence of Coffey and Stand Watie in the vicinity of Elk Mills and Cowskin Prairie, took one hundred and forty-six men of his battalion, and one howitzer, and started in search of them. When he arrived at Elk Mills he found that the rebel leaders had heard of his advance and nearness, and broke up their camp at Cowskin Prairie, one mile south of the mills, and disappeared among the thickly wooded hills and bluffs along the Cowskin River. Having taken several prisoners in the neighborhood, and finding no organized force of the enemy, Major Hubbard started back to Cassville, *via* Neosho, reaching the latter place on the evening of the 25th of April. His detachment was observed from a distance by some of Stand Watie's men, and the number of men in it very nearly ascertained.

Knowing very nearly the number of men in the Federal detachment, and believing that the commanding officer of it had become alarmed and decided to retreat in the direction of Neosho, Stand Watie collected some three hundred Indians and white men and pursued it to that place, and attacked it the next morning just at daylight. During the night he ascertained the position of the Federal camp, and dismounting his men about two miles from town, advanced on foot, surprised and killed the Federal picket, and, on arriving within two hundred yards of the rear of the Federal camp, delivered a volley into it. In a moment Major Hubbard had his men under arms. He ordered Lieutenant Amos S. Burrows to take parts of two companies and charge the Indians, which he did, putting them to flight with the assistance of a few rounds from the howitzer. Major Hubbard's men fired so rapidly with their Colt's revolving rifles that the rebel Indians and white troops could not be made to face the Federal line after the first volley. Colonels Stand Watie and Coffey kept their men in the woods near Neosho until three o'clock in the afternoon, and then fell back to Cowskin Prairie.

Major Hubbard reported that he took sixty-two prisoners and captured seventy horses and a large quantity of arms, and sustained a loss of three men killed and two wounded. He estimated the Confederate loss at thirty killed and wounded. The Indians showed no disposition to fight in line face to face with their opponents, and a shot or shell thrown at them sent them flying into the thick woods. They showed their fighting qualities to best advantage when they could shelter themselves behind trees and logs, and when they could get their foe on the retreat, or felt certain of having superior numbers to him.

Another important skirmish took place at Neosho on the morning of May 31, 1862, between two hundred and twenty-five Union militia under Colonel John M. Richardson, Fourteenth Missouri State Militia Cavalry, and five hundred Confederate white and Indian troops under Colonels J. T. Coffey, Stand Watie, and Livingston. On the morning of the 28th of May, Colonel Richardson, with two hundred and twenty-five men of his own regiment, consisting of parts of six companies and one company of the Tenth Illinois Cavalry, uuder Captain Wilson, left Mount Vernon for Neosho, and marched that day to Sarcoxie, eighteen miles west, and then went into camp for the night. The next morning the march was resumed, and the command arrived at Neosho, twenty-five miles southwest, before sundown, and went into camp on the McGinnis place, on the northwest side of town and about three hundred yards west of Hickory Creek. The camp was pitched on open ground, slightly undulating. On the south a growth of young oak woods came down within a hundred yards or so of camp. The command had four baggage wagons and ten tents. Picket guards were promptly put out half a mile from camp on all the roads leading into town, to guard against a surprise. A good many Union refugees came along with the troops, hoping to be reinstated in their homes. Colonel Richardson and several of his officers went up town that evening to ascertain if possible if any Southern troops were in that section. They were unable to obtain any information of the presence of any organized force nearer than Cowskin Prairie, about twenty-five miles southwest of Neosho. That night and the next day passed without alarm, and no danger from an attack was apprehended.

Captain Wilson, Tenth Illinois Cavalry, returned to Springfield with his company. That evening, however, after dark, there was a rumor in camp that the woods south of the old Academy on the hill overlooking the town and

Hickory Creek valley to the north, were full of men and horses. Colonel Richardson called a council of his captains to consider the question of putting his command in a defensive position and to investigate the facts connected with the rumor. Scouts were sent out to ascertain if there was any truth in the rumor, but after some investigation, returned and reported that they could find no signs of an enemy at or near the point where the men and horses were alleged to have been seen. The camp guards were doubled, the pickets were kept out as usual, and the night of the 30th also passed without alarm.

Colonels Stand Watie and Coffey had been encamped at Elk Mills, fifteen miles southwest of Neosho, for several days before Colonel Richardson's arrival at the latter place. On the 29th Colonel Stand Watie sent Captain Livingston with twenty-four mounted men to scout in the vicinity of Granby and Neosho. At noon that day Captain Livingston's detachment met and fired upon Colonel Richardson's advance guard near Granby and then fell back through Neosho towards Elk Mills, and sent forward a courier to report the Federal advance. On the morning of the 30th two hundred men of Stand Watie's Cherokee Indians, and about three hundred white men under Colonel Coffey, advanced in the direction of Neosho to ascertain the strength and movements of the Federal command that had come into that section. This force met Captain Livingston, who reported that the Federal cavalry, supposed to be four hundred strong, were in Neosho.

The Confederate force moved forward again, but when they arrived within a mile southwest of town on the Buffalo road, it was getting dark. The command halted and after a short consultation between the principal officers it was decided that it was too late to make an attack on the Federal camp that night. Guards were thrown out and the men quietly bivouacked in the woods near the road that night. Some of the men lived in and near Neosho, and knew every path leading into town. Several of those best acquainted with the approaches to town were detailed or volunteered to ascertain the exact location of the Federal camp, and to obtain any other information that would tend to enable the Confederates to surprise the Federal detachment. Directly west of town, but touching the town limits, there was a high and precipitous bluff out of which flowed the Big Spring off to the northeast. Along the ridge, back of this bluff, extending perhaps half a mile south and west, there was a heavy growth of young timber and some underbrush. This timber and woods extended north and south from where the Confederate force bivouacked down to within about one hundred yards of the Federal camp, and there was no road through it. In most places, however, it was open enough to ride through it on horseback with little inconvenience.

In the plan of the attack it was decided that two hundred of Coffey's white men and two hundred of Stand Watie's Cherokees should dismount as infantry and march down through the woods described, closely followed by the balance of Coffey's force, mounted, and open fire upon the Federal camp. As they took the precaution to march to the attack through the woods, they got in sight of the Federal camp before they were discovered by Colonel Richardson's pickets or camp guards. The attack was made about eight o'clock in the morning.

Colonel Richardson had taken the precaution, on the strength of the reported nearness of the enemy, to have his men keep their horses saddled and in readiness for an emergency. In a moment after the alarm was given of the approach of the enemy, Colonel Richardson commenced to form his companies in line. Lieutenant Peter Wilson formed his company on the left in advance of the camp, and Lieutenant Amos Norton formed on the Federal right. The companies of Captains S. H. Julian, Mastin Breedin, and William W. Hargrove were formed in the centre near the camp. As the Confederates advanced they fired much at random. When they came within range, Lieutenants Wilson's and Norton's companies each fired three volleys into their line, and checked their advance for a moment. At this instant, just as Colonel Richardson was turning to give orders for his troops to take a position which he had selected for the action, he was shot in the right arm, and his horse also being shot fell on his left leg, the fall at the same time dislocating the shoulder and spraining his wrist. In this condition he was unable to rise for a few moments. In the meantime the refugees fled without awaiting the result of the action. Observing their flight, Stand Watie's Indians raised the war-whoop, and the whole Confederate force moved forward, firing rapidly as they advanced. Colonel Coffey also extended his line, which threatened to flank the Federal position. Seeing the fall of their commander, and supposing that he was killed, observing the flight of the refugees and the threatened flank movement of the enemy, Colonel Richardson's line gave way and retreated from the ground in the utmost confusion. After he became disabled, there was no field-officer present to take command and rally the men, and no provision had been made for the ranking captain to assume the function of commanding officer. As most of the Confederate force was dismounted, that part of it which was mounted pursued the retreating Federal detachment only a short distance northeast of town.

Colonel Richardson lost all his wagons and teams and camp equipage, and reported a loss of eight men wounded and two missing. Stand Watie reported a loss of only one man killed. The Federal detachment continued the retreat to Mount Vernon. Colonel Richardson managed to save himself by taking to the woods afoot. He did not get back to his command for several days after this action. He made his way to the residence of a Mr. Greer, a Union man, who lived on Diamond Grove Prairie, about ten miles north of Neosho, and who kept him concealed in his house until he was able to travel and return to Springfield. Though the Confederates were much elated by their successful movement, they hastily gathered up the property they captured and retreated in the direction of Cowskin Prairie.

CHAPTER XXI.

ENGAGEMENTS AT SEARS' FARM AND BIG CREEK BLUFFS. SKIRMISH ON CLEAR CREEK.

OF the numerous skirmishes and engagements between the Federal forces and Confederate guerillas along the border, the engagement of a detachment of Missouri and Iowa cavalry, under Major James O. Gower, with Quantrill's band at Sears' farm and at Big Creek Bluffs, three miles northwest of Pleasant Hill in Cass County, on the morning of July 11th, was perhaps the fiercest. On the 8th of July, Major Gower commanding a battalion of the First Iowa Cavalry and two companies of Missouri Enrolled Militia stationed at Clinton in Henry County, received information through several Union citizens that Quantrill had brought his band from Jackson County, and was encamped on Sugar Creek in Bogard Township in the western part of Henry County, some fifteen miles northwest of Clinton. Lieutenants R. M. Reynolds and John A. Bishop were at once sent out with a detail of ninety men from the several companies of the First Iowa Cavalry stationed at Clinton, to the neighborhood where the guerillas were reported to be encamped, with orders to attack them, if not thought too strong.

Lieutenant Reynolds left Clinton at eleven o'clock at night and discovered Quantrill's camp the next morning shortly after sunrise. It was his intention to strike the guerilla camp at daybreak, but the troops did not make quite the time it was calculated they would. Although Lieutenant Reynolds knew that the enemy were aroused and prepared for him, he determined to make the attack, and at once formed his men and led them in a gallant charge against the guerillas. But finding their position very strong, and the ground unfavorable, he was obliged to retire with three men wounded, one mortally. On his return to Clinton, Major Gower dispatched couriers to the commanding officers at Butler, Harrisonville, and Warrensburg, for detachments from the commands at those places to meet him the next morning at Lotspeich's farm, one mile west of the place where Lieutenant Reynolds had had the skirmish on the 9th.

Early on the morning of the 10th, Major Gower took seventy-five men and four officers and marched to the place designated, and was joined there by Captain W. H. Ankeny with sixty-five men of the First Iowa Cavalry from Butler, Captain W. A. Martin with sixty-five men of the Seventh Missouri Cavalry from Harrisonville, and by Captain Miles Kehoe with sixty-one men of the First Missouri Cavalry from Warrensburg. Soon after the arrival of the detachments at the place appointed for their meeting, it was ascertained that Quantrill with his force, estimated at two hundred and fifty men, had left their camp on Sugar Creek the evening before. The several detachments immediately moved off in different directions to strike the trail of the guerillas. About two o'clock in the afternoon Captain Kehoe found their trail and at once sent word to Major Gower. The trail at first led in a northeasterly direction to the east of Rose Hill, thence up Big Creek bottom in a northwesterly direction. On striking the trail, Major Gower pushed on and overtook Captain Kehoe that evening just before dark, about four miles northwest of Kingsville. The Federal detachments now went into camp for the night, with the understanding that the pursuit of the guerillas would be resumed the next morning at daybreak.

Promptly at the time agreed upon Captain Kehoe and his men were in their saddles, notice of which was sent to Major Gower, whose command had not yet been aroused. Captains J. N. Coates and William Weaver of the Sixtieth Regiment Enrolled Missouri Militia were guides for the command and, of course, marched in the advance with Captain Kehoe. On resuming the march Captain Kehoe soon came to a farm-house where the guerillas had fed their horses the evening before. It was ascertained here that Quantrill was keeping along Big Creek timber, leaving Pleasant Hill to the east. Captain Kehoe marched along leisurely upon his trail until about nine o'clock, when he came upon two of his pickets near the timber on Big Creek near Mr. Sears' farm, about one half-mile from the guerillas' camp at Mr. Sears' house near the edge of the timber. Captain Kehoe's advance fired upon the pickets and then pursued them swiftly to their camp, his command charging through their camp, firing upon the enemy with revolvers.

Having travelled through the woods the night before, the guerillas had got their equipments wet from the heavy dew, and had that morning spread their blankets out on the fence along the road to dry. When, therefore, Captain Kehoe's command came charging down upon them, they quickly sought shelter behind their blankets on the fence, and in the house and barn, and fired upon the advancing Federal soldiers at short range and with terrible effect. In this charge Captain Kehoe had three or four men killed, and several wounded. The two guides, Captains Coates and Weaver, barely escaped falling into the hands of the enemy. In the excitement Captain Weaver's horse threw him, and he saved himself by getting behind a tree and remaining there until the fight was over at that point. The side of the tree between him and the enemy, and next to the enemy, to the height of a man's head, was scarred and thickly stuck with bullets from their guns. Captain Coates' horse became unmanageable, and ran away with him in the midst of the fight, and in the effort to turn it he dropped his navy revolver.

The fight lasted some twenty minutes, when the guerillas retreated to the woods and a ravine on Big Creek. Captain Kehoe's command was too badly crippled and too few in numbers to pursue them into the woods, and withdrew to a log-house in the prairie about one half-mile west of the scene of the conflict, and remained there until Major Gower's command came in sight, which was perhaps in less than half an hour. Captain Kehoe had sent a messenger back to him, stating that he had engaged the enemy, and requested him to push forward as rapidly as possible.

After coming up to where the fight had commenced at Sears' farm, Major Gower, with his own command and sixty-five men under Captain Martin, of the Seventh Missouri Cavalry, moved cautiously to the timber in the direction the guerillas had retreated, and soon found them strongly posted in the cliffs and ravines near Big Creek, about one half-mile from Mr. Sears' house. In the meantime Captain Kehoe had deployed a part of his command as skirmishers, thus holding the guerillas until Major Gower could arrive with the main command. The Federal troops all up, the attack upon the guerillas was vigorously renewed, and for nearly half an hour every tree and bush or object that could conceal a man appeared to send forth flashes of fire and volumes of smoke. Part of the Federal soldiers were dismounted in this attack, and fought from sheltered positions as much as possible. The guerillas were finally driven from their position, and retired northward, keeping the timber of Big Creek. In this last conflict Quantrill was wounded in the leg, but escaped, being borne off by his comrades. He was being pushed very closely, but managed to draw the attention of the Federal troops to a particular point while he and the main body of his men were escaping in another direction. The Federal troops pursued the guerillas only a short distance from the bluff and ravines from which they were routed, being unable to advance much farther on account of the thick foliage of the tangled woods through which the enemy retired.

The several Federal detachments engaged in the fight gathered up their killed and wounded and took them to Pleasant Hill that evening, where the dead were buried with military honors. After this the detachments marched to their respective stations.

In the Iowa cavalry Major Gower reported a loss of three killed and ten wounded. In Captain Kehoe's detachment there were six killed and nine wounded, Lieutenant William White being among the wounded. Captain Martin, of the Missouri cavalry, also had one man killed. The loss on the side of the guerillas was reported at eighteen men killed. The hardest fighting fell to the Missouri troops, as they were in advance and brought on the engagement. Captain Martin, Seventh Missouri Cavalry, with his sixty-five men charged the guerillas seven times during the fight, and drove them twice from a strong position which they were tenaciously holding between the banks of Big Creek. In one of the charges he had a hand-to-hand conflict with them. Captain Kehoe had two horses shot, and was himself wounded in the shoulder. He thought that if Major Gower with his Iowa cavalry had kept up and been on hand at the first engagement, the entire force of guerillas could have been captured or destroyed. Some thirty horses, most of the equipments, guns, coats, Quantrill's spy-glass, and the company roll of the guerillas fell into the hands of the Federal troops.

During the summer frequent demands were made upon the commanding officers of Federal troops stationed in the towns in Western Missouri for detachments of cavalry to operate against guerillas. On the 2d of August Colonel Fitz Henry Warren, First Iowa Cavalry, commanding the Federal forces stationed at Butler, Bates County, received information that some two hundred guerillas were in the neighborhood of Gordon's farm, on Clear Creek, in the western part of St. Clair County. He at once directed Captains Herman H. Heath and J. W. Caldwell, First Iowa Cavalry, to take one hundred and thirty-five men of their companies and proceed to the locality where the guerillas were reported to be encamped, and attack them. In marching to the locality Captain Heath kept a lookout for the enemy. But the guerillas, discovering the approach of the Federal cavalry some distance off, took position in a thick woods with heavy foliage within rifle range of a point which they knew that the Federal force would pass.

When Captain Heath came within range, the guerillas opened fire upon him, and the whole front of the brush blazed with the flash of small-arms. Not a man of the enemy was visible on account of the heavy foliage of the thick brush in which they were concealed. This sudden and terrific fire threw Captain Heath's detachment into a little disorder, but they soon rallied and opened a vigorous fire upon the guerillas, whose position was now disclosed. Captain Caldwell, with sixty men dismounted, took position behind a rail fence, and fought them for some time, and held his ground with commendable firmness until he heard firing in his rear. Thinking that his horses were in danger of capture, he fell back to secure them. This done, he returned to renew the attack, but found that the enemy had left, taking with them their dead and wounded. Immediately after their first attack, in which Captain Heath was wounded, a courier was sent back to Butler for reinforcements. Colonel Warren hastened to the relief of Captains Heath and Caldwell with every available man, but on reaching them, and after a short pursuit of the enemy, barren of good results, he returned to camp. The Federal loss in the skirmish was four killed and nine wounded. Colonel Warren estimated the loss of the guerillas at eleven killed and as many wounded, the latter being carried off in their retreat from the place.

CHAPTER XXII.

THE INDIAN EXPEDITION.

DURING the fall of 1861 Fort Scott had become the most important point south of Leavenworth and Kansas City for organizing and equipping troops and of operating from as a base. Its position being thus recognized, General David Hunter, the commanding general of the department in the winter of 1861–2, and in the early spring of 1862, ordered the following regiments there with the view of marching south as soon as spring opened.

Colonel Doubleday's Second Ohio Cavalry, Colonel Barstow's Third Wisconsin Cavalry, Colonel Powell Clayton's Fifth Kansas Cavalry, Colonel Judson's Sixth Kansas Cavalry, Colonel Salomon's Ninth Wisconsin Infantry, Colonel Bryant's Twelfth Wisconsin Infantry, Colonel Chapman's Thirteenth Wisconsin Infantry, Colonel Weer's Tenth Kansas Infantry, Captain Rabb's Second Indiana Battery, and Captain Allen's First Kansas Battery.

Colonel Deitzler, of the First Kansas Infantry, who had recovered from his wound received at the battle of Wilson Creek, was placed in temporary command of the troops thus rendezvousing at Fort Scott and vicinity. It was at first the intention that this force should cooperate with General Curtis, who started out from Rolla with his army about the 1st of February, in active operations against the armies of Price and McCulloch in Southwest Missouri. General Curtis had driven Price's army from Springfield to Fayetteville, Arkansas, without bringing on a general engagement, so that when the order came for the troops at Fort Scott to move south and join him, the battle of Pea Ridge had been fought and won by the Federal army. After the rebel armies at Pea Ridge had been defeated and dispersed, some of the troops at Fort Scott were ordered to other points, and Colonel Deitzler was relieved and sent to West Tennessee.

Colonel Jennison's Seventh Kansas Cavalry, that had been operating along the border counties of Missouri and Kansas, between Fort Scott and Kansas City, during the winter of 1861–2, were also sent to West Tennessee. Colonel Clayton's Fifth Kansas Cavalry, after encamping near Morris' Mill on Dry Wood, twelve miles southeast of Fort Scott, some two weeks, marched to Carthage, thence to Springfield through Southern Missouri and Northern Arkansas, to Helena on the Mississippi River.

Early in April Colonel Doubleday, commanding the Second Ohio Cavalry, marched into Southwest Missouri, where he was kept for a month or so actively employed in scouting and skirmishing with bushwhackers and recruiting detachments of rebels. In June he established a camp at Baxter Springs on the west side of Spring River, sixty miles south of Fort Scott, on the military road to Fort Gibson, and on what was known as the Government strip.

Colonel Judson's Sixth Kansas Cavalry, which had recently been reorganized, operated a few weeks in Jasper, Barton, and Vernon counties, Missouri, and then moved along up the State line in the direction of Kansas City, encamping a day or two at each of the places, Barnesville, Mine Creek, Trading Post, West Point, and Little Santa Fé. The headquarters of the regiment, however, were at Paola, Kansas, from April to June, during which period the different companies received their arms and cavalry equipments. Several of the companies were furnished with Austrian carbines, a weapon soon found to be utterly worthless. They were calibre 70, and the soldiers declared that when loaded and slung with the muzzles pointing downward the balls fell out of their own weight. But the companies soon exchanged this worthless arm for Sharp's carbines, which were then perhaps the best cavalry arm in the service. In the frequent contests with Quantrill's bushwhackers, the commanding officer of the regiment felt that his men should be furnished with the best cavalry arm in use. On the 10th of June the companies of the regiment that had been operating in Missouri from Paola, struck tents and started on the march for Baxter Springs, but went into camp for a week at Cato, fourteen miles south of Fort Scott, to await the arrival of a supply train from Fort Leavenworth. The march was resumed again to Baxter Springs.

At Baxter Springs nearly all the troops that were to make up the contemplated expedition into the Indian country had already arrived. On the 23d of June there were at that place ready to move south the Second Ohio Cavalry, the Sixth Kansas Cavalry, the Ninth and Twelfth Regiments Wisconsin Infantry, the Tenth Kansas Infantry, Rabb's Second Indiana Battery, the First Kansas Battery, and a large number of refugee Indians that were partly organized into companies. The Third Wisconsin Cavalry and the Ninth Kansas Cavalry were left at Fort Scott and at points along the State line, to guard the post of Fort Scott and to furnish escorts to supply trains.

Colonel James G. Blunt, late of the Third Kansas Infantry, had been recently promoted to Brigadier-General and assigned to the command of the troops in Southern Kansas and the Indian Territory, but Colonel William Weer, of the Tenth Kansas Infantry, was in command of the troops in the field at Baxter Springs.

On the 25th of June the whole command moved south on the military road to the south side of the Neosho River, a distance of about fourteen miles. Here a large number of other Indian refugees, men, women, and children, from the Cherokee, Creek, Seminole, and Osage tribes, most of whom had been along the southern line of Kansas for some time, met the troops of the expedition. In the summer and fall of 1861 the Confederate authorities sent agents among these tribes or nations to secure their allegiance to the Confederacy. A good many leading men of the tribes promised their allegiance to the Confederacy, and two mounted regiments of troops were raised for the Confederate service, but perhaps a majority of the people could not be induced to sever their relations with the United States Government without coercion. The Creeks in particular, under the leadership of their old chief, Hopoeithleyohola, firmly refused to treat with the Confederate agents. As a consequence their territory was invaded by Confederate white and Indian troops, and several battles fought, in one of which the old chief held his own by setting the prairie on fire between his forces and the enemy. He was finally obliged, however, to retreat, in mid-winter, in the direction of Kansas, for the Confederate forces were soon reinforced. In his retreat he took with him nearly all the men, women, and children of his tribe, together with such ponies and cattle as could be gathered up. His people suffered great hardships on their retreat to Kansas and after they got there, before the Government could adequately provide for them. And now when they heard that there was a prospect of returning to their homes, from which they had been exiled by the calamities of war and devotion to principle, the able-bodied men were anxious to volunteer their services to the Federal Government.

The First and Second Indian Regiments were at once raised, and Robert W. Furnas, of Kansas, was commissioned as Colonel of the First Regiment, and John Ritchie, Colonel of the Second Regiment. A short time after this the Third Indian Regiment was recruited and organized by Colonel William A. Phillips, an active and energetic officer. This regiment was all Cherokees, and the Second Indian Regiment was composed of companies from several tribes, but perhaps most of the companies were Cherokees. Shortly after these regiments were organized the men were furnished clothing by the Government the same as other soldiers. It was quite amusing to the white soldiers to see the Indians dressed in the Federal uniform and equipped for the service. Every thing seemed out of just proportion. Nearly every warrior got a suit that, to critical tastes, lacked a good deal in fitting him. It was in a marked degree either too large or too small. In some cases the sleeves of a coat or jacket were too short, coming down about two thirds the distance from the elbows to the wrists. In other cases the sleeves were too long, coming down over the hands.

At the time these Indian troops were organized the Government was furnishing its soldiers a high-crowned stiff wool hat for the service. When, therefore, fully equipped as a warrior, one might have seen an Indian soldier dressed as described, wearing a high-crowned stiff wool hat, with long black hair falling over his shoulders, and riding an Indian pony so small that his feet appeared to almost touch the ground, with a long squirrel rifle thrown across the pommel of his saddle. When starting out on the march every morning any one with this command might have seen this warrior in full war-paint, and he might have also heard the war-whoop commence at the head of the column and run back to the rear, and recommence at the head of the column several times and run back to the rear.

After encamping at Hudson's crossing of the Neosho River on the military road part of two days, to await the arrival of supply trains from Fort Scott, the troops of the Indian expedition resumed the march south down the west side of Grand River some twenty miles to Carey's Ferry, and then crossed over to the east side, and marched southeast to Round Grove on Cowskin Prairie some three miles from the ford. Colonel Weer had received information through his scouts that a considerable body of rebel Indian and white troops, under General Rains and Colonels Stand Watie and Coffey, were in the vicinity of Cowskin Prairie, and he determined, if he could find them, to give them battle if they would stand. But he was disappointed, for the enemy, from the reports they had received of the strength of the Federal command, had not confidence in their ability to meet it, and broke camp and moved south in several detachments. Colonel Weer soon ascertained that Stand Watie was encamped with his command at his mills on Spavinaw Creek, some twenty-five miles south, and that Colonel Clarkson, who had recently been assigned to the command of the northern part of the Indian Territory, was encamped at Locust Grove, near Grand Saline, on the east side of Grand River, fifteen to twenty miles farther south, with a regiment of Missourians and a large amount of powder and ammunition. To strike these commands, Colonel Weer saw that no time should be lost, and that it might be necessary to make one or two night marches. That his movements might be as free as possible from any embarrassment, he sent all his baggage and supply trains, part of his artillery, the Second Ohio Cavalry, and the Ninth and Twelfth Regiments Wisconsin Infantry, from Round Grove to the west side of Grand River, with instructions to march down on the west side of that river on the military road to Cabin Creek. At that point, that part of the command was to await further orders.

Colonel Weer took with him the available men of the Sixth Kansas Cavalry, under the command of Lieutenant-

Colonel Jewell, a detachment of the Ninth Kansas Cavalry, under Major Bancroft, a detachment of the Tenth Kansas Infantry, under Captain Quigg, in wagons, and a detachment of the First Indian Regiment, and a section of Captain Allen's First Kansas Battery, and marched down on the east side of Grand River, with the view, if possible, of striking and demoralizing Stand Watie's command, and of surprising Colonel Clarkson at Locust Grove. He had information that Stand Watie's and other Confederate troops operating in the Cherokee nation were to join Clarkson at once, or were to be concentrated at some point in the nation for the purpose of checking the Federal advance.

Having decided to strike Stand Watie first, Colonel Jewell, of the Sixth Kansas Cavalry, was sent east of Colonel Weer's column in the direction of Maysville, and in the afternoon of the first day's march he came upon the fresh trail of the enemy. He was informed by an Indian family that Stand Watie had passed, marching south, only an hour or so before, with three or four hundred mounted men. This news caused a ripple of excitement, and Colonel Jewell's cavalry at once struck up a fast trot in the pursuit, and after about two hours came in sight of Stand Watie, where he had stopped at an Indian house for supper. He had heard that the Federal column was moving south, and had taken the precaution to leave a guard in the road, who warned him of the nearness of the Federal advance in time to enable him to mount his horse and gallop off in sight of his pursuers. He soon overtook his command, but the Federal cavalry were right at his heels, the foremost troopers firing at him every time they came in sight of him and his attendants, killing one of his men. He made no effort to form his men in line, but every man seemed bent on saving himself. The chase was exciting for several miles, when darkness came on and then the enemy commenced to break up into small detachments and take to the hills and obscure paths and byroads. As the enemy had been forced from the main road leading to Locust Grove, and as the pursuit could not be kept up farther to advantage, Colonel Jewell halted a short time to allow his command to close up, which had not been practicable in the exciting chase of the last few miles. When his command had all closed up, a short consultation was held with his principal officers, and the march resumed for the purpose of joining Colonel Weer in the neighborhood of Grand Saline by daylight next morning. It was thought that Stand Watie's command was too badly demoralized to rally and reach Clarkson in time to do him any good, or to even warn him of the nearness of the Federal troops. An estimate of the time it would take to reach the enemy's camp was made, and the command at once put in motion.

Colonel Weer, who had taken a road west of Colonel Jewell's column, had guides along who knew the exact location of the enemy. On nearing the neighborhood of the Confederate forces, he ordered his troops to march in as close order as practicable, so that when the time came their movements could be directed as the situation required. Just before daylight the head of his column reached Locust Grove without opposition, and in a few moments he had ordered his troops into positions that surrounded Colonel Clarkson's camp, and at once opened fire upon it. The Confederates were completely surprised. They had not heard that there were any Federal troops in the Indian Territory nearer than Neosho River or Round Grove. When they were aroused by the Federal firing, so much confusion ensued that no regular line of battle could be formed. Some of the men, in a half-dressed condition, endeavored to shelter themselves behind the wagons of their train. Others endeavored to break through the Federal lines, and were shot down or captured. A few, on the first alarm, made their escape before the Federal line had closed around the camp.

Seeing that such resistance as he could make would entail a useless loss of life, Colonel Clarkson surrendered to Colonel Weer one hundred and ten men, all that had not escaped and that had not been killed or wounded, together with all his trains. Colonel Jewell's column came up in time to engage in the pursuit of the fleeing rebels. There were sixty-four mule teams in the baggage and supply trains thus captured, and the Confederate commissary had on hand a good supply of salt, flour, and other provisions. The Confederates had been working the salt-works at Grand Saline up to their full capacity in making salt for the use of the Confederate troops operating in Western Arkansas and in the Indian Territory. As salt was as plentiful as any other commodity all over the North, and as the Federal troops were abundantly supplied with it by the Government as a part of their rations, the salt-works at Grand Saline were destroyed to prevent their further use by the Confederates.

On the 4th of July, the day after the capture of Colonel Clarkson's camp, all the prisoners and public property captured were taken to Cabin Creek, on the west side of Grand River, some three miles west of Locust Grove, where Colonel Weer's supply and baggage trains and that part of his command that had marched down on the west side of Grand River had gone into camp. At this place the Fourth of July, Independence Day, was appropriately celebrated by the booming of cannon and a grand review of the troops in the beautiful prairie valley in which the Federal camp was pitched. The day was bright and clear, and the troops, with their new uniforms and beautiful flags and guidons yet little stained by service, made a fine appearance. The Indians present had never before seen such a display of the military power of the Government. The prisoners captured at Locust Grove were sent under guard to Fort Scott and thence to Leavenworth, and the public property captured, such as wagons and teams, was mostly disposed of amongst the Indian troops that were being organized, and who were without means of transportation.

The troops of the expedition encamped at Cabin Creek nearly two weeks, except that most of the cavalry were kept busily employed in scouting the country east of Grand River to the Arkansas line, extending south almost to the Arkansas River. While encamped at this place, hundreds of Cherokees who had endeavored to remain neutral, but who were in reality attached to the Union during the Confederate occupation of the nation, came in and enlisted into the Third Indian Regiment, which was being recruited and organized by Colonel W. A. Phillips, of Kansas. The Indians of the Cherokee nation, like the people of the States, were divided into two political parties or factions. The followers of Colonels Stand Watie and Boudinot were all secessionists and active supporters of the Confederacy, while the followers of the chief, John Ross, were generally opposed to taking any part in the war, endeavored to be neutral, and were mostly attached to the Union.

At the end of about two weeks, and after the arrival of the supply train from Fort Scott, the troops of the expedition again turned their faces to the south and marched down the west side of Grand River about forty miles to Flat Rock, where they went into camp again for nearly two weeks. From this point the cavalry were again sent out to the east and southeast, to ascertain if any of Colonel Cooper's force from Texas had crossed to the north side of the Arkansas River. The Federal cavalry, under Colonel Jewell, Sixth Kansas Cavalry, thus sent out, made a dash on Fort Gibson, the objective point of the expedition, and drove out a detachment of rebel cavalry and captured a few men.

On the 14th of July Captain H. S. Greeno, of the Sixth Kansas Cavalry, was sent out in the direction of Tahlequah with one hundred and fifty white cavalry and Indians, and reached that place on the 16th, and the next morning marched to Park Hill, about six miles south, where the chief, John Ross, was residing, and where there were two hundred Cherokees, who had lately belonged to Colonel Drew's regiment in the Confederate service, but who were waiting for an opportunity to join the Federal expedition. At this place Captain Greeno captured Lieutenant-Colonel W. P. Ross, Major Thomas Pegg, Lieutenants Anderson Benge, Joseph Chover, L. Hawkins, Archibald Scraper, Joseph Cornsilk, and John Shell, all of Colonel Drew's regiment, and brought them in as prisoners of war. These officers had only a few hours before their capture received orders from Colonel Douglas H. Cooper, commanding the Confederate forces in the Indian Territory, to report at once for duty at Fort Davis, near Fort Gibson. The chief, John Ross, had also just received a despatch from Colonel Cooper, calling upon him, in the name of the President of the Southern Confederacy, to issue a proclamation calling upon the Cherokee Indians for every man over eighteen and under forty-five years of age to take up arms to repel the invasion of the Federal army, according to treaty stipulations.

Chief Ross was now between two fires. In the treaty with the Confederate authorities he was bound to furnish his quota of troops for the Confederate service when called upon by the President of the Confederacy. It was true that the treaty had been made under pressure, in fact extorted, under circumstances that precluded the free expression of the people of the nation. In the absence of definite instructions, Captain Greeno concluded to make the chief, John Ross, a prisoner of war, and then left him at home on his parole until the matter could be brought to the attention of the commanding general. As a prisoner of war on parole, it was understood that he would not issue the proclamation demanded by Colonel Cooper. On Captain Greeno's return to the command, the two hundred friendly Indians at Park Hill came in with him, and in a few days most of them joined Colonel Phillips' Third Indian Regiment. Chief Ross had long been suspected by the secessionists of leaning toward the Union cause, and he was apprehensive of his personal safety, unless the Federal troops occupied the country east of Grand River, as well as that west of it. It was ascertained that Stand Watie and his followers had fled to the south side of the Arkansas River, and that the Indian Territory north of that river was now clear of any organized force of the enemy.

The expedition had now accomplished all that it was intended that it should accomplish. Some of the cavalry that had been scouting as far east as the Arkansas line obtained information, through Union refugees, that detachments of the enemy, of a hundred or so men together, had been passing through Cane Hill, Arkansas, for several days, on their way north to Missouri. As there was now practically nothing further for the troops of the expedition to do in the Indian Territory north of the Arkansas River, and as the army had been put on one half rations, toward the latter part of July the brigade and regimental commanders received orders to strike tents, and at once commenced a retrograde movement north, on the Fort Scott and Fort Gibson military road. While the main body of the troops and all the trains moved north, up the west side of Grand River, Colonel Cloud's Second Kansas Cavalry, that had joined the expedition after it left Neosho River, and Colonel Jewell, with part of the Sixth Kansas Cavalry, were sent to Tahlequah to bring out the chief, John Ross, and his family, and the archives and treasury of the nation.

When the old chief found that the Federal army was going to be withdrawn from the nation, and that he could no longer look to the protecting ægis of the United States for protection, he expressed a willingness to go north with his family. He felt certain that the Confederate forces would shortly follow the retreating footsteps of the Federal soldiers. After he joined the main command on the march with his train of carriages and attendants, a good many of the white soldiers were a little disappointed in not seeing an old Indian chief with squaws and papooses, but, instead, an intelligent-looking old gentleman, with only a slight trace of Indian blood, and with a white wife and daughters who appeared to have had many of the advantages of education and refinement.

On the return march the troops went into camp for a few days about six miles below Baxter Springs on the west side of Spring River, for the purpose of giving the soldiers and stock a little needed rest. The month of July had been very warm and dry; there had been scarcely any cloudy weather, and the heat had been oppressive to both troops and stock. The cavalry had been constantly engaged in marching and scouting in Southwest Missouri and the Indian Territory since early in the spring. And as the cavalry horses had performed the hard service required of them with little other food than that obtained by grazing upon the wild prairie grass while picketed out, they had run down very much in strength and flesh. The Second Ohio Cavalry started out from Fort Scott in the spring a finely equipped regiment, and the men were mounted upon fine horses that they had brought from Ohio. When the regiment returned to Hudson's Crossing of the Neosho River and to Baxter Springs with the troops of the Indian expedition the 1st of August, nearly, or perhaps fully, one half of the men were dismounted. Their horses had given out and were abandoned. In a good many instances the horses had, while picketed out on the prairies to graze, eaten each other's manes and tails off, so that there was a marked contrast in the appearance of the troopers when they marched south in the spring, and when they returned in August mounted upon poor, bobtailed, ragged-maned horses.

Three or four thousand horses and transportation animals, it was found, would eat the grass off the area of a large camp quicker than the inexperienced soldier at first thought had any idea of. While the horses of the other cavalry regiments showed that they had been subjected to hard service, it was plainly to be seen that the horses of the Second Ohio Cavalry had not stood the service as well as the native horses of the other regiments, although these native horses had performed fully as much service as the Ohio horses.

The troops of the expedition had been encamped on Spring River only two or three days when the scouts and Unionists from Southwest Missouri came in and reported that large bodies of rebels under Shelby, Coffey, and Jackman had recently passed through Neosho on the march north. Where they were intending to concentrate for an offensive movement could not be definitely ascertained. General James G. Blunt, who had recently arrived at Fort Scott, and who had been informed of these movements of the enemy through the border counties of Missouri, ordered all the white troops of the expedition to march to Fort Scott at once. The three Indian regiments that had been organized during the summer were left at Baxter Springs and vicinity, to cover any movements of the enemy that might be made from the direction of the Indian Territory, and to protect their families and property. Though the expedition had marched up the hill and marched down again, it had done something for the Union. It had been successful in every skirmish, and had driven the enemy from a territory larger than some of the States. It had given the loyal Indians an opportunity to organize for their own defence, and to gather up all their stock that had not been driven off by the rebels before the arrival of the Federal troops in the nation. It had also made it possible for these Indians to defend themselves if the Government could defend them from invasion by white troops.

It will be well now to notice briefly the operations of the Indian troops under Colonels Furnas and Phillips, after the white troops under Colonel Weer were withdrawn from the Indian Territory. When Colonel Salomon arrested Colonel Weer and assumed command of the troops of the Indian expedition, and ordered a retrograde movement of the command from where it was encamped on Grand River, twelve miles above Fort Gibson, he left the commanding officers of the three Indian regiments without definite orders or instructions. It was certainly not good policy to take the Indian soldiers out of their country the moment they were restored to it and organized for efficient service. Should they, too, be withdrawn, no one doubted but that the rebels would quickly return in marauding bands, and murder, rob, and persecute those who had declared for the Union during the temporary occupation of the country by the Federal army. A council of the commanding officers of the three Indian regiments was therefore held at the camp on Grand River, to determine what course should be pursued in the face of the embarrassing situation presented, and, as a solution of it, Colonel R. W. Furnas, the senior officer present, assumed command of them, and called them the Indian Brigade. In the discussion at the council, it was the opinion of the officers present that, by judicious management, the three Indian regiments could hold the country north of the

Arkansas River, which had just been subdued by the troops of the Indian expedition, provided that Colonel Cooper, who was commanding the Confederate troops in the Indian country, with headquarters at Fort Davis, on the south bank of the Arkansas River, opposite the mouth of Grand River, should not be reinforced by white troops.

Having determined to hold the Indian country north of the Arkansas with the Indian soldiers, Colonel Furnas sought Colonel Salomon, while his command was on the march northward, and, after laying the situation before him, got him to leave with the Indian Brigade, one section of Captain Allen's First Kansas Battery. Immediately after the white portion of the troops of the Indian expedition had commenced their march north, Colonel Furnas marched the Indian Brigade, except a detachment of two hundred men at Fort Gibson as an outpost of observation, to the Verdigris River, some twenty miles northwest of the camp at Flat Rock, on Grand River. The first night the command encamped on the Verdigris, one hundred and eighty Osages, who had joined the Second Indian Regiment, and who were unused to military discipline, deserted and went buffalo hunting. In compliance with instructions from Colonel Salomon of July 23d, Colonel Furnas marched his command to Horse Creek, some twenty miles below Hudson's Crossing, on the Neosho River, where the troops of the Indian expedition had gone into camp for some ten days, having met their supply train from Fort Scott.

On the 23d of July Colonel W. A. Phillips took the available men of his regiment from the camp at Wolf Creek and started on an expedition to the east of Grand River, in the neighborhood of Tahlequah and Park Hill, to punish some detachments of Stand Watie's rebel Indians, who had crossed from the south to the north side of the Arkansas River the moment the troops of the Indian expedition were withdrawn, and were committing depredations against those Cherokees who had declared for the Union. The Colonel having heard that a considerable force of the enemy were north of the Arkansas in the neighborhood of Fort Gibson, that place having been abandoned by the Federal detachment of observation, he determined to seek it and attack it. After leaving Park Hill his force was divided into three columns that marched on three roads in the direction of Fort Gibson. The three roads came together about seven miles northeast of that place, near Bayou Bernard. At the junction of the three roads the Confederate force under Lieutenant-Colonel Thomas F. Taylor marching from Fort Gibson, took the Park Hill fork, and soon met Lieutenant Haneway, commanding Colonel Phillips' right wing. The Lieutenant ordered his men to open fire upon the enemy, which they did, and then fell back in the direction of Park Hill, pursued by the rebels, who knew nothing of the near approach of the other two columns of Colonel Phillips. In pushing on after Lieutenant Haneway, Colonel Taylor's force was unexpectedly attacked in the flank by Colonel Phillips' left and centre, and after a short, sharp conflict completely routed. Colonel Phillips reported that he found thirty-two dead bodies of the enemy on the field in the prairie, and that among those killed and identified were Colonel Taylor and Captain Hicks, of Stand Watie's Cherokee regiment, and two captains of the rebel Choctaw regiment.

After the engagement of July 27th near Bayou Bernard, Colonel Phillips marched his command to Flat Rock, on the west side of Grand River, the point where the troops of the Indian expedition under Colonel Weer had recently encamped, so that he could have the assistance, if necessary, of a detachment of some two hundred men of his regiment that had fallen back to that point from Fort Gibson. But when he arrived at Flat Rock he found that the detachment had fallen back to a point higher up on Grand River, on account of the movement of a superior force of the enemy under Majors Buster and Boudinot to get into the rear of it and cut it off or capture it. Colonel Phillips sent a courier to the commanding officer of the detachment to join him at once with the section of artillery, and on their arrival proceeded to attack Colonel McIntosh, who was in command of the Confederate Choctaw regiment stationed between the Verdigris and Arkansas rivers. Colonel Cooper, commanding the Confederate forces at Fort Davis, hearing of Colonel Phillips' movement, ordered all the Confederate troops from the north to the south side of the Arkansas River, to prevent their being captured in detail by the Federal forces. Colonel Phillips' force pursued the enemy as far as the Creek Agency ford of the Arkansas, but as his troops were out of rations, and as the enemy were not inclined to fight, he fell back to Wolf Creek and from thence to Baxter Springs, where the main command was encamped. A large number of refugee Indians and their families followed his retreating column for protection. He also brought out not less than six hundred head of cattle and a large number of ponies, some of which belonged to the soldiers of his command, but many of which had belonged to the rebel Indians. The property which had been captured from the enemy he urged should be held for the use of the loyal Indians, instead of being sold to contractors for a small percentage of its actual value. His energetic action had the effect of keeping the marauding bands of rebel Indians south of the Arkansas River until his troops were ordered to Baxter Springs. But very soon after he commenced to retreat north Colonel Cooper's forces crossed the Arkansas River and advanced north until they came in contact with detachments of the loyal Indians, who had not yet rejoined the retreating troops.

CHAPTER XXIII.

BATTLE OF INDEPENDENCE.

AFTER the defeat and demoralization of the Confederate forces at Pea Ridge in March, and after the Missouri State Guard forces under General Sterling Price were reorganized and those who entered the Confederate service were sent east of the Mississippi River, those who remained in the State Guard service, and the guerilla organizations co-operating with them, commenced returning to Missouri in small detachments, and continued to so return during the spring and summer. In the spring and early part of the summer most of the regular Federal forces had been withdrawn from Missouri under General Curtis, and the loyal militia was not yet thoroughly organized. General John M. Schofield, who was in command of the department, embracing the regular and militia forces of the State, was called upon for troops to occupy every town of consequence in the State for the protection of the Union people.

The loyal militia that had been organized were therefore distributed in detachments of half-companies, companies, and battalions throughout the State. Even in towns where half a regiment was stationed, it frequently occurred that one half this force was absent, scouting or on escort duty to supply trains. The Confederate guerilla bands and recruiting detachments of course made no pretensions to holding any particular point, and were free to attack or retreat as they thought proper. As they had friends and sympathizers in every town, they had no difficulty in ascertaining the exact strength of the Federal force occupying any particular place, and the exact situation of the forces. When they determined to attack a place, they knew that they were strong enough to make the chances of success in their favor. There was the advantage, too, that a good many of these detached forces could concentrate, on short notice, to attack a given point or an escort to a train. They were always mounted upon the best horses in the country. They could encamp in some out-of-the-way or inaccessible place for almost any length of time, to await an opportunity for the Federal commanders to be off their guard. No section was better adapted for such guerilla operations than the heavily wooded country along the breaks of the Blue rivers and the Sni hills of Jackson County. Independence, the county seat of Jackson County, was a thriving town, in the midst of a rich country, and had been occupied by one or two companies of Federal troops almost continuously since the fall of 1861.

In the endeavor to distribute his troops to the best advantage to preserve order in his military district, General Totten assigned Lieutenant-Colonel James T. Buel, of the Seventh Missouri Cavalry, to the command of the post of Independence, on the 7th of June, 1862. The troops under his command consisted of three companies of the Seventh Missouri Cavalry, two companies of Colonel Newgent's Second Battalion, Missouri Provisional Militia, commanded by Captains Jacob Axline and Aaron Thomas, and Captain W. H. Rodewald's company of the Sixth Regiment of Missouri Enrolled Militia, attached to the Seventh Missouri Cavalry. When none of this command was detached scouting, there were probably between four hundred and five hundred men present for duty. This force was quartered and stationed in Independence as follows: Colonel Buel had his headquarters on the first floor of the Southern Bank building, two doors from the southwest corner of the Public Square, on Lexington Street. Captain Rodewald's company was quartered in a two-story brick building on the north side of Lexington Street, opposite Colonel Buel's headquarters. Lieutenant Charles W. Meryhew, Seventh Missouri Cavalry and acting Provost-Marshal, was stationed at the jail, one block north of the Public Square, on North Main Street, with twenty-five men. The rest of the command were encamped in tents on the south side of Lexington Street,—a street that runs east and west through the city,—near the western limits of the city. The camp was in a depression, and there were no defences to protect it should it be surprised. There was, however, a stone fence, nearly a half-mile long, running east and west, the east end of which came within about ninety feet of the southeast corner of the camp, and which might be used for defensive purpose if the attack should be made from the direction of the city. The troops at this camp were all cavalry. Colonel Buel's headquarters were at least a half-mile up town.

It was known to the officers of this camp, some days before the battle, that a number of Confederate officers had recently come up from the South, and were in that section recruiting and organizing companies of Confederate troops. Colonel Buel kept out as much as a company of cavalry, scouting all the time up to within a day or two of the attack. Only two or three days before the attack, Captain Breckenridge returned from a long scout of eleven days, and reported that he had not seen or heard any signs of an organized force of the enemy. It was taken for granted by Colonel Buel that he had used proper diligence in obtaining all possible information in regard to the movements of the enemy, and, as a consequence, that there should be no reasonable apprehension of an immediate attack. It created no surprise to hear of Quantrill's guerillas in Jackson County any day; but that a Confederate force of one thousand men or upwards should be able to concentrate in the county, without the knowledge of the Federal scouting parties, did not seem probable. But, in view of the alarming reports brought in by citizens living in the neighborhood of Blue Springs, picket guards were kept out by Colonel Buel from one to one and a quarter miles from camp on all the roads leading into town. The picket guard was mounted, but they were not instructed or cautioned to be more than usually vigilant, as Captain Breckenridge, on his return from a long scout, reported finding no signs of an organized enemy.

Every thing was quiet about camp Saturday and Sunday preceding the attack of Monday morning, August 11th, except that, about ten o'clock Sunday night, a lady, Mrs. —— Wilson, who lived about three miles north of Blue Springs, a village about eleven miles northeast of Independence, came into Colonel Buel's headquarters and reported to him, in the presence of Captains Rodewald and Thomas, that a big body of men from near Blue Springs, and, as she heard, another large number of men from the Sni, were coming, and would attack him that night. She also stated that she had seen the Blue Springs column, and that it was said that there were one thousand to twelve hundred men in it. Colonel Buel replied to Mrs. Wilson: "Madam, we have heard such reports several times lately, and don't you see we are here yet!" He further remarked to her that she had better go home, or go and stay all night with some friend, and go home in the morning.

Mrs. Wilson, leaving Colonel Buel's office, had just reached the street, when she turned around and started back to ask where General Samuel D. Lucas, a prominent Union citizen, lived, and was met by Captain Rodewald, to whom she repeated what she had said to Colonel Buel, and assured the Captain that she had seen the rebel forces near Blue Springs, and that they would be in that night. Captain Rodewald directed her to where General Lucas lived, and returned to Colonel Buel's headquarters. In about half an hour General Lucas came down to Colonel Buel's headquarters, and stated that Mrs. Wilson had just come to his house and told him what she had seen and heard, and wished him to impress Colonel Buel with the danger with which he was threatened. General Lucas assured Colonel Buel that Mrs. Wilson was a truthful lady. Then Colonel Buel replied that he had had Captain Breckenridge out on an eleven days' scout, and that the Captain had returned and reported that he had found no signs of an organized force of the enemy, and that he wished that people would stop bringing in such reports,—" that we always know how to take care of ourselves." General Lucas turned suddenly, as if his feelings had been a little ruffled, and left the office without further remark.

After General Lucas left, Colonel Buel issued no orders of extra precaution to the guards or the camp at the western limits of the town, and gave the officers, Captains Rodewald and Thomas permission to go to their homes in town, where they sometimes stayed when there was no excitement or threatened danger. Captain Rodewald, however, being impressed with the danger, after hearing Mrs. Wilson's report, instead of going home shared the quarters of his company opposite Colonel Buel's headquarters. Captain Thomas went to his home. Captain Rodewald, before retiring, informed his men of the report of the threatened attack, and instructed them to load their carbines and have them ready for an emergency. At twenty minutes to four o'clock Monday morning, the guard for Captain Rodewald's company quarters, and for headquarters, was heard to call out in the stillness of the night: "Halt! halt! halt!" and by the time that he had called out halt the third time, fired upon the advancing enemy, who had dismounted and hitched their horses around Court-house Square, and were marching down Lexington Street in the direction of the main camp, in double-quick time. After discharging his carbine the guard came immediately rushing into the guard-room and closed the door behind him. The discharge of his gun had awakened the guard in the guard-room down-stairs, and also the soldiers of Captain Rodewald's company in their quarters on the second floor. Lexington Street in front of the company quarters was in a moment full of Confederate soldiers, seeing which Captain Rodewald's men from the front second-story windows fired into them about half a dozen shots. The Confederates did not return the fire, and some one in the darkness called out: "For God's sake don't fire, it 's your own men."

The firing then ceased, and Captain Rodewald led his company out of the building on to the street, and the first man he met he recognized as a Confederate soldier who lived in Independence, and caught him by the arm and took him prisoner on the spot. The Captain then called out, so that his company could hear him, that the men in the streets were rebels, and ordered his men to fall into line. By bringing his men into the street and forming a line he cut off a few of the rearmost rebels from the main column that continued to march rapidly down the street to the Federal camp. As soon as his company formed he ordered them to fire upon the rebel column that had just passed, but that was still in range. The volley killed the Confederate colonel, Kit Chiles, as was discovered when daylight came. Captain Rodewald, almost at the same moment, ordered a part of his company to fire a volley into a number of the enemy who were up the street in the direction of the court-house. He held his position at the crossing of Lexington and Liberty streets until about six o'clock, having repulsed three attacks of the enemy, the first two from East Lexington Street, and the last from West Lexington Street, from the main column of the enemy that had passed down the street in the direction of the Federal camp. In this last attack, or charge, the Confederate officer, Major Hart, was mortally wounded, and one of his Arkansas lieutenants and eleven private soldiers were captured, two of whom were wounded.

Immediately after this attack Colonel Buel ordered Captain Rodewald and his company into his headquarters building, and to take possession of all the windows or openings of the first and second stories of the building, and of the open space or yard on the west side of it, as there was but one opening in the building up-stairs on the west side. There were three windows to the front and rear of the second story, three windows in the rear of the first story and two windows and a door in the front.

The enemy surrounded Colonel Buel soon after he drew his men in from the street, and the fight, until fifteen minutes after nine o'clock, when he surrendered, was mainly carried on by sharp-shooting. The rebels got into a large brick store on the east side of Liberty Street, and opposite headquarters building, and by keeping up a constant firing into a window on the east side, but near the rear, completely commanded it. This was the only window which Colonel Buel could not use during the engagement. The firing was almost constant from all his windows to the close of the fight.

At about half-past seven o'clock, Colonel Buel asked Captain Rodewald where his flag was, and stated that he wanted the Federal flag to hoist over headquarters, to show to the camp that he was still holding out. Captain Rodewald replied that it was at the company quarters, across the street. One of his company, a bugler, a youth about sixteen years old, named William O. Buhoe, having heard the conversation about the flag, volunteered to go across the street to the company quarters and get it, which he did, amid a shower of bullets, as he swiftly crossed and recrossed the street barefooted. It was a daring act. After the flag had been brought over to his headquarters, Colonel Buel wished it to be hoisted over the building. As there was no flagstaff on the building to which it could be fastened, two men of Captain Rodewald's company were detailed to fasten it as best they could to the chimney, and were shot and killed while endeavoring to perform this duty. After this, two of the Confederate prisoners—the recently captured lieutenant and one private—were required to fasten the flag to the chimney, and did it without getting wounded, being recognized by the rebel sharp-shooters.

About four o'clock, or shortly after the enemy had entered the city, two of the Provost Guard stationed at the jail made their escape therefrom, and came into Captain Rodewald's quarters and reported that Lieutenant Meryhew had abandoned the jail and had gone either to the camp or to Kansas City. Lieutenant Meryhew got to Kansas City some time in the afternoon, with thirteen to fourteen men, having travelled through the woods north of Independence. The rebels took possession of the jail, released the rebel prisoners, and killed the City Marshal of Independence, who had been confined there on a charge of murder.

Let us now turn to the main camp, and see what took place there. About twenty-five minutes after the main column of the enemy had passed Colonel Buel's headquarters, a heavy volley was heard in the direction of the camp. The Federal camp was approached by two columns of the enemy. One column, under Colonels Thompson and Chiles, marched down Lexington Street; and the other, under Colonel and acting Brigadier-General John T. Hughes and Colonel Upton Hays, marched down Walnut Street. The camp lay between Lexington and Walnut streets. The enemy formed behind a board fence—picket style—that ran from Lexington to Walnut Street, about twenty to twenty-five yards east of the line of tents. The men in the camp, not having heard the firing at headquarters, were taken completely by surprise, and the first volley of the enemy was delivered with terrible effect, while most of the Federal soldiers were in their tents asleep. This volley, of course, instantly aroused the camp. The first word heard from any of the officers of the camp was from Captain Breckenridge, who spoke out in a loud voice and said: "Boys, we are completely surrounded, and we had better surrender." Captain Axline, hearing this remark, at once called out, so that he could be heard: "Boys, get your guns and ammunition and rally behind the rock fence."

The enemy, after delivering his first fire, commenced to plunder the camp, which had been abandoned. In the meantime the Federal soldiers were rallying behind the rock fence under Captain Axline, which position he held during the fight. About daylight, Colonel Hughes, while endeavoring to turn the Federal right, which was behind the stone fence, was killed, and also a number of his men were killed and wounded. After Colonel Hughes was killed Colonel G. W. Thompson took command, and attempted to turn the Federal right; but his force was also repulsed, and he too was wounded in the knee. After this, Colonel Upton Hays took command of the Confederates, but made no more assaults on the Federal position. He used his force in sharp-shooting during the rest of the engagement. He got wounded in the foot, but the wound was not of such a serious nature that he was obliged to leave the field.

The Federal position was impregnable unless the enemy flanked it on the right. Immediately after the Federal troops rallied behind the stone fence, Captain Axline ordered Lieutenant Herrington to take forty men and report to Colonel Buel at headquarters. He started to headquarters with his forty men, but for some reason took position in Mr. McCoy's brick house, that stood to itself several hundred yards north of the camp, and after firing a few shots at a small squad or so of the enemy, retreated to Kansas City, where he arrived with his men early in the morning. At a quarter past nine o'clock Captain Rodewald's company at headquarters were ordered to cease firing, and Colonel Buel sent his Adjutant, Lieutenant Preble, with a flag of truce, a piece of bed-sheet fastened to a ramrod, to the officer commanding the Confederate forces, requesting an interview. About eleven o'clock the flag of truce returned, with Colonel Upton Hays accompanying Colonel Buel's Adjutant. A few moments after this Captain Rodewald's company of ninety-one men were ordered to march out of headquarters, and were drawn up in line in front of the building, where they stacked arms in presence of Colonels Buel and Upton Hays.

In the meanwhile the Federal soldiers behind the stone fence near the camp had surrendered, and reached headquarters about twenty-five minutes after Captain Rodewald's company had stacked arms. All the several companies of Federal soldiers were surrendered except some forty men under Lieutenant Herrington and some fifteen to twenty men under Lieutenant Meryhew, Provost-Marshal, who escaped to Kansas City. Just before the Federal soldiers from the camp were marched up to headquarters, Colonel Thompson, the senior officer commanding the Confederate forces after the death of Colonel Hughes, was brought in from the direction of the camp, though severely wounded, and paroled the Federal prisoners, officers and enlisted men, from Colonel Buel's headquarters. It was stipulated that none of the Federal prisoners should be murdered by Quantrill's men.

The Federal forces sustained the heaviest loss when the enemy fired his first volley into the tents. When the battle was over twenty-six Federal soldiers were found killed in and around the camp. There were seventy-four Federal soldiers and officers wounded in the battle, eleven of whom were mortally wounded. Captain Aaron Thomas, of Colonel Newgent's battalion, was killed while endeavoring to reach the Federal camp from his hotel. He was a brave and an efficient officer. Sergeant John T. Blake received a serious wound in the arm and ankle. Captain Breckenridge received a slight wound on the arm.

The Confederates left in town twenty-three men killed, ten of whom were officers, and nine men mortally wounded. Of the officers killed and who died immediately after the engagement, there were Colonels John T. Hughes, Kit Chiles, and Boyd; Majors Hart and Wortle; Captains Brown, Clark, and Chambers; and Lieutenants Jones and R. Johnson.

In the two assaults on the Federal position behind the stone fence the Confederate losses were heavy, and Captain Rodewald reported that their total loss in killed and wounded was equal to if not greater than the Federal, for it was known that a good many of their wounded were sent to their friends in the surrounding country. After gathering up the captured property, such as they did not burn, the Confederate forces marched out of Independence, in the direction of Blue Springs, about five o'clock in the afternoon. The arms, ammunition, quartermaster and commissary stores captured, made a train of fifteen to twenty wagons. The ordnance and quartermaster's stores were much needed by the Confederates to arm and equip new recruits. From the manner in which we have seen that the Federal troops were stationed about town, at the camp, near headquarters, and at the jail, it is easy to see that they could not co-operate to the best advantage after the enemy had once got into town.

The Union citizens and soldiers charged that Colonel Buel and Captain Breckenridge had an understanding with the Confederate officers to surrender the Federal forces without offering any resistance. Whether there was any truth in the charge or not, there certainly appeared to be some grounds for making it, in view of the fact that Colonel Buel had been thoroughly warned that the enemy were only a few miles distant, and would attack him that night. It was also claimed that, scattered as they were, there was no necessity for the Federal troops surrendering to the enemy; that after those from the camp took position behind the stone fence they repulsed every assault of the Confederates and killed and wounded most of their field-officers. Several days before the attack was made, a number of Union citizens were so fully convinced, from what they could hear and see of the secessionists, that it would be made, that they left Independence the day before and went to Kansas City and Leavenworth, Kansas.

The paroled Federal prisoners stayed in Independence several days after the battle, gathering up and taking care of the wounded of both sides and burying the dead. During all this time no Federal troops from any quarter came in, and on the morning of the third day Colonel Buel, with his officers and enlisted men, somewhat over one hundred and fifty in number, started on foot for Kansas City and Leavenworth to be exchanged. After waiting at Leavenworth some one to two weeks, these paroled prisoners were ordered to Benton Barracks, St. Louis, and were mustered out of service.

After the fatal mistake had been made, of taking measures to guard against a surprise, it was easy to see that had Colonel Buel put two companies of his command into the court-house, they could have held it against the enemy any length of time. But Captain Rodewald, whose loyalty to the Government was never questioned, stated that "if I were upon my oath I should say that I believe that Colonel Buel acted in good faith, and did not betray his command into the hands of the enemy; that he did not display any lukewarmness during the fight, but even seized a musket and fired several shots into the rebel attacking force."

CHAPTER XXIV.

BATTLE OF LONE JACK.

IN the early part of August, reports were almost daily coming to General James Totten commanding district of Central Missouri, headquarters at Sedalia, and to Colonel Daniel Huston, Seventh Missouri Cavalry, commanding post of Lexington, that large detachments of Confederate forces were arriving in the counties of Jackson, La Fayette, and Johnson from the south; that these fragmentary commands were being rapidly augmented by recruits from those counties, in which there were large numbers of men who preferred to join the Confederate service to joining the loyal militia; and that the Confederate officers were preparing to concentrate their forces in the neighborhood of Lone Jack, in the southeast corner of Jackson County, with the view of marching on Lexington. The receipt of the information of the surrender of Colonel Buel's Federal force at Independence on the 11th produced a profound impression, and led General Totten to immediately send troops into the section reported to be overrun by the enemy.

Major Emory S. Foster, Seventh Missouri State Militia Cavalry, had already rendered distinguished service in fighting guerillas in Central and Western Missouri, and his bravery and efficiency had been brought to the notice of the commanding general. He was therefore directed by General Totten to proceed to Lexington with a detachment of two hundred cavalry; and at that place Colonel Huston was instructed to detail a force of as many men as could safely be spared to report to him. In view of the threatened danger, Colonel Huston had strengthened his position at Lexington. On the 10th he ordered Colonel Newgent's Second Battalion Missouri State Militia, stationed at Chapel Hill, to march to Lexington, which they did, arriving there on the 11th.

Major Foster's force of eight hundred and six men consisted of details from the Sixth, Seventh, and Eighth Regiments Missouri State Militia Cavalry, a detail from the Seventh Missouri Volunteer Cavalry, a detail from Colonel Newgent's Second Battalion Missouri State Militia Cavalry, and a section of two pieces of the Third Indian Battery six-pounders, under Lieutenant J. S. Devlin. Surgeon W. H. H. Cundiff, of the Second Battalion Missouri State Militia, was the chief medical officer of the command. After his command was made up for him, Major Foster was instructed by General Totten to proceed to the neighborhood of Lone Jack, where Colonel FitzHenry Warren, First Iowa Cavalry, from Clinton, Henry County, was directed to join him by the evening of the 15th or morning of the 16th. He might also be joined by General Blunt's forces from Kansas, as a request had been sent to that officer for co-operation by General Schofield commanding the Department of the Missouri.

At sunrise on the morning of August 15th, Major Foster moved out of Lexington with his command, and reached Lone Jack about nine o'clock at night, having marched thirty-three miles on an exceedingly hot day. About one half-mile northeast of town his advance guard encountered and captured the enemy's pickets, from whom he obtained a good deal of information in regard to the strength and location of the rebel forces in the neighborhood. He ascertained that Colonel Coffey was encamped with a force of at least twelve hundred men about one mile south of town, and that Colonel Cockrell, with the main rebel force, was encamped that night about three miles northwest of town. Having decided to attack the rebel force near him that night, he continued his march through Lone Jack, and from thence nearly a mile south to the cross-roads, where the enemy's pickets were again encountered and fired into, and a commissary sergeant captured, from whom further information was obtained in regard to the large rebel force northwest of the village. The exact location of the enemy in his immediate front was also ascertained.

In the meanwhile the moon had risen, which very soon dispelled the darkness to a considerable extent. Major Foster now halted his command and ordered up his artillery, and directed Lieutenant Devlin to throw a few shells into the area where the Confederate camp was pointed out to him. The shells appeared to have dropped in the rebel camp, for in a few moments the rebel command moved out in the utmost confusion. Major Foster had kept out skirmishers on his flanks when he found himself in the vicinity of the enemy, and when the advance skirmishers on his left fired upon the enemy's pickets near the Cross Roads, the rear skirmishers on the left mistook the fire as coming from the enemy, and opened fire upon their comrades in advance, and killed two of them. The advance skirmishers had got farther off to the left of the command marching than the rear skirmishers had anticipated, and this led to the fatal mistake. This mishap determined Major Foster to return to Lone Jack, and make preparations to renew the attack the next morning. His troops and animals were fatigued from the hard day's march, and needed food and rest. They were not in condition to pursue a flying foe, mounted upon fresh horses, even had the accident referred to never occurred.

The shells thrown into Coffey's camp had had the effect of demoralizing his command, so that, after moving out that night, it made a detour from the southeast to the west of Lone Jack, with the view of joining the main rebel force under Cockrell. Coffey was commanding troops that belonged to the Missouri State Guard, and, up to this time, was acting independently of the Confederate officers.

Major Foster ascertained that Cockrell's command consisted of the regiments of Colonels John C. Tracy, Tom Hunter, Dick Hancock, Gid Thompson, Upton Hays, Bohannon, and S. D. Jackman, besides Quantrill's guerilla band. After returning to the village that night with his command, Major Foster encamped in an open square, lying on the east side of the street, which had a *bois d'arc* hedge on the north, east, and south sides of it. He put out pickets on all the roads leading into town, but his position was accessible from the corn-fields on the west and east, there being no roads leading into his camp from those directions. His position was not a well-chosen one for receiving an attack, nor was it so intended. But it was better than an open field, for the buildings in town and the hedges would afford some shelter for his troops, in the event of attack that night or the next morning. He was inclined to regard the reported strength of the combined forces of the enemy in the vicinity as exaggerated, and hardly believed that they would attack him. Any way he could await their attack, for he expected to meet Colonel Warren with his command from Clinton, Henry County ; but that officer for some cause took the wrong road, and failed to reach the designated point at the designated time. Major Foster was, therefore, left to his own resources. He was surrounded by an enemy that outnumbered him more than five to one, and that was elated by its recent success in the capture of Colonel Buel's command at Independence on the 11th.

During the night the Confederate officers had a conference, and agreed upon the plan of attack, which was to be made the next morning at daylight. Their different commands were put into their positions during the night. Major Foster also had a conference with his officers after he got into camp, and it was decided to find out the exact location of the enemy, and renew the attack if they could be found. The delay in making the attack until the next morning would also give Fitz-Henry Warren time to come up, or attack the enemy on the south side of Lone Jack. Although no recent couriers had come in with information showing just where Warren was that evening, his arrival from Clinton, Missouri, was expected at any moment. Major Foster thought that, if Colonel Warren did not arrive in time to join forces with him, he would certainly be within striking distance, and that on hearing the firing of artillery, in the event of an engagement being brought on, he would hasten to the scene of conflict and attack this large rebel force south of Lone Jack in the rear, and give them a genuine surprise. But, unfortunately, Colonel Warren had allowed himself, on some account unexplained, to be led around *via* Harrisonville, some twenty miles west of a direct line from Clinton to Lone Jack, instead of *via* Kingsville. The blunder could not in justice be chargeable to his guide, for if he had a map of the section he could easily have seen where his direct route lay between the two points, and the creeks and little towns, that he would necessarily pass on his line of march, would have served to guide him aright. As it was, his detour to the west had taken him so far out of the way that he did not reach Lone Jack until ten o'clock Sunday morning, August 17th, nearly twenty-four hours after the battle had closed.

Thus it turned out that the Federal force that was expected to join Major Foster in the neighborhood of

Lone Jack on the evening of the 15th or morning of the 16th, failed to do so, leaving him to fight the combined forces of the enemy of not less than three thousand men, with his little command of seven hundred and forty men. His men slept in line, and got a few hours of much-needed rest. At daylight his pickets came in and reported that the enemy were advancing in strong force. In the conference of the Confederate officers it was decided that Hunter's, Tracy's, and Jackman's forces should be dismounted and used as infantry in making the attack, with Hunter on the right, Jackman in the centre, and Tracy on the left. The forces of Hays and Quantrill were to remain mounted and bring on the attack at daylight. In this order they marched to the attack of Major Foster's force at daylight, but for some reason did not make the attack for nearly three quarters of an hour after the Federal pickets had fled to their camp. This delay gave Major Foster time to get every thing in readiness for the assault. His rear was protected by a small deep stream, the crossing of which was held by a small force. And the *bois d'arc* hedge would prevent the enemy from charging his force on two sides.

After the brief halt referred to, the Confederate forces, under Hunter, Jackman, and Tracy, advanced and opened the fight. When approaching the Federal position and about forty yards from it, they encountered a rail fence running parallel with their line, and were there met with a terrific fire of grape and musketry, which checked their advance and sent a good many flying in confusion to the rear. Major Foster, observing the movement, directed his troops to reserve their fire until the enemy came within easy range, and then to aim low. A few rounds of grape from his section of artillery, and the well-directed fire of his troops, repulsed the enemy, who retired from the field. In the charge they lost several officers killed and wounded, and others had become less anxious to press to the front. The Federal troops did not run after the first fire, as had been predicted the night before by some of the Confederate officers in their harangues to their men and in the council. In a short time, however, after the first repulse, the Confederates rallied and returned to the attack. This time they also attempted to turn the flanks of the Federal position, but Major Foster had posted a part of his force behind the *bois d'arc* hedge, and this force kept up such a hot fire that the rebels were obliged to retire and join the force making the attack in front.

After four hours of desperate fighting the enemy fell back. They had, however, killed all the horses hitched to the two pieces of artillery and their limbers and caissons. Several of the artillerymen had also been killed and wounded. At this point of the battle Lieutenant Devlin came on the field and ordered his men to fall back, which they did, leaving their guns. Seeing this, the enemy rallied and made a furious charge to capture the guns, but were again repulsed. Of sixty men led by Major Foster in the charge to save the guns, only eleven reached them, and in dragging them out of the enemy's reach Major Foster was shot down. Captain Milton Brawner, the next officer in rank to Major Foster, then took command. After a hand-to-hand fight for nearly half an hour the enemy again retreated, leaving the Federal forces in possession of the field and artillery.

It was now after eleven o'clock, and Colonel Cockrell, who had been in command of the rebel forces engaged, was reinforced by twelve hundred men under Colonel Coffey, who had been driven from their camp the night before by Major Foster. The Federal force had now suffered a loss of nearly one third their number in killed and wounded. In view of this heavy loss and of the reinforcement of the enemy, Captain Brawner thought that the safety of the command depended upon his withdrawing from the field, and he did so, leaving the two guns. The artillery horses that were hitched to the limbers and caissons at the beginning of the action were all killed and wounded, and it became necessary to cut the harness to free the limbers and caissons from the dead and wounded horses. In this way the artillery harness was scattered and destroyed.

After calling in the several detachments holding different points, Captain Brawner marched out of Lone Jack on the Lexington road unmolested by the enemy, and arrived at Lexington that evening. An hour after his departure the enemy marched into the village and took possession of the two guns which had been left. One of them had been spiked by Captain Brawner's order. In the course of the engagement the sharp-shooters on both sides secured sheltered positions as best they could, to enable them to render as effective service as possible. Early in the action a few of Major Foster's best marksmen took positions in some of the buildings in town, and were very annoying to the Confederates, for their attention was mainly directed to Confederate officers leading their men into action and to squads of sharpshooters endeavoring to secure sheltered positions. The whizzing of bullets from the rifles of the unerring Federal sharp-shooters felled many a Confederate officer prone in the dust.

Confederate Colonel Jackman stated that he, Captain Bryant, a lieutenant, Sergeant Montgomery, and a Southern soldier took position behind an old log-cabin, and that in a few moments they were discovered by the Federal sharp-shooters; that Captain Bryant, Sergeant Montgomery, and the soldier were shot one after the other, each through the temple, and fell dead upon each other by his side; that the lieutenant also was wounded in the arm and had to leave the field; and that all these men were killed and wounded by the same Federal sharp-shooter.

Into other quarters of the field, too, where isolated groups of the enemy were found loitering or peering around, these sharp-shooters sent their death-dealing missiles. Some of the Confederate officers thought that the fatal shots came from men sheltered in the hotel, a frame structure, and they determined to fire it. The rebels moved up in strong force so as to completely command one side of the building, and then sent forward two men who had volunteered to fire it. As they approached near the building a Federal squad came around each end of it to fire upon or capture them, but were driven back by a heavy fire from the enemy in position. The burning of the building was of no consequence except the relief it gave the enemy in that quarter while it was burning, for there were other buildings near at hand in which the Federal sharp-shooters could find shelter to continue their effective work.

The loss of the Confederates in the battle is not known, only that it is known to have been much heavier than the Federal loss, for the Confederates were the assaulting party. Every time that the Federal force charged them and made them show their backs they suffered severely from Foster's grape-shot and musketry.

Colonel Jackman reported that he went into the battle with five hundred men, and that out of ten captains four were killed and three wounded. If the other regiments of the seven or eight Confederate colonels on the field were as strong as Jackman's, and each sustained a loss of officers and enlisted men as heavy as his, the Confederate killed and wounded would almost equal the Federal force engaged in the battle. Colonel Coffey's command took very little if any part in the battle, and should not therefore figure in the estimate of the Confederate loss. The Confederate forces of Thompson and Hays had captured a considerable supply of arms and ammunition at Independence on the 11th, so that the combined forces fighting Major Foster were fairly well supplied in this respect. Indeed, five hundred men to the regiment would be a low estimate of the number of men engaged on the Confederate side, for Colonel Jackman reported that, when he came into Western Missouri for the purpose of recruiting, he found "the woods full of men" ready to enter the Confederate service, on account of an order of the Governor of Missouri having been issued about that time, requiring all able-bodied men to join the loyal militia or leave the State. The heroic conduct of Major Foster and his devoted little band is without a parallel in the history of modern wars, and must live as long as military history lives.

The official statement of casualties showed that, on the Federal side, there were two officers and fifty-one enlisted men killed; thirteen officers and one hundred and forty-four enlisted men wounded; and one officer and forty-three enlisted men missing. Thus, as Captain Brawner reported, nearly every officer of Major Foster's command was killed and wounded. He also stated that the enemy acknowledged a loss of one hundred and eighteen men killed. Lieutenants A. M. Baltzell and Samuel M. Baker, Seventh Missouri Cavalry, were killed on the field, while leading their men into action. And Captain Wm. A. Long, Second Battalion Missouri State Militia Cavalry, was mortally wounded in leading his men in a charge against the enemy to save the artillery from capture. Lieutenant E. F. Rogers, of the same battalion, was at the same time shot through the body, but recovered.

CHAPTER XXV.

BATTLE OF LONE JACK.—CONCLUDED.

GENERAL JAMES G. BLUNT, commanding the Department of Kansas, including the Indian Territory, assumed command in person of the troops that had just returned from the *Indian Expedition* into the Indian country. While his command of three or four thousand men were resting a few days at Baxter Springs, sixty miles south of Fort Scott, he received despatches from General Schofield, commanding Department of the Missouri, and information from his scouts, scouting parties, and Union people who came into his camps from the border counties of Missouri, that detachments of rebels from the South were passing through the country, marching northward, every day. His troops arrived at Fort Scott August 9th, and the reports constantly coming in indicated that the rebel detachments marching northward through the border counties of Missouri were intending to concentrate at some point near the Missouri River, but south of it, and attack the Federal forces stationed at Independence, Lexington, or Warrensburg. Some of General Blunt's cavalry scouts skirmished with the rebel detachments in their march northwards, and in other instances came upon their trails where they had marched through the high prairie grass of Vernon and Bates counties, Missouri. From the number of colonels ascertained to be commanding the different detachments of the enemy, it was thought that they would be able to concentrate a force of several thousand men to attack any given point.

Most of the rebel detachments, however, had arrived in Jackson and Lafayette counties, south of the Missouri River, before General Blunt's troops arrived at Fort Scott. These detachments, that were mere skeletons of companies when they passed from Arkansas into Missouri, grew into full regiments by recruiting by the time that they reached the Missouri River. Bushwhackers and Southern sympathizers from every neighborhood through which they passed flocked to them. General Totten, who commanded the district of Central Missouri, from Sedalia to Kansas City, became alarmed at the concentration of such large rebel forces in the immediate vicinity of some of his posts, and sent a despatch to General Blunt, requesting his co-operation in attacking the enemy, or in moving against him. In the three months' campaign in the Indian country a considerable portion of General Blunt's cavalry had become dismounted on account of the breaking down of their horses, caused by hard marching and lack of sufficient and proper forage. The expedition showed very conclusively that good cavalry horses will very soon break down when corn and oats are denied them, and they are obliged to live on wild prairie grass.

The Second and Sixth Regiments, Kansas Cavalry, that had returned from the Indian expedition, had also lost some horses. A few days at Fort Scott were therefore required to reorganize and outfit the troops just returned, before starting out on another long and arduous expedition. In order that all the troops not needed at Fort Scott and Baxter Springs might be put into the expedition, General Blunt ordered that the available infantry of the Tenth Kansas and of the Ninth and Twelfth Regiments from Wisconsin, and a battalion of dismounted troopers of the Second Ohio Cavalry, in all about two thousand men, be put into Government wagons, each wagon drawn by four mules, so that they could keep up with the cavalry and light artillery.

The cavalry detailed for the expedition were the Second and Sixth Regiments, Kansas Cavalry, and a battalion of the Third Wisconsin Cavalry. The whole force was accompanied by Captain Allen's First Kansas Battery, six pieces; Captain Rabb's Second Indiana Battery, six pieces; and two twelve-pound howitzers of the Sixth Kansas Cavalry. There were probably one hundred wagons provided to transport the infantry, and the wagon bows and covers were removed, so as not to interfere with the contemplated rapid transit.

About two o'clock Friday morning, August 15th, General Blunt took command of this force and left Fort Scott and marched directly east about twelve miles on the Fort Scott and Nevada road, and then turned north and crossed the Marmaton and Osage rivers and halted an hour, from one to two o'clock, about three miles northeast of Balltown, to rest and refresh his troops and animals. After this short halt the march was resumed in a northeasterly direction until the command came near the Saint Clair or Henry County line, where it went into camp about ten o'clock at night. The next morning before daylight the troops again moved out on the march, northward, and at night reached a point near the southeast corner of Cass County, where another halt was made until morning. The march since leaving Fort Scott had been over broad prairies covered with grass, in some places high as a man's head, except that on the creeks and rivers crossed there were skirts of timber passed through. On account of there being very little regular travel upon the county and State roads, and of their neglect by the county authorities since the war had commenced, they had in many places been washed out considerably, and the grass and weeds had grown up in them, so that the march of the cavalry and artillery was frequently on one or the other side of them through the high prairie grass, leaving a regular trail with the grass tramped flat down.

In the afternoon of the second day's march General Blunt's advance noticed that several fresh trails, each indicating that a considerable cavalry force had entered the road he was marching upon and were marching in the same direction. He had also received information from his scouts and from some of the few people still living in the country, that the trails observed were those of the enemy, who had recently marched north in large force. At daybreak Sunday morning the third day's march was resumed along the western part of Johnson County, and it was soon understood that Lone Jack was the objective point, for some reports had reached General Blunt that a battle had been fought there, and that the enemy were yet on the ground. It had been warm and clear since leaving Fort Scott, and the roads were in good condition with few exceptions, and the troops had marched forty miles a day.

As the troops moved forward on the third day, they every now and then met citizens who were able to give more definite information of the battle that had taken place between the Federal and rebel forces at Lone Jack on Saturday, from morning until noon. Some stated that they had plainly heard the sound of artillery, and others that they had heard the sound of the firing of small-arms in the direction of Lone Jack. Others again, stated that they had seen parties who were in the battle and that the Federal troops had been defeated. General Blunt pushed forward his command in the direction of Lone Jack with the determination of attacking the enemy if they were yet in the vicinity. His command passed Kingsville early in the afternoon, near which place it met General Fitz Henry Warren's command retreating from the direction of Lone Jack.

General Blunt did not halt his troops, but continuing

the march arrived within a mile of Lone Jack Sunday evening about six o'clock on the 17th, thirty hours after the battle had been fought, and found the enemy encamped in large force in and around the village. At the point where the head of his column halted, the enemy could plainly be seen in force about half a mile to the front. A threatening rain and thunder-storm was rapidly approaching from the northwest, but General Blunt formed his troops in line as fast as they came up, intending to give battle at once if the enemy did not attack first. A heavy timber and woods extended for several miles on his right, and it was soon observed that the enemy were advancing towards his front, and that when they came some distance down the road they turned to the left, passing out of sight into the timber and woods described. General Blunt at once threw out skirmishers into the timber and woods on his right, but now the storm burst forth, the rain came down in torrents, and it was soon intensely dark.

After the troops had been standing in line a short time, a detachment of the Sixth Kansas Cavalry under Lieutenant-Colonel Jewell, that had been sent out on the right flank, discovered that the enemy, instead of preparing to fight, were passing around General Blunt's right flank, and had nearly all got by and were in full retreat. Although intense darkness prevailed, the Federal troops were ordered to face about, and with guides, advanced cautiously in a southeast direction, endeavoring to strike the road the enemy were retreating upon. The locality where the Federal troops halted was cut up by ditches and washouts, so that the ambulances, artillery carriages, and caissons could not be moved without much difficulty, being frequently on the point of upsetting in the ditches, and requiring much labor to extricate them.

On account of the darkness and rain, General Blunt did not march during the night more than five or six miles in pursuit of the retreating rebels. But the enemy also had made little progress marching during the night, and when daylight came General Blunt's advance was in sight of Cockrell's rear-guard. General Blunt now commenced a vigorous pursuit of the enemy, and continued it for three days and nights, stopping only an hour or so twice a day to allow his troops and animals a little time for taking food and rest. His advance under Colonel Judson, Sixth Kansas Cavalry, overtook the rebel rear-guard several times before reaching the Osage River, eighty miles south, and skirmished with them, but they could not be held long enough for the main command to come up. In the excitement of the pursuit, the Federal troops were obliged to march in open order, the command frequently covering a distance of four or five miles along the road over the rolling prairies. The troops picked up in the pursuit a good many rebel stragglers who had fallen asleep by the roadside, and who had failed to get waked up when their commands moved on the approach of the Federal cavalry.

The marching day and night became very exhausting to both parties. Between midnight and daylight many of the soldiers became so drowsy that they slept in their saddles. Many a nodding soldier lost his hat or cap while thus sleeping. General Blunt's cavalry under Colonel Jewell, Sixth Kansas, pursued the enemy to Carthage, seventy-five miles south of the Osage River, but being unable to bring them to a stand, and his horses and men being worn out from a week's constant marching, he relinquished the pursuit.

At Carthage the Kansas troops under Colonel Jewell were relieved by a force of fourteen hundred Missouri cavalry of General E. B. Brown's command under Colonel Clark Wright, who came in from the direction of Stockton, and who continued the pursuit of the rebels to Neosho and Pineville, near the south line of the State, with comparatively fresh horses. On the evening of the 21st Colonel Wright overtook the enemy at Neosho and drove them out of town, and in the pursuit toward Pineville killed several and captured thirty prisoners. He also captured a despatch from Coffey to Colonel Hays at Lone Jack, requesting him to press forward and join him, thus showing a considerable rebel force was yet in the rear of the Federal troops.

After part of the Sixth Kansas Cavalry gave up the pursuit of the enemy at Carthage, and had turned back to join the main command at Fort Scott, they fell into Colonel Cloud's command.

Colonels Shelby and Hays, with a Confederate force of twelve hundred men, marched south from the Missouri River two days in the rear of General Blunt's command, and on the 24th went into camp in the timber on Coon Creek, twelve miles northeast of Carthage. Colonel Cloud, of the Second Kansas Cavalry, who had participated in the pursuit of the main rebel force under Colonels Cockrell and Coffey, and who was returning to Fort Scott by easy marches, heard of the rebel force under Shelby and Hays encamped in the timber on Coon Creek, and without ascertaining their strength, ordered Captain H. S. Greeno, Sixth Kansas Cavalry, to take his company, dismounted, and move forward through the woods to develop the position of the enemy. Captain Greeno had not proceeded far into the woods, when the enemy, who were watching his movement, placed themselves in an advantageous position, and as soon as he came within easy range, poured a volley into his company. The brush appeared to be full of rebels, and the captain was obliged to fall back to the main command near at hand. In the affair he had three men killed and twenty-one wounded. He was also seriously wounded through the hand. No further attack was made upon the enemy, and after resting they continued their march southward.

Statement of casualties on the Federal side in the battle of Lone Jack, August 16, 1862:

Command.	Killed.		Wounded		Missing.	
	Officers.	Enlisted Men.	Officers.	Enlisted Men.	Officers.	Enlisted Men.
Seventh Missouri Cavalry	2	19	3	62		11
Sixth Missouri State Militia Cavalry		9	5	35		17
Seventh Missouri State Militia Cavalry		6	1	14		6
Eighth Missouri State Militia Cavalry		9	2	28		4
Second Battalion, Mo. State Militia Cavalry		4	1	5	1	5
Third Indiana Battery		5				
	2	52	12	144	1	43

The surrender of Independence, the defeat of Major Foster's force at Lone Jack, and the report that the combined rebel forces in Jackson and La Fayette counties were four thousand or five thousand strong, created much anxiety in the minds of the people in the border counties of Kansas. And there were good reasons for such anxiety. It was known that a good many rebels in the border counties of Missouri were smarting to avenge the conduct of Colonel Jennison and the lawless bands of Red Legs from Kansas. These rebel sympathizers alleged that Jennison's men and the Kansas Red Legs robbed and plundered the people of Missouri of personal property which could not in any manner be applied to military purposes, and it was sometimes hinted that the secessionists would get even with General Lane for wantonly burning Osceola. There was a general feeling along the Kansas border that, on account of the alleged depredations referred to as not justifiable acts of war, the organized rebels of Missouri would, if an opportunity offered, retaliate with interest.

Complaints of Union men, men, too, who were serving as soldiers in Union regiments from Missouri, were made, charging Jennison's men with committing all sorts of depredations. To guard against raids of rebel guerillas from Missouri into Kansas, there were small military posts at convenient distances from each other along the State line between Fort Scott and Kansas City. Major W. C. Ransom, of the Sixth Kansas Cavalry, was stationed at Little Santa Fé, twenty-five miles south of Kansas City, with four companies of cavalry, and patrolled the State line between that point and Kansas City, and Cold Water Grove, twenty-five miles south. But after the fall of Independence, being threatened with attack by a superior force of rebels under Colonels Hays and Thompson, he fell back to Kansas City, and strengthened his position there by repairing the fortifications which had been thrown up by Major Van Horn in 1861. As he was unable to communicate with Colonel Fitz Henry Warren at Clinton, or General Blunt, who, as he was informed, was moving from Fort Scott to Lexington, and being apprehensive that the large rebel force in the neighborhood was intending to attack him at Kansas City, he telegraphed Colonel J. T. Burris, commanding the post of Fort Leavenworth, Kansas, for assistance. On the arrival of Colonel Burris, he and Major Ransom joined forces and marched on Independence with seven hundred men. At that place they found only Colonel Buel's Federal and the rebel wounded left there from the engagement of the 11th, but received information that the rebel force of three thousand or four thousand men was on the Blue River about eighteen miles southeast of Independence. Feeling that they were not strong enough to move forward and attack the enemy, they fell back to Kansas City, and Colonel Burris returned to Fort Leavenworth.

In the meantime the battle of Lone Jack had been fought, and General Blunt, coming up, compelled the main body of the Confederates to retreat south. But on the night that they commenced the retreat, Colonels Hays and Thompson took their commands and moved into the Sni Hills region east of Independence, with the view of falling upon some detachment or weak point in the absence of the Federal troops engaged in the pursuit of Colonel Cockrell. General Blunt did not know that this large rebel force of about twelve hundred men was left in his rear, and no sooner were his troops out of reach than Hays and Quantrill commenced to make hostile demonstrations in the direction of Kansas City and the Kansas line. To check this apprehended movement, Major Ransom, commanding the post at Kansas City, again despatched Colonel Burris at Fort Leavenworth for assistance. On his arrival, and agreeing upon a plan of movement, Major Ransom, with his battalion of cavalry, marched by land to Independence, while Colonel Burris, with a battalion of infantry and a battery of artillery under Lieutenant Charles S. Bowman, Fourth U. S. Cavalry, were transported by steamboat to a point three miles north of Independence, and landed and marched into town.

No definite information was obtained there of the movements of the enemy, and the next morning Colonel Burris left Independence with his entire command and marched in the direction of Harrisonville, near which place he received information that the enemy were encamped. After marching twelve miles south on the Harrisonville road near the crossing of the Little Blue River, he ascertained that the enemy, reported to be one thousand strong, were near at hand, strongly posted along the cliffs and deep ravines of the Little Blue River. He proceeded cautiously a mile or so, and then came upon and drove in their pickets, capturing one. After some reconnoitring by the cavalry under Major Ransom, approaching darkness determined Colonel Burris to cease operations, and he bivouacked his command at a watering-place near by until three o'clock the next morning, when he marched to the nearest point to the enemy's camp accessible for posting his artillery. Here he formed line of battle and sent Captain Derry with two companies of cavalry to reconnoitre the position of Hays and Quantrill, and, if possible, draw them out into open ground. But they declined to be drawn into an open field, and Colonel Burris, not feeling strong enough to attack them in their chosen position, marched to Hickory Grove, a mile or so west. In marching to this new position, the enemy moved out and attacked his rear. He quickly formed his troops in line of battle on a high piece of ground in the prairie near Hickory Grove, and awaited the enemy. They formed in line about one thousand yards off, and were preparing to advance, when Colonel Burris directed Lieutenant Bowman to open on them with his battery. A few rounds of shot and shell thrown by the guns into their ranks threw them into confusion, and they resumed their march south.

This was the last time that Jackson County was troubled with the guerilla operations of Colonel Upton Hays. He continued his march south from the skirmish at Hickory Grove, and joined Colonel Shelby, in his retreat from the Missouri River, and was with him in Northwestern Arkansas. After some reorganization of their forces, General Hindman placed Colonel Shelby in command of the cavalry brigade, composed of his own regiment and the regiments of Colonels Hays and Coffey. The command then moved from the mouth of Elk Creek, in McDonald County, to Camp Kearney, on Indian Creek, six miles south of Newtonia, reaching the latter place about the 12th of September. While encamped at this place, Colonel Shelby's command attacked a detachment of Missouri cavalry at Newtonia, and drove them about ten miles northeast, and in the engagement Colonel Hays was killed.

CHAPTER XXVI.

BATTLE OF NEWTONIA.

SHORTLY after the return of the troops to Fort Scott and vicinity from the Lone Jack expedition, the Twelfth and Thirteenth Regiments, Wisconsin Infantry, were ordered out of the Department of the Missouri to join divisions of the army operating east of the Mississippi River. There was also some reorganization of the troops operating in Southern Kansas. The Second and Sixth Regiments, Kansas Cavalry, that had taken an active part in the Indian and Lone Jack expeditions, and that had lost a good many horses by being broken down from hard service, went into camp six to eight miles southeast and northeast of Fort Scott, on good grazing ground, to await the filling of the requisitions of their quartermasters for new horses and equipments. At their camp, northeast of Fort Scott, most of the dismounted troopers of the Sixth Kansas Cavalry were remounted upon Government horses. They had, from the organization of the regiment to this time, furnished their own private horses and equipments, for the use and risk of which they received pay from the Government.

In fact, in a few days all the troops operating from Fort Scott were receiving the necessary supplies and equipments for another campaign south. The soldiers were getting inured to the service, and they were chafing to carry their banners into the enemy's territory. The enemy, under Colonels Shelby, Cockrell, and Coffey, who had just been driven from Lone Jack out of Missouri, met large reinforcements, under General Hindman, in Northwestern Arkansas. The three thousand or four thousand recruits brought out of Missouri by Cockrell, Coffey, and Shelby, were organized into regiments, and a cavalry brigade formed, of which Colonel J. O. Shelby was given the command by General Hindman. This cavalry brigade, with Stand Watie's Cherokee regiment, the Choctaw regiments, and the regiments from Texas, constituted a force of upward of seven thousand men. With this force General Hindman commenced to move north early in September for the invasion of Southwest Missouri. Scouting parties from the Indian troops left at Baxter Springs, under Colonels Phillips and Ritchie, were constantly kept out in Southwest Missouri and along the State line as far south as Arkansas, and now and then skirmished with detachments of the rebel cavalry. The Missouri Union militia and other troops operating from Springfield, under General Brown, in scouting expeditions, also met and exchanged shots with some of General Hindman's outposts in Southwest Missouri, near the Arkansas line.

General Blunt was kept advised of the aggressive movements of the enemy, and determined to commence active operations against him at once. On the 1st of September, therefore, after a week's rest and recuperation, the different regiments and batteries of his command at Fort Scott and vicinity took up the line of march for an active campaign in Southwest Missouri and Northwest Arkansas. His command was composed of the following regiments and batteries: The Third Wisconsin Cavalry, the Second Ohio Cavalry, the Second, Sixth, and Ninth Regiments, Kansas Cavalry; the Ninth Wisconsin Infantry, the Tenth Kansas Infantry, Captain Rabb's Second Indiana Battery, Captain Allen's First Kansas Battery, and the three Indian regiments recently organized, and encamped at Baxter Springs and vicinity.

General Salomon, who had been promoted to brigadier-general from the colonelcy of the Ninth Wisconsin Infantry, on the return of the Indian expedition to Kansas, commanded the first brigade, and Colonel William Weer, Tenth Kansas Infantry, commanded the second brigade. After three days' march over rolling prairies, the command went into camp for a week a mile southeast of Carthage, sixty miles southeast of Fort Scott. The camp was pitched only a short distance from the south bank of Spring River, and many of the soldiers enjoyed themselves bathing in the clear running waters of that beautiful stream. In this section the people had raised fair crops of corn, oats, and wheat, and as a consequence the cavalry horses were better supplied with forage than they had been in the earlier part of the summer. Experience had taught officers and soldiers the importance of looking after their horses, and it was now possible to keep them in good condition.

But the bountiful supply of forage obtained for the cavalry horses was generally at the expense of the people, who had worked hard through dangers and difficulties to raise something to subsist upon and to feed to the few head of horses, cattle, and hogs still left to them after being plucked by both parties. Sometimes receipts and vouchers were given the owners by officers of detachments and commands for forage and property taken from them, but in most cases nothing was given to them to show that such seizures had been made. In some cases, on the approach of troops, the owners of farms left their homes, crops, and every thing except a team or so with which to move away with some of their most necessary household goods. Only women and children were usually at home when the army was passing through the country, and when the troops took horses, mules, forage, or cattle from families, the women rarely had the courage or facilities to go to the commanding officer and demand the return of or payment for their property. Now and then, however, sheer necessity compelled the wife or mother, the head of the family at home, to go to the camp and appeal to the commanding officer for the return of an only horse for the children to use to take the corn or wheat to mill, or to stop the taking of the last load of corn from the crib, or the last ham or side of bacon from the smoke-house. The wife and mother whose husband was off in one or the other armies, or widow whose husband had recently been killed in the war, when she thus appealed to be allowed to keep a pittance of her property for the use of her children, sometimes looked the very picture of despair.

While encamped near Carthage Colonel Phillips' Third Indian Regiment joined the main command. He had just made a reconnoissance to Elk Mills on Cowskin River in the southwest part of McDonald County, and skirmished with the enemy until he deemed it advisable to fall back within supporting distance of the other troops. The rebel cavalry followed him as far as Neosho, occasionally firing on his rear-guard. About this time, Colonel Ritchie, commanding the Second Indian Regiment at Baxter Springs, moved about fifteen miles up Spring River and encamped near Shirley's Ford. The families of the soldiers or warriors of this regiment accompanied it in its movements and encamped near it. In the face of the enemy this large refugee camp of twelve hundred to fifteen hundred women and children was an embarrassment to the operations of the Indian troops, and should have been in a place of safety in the rear. The regiment was stationed in an important position—a position which, if held, with proper scouting parties kept out, would prevent detachments of the enemy from passing around the right flank of the brigades of General Salomon and Colonel

Weer, then encamped a few miles south of Carthage. But Colonel Ritchie was continually in trouble with his superior and subordinate officers, came near inciting a mutiny in his portion of the command at Baxter Springs, and through his incompetency neglected to have his cavalry thoroughly reconnoitre the country in his front to keep him informed of the movements of the enemy. He therefore allowed himself to be surprised by the rebels, resulting in some loss and confusion in his command.

About eight o'clock on the morning of the 20th of September, Colonel Ritchie's picket guard was fired upon, and in a few moments after the alarm was given of the presence of the enemy, the women and children and camp followers became almost panic-stricken and crowded into camp for protection. About two hundred Indian soldiers were at once sent forward to the front to check the advance of the enemy, while Major M. B. C. Wright took another detachment and moved around to attack them in the flank. A strong guard having been put around the supply train and the camp, Colonel Ritchie ordered his dismounted Indians that were placed in the centre, and the mounted detachments operating on the flanks, to move forward, which they did with a war-whoop, firing as they advanced. A hot fire was now kept up for an hour or so between the opposing forces, when the Confederates retreated, leaving on the field twenty of their number dead, among them two officers. Colonel Ritchie reported that his command captured one rebel flag, and that the Confederate force was composed of part of Colonel Hawpt's Texan regiment, part of Stand Watie's Cherokee regiment, and Major Tom Livingston's Rangers that were operating in Jasper and Newton counties.

On the Federal side, Colonel Ritchie reported a loss of twelve to twenty men killed, including Captain George Scraper, and nine men wounded. His command slept on the battle-ground that night, but fearing that the enemy might return reinforced to renew the attack, he fell back and marched his command, starting the next morning at sunrise, to Cow Creek, Kansas, the point where his trains and the refugees had already been ordered. Colonel Cloud, who had been sent on a scout through Southern Kansas from Fort Scott with three companies of cavalry, arrived at Colonel Ritchie's camp just one day after the engagement at Shirley's Ford on Spring River.

Colonel Ritchie's conduct in this section was not such as to commend it to the favorable consideration of right-minded men. He ordered or permitted the burning of houses and the destruction of private property along Spring River without the slightest pretext of a military necessity. On the day of the engagement at Shirley's Ford, he ordered or permitted to be shot five citizen prisoners, two at least of whom were unquestionably Union men. And he permitted the plundering and robbing of the families of Union soldiers of Colonel Weer's command. For certain of his actions that could hardly be considered the actions of a sane man, he was placed in arrest and recommended by Colonel Weer for dismissal from the service.

Detachments of cavalry were sent out every day by Colonel Weer to watch the movements of the enemy, but very little information could be obtained of General Hindman's intentions. From the camp near Carthage the Federal troops marched about eight miles southeast in the direction of Sarcoxie, and then turned and marched about forty miles northeast to Turnback in Lawrence County. Very few, if any, of the troops had any idea of the object of this movement, as it was directly away from the enemy, who were at Neosho and Newtonia. It turned out, however, that General Salomon, who had just arrived from Fort Scott with the first brigade, had information that the enemy were preparing to attack Springfield, and that he marched his command to Turnback Creek and Sac River to head them off.

The troops encamped on Turnback only one night, and then faced about and marched to Mount Vernon, where they met Colonel Geiger's Eighth Missouri Cavalry, and parts of Colonels Hall's and King's Fourth and Sixth Regiments Missouri State Militia Cavalry, of General Brown's command. Two or three companies of the State militia had been stationed at that place during the spring and summer for the protection of the Union people who had moved into that section from Newton and Barry counties and from Northwest Arkansas. General Salomon and Colonel Weer, commanding the two brigades of General Blunt's army, halted at Mount Vernon only one day, and then resumed the march to Sarcoxie, eighteen miles west. Here the command encamped about one week, directly in front of the enemy. The main body of General Hindman's army was encamped on Indian Creek, some twenty-five miles southwest, but he had strong outposts at Neosho and Newtonia.

While the two brigades of General Blunt's division and General Brown's brigade were facing the enemy at Sarcoxie, two other divisions of Federal troops were being organized at Springfield and Rolla under Generals Totten and Herron, with the view of marching against the enemy in Southwest Missouri. These three divisions and General Brown's brigade were to be in readiness to support each other in a movement against General Cooper, who had assumed command of the Confederate forces in the absence of General Hindman, by the first of October.

The enemy were also displaying much activity. Colonel Emmet McDonald of the Confederate army, who had lately been appointed Provost-Marshal-General of Missouri, came to Neosho toward the last of September and gathered up all Southern men who were able to bear arms, and put them into companies for temporary service. A good many secessionists from different parts of the State, who had gone to Texas and Arkansas from time to time as the Federal troops occupied every part of Missouri, and who had heard of General Cooper's contemplated invasion, thought it would be a good time to return to their homes, and had done so, or were on the way. They were not, however, generally a class of men who were anxious to fight for their cause. Some of these secessionists, who had gone to Texas that they might be away from the exciting scenes and dangers of the war, had not been very hospitably received by their brethren there, but were taunted for running away from their homes instead of staying and fighting the Federal minions.

So provoked were some of the Missouri secessionists at the conduct of their brethren in Texas that they declared that they would have gladly seen Texas invaded by the Federal army. Some men who went to Texas in 1861, strong secessionists, had their feelings so wounded by the Texans that they came back to Missouri in 1862 staunch friends of the Union, and even became republicans. Those most deeply offended were generally men who were not owners of slave property. It was the prevailing notion that every man from Missouri who did not own slaves, and who was able to bear arms, should be in the Southern army. He might not be good enough to admit into the social circle, but he was considered good enough food for powder.

General Salomon, temporarily in command of Blunt's division encamped at Sarcoxie, sent out reconnoissances every day, and kept himself advised of the enemy's movements. He had no intention, however, of bringing on a general engagement, for there was a tacit understanding with Generals Schofield, Totten, and Brown that no general attack should be made until their troops arrived in supporting distance. There might be policy, too, in acting a little timid, with the view of encouraging the enemy to advance into a more open country than the rugged hills along Indian Creek and Cowskin River.

About the 28th of September, General Cooper moved up from Indian Creek to Newtonia and vicinity with his entire force. The Federal and Confederate forces were now within fourteen miles of each other, with only Shoal Creek between them. General Salomon had not yet heard that General Cooper had moved to Newtonia with his entire force, and on the night of September 29th sent out a reconnoissance under Colonel E. Lynde, of the Ninth Kansas Cavalry, consisting of three companies of his own regiment, two companies of the Sixth Kansas Cavalry, under Captain David Mefford, and a battalion of the Ninth Wisconsin Infantry, under Lieutenant-Colonel Jacobi, to feel the strength of the enemy at Newtonia. This little college town of four or five hundred people was located on a branch in the prairie that flowed off to the north in the direction of Shoal Creek, and on the west and northwest of it, one half to three quarters of a mile off, there was a high rolling ridge of prairie, perhaps seventy-five feet above the town, that extended to Shoal Creek timber. The Sarcoxie road came over the ridge from the northwest, and the Granby and Neosho roads came over the ridge from the west, and these roads entered town from the west side.

Colonel M. H. Ritchie, a prominent Union man of Newtonia, had a farm that joined the town limits on the southwest, south of the Neosho road. His dwelling-house, stone barn, and barn lots were adjoining the town. On the north side of his farm there was a stone fence that extended from his house to a quarter of a mile or upward along the Neosho road. His barn lot, of about two acres, was also enclosed with a stone fence. This lot was west of north of his house. The south-side stone fence of it and the farm fence made a lane fifty to sixty feet wide, and some two hundred yards long.

Early on the morning of September 30th, Colonel Lynde passed over the ridge described to the northwest of town, marching directly towards Newtonia. The enemy plainly saw his command marching over the ridge, but he could see very little of them on account of the shade trees, buildings, and a slight elevation behind which they had their camps pitched. When General Cooper saw the Federal column approaching, he posted his dismounted cavalry behind the stone fences of the barn lot and field described, and sent out six hundred or seven hundred cavalry to meet the Federal advance. He also had his artillery placed in position to open fire upon the Federal troops as soon as they came in range. After a little skirmishing, the rebel cavalry fell back to town through the lane made by the stone fences, pursued by Colonel Lynde's force up to near the west end of this lane. Here the enemy opened upon him with artillery, and the rebel infantry posted behind the stone fences commenced a brisk fire of musketry upon his advancing line. The volleys of this sudden attack from the concealed foe soon threw the Federal force into some disorder, and a retreat was at once sounded. The rebel cavalry at once returned to the attack, and pursued Colonel Lynde vigorously, and flanked him and almost surrounded him several times before reaching the Shoal Creek timber, some two and a half miles northwest of Newtonia.

Up to this point the well-directed volleys of Major Jacobi's infantry had kept the rebel cavalry from crowding on the rear, and Colonel Lynde's cavalry, with their long-range Sharp's carbines, had been able to keep them off at a distance on the flanks. At the edge of the timber the rebel cavalry and Choctaw Indians came charging up on the Federal flanks in overwhelming numbers, and surrounded Colonel Lynde's force. But a volley from his carbines fired right into the rebel line in front opened a gap in it, and he ordered his men to draw sabres and charged through it. The enemy now closed in behind him quickly and cut off Major Jacobi's infantry, nearly all of which, to the number of about 166 men, were captured, killed, and wounded. In this fight nine Federal soldiers were killed and stripped of their clothing by the Confederate Choctaw Indians. In the fight near the end of the land described, four or five Federal soldiers were also killed and wounded. The Confederate cavalry and Indians pursued Colonel Lynde's cavalry about a mile into the timber, and nearly to Shoal Creek, and then they returned to Newtonia. The troops at Sarcoxie heard the artillery firing in the direction of Newtonia in the morning, and fearing that Colonel Lynde had met a larger force of the enemy than was anticipated, General Salomon and Colonel Weer took all the companies of the Sixth and Ninth Regiments Kansas Cavalry that were in camp, two companies of the Third Wisconsin Cavalry, two companies of the Second Ohio Cavalry under Captain Smith, nearly all of Colonel Phillips' Third Indian Regiment, the Tenth Kansas Infantry, two companies of the Ninth Wisconsin Infantry, Captain Allen's First Kansas Battery, and Rabb's Second Indiana Battery, and started to the relief of Colonel Lynde's force.

Major Blair's Second Kansas Battery that had joined the command at Sarcoxie, part of the Ninth Wisconsin Infantry, and three or four companies from other regiments, were left to guard the camp and trains. General Salomon's advance under Colonel Judson of the Sixth Kansas Cavalry, met Colonel Lynde's force just north of Shoal Creek, and saw a number of the men bloody from the wounds they had received in the fight just ended. After briefly ascertaining from Colonel Lynde the situation as nearly as possible, the march was resumed, but with caution, as it was not known but that the enemy had massed their whole force in the dense woods south of Shoal Creek. Presently the spot was reached where the soldiers of the Ninth Wisconsin had been killed and stripped of their clothing on the southeast side of a little field, and three or four rail pens were hastily built and the dead soldiers put into them to keep the hogs that had already come on to the ground from mutilating their bodies. Brave soldiers who have a proper sense of honor would not thus treat their fallen foe.

In a few hours after Colonel Judson, commanding the advance, passed the scene of the recent fight, General Salomon's command was marching to positions on the ridge west and northwest of Newtonia. From these heights the Federal troops could discern the movements of the enemy in the western part of town. It was now between one and two o'clock when General Salomon and Colonel Weer commenced directing the movements of the troops on the field. The Sixth Kansas Cavalry, under Colonel Jewell, was ordered to the right along the ridge overlooking town, and Colonel Phillips, with his Third Indian Regiment, was ordered to the left, where part of his command was dismounted, and fought the enemy on foot along the branch north of town. The batteries took up positions along the ridge northwest of town, supported by the infantry a short distance in the rear, but perhaps out of sight of the enemy. As soon as the troops came in sight of town, Colonel Weer, through his field-glasses, noticed a considerable force of the enemy around Ritchie's stone barn, and at once directed Captain Allen to open fire upon them with shells from his long-range rifled guns. The guns from their elevation held up well, as could be seen and heard when the percussion shells from them flew to the marks at which directed and exploded. The first round from the Federal batteries soon brought a reply from the rebel batteries that had been behind the stone barn. As the position of each of their guns could now be seen every time it was fired, from the smoke arising from it, Captain Allen directed the guns of his battery to play upon them, and in a short time killed all the rebel battery horses, and killed and wounded several rebel artillerymen.

After the artillery duel had lasted for some time, General Cooper sent out parts of two Texas cavalry regiments to the west on the Neosho road, as if intending to flank the Federal position. As soon as the enemy emerged from the lane made by the stone fences described, they came into line and marched over the open prairie in fine order, until they reached the summit of a low ridge, when they came in plain view of the Federal cavalry under Colonel Jewell, who was marching in line directly toward them. In a few moments the eyes of officers and troops from Colonel Weer's position, and from the position of the enemy in town, were anxiously directed to the movements of the two hostile forces approaching each other. Presently they had approached within little over a hundred yards of each other, when the hostile forces opened fire. After a round from his Sharp's carbines, Colonel Jewell ordered his men to draw sabres and charge, and away they flew over the prairie, raising a cloud of dust in their rear. When the Confederates saw the Federal sabres flashing in the sunlight, and the dust arising from the horses' feet of the advancing foe, they instantly wheeled about and galloped back to town. Colonel Jewell pursued them to within about two hundred yards of the stone fence, behind which General Cooper had posted several thousand dismounted cavalry, with the hope of again surprising the federal forces.

The moment the rebel cavalry had reached low ground near town, the rebel battery near the stone barn was turned upon Colonel Jewell's force, which shortly returned to the high ridge west of town, having had several men wounded and two or three horses of his command killed by cannon-shot.

While these movements were going on on the Federal right, Colonel Phillips, with his Indian troops, was hotly engaged with the enemy on the Federal left. His men got into the plum thickets and brush along the branch that runs north from Newtonia, and behind the rail fences of a field north of town, and by sharp-shooting drove the enemy into town. The hardest fighting of the afternoon was along this branch, and Captain William Webber and one or two Indian soldiers were killed and some sixteen wounded. The batteries of both sides kept up the cannonade until sundown, when the Federal troops commenced to withdraw from the field in the direction of Sarcoxie. No sooner had the Federal skirmishers been called in and the retreat commenced, than the Confederate cavalry moved out in pursuit, as if the morning scene were to be re-enacted. When the Federal troops reached the timber northwest of Newtonia, the rebel cavalry literally covered a ridge in the prairie that ran nearly east and west about a quarter of a mile south of the timber. A few shots were exchanged between the Federal rear-guard flankers and the rebel advance.

At the edge of the timber just as the twilight was fading away, General Salomon's command met some two thousand Missouri troops and Captain Murphy's battery First Missouri Artillery, under Colonel George H. Hall, commanding a brigade of General Brown's command, who had heard the artillery firing during the day, and who had hastily marched to the scene to join in the fight. Captain Murphy's battery was carefully masked behind thickly leaved clumps of small black-jack and post oak near the prairie, and was supported by the fresh troops and by part of the troops that had been withdrawn from the field. The enemy were marching up rapidly in line as if they felt certain that they were following a demoralized foe. As it was now getting dark the advancing Confederates could not see the Federal troops in the timber, but the Federal troops could easily see the Confederates in the open prairie. The Confederate cavalry therefore steadily advanced to within a hundred or so yards of the Federal batteries, when suddenly they belched forth a stream of grape and canister shot and shell that fairly made the earth tremble. Round after round of canister was fired by Captain Murphy's six guns into the ranks of the enemy, knocking horses and riders into confused heaps upon the prairie, and throwing their lines into wild confusion. General Cooper's artillery followed his cavalry closely, and from the ridge in the prairie shelled the Federal position in the woods for a short time. The terrific shock of the Federal batteries was more than the Confederate cavalry could stand, and in a few moments they broke and were sent flying back over the prairie in the direction of Newtonia, leaving their killed and wounded on the field.

The sight of bursting shells and screaming shot at night was more impressive than dangerous. When the splinters and limbs of trees and pieces of shell are falling thick around, there is a kind of grandeur in such a sight that is more pleasant to contemplate than to witness. Most of General Salomon's command had exhausted the water in their canteens by the middle of the afternoon, and as soon as the enemy had left the field, gladly resumed the march to Shoal Creek to quench their thirst. All the Federal troops fell back that night to the north side of Shoal Creek and to Sarcoxie, bringing along the wounded in ambulances. A good many of the troops who were fatigued by the day's operations, bivouacked on the open prairie north of Shoal Creek that night, and were drenched by rain before morning. Early on the morning of October 1st the Federal troops were all in camp at Sarcoxie, not demoralized, but confident of success when the attack should be renewed in a few days.

On October 2d General Blunt arrived from Fort Scott and took command of his division, and at once commenced preparations to move against the enemy. General Totten's division had marched from Springfield, and were now in the western parts of Barry and Lawrence counties, not more than twenty miles off.

General Schofield, who had arrived, met Generals Blunt

and Totten, commanding the two divisions, and they agreed upon a plan of movement to be made against the enemy on the morning of October 4th. It was thought that General Cooper would accept battle, as he seemed to think his position a strong one on account of the shelter the stone fences in and near town would afford his troops in the event of an assault by the Federal soldiers. In the movement against the enemy on the 4th of October, General Schofield commanded the combined Federal forces, but General Blunt commanded the right wing, and marched over the road that his troops had marched over on the 30th of September, and took up his position on the ridge northwest of Newtonia. General Totten, commanding the left wing and centre, marched to positions north and east of town.

A brisk cannonade was opened upon the enemy for half an hour or upward from the batteries of the three divisions, when at a signal the troops of these divisions unfurled their flags, sounded the march from their bugles, and moved forward to battle, marching in columns of companies and squadrons. As the troops came near town, rail fences were thrown down where they were in the way, and the infantry came into line with the cavalry marching on the flanks. As soon as the rebel pickets and outposts ran in and announced the Federal advance, General Cooper posted his troops behind the stone fences and other advantageous positions. He then watched the advancing columns as they came steadily on, until he became satisfied that they were going to meet him, man to man, on ground of his own choosing, and then he ordered a retreat, after firing a few scattering shots from his small-arms. When the Federal commanders saw that the enemy were abandoning the town without a fight, they ordered the cavalry forward to attack their rear columns, and a running fight was kept up nearly all day without any important result. General Cooper retreated down Indian Creek until he struck the

Pineville and Neosho road, and then he passed through Pineville, and from thence into Northwest Arkansas. The Federal cavalry pursued him a few miles south of Pineville, and then returned to the main command that had marched to Indian Creek and gone into camp some twelve miles southwest of Newtonia.

When the Federal troops passed through Newtonia they saw on every hand the effects of the Federal artillery, on September 30th and on the morning of October 4th. There were dead horses all through town, torn by shells, and there were cannon-ball holes through Colonel Ritchie's house and barn, through the college buildings, and through other buildings in town. In one spot there were six artillery horses that had been killed by an exploding shell from the Federal guns. The casualties on the Confederate side, as reported by General Cooper, were seventy-five men killed and wounded. On the Federal side there were fifteen men killed and thirty-two wounded in the operations of September 30th. In the movement on the morning of October 4th the Federal forces sustained no loss.

CHAPTER XXVII.

BATTLE OF FORT WAYNE, CHEROKEE NATION.

THE two divisions of Federal troops that encamped on Indian Creek, south of Newtonia, after driving the enemy from there, were now called the Army of the Frontier. General Schofield was the senior officer, and in command. This army had in a few hours changed the offensive movements of the enemy into a demoralized retreat. General Cooper's Choctaw Indians, who had been lauded for their bravery in firing upon Colonel Lynde's force from behind the stone walls in the engagements at Newtonia, and for their swiftness in the pursuit of the retreating Federal detachment, were now vying with each other in the race that had for its goal their escape from the Federal cavalry. No thought of prizes gained by stripping the clothing from the Federal dead slackened the pace of their savage feet.

The belligerent tone of the Southern sympathizers of the non-combatant classes had changed from confident and expressive hope to silent and sullen disappointment. Very few people had the means of looking over the field of operations of the contending forces, except from their own narrow standpoint, and were therefore easily carried away by a feeble tide of success of their party. The news they read or heard of army operations was nearly always from a biased source.

After the trains had arrived, and after encamping on Indian Creek three days of rainy weather, during which time the troops were paid off, the Army of the Frontier marched about twenty-five miles southeast to Keetesville, in the southwest corner of Barry County. This section is high and comparatively level, being the watershed of the waters flowing east into White River, and west and northwest into Grand River. There were good farms in the neighborhood that afforded forage for the cavalry horses that were obliged to be foraged off the country. Every day detachments of cavalry were sent out to the south and southwest to reconnoitre the country, and from the information they obtained it appeared that the enemy were displaying very little activity except in efforts to secure recruits by conscription. Colonel Brooks was at the head of the Confederate recruiting service in Northwestern Arkansas, and had gathered up nearly a regiment of conscripts about Fayetteville and Elm Springs.

The Confederate authorities were sending out over the country detachments of half a dozen to a dozen or more soldiers to arrest and bring into camp all men not under or over the military age, who were thought to be able to bear arms, and who did not own over a certain number of slaves, and put them into the service. Men suspected of sympathizing with the Union cause were generally among the first to be thus arrested and brought in, whether they were of the proper military age and soundness, or not. From the statements of Unionists who escaped to the Federal army, these Confederate recruiting parties frequently played the part of organized bands of thieves. In many instances they arrested men and afterward arranged to let them get away by leaving their horses and saddles in their possession. A man who escaped under such circumstances would not likely venture into the camp of the recruiting squad to claim his property, for fear of worse treatment befalling him. But this kind of conduct of the Confederate recruiting officers had an effect beneficial to the Union cause. It drove a good many men, who did not wish to serve in the Confederate army, into the Union lines, where they enlisted into companies of the First Arkansas Union Cavalry, that were being organized at this time.

The two divisions of the Army of the Frontier, after encamping around Keetesville several days, struck tents and marched into Arkansas about fifteen miles south, and went into camp, for upwards of a week, on Pea Ridge battle-ground. Here the third division, under Brigadier-General F. J. Herron, came up. The divisions of Generals Herron and Totten formed the left wing of the army, and extended their operations to the east and southeast, while General Blunt's division formed the right wing, and extended its operations to the west and southwest. The signs of the great battle fought in March, between the Federal forces under General Curtis and the Confederate forces under Generals Van Dorn, Price, and McCulloch, were still visible on every hand, and many of the soldiers availed themselves of the opportunity of going over the field which had recently been the scene of blood and strife, for the purpose of picking up something, such as a piece of shell, or bullet, or buckle, as a souvenir to be sent north to relatives or friends.

While the army was encamped at Pea Ridge, a detachment of cavalry from General Herron's division, which had been sent out in the direction of Huntsville on a reconnoissance, had a brisk skirmish with a force of several hundred rebel cavalry, which resulted in the wounding of two or three soldiers on each side. The enemy retreated, followed some distance by the Federal cavalry. General Blunt's cavalry were also busy in scouting the country off to the south and west.

On the 18th of October part of the Second Kansas Cavalry, under command of Lieutenant-Colonel O. A. Bassett, were sent forward on the Fayetteville road and struck a detachment of some two hundred rebel cavalry about two o'clock in the afternoon, about four miles north of Cross Hollow. After a light skirmish the enemy fell back, and were pursued by Colonel Bassett to Cross Hollow. At this place a sharp skirmish ensued, resulting in the complete rout of the enemy. The Federal cavalry encamped on the field for the night, and at daylight next morning marched to Elm Springs, the point of destination. From this point the detachment returned and rejoined the main command at Pea Ridge late in the afternoon of the 20th.

When the troops got into camp they found that the army was under marching orders. The Second Kansas Cavalry, under Colonel Bassett, were assigned to the advance, and at six o'clock the regiment struck tents and marched toward Bentonville that night, arriving there about eight o'clock on the morning of the 21st. The regiment halted in an open space in the town limits, fed their stock, and rested during the day, having been several days and nights without sleep and rest. Late in the afternoon the main command arrived, and halted long enough to allow the troops to get supper and feed their stock. Owing to some delay in filling requisitions for rations for some of the regiments of Colonel Weer's brigade, the last of the troops did not leave camp at Pea Ridge until about two o'clock on the morning of the 21st. All the troops, therefore, except the Second Kansas Cavalry, were in line ready to march, or on the march, all the night of the 20th and nearly all day of the 21st.

About six o'clock on the evening of the 21st, the army resumed the march, as was generally understood, to Maysville, a distance of about twenty-five miles nearly due west, where it was reported by the scouts that General Cooper was encamped with a large force of Confederate troops. General Blunt determined to make the march during the night and strike the enemy by daylight. He placed Colonel Bassett, with the Second Kansas Cavalry, in advance, and with his staff marched with Colonel Cloud at the head of the column all night. The Second Kansas having rested at Bentonville during the day, resumed the march with greater freshness and buoyancy perhaps than any of the other troops. A good many of the officers and soldiers who had marched all day and part of the previous night from Pea Ridge, and rested only an hour or so at Bentonville, craved sleep and rest before midnight. The Sixth Kansas Cavalry, under Colonels Judson and Jewell, followed the Second Kansas. Then came parts of the Third Wisconsin Cavalry and the Ninth Kansas Cavalry under Colonel Lynde, followed closely by the artillery and infantry. The cavalry had marched off so briskly that at midnight there was quite an interval between them and the infantry. General Blunt, therefore, ordered the cavalry to halt for an hour to allow the infantry and artillery to close up. The officers and soldiers dismounted, and, with few exceptions, they were soon oppressed with sleep. As the advance infantry came up, they, too, halted to allow the troops in the rear to close up all the gaps. The infantry were perhaps more fatigued than the cavalry, and, naturally enough, when a halt of a few moments was made, threw themselves down upon the ground by the roadside for a short nap. Most of the troops, therefore, got nearly an hour's rest at an hour of the night when sleep sits heaviest on the eyelids. At one o'clock the march was resumed on the Maysville road, General Blunt and staff still marching at the head of the column.

Thinking that the enemy might have pickets far out on the road he was marching on, and as he did not wish to give them warning of his approach, the General directed that the march be resumed without sounding the bugles. Captain S. J. Crawford, who commanded a battalion of the Second Kansas Cavalry, and who was riding at the head of the column with General Blunt and Colonel Cloud, took the precaution to send an orderly back to each of the commanding officers of companies of his regiment, with instructions to see to it that every man be waked and take his proper place in his company. After marching some three hours, and having arrived at about midway of a prairie four miles east of Maysville, General Blunt and his advance saw directly in his front, perhaps a half-mile off to the farther edge of the prairie, the camp-fires of the Confederate pickets. He at once ordered a halt, so as to allow the command to close up and prepare for action. He also directed the field-officer of the day, Major Fisk, of the Second Kansas Cavalry, to see that the troops were in their proper positions.

That officer rode back to the rear of his regiment and beyond, and seeing no other troops in sight returned and reported the fact to General Blunt. The General was perplexed at the situation in which he found himself. The earliest rays of the light of day were beginning to streak the east. The enemy were near at hand. He was uncertain whether the remainder of the army had taken the wrong road in the darkness of the night, or were yet at the point where he had halted at midnight. The order to resume the march at one o'clock was given only to the commanding officer of the Second Kansas Cavalry, and as this regiment moved out noiselessly in the darkness, some time elapsed, perhaps half an hour, before Colonel Jewell, of the Sixth Kansas Cavalry, noticed that the troops in advance of him had marched away. It was now plain that General Blunt had neglected to send an officer or aid back to see that the troops were all moving at the same time. The moment that Colonel Jewell found that the Second Kansas were gone he pushed on after them, his squadrons gradually quickening their pace until the horses struck a lively trot, which was kept up until the Colonel caught sight of the rearmost squadron of the Second Kansas as they passed into the timber from the western edge of the prairie east of Maysville.

After discussing the situation a few moments with his

officers where he halted on the prairie, General Blunt became satisfied that the rebel pickets directly in his front would at once give the alarm of his approach. He therefore directed Major Fisk, the officer of the day, to find and bring up the remainder of the army with as little delay as possible. He then took the Second Kansas Cavalry and pushed forward to capture or drive in the rebel pickets, intending to force the enemy into line and to hold them until the rest of his troops could reach the field. He dashed forward and put the first picket to flight, without firing a shot, and then moved on rapidly toward the Confederate camp.

In passing through Maysville, just at sunrise, he met and captured a negro servant of a rebel officer, coming in from the rebel camp, and who, after being questioned by the General, told in a few words where and how the enemy were encamped, and something of the roads and the general formation of the country. He had missed the rebel pickets, who, in their flight to camp, had taken a different road from the one on which he was coming to town. He was a little frightened at first, but was told that he need have no fear, that he was now a *free man*. His countenance now brightened, and he was willing enough to give any information in his possession. Being well mounted on a rebel officer's horse, he was *persuaded* to accompany the General and his command, and to point out the way to the rebel camp.

The distance from Maysville to the camp was about four miles, mostly over a smooth prairie, with here and there small groves of timber on each side of the road. Soon after leaving Maysville, General Blunt and Captain Crawford, being in advance, came in full view of a small detachment of rebel cavalry. Orders were given for the Second Kansas Cavalry, the only troops yet in sight, to move forward at a brisk trot, and at the same time the General and Captain Crawford put spurs to their horses and pursued the rebel detachment to a distance that came near putting an end to their military career. They were accompanied by Sergeant Cooper, three soldiers of the General's body-guard, and the contraband or colored man picked up near Maysville. The chase was across the prairie southwest of Maysville in the direction of the main body of the enemy, which had by this time moved out and was forming in line to receive the Federal troops. General Blunt and Captain Crawford, being mounted on fleet horses, were gaining rapidly on the rebel detachment when, suddenly coming to a sharp curve in the road, they found themselves face to face with the enemy's grand guard of perhaps not less than eighty men, mounted and in line. The General and Captain Crawford checked their horses suddenly, but Sergeant Cooper's horse could not be stopped, and carried him right through to the Confederate line, and he was captured. This left General Blunt, Captain Crawford, three soldiers, and the unarmed colored man facing about eighty rebel soldiers not more than two hundred yards distant—the Second Kansas not yet having come in sight.

The opposing parties eyed each other intently for a moment, as if undecided as to the next movement, and then one of the rebel officers ordered a charge, and at the same instant one of his men fired a shot which passed directly over the heads of General Blunt and his party. Captain Crawford, who was carrying his Colt's army revolver in his hand, immediately brought it in line with his eye and fired two shots into the rebel guard, which seemed to disconcert the rebel officer who had just ordered the charge, for the charge was not made, and the two foes sat on their horses facing each other until the Second Kansas Cavalry came in view, when the rebels broke into columns and moved off in quick time in the direction of their camp.

The reckless daring of General Blunt and Captain Crawford had got them into the scrape, and stubborn impudence brought them safely out of it. As soon as the Second Kansas Cavalry arrived, General Blunt directed Captain Crawford to take a battalion of five companies and move through the timber directly toward the enemy's camp, which was east of the lower end of the prairie on which the battle was subsequently fought. Having now directed this movement, the General took the balance of the regiment and two howitzers and moved rapidly forward, following the route taken by the pickets and grand guard in their flight.

On reaching the lower end of the prairie some four miles southwest of Maysville, the General found the whole rebel forces, about three thousand strong, with four pieces of artillery, in line. The enemy had formed with their backs resting against the timber and both flanks protected by the timber. Their battery was stationed on an elevated piece of ground near their centre. As soon as General Blunt ascertained their position he despatched an order to Captain Crawford to rejoin him at once, and immediately the five companies and howitzers he had taken with him were posted to the best advantage, and then he opened the battle. He had stationed one company and the howitzers in front of the enemy's left; two companies on the right, one company on the left centre, and one company on the right centre, leaving a wide gap in his own centre directly in front of the enemy's battery. Of course five companies and two howitzers could not very well cover the front of the large force of the enemy.

On receipt of General Blunt's order, Captain Crawford moved to his assistance as rapidly as possible, and reached the field about fifteen minutes after the firing commenced. On approaching the field at a swift gallop, and when within a half-mile of the centre of the Federal line, the enemy turned their artillery upon Captain Crawford's battalion. As he dashed up he was met with an order from General Blunt to dismount his men and form in the centre fronting the rebel battery. Between the Captain's battalion and the battery there were two rail fences. He dismounted his men and moved them forward a distance of about two hundred yards from the enemy's line, and immediately opened fire upon it with carbines.

The rebels replied with volleys of musketry, and at the same time kept up an incessant fire at his battalion with their artillery. At first the enemy used shell, which passed over the heads of Captain Crawford's command, but finally they brought their guns down to the proper range and began to use them with telling effect. Captain Crawford soon discovered that he could not hold his position under a heavy fire of musketry and a raking fire of artillery at the same time. He became convinced that there was but one of two things to do—either to charge the rebel battery or fall back. To fall back he saw was certain defeat of the Federal force then engaged, for the main part of the army had not yet made its appearance. Glancing at the situation, he saw that he had nothing to fall back on except the open prairie. He therefore determined to charge the enemy and break their line and take their artillery or lose what he had. General Blunt was too far away to communicate with at such a critical moment, and he stated to Captain A. P. Russell of his battalion what he was going to do. Captain Russell seconded the movement, and then Captain Crawford ordered his battalion forward with instructions to keep up a continuous firing as they advanced. On reaching the fence between the two lines, he ordered his men to load and cap their carbines. Then he ordered them to cross the fence and charge the battery. As the men crossed the fence they received a galling fire from the rebel small-arms, and also from their artillery, but the firing from both soon slackened. As soon as his men crossed the fence they poured one volley into the battery and brought down horses enough to hold the limbers and caissons, and at the same time drove the men from the guns. A second volley as his men advanced, then within fifty yards of their guns, broke their line of infantry. Captain Crawford then advanced until he passed the battery and drove the rebel troops from the field. As he passed the battery he ordered Captain Hopkins, who had been an artillery officer in another field of service, to turn the guns on the enemy. That officer, however, soon reported that he could not do so for want of fuse. Captain Crawford then directed Lieutenant H. L. Moore, commanding a company of his battalion, to take part of his men and run the guns to the rear. As he did this he met the Second Indiana Battery, under Captain Rabb, coming up at full gallop. Captain Rabb, not having been informed what had just taken place, called General Blunt's attention to the fact that the enemy were moving their guns forward into position. The General ordered him to go into battery and open upon them, not knowing up to this time that Captain Crawford had captured the battery. Before he went into battery, however, one of Captain Crawford's men reached him and General Blunt, and informed them what had happened. Captain Rabb then quickly moved forward to that part of the field where Captain Crawford was still holding the line, and opened fire upon the enemy, which had by this time been driven into the dense woods to the south and west.

In the meantime the Sixth Kansas Cavalry and other regiments had arrived and were skirmishing with and driving the enemy out of the woods on the extreme right of the Federal line. The Federal attack was so vigorous at every point that the rebels were in less than half an hour driven from their camp and obliged to retreat in the utmost confusion, leaving their artillery and part of their camp equipage on the field.

After the battle was over the bravery displayed by Captain Crawford and his comrades was the theme of universal commendation among the officers and soldiers of the army. As soon as he found himself fully in possession of the field, General Blunt sent part of his cavalry in pursuit of General Cooper's demoralized and retreating forces; but the country south of Maysville soon became so broken and hilly that nothing further could be accomplished beyond picking up a few rebel stragglers and breaking up the rebel command into small detachments. It was stated by prisoners captured a week after the engagement, that General Cooper and his Choctaw Indians did not stop running from the battle-field of Fort Wayne until they got to the Arkansas River, and that they crossed the river as quickly as possible, by fording it.

The casualties on the Federal side were five men killed and five wounded. General Cooper reported a loss of six killed, thirty wounded, and twenty-six missing. He had been ordered by General Rains to move north immediately, invade Kansas, and attack Fort Scott, and was to have marched the morning he was attacked by General Blunt. Had General Blunt's command delayed movement for another day, the Confederate force would have got so much the start that they could not have been overtaken before penetrating Kansas, and perhaps not before reaching Fort Scott. This brilliant movement of General Blunt cleared the Indian Territory north of the Arkansas River of the enemy again, and enabled many of the loyal Cherokees to return to their homes.

CHAPTER XXVIII.

OPERATIONS IN NORTHWESTERN ARKANSAS.

THE complete rout and destruction of organization of Cooper's command at Old Fort Wayne left the right flank of the Army of the Frontier free from danger of being turned, and saved Kansas from the contemplated invasion of the Southern forces that were to advance up through the Indian Territory. Nearly all the Confederate leaders operating in the Southwest had threatened to invade and lay waste Kansas, and the immense amount of army supplies stored at Fort Scott afforded an additional incentive for the contemplated invasion. But now that the foe had been driven in a demoralized condition to the south side of the Arkansas River, the people of Southern Kansas might well feel secure, and the loyal Indians could return to their homes, and, scattering over the country, would give notice should detachments of the enemy attempt to move north

General Blunt remained in camp, with the first division, at Fort Wayne until the 29th of October, awaiting the arrival of his supply train from Fort Scott. His command was out of rations, and he could not depend upon the country to furnish all that he required. He sent out detachments to take charge of the mills for about ten miles around, and gathered up wheat in the country, and had it ground, and obtained sufficient flour to supply his troops until his trains arrived. On the 30th he moved his command, *via* Maysville, about ten miles east on the Bentonville road, where the supply train was met, and full rations for ten days issued to the troops.

The night that General Blunt marched from Pea Ridge to attack Cooper near Maysville, General Schofield took the second and third divisions of the Army of the Frontier, also encamped at Pea Ridge, and marched in the direction of Huntsville in pursuit of the Confederate forces under General Rains. After a hard day and nights march, the advance of General Herron's division on the morning of the 22d drove Rains' rear-guard from Huntsville. General Schofield ascertained that the enemy were retreating across the Boston Mountains to the Arkansas Valley, and as he had supplied his troops with only five days' rations, he deemed further pursuit impracticable. On their return, General Totten's second division was posted at Osage Springs, and General Herron's third Division at Cross Hollows, twelve miles south of Pea Ridge, to meet a possible movement of the enemy from the direction of Fayetteville and Fort Smith.

The troops had been in camp hardly three days when General Schofield received reliable information that Major-General Hindman, the commanding-general of all the Confederate troops in Northern Arkansas, was with the force that retreated through Huntsville on the 22d, and that he had subsequently been to Fayetteville with some three thousand cavalry, which were still north of the mountains, on White River, about eight miles east of Fayetteville. General Schofield determined to attack this force of the enemy, if they were inclined to fight. He directed General Herron to take the available cavalry of his division and cross the White River Mountains and attack the enemy in the rear. And General Totten was directed to take the available cavalry of his division and a battery of artillery, and move forward *via* Fayetteville and attack the enemy in front. The rest of his division was ordered to march to Fayetteville to support him if necessary.

General Schofield accompanied the column under General Totten. Both columns made a night march. General Herron, with the First Iowa and Seventh Missouri Cavalry, found the enemy, under Colonel J. L. Cravens, who had recently superseded General Rains, about three thousand strong at daylight on the morning of October 28th, some six miles east of Fayetteville, and at once commenced a vigorous attack. After skirmishing and fighting for an hour the Confederate force was routed, with the loss of all their camp equipage. General Marmaduke, commanding the Confederate cavalry division, was encamped about five miles in the rear of Colonel Cravens' advance cavalry brigade, on the Fayetteville and Frog Bayou road, and General Hindman, commanding all the Confederate troops in the district, was encamped near at hand with his infantry and artillery. When Colonel Cravens' men came rushing back in the utmost confusion and reported the Federal troops advancing, General Marmaduke ordered his men into line, and notified General Hindman of the situation.

Feeling that he was not strong enough to successfully resist the probable Federal attack, General Hindman retired towards the Arkansas River on the Fayetteville and Ozark road, and directed General Marmaduke to march with his cavalry division around south of the mountains and take up a position in the Boston Mountains, between Van Buren and Fayetteville, so as to cover Fort Smith and Van Buren. His position east of Fayetteville left Van Buren and Fort Smith entirely unprotected. General Totten's column did not arrive in time to participate in the attack on Colonel Cravens' camp, and as General Schofield did not know at that time that Generals Hindman and Marmaduke were so near at hand with a large force of infantry, cavalry, and artillery, he soon gave up the pursuit of Cravens, and returned to Fayetteville. The expedition of General Schofield had the effect of driving Generals Hindman and Marmaduke south of the Boston Mountains into the Arkansas Valley, and of giving the Union men of Northwestern Arkansas an opportunity of coming into the Federal lines for protection, and for the purpose of organizing for self-defence. Having accomplished all that was then practicable, he returned with the troops of Generals Totten's and Herron's divisions, and took up positions again at Osage Springs and Cross Hollows on the 30th of October.

On the morning of the 3d of November, General Blunt marched the first division from the camp on the Bentonville and Maysville road to a position on Prairie Creek, about five miles southwest of Bentonville. The three divisions of the Army of the Frontier, having now driven the Confederate forces out of Northwestern Arkansas, and out of the Indian Territory north of the Arkansas River, were again encamped within eight to ten miles of each other, ready for another forward movement, if military operations in the eastern part of the State were far enough advanced to make such movement advantageous.

General Curtis, the department commander at St. Louis, having been kept advised of the successful operations of these divisions, and believing that General Blunt, with his division, could hold Northwestern Arkansas and the Indian Territory, directed General Schofield to order Generals Totten's and Herron's divisions back in the direction of Springfield, with the view of aiding General Steele's movement in the direction of Little Rock, and covering Springfield, which was thought to be threatened by a large Confederate force under General Parsons at Yellville, Arkansas, about eighty miles south of Springfield. Generals Totten and Herron marched immediately with their divisions to Crane Creek, and from thence to the neighborhood of Ozark, about twenty-five miles south of Springfield. But when they arrived near Ozark, the danger of attack on Springfield from the direction of Yellville had passed, for General Parsons, commanding the Confederate forces in that section, had been ordered by Hindman to join him near Van Buren with all his available troops as early as practicable, and was then on the march to that place.

In the meantime, the scouts and spies which General Blunt had sent to Fort Smith and into the Arkansas Valley had returned, and reported that General Hindman was concentrating all his available forces in the vicinity of Fort Smith and Van Buren, and was making extensive preparations to march north and invade Southwest Missouri with an army of twenty-five thousand men. General Blunt also received information that General Marmaduke's Confederate cavalry division, composed mainly of Missouri troops, had crossed the Boston Mountains and were encamped at Cane Hill and Rhea's Mills, and engaged in collecting flour and provisions for the Confederate forces. General Hindman was informed by his spies of the retrograde movement of General Schofield's two divisions, and thought that the time had come when he should march across the mountains with his whole force and attack General Blunt's division of Kansas troops and Indians, and if successful in defeating him, march into Missouri and call his corps the Army of Missouri. General Blunt charged Colonel Phillips, commanding the Indian brigade, with guarding his right flank as far west as Grand River, and used his regular cavalry in making reconnoissances directly in front. On the 12th he advanced ten miles southwest to Lindsay's Prairie on the Line road near Flint Creek, where it was reported forage was more plentiful. He would be in a better position to watch the movements of the enemy, and to beard them with strong reconnoissances.

The opposing forces were now scarcely twenty-five miles apart. General Marmaduke was reported to have six thousand men and six pieces of artillery. General Blunt advised General Schofield at Springfield, and General Schofield advised General Curtis, commanding the department at St. Louis, of General Hindman's extensive preparations to march north from Van Buren for the invasion of Missouri. General Curtis therefore directed General Schofield to order Generals Totten's and Herron's second and third divisions, then encamped eight miles east of Ozark, Missouri, to march at once to reinforce General Blunt. For several weeks after Cooper's force was broken up at Maysville, and the Southern troops were driven from Northwestern Arkansas, Generals Curtis and Schofield could not obtain reliable information in regard to General Hindman's further plan of operations; whether he intended to take most of his forces from Western Arkansas to operate against the Federal forces under General Steele in the northeast part of the State, or whether he meditated another movement into Northwestern Arkansas and the invasion of Southwest Missouri. His intentions were now developed, but his preparations for movement were incomplete. His conscript regiments were not armed and had received no clothing whatever.

General Blunt determined to attack General Marmaduke's force at Cane Hill before General Hindman could arrive with his other divisions, and made preparations to move on the morning of the 17th of November. But before the Federal troops marched from camp, a reconnoitring party, which had been sent to the front under Colonel Jewell, Sixth Kansas Cavalry, returned and reported to General Blunt that the Confederate forces had retreated from Cane Hill across the mountains in the direction of Van Buren, their baggage having been sent back on the night of the 14th. General Blunt advised Schofield of the retreat of the Southern forces south from Cane Hill, and the divisions of Generals Totten and Herron were halted at Crane Creek, thirty miles southwest of Springfield, to await further orders.

The retreat of the enemy, however, did not cause General Blunt to relax his vigilance or aggressiveness. Having received information that Stand Watie had crossed to the north side of the Arkansas River, between Fort Gibson and Fort Smith, with a force of rebel Indians, the General sent Colonel Phillips, with a detachment of the Federal Indian Brigade, to chastise him or give him no rest until his force was driven back south of the Arkansas River. That the country might be made to subsist his troops as far as practicable, General Blunt sent out detachments under officers to take charge of the mills of the section in which he was encamped, to purchase wheat from the Union citizens and take it from the disloyal, and manufacture flour sufficient to supply his command. Other articles of subsistence supplies were obtained in that section in sufficient quantities to supply the Federal troops for several weeks. To consume such supplies as could be obtained in that region would not only prevent the Confederate forces from wintering there in the event of the Federal army being obliged to fall back, but it would lessen materially the amount of transportation required to haul supplies from Fort Leavenworth, a distance of two hundred and fifty miles.

While General Blunt thus maintained his position southwest of Bentonville, and kept the enemy from getting a footing north of the Boston Mountains, his left flank and rear was threatened by a Confederate force of about one thousand men at Yellville, some seventy-five miles east. Lieutenant-Colonel A. W. Bishop was stationed with his regiment, the First Arkansas Union Cavalry, at Elkhorn Tavern, a telegraph station at the terminus of the telegraph line from St. Louis, to keep the line of communication open between Generals Blunt and Herron, and also to forward despatches to and from General Blunt. Colonel Bishop kept out scouting parties to the east and southeast, and reported to Generals Blunt and Herron such information as he could obtain of the movements of the enemy. His men were mostly from Northwestern Arkansas, and, through their relatives and friends, it was not difficult to obtain information of the movements of the Confederate forces in that section.

On the 16th of November a detachment of seventy-five men, under Captain John I. Worthington and Lieutenant Thomas Willhite, First Arkansas Cavalry, attacked and dispersed Captain Ingraham's company of Southern Home Guards, thirty miles east of Elkhorn, and captured a number of horses. Colonel Bishop sent out a detachment of two hundred men, under Major Johnson, First Arkansas Cavalry, to scout the country in the direction of Huntsville. When the detachment arrived near that place, Major Johnson received information which he deemed reliable, that a brigade of Confederate infantry, cavalry, and artillery was encamped there. As his command was too small to attack such a large force, he returned to Elkhorn, and reported to Colonel Bishop on the 19th of November, the result of his scout.

The Confederate force encamped at Huntsville belonged to Colonel Burbridge's command, and moved immediately in the direction of Yellville, where there were saltpetre works, and where the rebels were collecting supplies for a large force.

About this time General F. J. Herron, commanding the Second and Third Divisions Army of the Frontier, then encamped at Crane Creek, heard of the operations of the Confederates about Yellville, and at once sent out a cavalry expedition against them under Colonel D. Wickersham, Tenth Illinois Cavalry. This force under Colonel Wickersham consisted of the First Iowa Cavalry, one battalion of the Second Wisconsin Cavalry, and the Tenth Illinois Cavalry. The troops marched day and night over a rough country, crossed White River, and attacked and drove the Confederates out of Yellville, captured sixty men of Colonel Burbridge's command, destroyed the saltpetre works, burned the arsenal and store-houses, broke up and destroyed five hundred shot-guns and rifles, and brought out one hundred horses. After the return of Colonel Wickersham General Herron was satisfied that the Confederate forces had been so thoroughly demoralized that they would not threaten him again soon from the directions of Yellville or Berryville. He kept his cavalry actively employed, however, scouting the country to the south and southeast, to prevent the dispersed detachments of rebels from concentrating at any place in Northwestern Arkansas, or from passing north into Missouri. But in spite of his vigilance and activity, small bands of guerillas did pass around him and return to Missouri, to resume their outrageous acts of murdering and robbing Union citizens in different parts of Southwest Missouri.

CHAPTER XXIX.

ACTION AT CANE HILL, ARKANSAS.

ON the 23d of November Lieutenant-Colonel L. R. Jewell, Sixth Kansas Cavalry, who had been sent out by General Blunt with a detachment of six hundred cavalry and two mountain howitzers to make a reconnoissance in the direction of Van Buren, returned and reported that he advanced within fifteen miles of that place and met and drove in the enemy's pickets. He also reported that he obtained information that General Hindman's forces, estimated as high as twenty-five thousand men, were encamped around Fort Smith and Van Buren, and that most of them had already crossed the Arkansas River, and were preparing to move northward immediately for the invasion of Missouri. The reconnoissance showed that the Confederate leaders were unquestionably displaying great activity.

General Blunt received information on the 24th that General Marmaduke with seven thousand cavalry and some artillery, had moved north from Van Buren, scarcely twenty-four hours in the rear of Colonel Jewell, and had halted at Cane Hill to await the arrival of General Hindman with the Confederate infantry and main park of artillery. It was evident that the contest was to commence at once for the possession of Northwestern Arkansas and the Indian Territory. General Blunt determined to move forward with a well equipped force of infantry, cavalry, and artillery and strike Marmaduke a hard blow before he could receive reinforcements. Cane Hill is thirty miles

25

south of Lindsay's Prairie, where the Federal troops were encamped.

On the morning of the 27th of November General Blunt, at the head of five thousand men and thirty pieces of artillery, took up the march for Cane Hill. The day was clear and delightful, and a soft haze of the lingering Indian summer pervaded the atmosphere. The troops were well rested, and many of them expressed themselves as eager for a fight. They carried in their haversacks four days' rations of hard bread, coffee, bacon, and salt. They marched that day upwards of twenty miles, and bivouacked that night about ten miles north of Cane Hill. From that point General Blunt sent several spies into the Confederate camp to ascertain their position, and to obtain any other information having a bearing on his future operations. On the return of the spies they reported that General Marmaduke had a strong picket guard occupying a good defensive position about two miles north of Cane Hill on the road upon which the Federal column was marching. The Confederate officers had heard in the early part of the evening of the approach of General Blunt, and were making preparations to fight him the next day.

At daybreak the Federal troops were aroused without beat of drums or sound of bugles, and devoting a few moments to satisfying the calls of hunger with rations from their haversacks, and coffee made upon their camp-fires, moved forward again to engage the enemy. Instead of moving forward on the direct road to Cane Hill, General Blunt made a detour to the east, advanced on an obscure road and approached within half a mile of the Confederate camp without meeting any resistance. In a few moments, however, a considerable force of Confederate cavalry appeared in his front drawn up in line. On looking around he saw that he was not prepared to bring on a general action at once, for in making the detour some six miles back his main column had been detained in ascending a mountain, and was not yet in sight. His advanced guard, consisting of four companies of the Second Kansas Cavalry, under Major Fisk, and two howitzers under Lieutenant Stover, at once commenced to skirmish with the enemy, and with the assistance of Captain Rabb's Second Indiana Battery, held the Confederates in check until the main Federal column came up.

With his advance guard General Blunt made a vigorous attack upon the Confederate grand guard, and putting them to flight pursued them until he came in full view of General Marmaduke's main force drawn up in line of battle on the right of the road, on high ground with timber in their rear. The moment General Blunt's advance came in sight and within range of the Confederate battery, which was posted so as to command the road the Federal troops were advancing on, it opened a brisk fire upon them. General Blunt ordered up the two mountain howitzers of the Second Kansas and Captain Rabb's Indiana Battery, and then an artillery duel commenced, and lasted until nearly eleven o'clock, when, the different regiments and batteries of the Federal column having arrived, they commenced to move to the positions assigned them for a general advance.

General Marmaduke's division consisted of Colonels J. O. Shelby's and Emmet McDonald's brigades of Missouri cavalry, Colonel Carroll's brigade of Arkansas cavalry, Captain Bledsoe's six-gun battery, and a company of Quantrill's guerillas from Missouri.

While engaging the enemy with his artillery and waiting for his main column to come up, General Blunt reconnoitred Marmaduke's position, and found an approach by which a force could be brought forward to attack his left flank with advantage, and perhaps turn it. He ordered Major Van Antwerp of his staff to hasten back and meet his advance, consisting of Colonel Thomas Ewing's Eleventh Kansas Volunteers, and Captain Hopkins battery, and to bring them forward on the double-quick. The troops were so far back, that, having moved forward at a quick step, and at a double-quick, they were very much fatigued and nearly exhausted when they came up. A good many of the men were obliged to drop out of ranks by the roadside and rest a little before resuming the march. On the arrival of the Eleventh Kansas to the front, Major P. B. Plumb was directed to take four companies and march down the road to the support of Rabb's battery, and Colonel Ewing took six companies and accompanied General Blunt to the right, followed by Hopkins' four-gun battery.

The Federal batteries now opened fire vigorously upon every exposed point of the enemy, and in a short time compelled them to abandon their position and retire nearly a mile south, near the little village of Boonsborough, where they again formed in line. By this time all General Blunt's troops and artillery had arrived, and were being placed in position for making a general attack. Colonel William Weer's Tenth Kansas Infantry, Colonel William A. Phillips' Third Indian Regiment, and Colonel Judson's Sixth Kansas Cavalry, formed on the left of the Federal line, and soon commenced to drive the enemy from the village and adjacent hills.

General Marmaduke being compelled to fall back again, took up another position behind a low ridge running east and west just south of town. He concentrated his entire force along this ridge, and his line of battle was about half a mile long. There was a deep ravine in his front, which the Federal troops would be obliged to cross before attacking him with small-arms. In moving up his troops, General Blunt saw that the position of the enemy was a strong one, and that it would require careful disposition and great determination of his forces to carry it. He ordered up some twenty pieces of artillery, and opened a hot fire of shot and shell upon the Confederate line, and soon demoralized it so much that his infantry crossed the deep ravine without serious resistance. Having crossed the ravine, he commenced at once to deploy his infantry to charge the enemy, when General Marmaduke again retreated before the Federal line had advanced within musket range. Captain Tenney, commanding the First Kansas Battery, came up in time with his long-range rifled guns to throw a few percussion shells into the rear of the retreating Confederates.

General Blunt ordered immediate pursuit, but owing to the hilly and broken condition of the country it was impracticable for his troops to move forward very rapidly. His infantry and cavalry, too, were beginning to feel the effects of hard marching. The road on which the Confederate forces were retreating in the direction of Van Buren runs through a valley for about three miles south of Boonsborough. In the valley on each side of the road there were several farms alternating with low hills and ravines covered with thick woods and brush. As the Federal troops advanced along this road they skirmished with General Marmaduke's rear column until it reached a large mound-shaped hill near the base of the Boston Mountains. Here the Confederate leader determined to make another stand, and quickly put his troops in position to check the progress of the Federal forces. His artillery commanded the road from the north, but his position was not impregnable.

General Blunt, who had kept up with his cavalry, at once commenced to make preparations for an assault. In a few moments his troops and batteries had come up in sufficient force to commence the attack. Lieutenant H. H. Opdyke, commanding two mountain howitzers attached to the Ninth Kansas Cavalry, was directed to a position on the right where he could shell the enemy's flank, while Captain Rabb opened upon them in front with his six brass field-pieces. This was an excellent battery, and, after throwing a few rounds of shot and shell, knocked to pieces a gun carriage, and dismantled one of the guns of the Confederate battery and forced the others to retire out of range. The storm of shot and shell from the Federal batteries having crippled one of his guns and forced the others to retire, and seeing the columns of Federal infantry and cavalry advancing steadily over the ridge about three quarters of a mile off, General Marmaduke could not make up his mind to engage the Federal forces at close quarters, and after some skirmishing with small-arms ordered his division to retreat again, and to take up a position in the Boston Mountains four miles south of Cane Hill. He dismounted his men and formed them in line along the side of the mountain and on its summit, and ordered his artillery placed in position to command the approaches. He did not have to wait long for the Federal troops to appear, and he soon saw that General Blunt was not going to depend upon his artillery this time to dislodge him, but upon his small-arms.

In his attack on this position of the enemy, General Blunt had with him Colonel Bassett's Second Kansas Cavalry, part of Colonel Judson's Sixth Kansas Cavalry, Colonel Ewing's Eleventh and Colonel Bowen's Thirteenth Kansas Volunteers, Colonel W. A. Phillips' Third Indian Regiment, part of the First Indian Regiment, under Major Ellithorp, and the four twelve-pounder mountain howitzers attached to the Second and Ninth Regiments Kansas Cavalry. The ascent of the mountain was too steep to move forward his field batteries, except along the main road. They were, however, brought to the front, and placed in position near the base of the mountain, and supported by Colonel Weer's infantry. General Blunt dismounted most of the Second and Sixth Regiments Kansas Cavalry, and Colonel Phillips' Third Indian Regiment, to co-operate with the Eleventh and Thirteenth

Regiments Kansas Infantry in storming the heights of the mountain. With desperate courage and resolution these troops charged up the steep acclivity, and soon came in range of the Confederate small-arms and artillery, when the rattle of musketry and roar of artillery burst forth in great fury along the side of the mountain. Onward and upward the Federal forces moved, springing from one ledge of rocks to another, and firing as they advanced, until they approached within a hundred yards or so of the Confederate troops in line, when they again broke and fled in the utmost confusion. In a few moments they reached and mounted their horses, which had been held a short distance in the rear, and were soon after beyond the range of the Federal small-arms. The exertion of ascending the mountain had so much fatigued the Federal troops when they reached its summit, that they required a few moments' rest before renewing the pursuit. When General Blunt saw that his forces had carried the heights he ordered up his four howitzers and Rabb's battery, and on their arrival again moved forward to attack the Confederates.

General Marmaduke had in the mean time rallied his troops about three quarters of a mile back, and formed them in line to make another stand. They made a feeble resistance, however, and fled again when General Blunt came up with his howitzers and the troops with which he had driven them from the summit of the mountain, and opened fire upon them. The ground was too rough and broken for the cavalry of either side to be used to advantage. General Blunt had prudently kept Colonel Ewing's Eleventh Kansas Volunteers and Colonel W. A. Phillips' Third Indian Regiment, dismounted, to the front, and quickly formed them in line on either side of the road along the sides of the mountain, or across ravines, and routed the Confederates every time their leaders endeavored to make a stand.

From the summit of the mountain, advancing south, the Cane Hill and Van Buren road gradually descends into Cove Creek Valley. This valley is very narrow, and on descending it the mountains on each side gradually rise to great height, perhaps to one thousand feet in some places. In the pursuit and fighting down the narrow valley of Cove Creek, General Blunt's infantry and artillery, except his howitzers and part of his cavalry, had fallen behind out of sight.

The sun had sunk behind the mountains, and the day was drawing to a close. In the deep hollow, and within the dark shadows of the mountains, the day appeared to be further spent than it really was. General Marmaduke had taken up another position with his artillery nearly a mile in advance of his rear-guard, and his troops, as they came up, formed on the side of the mountain. Having come up with the Confederate rear-guard, General Blunt determined to make another vigorous assault before darkness set in, and endeavor to capture the battery which was being used to cover the Confederate retreat. The Federal commander saw that the Confederate troops were being crowded into the narrow gorge of Cove Creek in such a mass that they were obstructing one another's movements in the retreat. Turning to order his troops forward into action, he found only the Sixth Kansas Cavalry, his four howitzers, and part of his body-guard in sight. Impatient of waiting for his infantry and the rest of his cavalry and artillery to come up, he called for volunteers to charge the enemy. Lieutenant-Colonel L. R. Jewell, who was at hand with about one half of his regiment, the Sixth Kansas Cavalry, offered to lead the charge. The bugles sounded the charge, and Colonel Jewell dashed forward at the head of his command, and in a moment more the opposing forces were joined in a fierce struggle. After firing several rounds with their Sharp's carbines and Colt's revolvers into the ranks of the enemy, Colonel Jewell ordered his men to draw sabres and charge into the midst of the Confederates, which they did, sabring them from right to left for about half a mile, and causing the greatest consternation. Many of the Confederate soldiers threw down their arms and fled in the wildest disorder, and spread the report that the Federal cavalry were advancing impetuously, and sabring their comrades in their progress down the valley.

Presently Colonel Jewell reached a point where the valley became a narrow defile, to defend which General Marmaduke had formed several dismounted regiments upon a narrow bench on the side of the mountain, prepared to open fire upon the Federal column the moment it reached the defile. In the excitement of the charge, Colonel Jewell and his men had not noticed the enemy formed on the left, partly concealed from view by the contour of the ground, until they saw the flashes from their guns only a few yards distant. In this volley, Colonel Jewell, Sergeant Ritchey of Company K, several enlisted men of the Sixth Kansas, fell, mortally wounded. Captains Greeno, Mefford, and John Rodgers, commanding the Federal companies in the charge, seeing that the defile was defended by a superior force of the enemy, who were preparing to charge them in flank, rallied their men and fell back until they met General Blunt with his howitzers and some detachments of other regiments that had come up. The General, with the assistance of Colonels Judson and Phillips and some of his staff, rallied and formed the retreating companies of the Sixth Kansas across the valley, and with the aid of his howitzers checked and drove back the Confederates under Shelby and McDonald, who were rapidly advancing up the hollow with wild yells, confident of turning the tide of battle.

The position was a strong one, and to carry it by assault General Blunt needed his whole force of infantry and artillery, instead of four companies of cavalry. Even had Colonel Jewell succeeded in forcing the passage of the defile, he could not have returned without running the gauntlet of another heavy fire from the enemy who were posted behind logs and rocks on the narrow bench of the mountain, about fifty feet above the road. Having checked the advance of the rebels, and turned and driven them again some distance down the valley, General Blunt expressed a determination of forcing his way through the gorge at all hazards. In the meantime, Colonel Ewing came up in sight with part of his regiment and a section of Rabb's battery. General Blunt ordered his four howitzers and the section of Rabb's battery loaded with double canister, and was advancing, with the companies of the Sixth Kansas supporting his guns, to the assault again. He had arrived within less than four hundred yards of the position defended by the Confederates, and was in the act of opening fire, when an officer from General Marmaduke came galloping up the road with a white flag. General Blunt sent forward Colonel W. F. Cloud, Second Kansas Cavalry, to receive it. Colonel Emmet McDonald, the bearer of the flag of truce, stated that General Marmaduke requested the privilege of taking his dead and wounded off the ground.

In view of the fact that Colonel Jewell, Lieutenant John A. Johnson, of Company A, Lieutenant John G. Harris, of Company K, and several enlisted men of the Sixth Kansas, who were wounded in the charge down the valley, were still lying upon the ground occupied by the enemy, and as darkness was coming on, General Blunt granted the request and hostilities for the day ceased. General Marmaduke continued his retreat toward Van Buren that night, and General Blunt, having gathered up his dead and wounded and placed them in ambulances in charge of his surgeons, returned to Cane Hill, some five miles back, where his infantry, on preparing to go into the fight, had divested themselves of their knapsacks and blankets. The exertions had been so severe during the day by marching and manœuvring and climbing the hills and mountains and fighting, that toward night the infantry regiments could bring into line scarcely one half the number of men they started out with in the morning. The men had dropped out of ranks from exhaustion. The cavalry were also much worn, for at one time detachments were sent out to operate on the flanks; at another time the men were dismounted to fight on foot over the hills and mountains, and then required to return to and remount their horses and move forward again in pursuit of the enemy.

Colonel Jewell died on the 29th of November, and was sent back to his family, near Fort Scott, for interment. He had distinguished himself all through the campaign, and was known as a bold and intrepid officer. Possessing a kindly and generous nature, he never asked his men to go where he dared not lead them, and they loved him and had unbounded confidence in him. Even if he knew that he was to lead a forlorn hope, he would not hesitate to offer up his life if his country demanded it or the reputation of his regiment was at stake. But when left to act on his own judgment and responsibility, he always mingled a proper caution with boldness, and thus escaped the charge of rashness.

General Blunt reported his casualties during the day at four men killed and thirty-six wounded. He also reported that the Confederates left seventy-five men killed and mortally wounded upon the ground fought over. The number of Confederates wounded and taken off the field during the action and under the flag of truce is not known. On his return to Cane Hill that night, General Blunt sent a courier back with orders for his trains and the rest of his troops under General Salomon at Camp Babcock, on Lindsay's Prairie, to move forward and join him at Rhea's Mills, a few miles north of Cane Hill. He kept part of his troops, however, at Cane Hill, that place being a more convenient point from which he could send out detachments to guard the passes in the mountains.

CHAPTER XXX.

BATTLE OF PRAIRIE GROVE, ARKANSAS.

ON the arrival of the trains and the rest of the troops at Rhea's Mills and Cane Hill, General Blunt at once commenced collecting subsistence and supplies for his men and forage for his animals. Between Fayetteville and Cane Hill was the finest agriculture section of Northwestern Arkansas, and most of the farms had raised on them good crops of corn, oats, wheat, potatoes, and apples. The possession of this fair valley, lying directly north of the Boston Mountains, had been won by the Federal General after a short, sharp contest; but to hold it, he soon became convinced that he would shortly be obliged to engage in a fierce struggle, for his troops had scarcely pitched their tents in their new camps when his scouts brought him information that General Hindman's army had all crossed the Arkansas River at Van Buren and advanced north fifteen miles, until General Marmaduke's retreating division was met on Lee's Creek.

Having made extensive preparations for the campaign, General Hindman, on meeting General Marmaduke, determined to move north rapidly with his entire army, and attack and, if possible, overwhelm General Blunt before his reinforcements could reach him. Finding that General Hindman, with an army upwards of twenty thousand strong, was advancing to attack him, General Blunt advised General Curtis in St. Louis of the situation by telegraph from Elkhorn, and requested him to order the

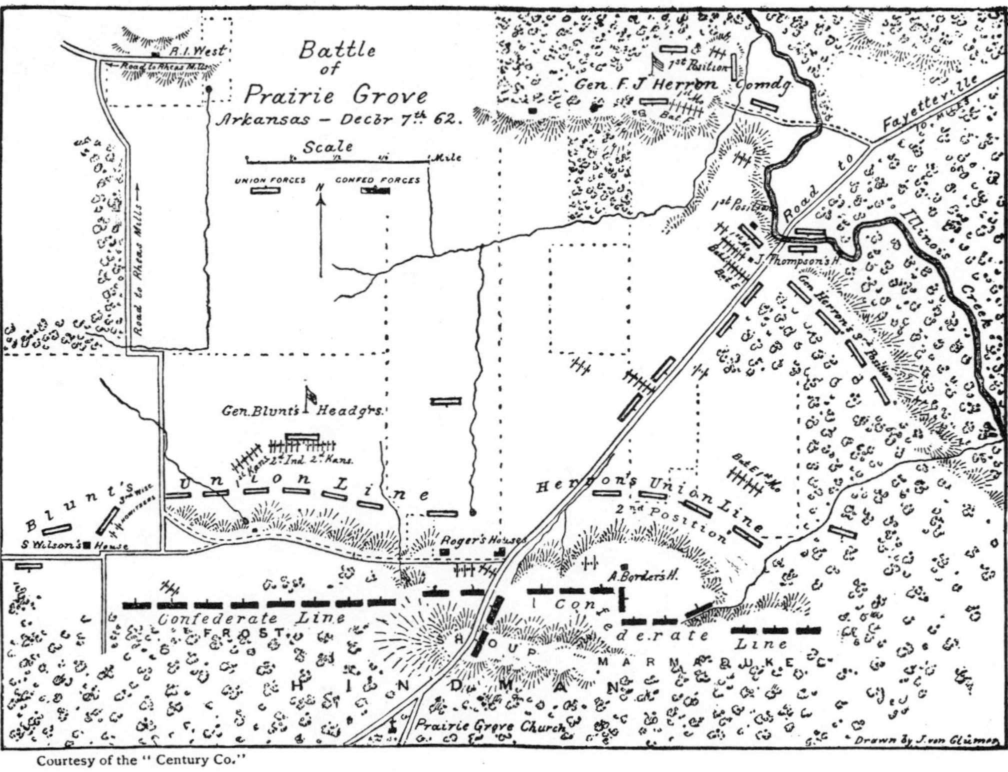

Courtesy of the "Century Co."

Second and Third Divisions Army of the Frontier, then encamped at Wilson Creek, ten miles southwest of Springfield, Missouri, to move forward by forced marches to reinforce him. On receipt of this despatch, General Curtis, by telegraph, ordered General F. J. Herron, commanding the two divisions, to push forward with them as rapidly as practicable to the assistance of General Blunt. General Herron received General Curtis' telegraphic order at eight o'clock on the morning of December 3d, and by twelve o'clock that day his troops were in motion and on the march in the direction of Fayetteville.

From Wilson Creek, Missouri, to Fayetteville, Arkansas, the point to which he would be obliged to march upon the telegraph road, was one hundred miles, and Rhea's Mills, where General Blunt's troops were encamped, was sixteen miles southwest of Fayetteville. This was a long distance for infantry to be put on forced marches, and would tax their power of endurance to the utmost limit. The Springfield and Fayetteville road, known also as the wire or telegraph road, was the nearest practicable route by which General Blunt could be reached. This road was in splendid condition on the eve of the march, for it had been much used the past year by large armies and their trains passing over it.

General Herron at once sent a despatch to General Blunt, stating that he would make the best time possible on the march, and keep him constantly advised of his position *en route*. His baggage trains followed in the rear of each division, and carried the knapsacks of his men, thus relieving them of a burden that would have been much felt in the long march before them, had they been obliged to carry them on their backs. General Herron arrived at Elkhorn with the cavalry of the second division on the evening of December 5th. Here he received an order from General Blunt to send forward all of the cavalry that he could spare. He ordered forward

Colonel Dudley Wickersham with the Tenth Illinois, First Iowa, battalion of the Second Wisconsin, and Colonel Geigers, Eighth Missouri Cavalry, to report to General Blunt. General Herron stayed all night at Elkhorn, waiting for his infantry and artillery to come up. He moved forward the next day to Cross Hollow, fifteen miles, and halted again for his troops to close up. Colonel Daniel Huston, commanding the second division, arrived at Cross Hollow at seven o'clock on the evening of December 6th, and rested until midnight, and then resumed the march, arriving at Fayetteville the next morning at sunrise. General Herron, who had moved forward at the head of his troops, arrived at Fayetteville about three hours in advance of Colonel Huston's second division.

While the second and third divisions were thus moving to his assistance at the rate of thirty-five miles a day, General Blunt was busily employed in skirmishing with the Confederate advance and endeavoring to keep General Marmaduke's cavalry from forcing the passes in the Boston Mountains. He determined to hold his position at Rhea's Mills and Cane Hill until his reinforcements under General Herron arrived. His information led him to believe that General Hindman was preparing to cross the mountains by taking either the telegraph road, which passed about ten miles east of his camp on Cane Hill, or by taking the Cove Creek road, which forked on the mountains, the left-hand fork of which led directly to Cane Hill and the right to Fayetteville. From the point where this road forked to General Blunt's position on Cane Hill, was about six miles. The Fayetteville branch of the Cove Creek road was crossed one and two miles north of the point where it united with the Cane Hill branch, by two roads running west and southwest from the telegraph road to the Newburg and Cane Hill road.

General Blunt saw the importance of keeping a strong

outpost at the junction of the Cane Hill road with the Fayetteville and Cove Creek road, and at the crossings of the other roads described. He saw also that if General Hindman was allowed to advance on the Cove Creek road to the point where it forked, he could, by making a strong feint, threaten a direct attack, while his main army moved north on the Fayetteville road to turn the Federal left flank.

On the 4th, General Blunt strengthened his outposts in the mountains, and sent forward a cavalry scout on the Cove Creek road in the direction of Van Buren to ascertain if the enemy were advancing in force. The Federal scout met the Confederate advance under Colonel Shelby, and after a slight skirmish fell back to the outpost on the mountain. The next morning Colonel Shelby threw forward a regiment and attacked the Federal outpost, but his force was soon repulsed and driven back several miles through the mountains. Anticipating another attack upon this outpost, General Blunt on the night of the 5th directed Colonel Cloud, commanding the third brigade, to strengthen it by daybreak the next morning with one hundred cavalry and two mountain howitzers. In the meantime, Colonel Shelby advanced up the Cove Creek road with a brigade of cavalry, and encamped that night within a mile or so of the Federal outpost, and the next morning at daylight dismounted part of his command, made another attack, and before Colonel Cloud's support arrived, forced the detachment of the Second Kansas at the station to fall back about three miles in the direction of Cane Hill. Colonel Emmet McDonald, who had crossed over the mountains on the telegraph road with a brigade of Missouri Confederate cavalry, joined Colonel Shelby shortly after he had driven in the Federal picket. Immediately after taking possession of the Fayetteville branch of the Cove Creek road, General Marmaduke advanced the brigades of Colonels Shelby, McDonald, and Carroll to within three miles of General Blunt's position on Cane Hill, where they came in sight of part of the Federal cavalry under Colonel Cloud drawn up in line.

The opposing forces consumed the day in skirmishing, each side sustaining a few casualties in wounded. While the Confederate cavalry were thus threatening General Blunt with an attack in front, General Hindman was bringing forward his infantry and artillery on the Cove Creek Road. As General Marmaduke's cavalry were now in possession of the Fayetteville branch of the Cove Creek road at its junction with the Cane Hill road, General Blunt was apprehensive that an effort would be made by the Confederate generals to turn his left flank, so as to get between him and his reinforcements under General Herron. That he might be advised at once if there were any indications of such a movement in progress, on the morning of the 6th he ordered Colonel John M. Richardson, Fourteenth Missouri State Militia Cavalry, who had arrived from Cassville the night before, to take a force of one hundred mounted men and proceed east on the Hog Eye road to the crossing of the Cove Creek and Fayetteville road, and on arriving there to send part of his men south on it to ascertain if the enemy were advancing.

On arriving at the intersection of the roads described, Colonel Richardson ordered Captain Julian with his company to take the advance, and proceed south on the road in the direction of Cove Creek. Captain Julian had not advanced more than two miles, perhaps, when he captured three Southern soldiers and sent them back, and advancing again a short distance, came in sight of the camp of the Southern troops, containing, as he thought, at least two thousand men.

Colonel Richardson examined the prisoners and obtained from them the information that he was within a mile of the main Confederate army, which was then moving up the mountain on the direct road to Cane Hill. The Colonel immediately fell back a mile or so, and sent messengers to report to General Blunt the presence of this large Confederate force within a few miles of his headquarters. The General could not feel certain whether the main Confederate force was being massed in his front to fight him early the next morning, or whether the Confederate cavalry, with which his troops had been skirmishing during the day, were concealing the real movements of the main force under General Hindman.

In view of the strong probability of a general engagement the next day, Colonel Cloud's third brigade were ordered to bivouac on their arms that night in front, just south of Newburg. At two o'clock on the mornings of the 5th, 6th, and 7th the Federal troops at Cane Hill and Rhea's Mills were ordered to strike tents and load up their baggage; and the teams were harnessed and hitched up, and the wagon trains stood ready until daylight to move at a moment's notice. In the midst of his preparations for the coming struggle, General Blunt was much gratified to have Colonel Wickersham report to him about ten o'clock on the night of the 6th with a brigade of cavalry, which General Herron had sent forward from Cross Hollow. He also received a despatch from General Herron stating that he would reach Fayetteville by daylight Sunday morning the 7th.

Shortly after midnight on the morning of the 7th, General Blunt again directed Colonel Richardson to proceed with his own battalion and Captain Conkey's company, Third Wisconsin Cavalry, east on the Hog Eye road to the crossing of the Fayetteville and Cove Creek road, to ascertain if the Southern forces were moving in the direction of Fayetteville, and if they were, to resist them to the last extremity, and to promptly notify him of their movements. The Colonel moved forward with his detachment, but before reaching the intersection of the roads met Captain Coleman, of the Ninth Kansas Cavalry, with

26

thirty men, who had just been driven from the junction of the roads by the enemy, and who reported that the Confederates were advancing up the Cove Creek road in strong force. Thinking that the Southern forces were advancing on Cane Hill, Colonel Richardson fell back about a mile, and took up a strong position to resist them, and sent a messenger to report to General Blunt. Waiting for a short time, and finding that the enemy were not advancing, the Colonel sent Captain Julian forward again with a small detachment to ascertain their movements. The Captain soon discovered that the Confederate forces were marching in the direction of Fayetteville, and then hastily returned and reported, and General Blunt was promptly notified.

Acting on the information that the enemy were advancing on Cane Hill, General Blunt and staff at seven o'clock left his headquarters and rode to the front, expecting soon to open the battle. Although a considerable force of Confederate cavalry were yet on the mountain in his front, he soon received information that the main Southern army were marching northeast in the direction of Fayetteville, on the Cove Creek road, and had already passed the point where that road was intersected by the Hog Eye road.

On the receipt of this information he immediately ordered all his transportation to Rhea's Mills, guarded by Colonel Phillips' Third Indian Regiment, and directed Colonel Judson to take his regiment, the Sixth Kansas Cavalry, and two howitzers, together with Colonel Richardson's detachment, and proceed as rapidly as practicable on the Hog Eye road, and if, on arriving there, the enemy had passed in the direction of Fayetteville, to follow them and attack them vigorously. Colonel Wickersham was ordered to proceed at once with his brigade of cavalry on the Cane Hill and Fayetteville road in the direction of Fayetteville, to form a junction with General

Herron. General Salomon, commanding the first brigade, was ordered to follow Colonel Wickersham. The second brigade, under Colonel William Weer, and the third brigade, under Colonel W. F. Cloud, were withdrawn from the front south of Newburg about nine o'clock, and directed to follow close in the rear of the first brigade. The moment General Blunt decided to make these movements, he sent two mounted messenger parties with despatches to notify General Herron; but failing to take the precaution to send his couriers *via* Rhea's Mills, they were cut off by General Marmaduke's advance.

Colonel Wickersham, who had moved in advance, instead of keeping on the direct road toward Fayetteville, about three miles north of Cane Hill, took a left-hand road leading to Rhea's Mills. The infantry and artillery following the cavalry, kept the same road until General Blunt rode forward and overtook Colonel Wickersham and directed him to proceed in the direction of Fayetteville, and endeavor to open communication with General Herron. General Salomon, with the first brigade was sent to Rhea's Mills to guard the Federal trains, arriving there about twelve o'clock. General Blunt then took the second and third brigades and marched on an obscure road in a northeast direction, the direction in which artillery firing had just been heard.

General Hindman had, up to a late hour on the night of the 6th, made all his preparations to fight General Blunt in his position on Cane Hill. His infantry and artillery had moved up, and were in position to make an attack on the Federal troops the next morning. He had heard of the arrival of Colonel Wickersham's cavalry brigade to reinforce General Blunt, but this information did not change his purpose to make the proposed attack. On the night of the 6th, however, after his generals had assembled to receive their final instructions in regard to carrying into effect the movements decided upon, he received information that General Herron would reach Fayetteville that night with large reinforcements of infantry and artillery for General Blunt. After some consideration, he came to the conclusion that, if he attacked General Blunt in front and forced him from his position, he would fall back until he met his reinforcements, after which he would probably assume the offensive. General Hindman, therefore, decided to abandon the proposed attack on the Federal position at Cane Hill, to withdraw his troops from their several positions, and to push them forward on the Cove Creek and Fayetteville road, and attack the Federal column under General Herron, and if possible crush it before General Blunt could come to its assistance.

To deceive General Blunt as completely as possible in regard to this new movement, General Hindman left Colonel Monroe with a brigade of Arkansas cavalry on the crest of the mountain in front of the Federal position, with instructions to dismount his men at daylight and skirmish as infantry with the Federal troops, and detain them as long as possible. In the next place, orders were issued to brigade and division commanders of the Southern army, to have their troops in their proper positions and in readiness to march at three o'clock on Sunday morning, the 7th. But on account of some unavoidable detentions, the troops were not all in motion until nearly four o'clock. The road was very rough, so that the artillery and infantry were obliged to move slowly.

General Marmaduke's cavalry division, consisting of Colonels Shelby's and McDonald's brigades, marched in the advance with a battery of light artillery. Moving down the northern slope of the mountain a distance of about eight miles northeast of Cane Hill, General Marmaduke's advance at daylight came in sight of Colonel M. La Rue Harrison's First Arkansas Union Cavalry, and detachments of the Sixth and Seventh Regiments Missouri Cavalry, marching southwest on the Cane Hill road near its junction with the Cove Creek and Fayetteville roads, to reinforce General Blunt. Colonel Harrison had been ordered forward from Elkhorn, and on the night of the 6th encamped on the Fayetteville and Cane Hill road near Illinois Creek. Major Bredett, commanding the detachments of the Seventh and Sixth Missouri Cavalry, had marched nearly all night, and having received no information that the enemy had flanked General Blunt, halted a few moments at daylight near the camp of the First Arkansas Cavalry, to feed and rest his tired and much-worn horses. Lieutenant L. Bunner had been marching with his company since two o'clock in the morning about half a mile in advance of the other companies of the regiment, to guard against a surprise.

Shortly after Major Bredett's command had halted near the entrance to a lane to feed their horses, a company of the Eighth Missouri Cavalry, also *en route* to Cane Hill, passed them, and entering the lane had got nearly through it, when a volley was fired into them by an unseen foe from the thick woods on their left front. The company instantly retreated, falling back through Major Bredett's column. On hearing the firing, the Major ordered his men to mount their horses and form in line to resist the enemy, who were seen approaching. He had scarcely formed his men in line when Colonel McDonald's Confederate Cavalry Brigade rapidly advanced within range and commenced pouring such heavy volleys of musketry into his line from his left, front, and rear, that he was obliged to order the retreat sounded. After retreating a short distance, he rallied and formed his men in line, but being pressed by a vastly superior force from all sides, he was wounded and killed and his men dispersed and pursued.

Colonel McDonald, in crossing over from the Cove Creek and Fayetteville road to the Cane Hill road, got between Major Bredett and his advance guard under Lieutenant Bunner. On hearing the firing in his rear, the lieutenant turned back with his company to join his command, but had proceeded only a short distance, when he saw advancing directly in his front a full company dressed in the Federal uniform. Supposing the company to belong to the First Arkansas Cavalry, he allowed them to approach within fifty yards, when they opened fire upon him. Still thinking that they were Federal soldiers, he called out to them to cease firing, that "we are friends." In another instant he became satisfied that they were rebels, and then withdrew his company with the loss of one man severely wounded and five horses killed and wounded. The rebels who were thus dressed in the Federal uniform proved to be Quantrill's company of bushwhackers and desperadoes, whose hands were reeking with the blood of murdered Union citizens of Missouri.

After the fall of Major Bredett, his command dispersed in every direction, but the men of each company kept together, and rallied and fought when not pressed by greatly superior numbers. Captain William McKee, in making a stand with his company, became surrounded, and was killed while trying to cut his way through the rebel line. In their rapid movements, Colonels McDonald's and Shelby's brigades soon came up and attacked and routed the First Arkansas Cavalry, capturing all their wagons and baggage. In pursuing the detachments of the Sixth and Seventh Regiments Missouri and Arkansas Cavalry, the Confederate cavalry also became much dispersed. It was at this time that a company of the Seventh Missouri Cavalry rallied and captured Colonel Shelby and two pieces of the Confederate artillery. The Federal detachment, however, were unable to hold their prizes very long, for on returning from the pursuit of the main body of the Federal cavalry in the direction of Fayetteville, Colonels Young and Crump, of McDonald's cavalry brigade, recaptured Colonel Shelby and his battery.

After resting an hour at Fayetteville, General Herron,

at four o'clock, pushed on with such of his troops as had arrived, sending forward Major Hubbard with two companies of the First Missouri Cavalry as an advance guard. When about ten miles southwest of Fayetteville, the Major met the First Arkansas Cavalry and detachments of the Seventh Missouri Cavalry retreating in great disorder. He succeeded in rallying part of the retreating troops, and ordering the fence thrown down on the left-hand side of the road, threw his two companies into line in a wheat-field to check the enemy. The Confederate cavalry soon approached in large numbers within two hundred yards, and filing off to the right and left of the road, commenced to flank him. Seeing that the Confederate force was too strong to contend with, he was obliged to order a retreat, but having several fences to throw down, his command was much impeded in its movements. The Confederate officers, seeing the situation, ordered a charge, and dashing upon the Federal cavalry, cut off and captured Major Hubbard and several of his men while trying to cross a fence.

Captain A. L. Burrows then took command of the two companies and marched them rapidly in the direction of the mountain, a mile or so distant, and on arriving near its base fell in with some two hundred stragglers of the First Arkansas and Sixth and Seventh Regiments Missouri Cavalry, and ordered them into line to make a stand to check the enemy who were still pursuing them. On seeing the Federal cavalry forming in line, the Confederate column soon came to a halt, and after some skirmishing commenced to fall back.

In the meantime detachments of the First Arkansas and Seventh Missouri Cavalry, which had retreated on the Fayetteville road, met General Herron with his escort, consisting of one company of the First Missouri Cavalry, under Captain J. M. Adams. The General, after some severe threats and decided action, halted his retreating troops, and formed them in line. He saw that the situation required energetic action to save his command from possible disaster. He immediately ordered forward two regiments of infantry and Captain Foust's battery, Missouri Light Artillery. When his infantry and artillery arrived at the front, General Marmaduke's cavalry had approached in strong force and formed in line of battle. General Herron at once opened fire upon the Confederates with Captain Foust's battery, and soon put them to flight, and pursued them four miles to the crossing of Illinois Creek. The course of this creek through the county is from the southeast to the northwest, but at the point where the Fayetteville road crosses it it flows nearly due west, and a short distance below the ford it changes its course and flows nearly due north for about one mile parallel with the road, when it again changes its course to the northwest.

On reaching the high ground just north of the creek, General Herron discovered the Confederate army in position, occupying the high ridge covered with a thick growth of young timber and underbrush, about three quarters of a mile south of the ford. On the left-hand side of the road, for a distance of half a mile south of the creek, the ground was a high plateau covered with timber. South of the timber extending to the foot of the ridge on which the enemy were posted, there were several cultivated fields.

On the right of the road from a short distance south of the creek to the foot of the ridge, there were several fields with intervening open ground. Prairie Grove Church was two miles southwest of the crossing of Illinois Creek, near the junction of the Cane Hill with the Cove Creek and Fayetteville roads. The two hostile armies were now confronting each other, and ready to engage in fierce conflict. After reviewing the situation for a moment, General Herron was satisfied that the Confederate army had passed General Blunt by turning his left flank. Though he was not fully advised of the strength of the Southern army, he determined to attack it at once, hoping that the artillery firing would bring up the Kansas General with his division. He crossed the creek with one of his staff, and rode forward a short distance to examine the ground in his front, on which he wished to place his infantry and artillery in position to open the battle. Inspired by the courage and devotion of their gallant leader, his artillery companies were bringing up his twenty pieces of artillery at a gallop, and his foot-sore infantry were coming forward on the double-quick.

After a careful inspection of the ground in front, General Herron ordered Lieutenant C. L. Edwards to cross the creek with a section of Foust's battery, First Missouri Light Artillery, advance to the high ground on the left of the road in the edge of the timber, and open fire upon the enemy with shot and shell. Lieutenant-Colonel McNulta, commanding the Ninety-fourth Regiment Illinois Volunteers, was directed to support Lieutenant Edwards' section of artillery in the movement thus ordered. The Lieutenant soon reached a point with his guns from which the enemy were seen drawn up in line about half a mile off, and at ten o'clock opened fire upon him. In a few moments the Confederate batteries replied with twelve pieces, and with such energy that General Herron withdrew the section of artillery and the Ninety-fourth Illinois from the advanced position thus taken. He saw that it would not be prudent to order his troops to cross the stream at the ford, unless he could draw the attention of the Confederate batteries to some other point, as they were posted so as to command the ford by concentrating the fire of all their guns upon it. His infantry and artillery were rapidly coming up and forming in line, and he determined to cross the creek without unnecessarily exposing his troops to an enfilading fire of the Confederate artillery. After some further examination, he found that the stream could be crossed about half a mile below the regular ford by cutting a road through the timber. This proposed crossing would enable him to take up a position south of the creek beyond the range of the Confederate batteries. He therefore ordered Colonel Huston, commanding the second division, to have a sufficient number of men detailed to cut out the proposed road with as little delay as possible.

The plan of the General was to have one of his batteries cross the creek by the new road, advance to the high open ground on his extreme right, and open fire upon the enemy, hoping to draw the fire of their batteries, so that the infantry and artillery of his third division could cross the creek at the regular ford without having to face a storm of shot and shell. The moment that the new road was open, Colonel Huston moved Captain David Murphy's long-range rifled battery, First Missouri Light Artillery, across to the south side of the creek, and then, dividing it into half batteries, placed the left half of three pieces, under Captain Murphy, in a commanding position north of the Spring branch on the extreme right; and the right half of three pieces, under Lieutenant James Marr, in a good position four hundred yards to the left on the south side of the Spring branch in front of the Confederate centre. The section of the Peoria Battery Illinois Light Artillery under Lieutenant Borris was posted about three hundred yards to the left of Lieutenant Marr, near the Fayetteville road.

Colonel William McE. Dye, commanding the second brigade, second division, was ordered to support the two batteries. He directed Colonel John C. Black, commanding the Thirty-Seventh Regiment Illinois Volunteers, to move to the right to support the pieces under Captain Murphy. Lieutenant-Colonel J. B. Leake, commanding the Twentieth Regiment Iowa Volunteers, was directed to support the pieces under Lieutenant Marr on the left.

Colonel J. G. Clark, commanding the first brigade,

second division, was ordered to occupy with his regiment, the Twenty-sixth Indiana Volunteers, a position one hun dred yards in the rear of the centre of Colonel Dye's brigade, as a reserve. At twelve o'clock the three regiments, following Captain Murphy's battery, waded the creek and marched to the positions assigned to them. While Colonel Huston was thus moving into position on the right with the troops and artillery of the second division, General Herron was preparing to cross the creek at the regular ford with the troops and artillery of the third division under cover of the fire of Captain Murphy's battery.

At 12:30 o'clock Captain Murphy fired the signal-gun, and a moment later the other two pieces, the half-battery under Lieutenant Marr and the section under Lieutenant Borris, opened fire upon the Confederates, who replied with twelve pieces with much energy. The moment the signal-gun was fired by Captain Murphy's battery, Colonel W. W. Orme, commanding the second brigade, third division, consisting of the Ninety-fourth Illinois Volunteers under Lieutenant-Colonel James McNulta, the Nineteenth Iowa Volunteers under Lieutenant-Colonel Samuel McFarland, and Captain Foust's battery, First Missouri Light Artillery, moved forward and crossed the creek at the regular ford, under a heavy fire from the Confederate artillery, and immediately prepared for action.

Colonel Henry Bertram, commanding the first brigade, third division, moved forward with the Twentieth Regiment Wisconsin Volunteers, and Captain Frank Backof's battery, First Missouri Light Artillery, following close upon the rear of Colonel Orme's brigade, also received a heavy fire from the Confederate batteries before his command had crossed the creek. The artillery companies of Captains Foust and Backof came to the front on a gallop, and went into battery a short distance in advance of the infantry, on the right and left of the road, and opened fire upon the Confederate batteries and position, and in less than fifteen minutes after his signal-gun was fired, General Herron had eighteen pieces of artillery on the south side of the creek playing upon the Confederate position on the ridge with shot and shell. This storm of shot and shell sent by his batteries screeching into the Confederate lines, exploding and tearing the timber into splinters, soon brought out all General Hindman's artillery, consisting of twenty-two pieces.

After crossing the creek, Colonels Orme and Bertram formed their brigades in line under cover of the bluff on the left and right of the road. Colonel McNulta, with the Ninety-fourth Illinois, formed on the left of the line; Colonel McFarland, with the Nineteenth Iowa, formed in the centre; and Colonel Bertram, with the Twentieth Wisconsin, formed on the right, the right of his line extending nearly to Colonel Huston's left. After the firing of General Herron's signal-gun, the batteries of the opposing armies engaged in a furious contest, and the roar of artillery and of exploding shells was continuous for nearly an hour, when the superior handling of the Federal batteries had silenced nearly every gun of the Confederate batteries, and compelled them to seek shelter behind the thick woods. During this artillery combat preparations were rapidly made on both sides for engaging in conflict with small-arms at close quarters. The detachments of the First, Sixth, and Seventh Regiments Missouri Cavalry, which had been dispersed in the morning by General Marmaduke's cavalry division, had now nearly all been collected under their proper officers, and, after reporting to General Herron, were assigned to duty on his flanks and as support to Lieutenant Borris' section of the Peoria battery. Having used a large amount of shot and shell during the day, the Federal batteries replenished their ammunition chests with grape and canister for close work.

On the Confederate side, General Hindman had not yet

been able to bring to the front all his forces to hurl against General Herron, as he had intended. His rear-guard, trains, and a force detached to guard the prisoners and wagons captured in the morning had been attacked by Colonel Judson, who had been sent out by General Blunt from Cane Hill with the Sixth Kansas Cavalry, two mountain howitzers, and Colonel Richardson's detachment. The booming of artillery in his rear alarmed General Hindman, and he detached General Parsons' division of infantry and sent it back to check the advance of the Federal force under Colonel Judson. Shortly after twelve o'clock he received information that General Blunt had left Cane Hill, was approaching rapidly, and would probably form a junction with General Herron before General Parsons could reach the field with his infantry. He was therefore greatly mortified when he saw that the time had passed for attacking with his combined forces the Federal divisions defiantly drawn up in his front. He was also astonished at the boldness of General Herron in crossing Illinois Creek in the face of the superior force and commencing the attack, instead of waiting behind that stream to be attacked.

Having compelled the Confederate batteries to retire out of sight, and having replenished his ammunition chests with grape and canister, General Herron ordered forward his left wing, consisting of the brigades of Colonels Orme and Bertram. In this movement Captain Foust's battery was flanked on the left by the Ninety-fourth Illinois Infantry, and on the right by the Nineteenth Iowa Infantry. And Captain Backof's battery was flanked on the left by the Nineteenth Iowa, and on the right by the Twentieth Wisconsin Infantry. Colonel McNulta, with the Ninety-fourth Illinois Infantry, advanced through the woods and brush on the left to an open field and engaged the Confederate infantry, and after several volleys of musketry compelled them to fall back to a position behind the fence on the south side of the field. To follow up the advantage thus gained, the Colonel moved his regiment by the left flank farther to the left through the woods and formed in line within two hundred yards of the Confederate infantry, again opened a hot fire upon them, and after a short conflict forced them to retire over the hill.

Colonel McFarland, in compliance with instructions from Colonel Orme, detached three companies of the Nineteenth Iowa Infantry, under Lieutenant Richard Root, and sent them forward under a heavy fire from the enemy as skirmishers to cover his advance, and to protect Captain Foust's battery, which had taken up a position in a wheat field on the left of the road, about one hundred and fifty yards from the foot of the ridge on which the Confederate infantry were formed in line. The Twentieth Wisconsin Infantry, under Major A. H. Starr, advanced on the right of the road across an open field a distance of five hundred yards, when Colonel Bertram ordered the men to lie down under cover of a fence. Captain Backof moved forward his battery close on the right of Major Starr, pouring a destructive fire of grape and canister into the Confederate line below the brow of the ridge as he advanced.

In another moment General Shoup's division and Colonel Shelby's brigade of Confederates were seen advancing against the Federal left and threatening Captain Foust's battery. To check this movement of the enemy, and to protect his battery, Colonel Orme ordered Colonel McNulta to withdraw the Ninety-fourth Illinois Infantry from their position on the extreme left, and place them in position on the outside of the fence near the battery, and to support it at all hazards. Captain Foust then divided his battery into three sections, placing the first section under Lieutenant C. L. Edwards, the second section under Lieutenant J. B. Atwater, and took charge of the third section himself. All the pieces now opened upon the Confederate infantry not more than one hundred and fifty yards distant, and drove them back into the woods on the ridge with great slaughter.

Colonel McNulta now moved forward again to the position from which he had been withdrawn near the southeast corner of the wheat field, and opened a heavy fire of musketry on the enemy, causing them to fall back over the hill in much confusion. While Colonel McNulta was thus engaged on the left of the Federal line, Colonel Bertram observed a Confederate battery supported by infantry about two hundred yards in his front near the brow of the hill, preparing to open fire upon him. He therefore ordered the Twentieth Wisconsin Infantry to rise from where they were lying down and charge and take the battery. The regiment under Major A. H. Starr moved forward in gallant style, shot down most of the artillery horses and gunners, captured the battery, and advanced to the crest of the hill, where they received a terrific musketry fire from four or five regiments of General Shoup's infantry division, which for a moment caused them to recoil, but rallying again returned the fire with great firmness and resolution. The enemy continuing to press forward in overwhelming numbers, Major Starr was soon obliged to fall back with his regiment much weakened by casualties, leaving the captured battery on the ground after destroying as much as possible of it and rendering it temporarily unfit for further use.

In the meantime the Nineteenth Iowa Infantry, led by Colonel McFarland, had been ordered to move forward to support the Twentieth Wisconsin Infantry in their fierce struggle in the woods. Ascending the hill to the left of the white house, near the road, Colonel McFarland advanced across the orchard back of the house to within a few yards of the fence, when the Confederate infantry, who had been lying down concealed in the brush behind the fence, arose three regiments deep, and poured a terribly destructive fire of musketry into his regiment from three sides, causing them, after a short, fierce struggle, to fall back to Captain Foust's battery on the left of the road near the foot of the hill. In this furious charge Colonel McFarland fell shot through the body, and his regiment sustained a heavy loss in killed and wounded. After the death of Colonel McFarland, Major D. Kent took command and rallied the regiment, and in retiring recovered and brought off the field the colors of the Twentieth Wisconsin Infantry, which had been dropped by the color-bearer, who had been shot by the enemy when the regiment commenced to fall back.

Finding it impossible to hold the position on the ridge with the force engaged, Colonel Orme rode up and ordered the rallied portions of the Nineteenth Iowa Infantry to fall in and rally with the Ninety-fourth Illinois Infantry on the left. And then leading these troops in person, Colonel Orme opened a heavy fire of musketry into the advancing line of Confederate infantry, and with the assistance of Captain Foust's battery, every piece of which was rapidly belching forth a perfect storm of canister into the Confederate line, succeeded in checking and driving it back into the woods on the brow of the hill. While the infantry of the third division were thus engaged in the desperate assault on the ridge, General Herron ordered Colonel Huston to bring up to their support two regiments of infantry from the second division on the right. The Colonel, leading his troops in person, brought forward at double-quick the Twenty-sixth Indiana Infantry, under Colonel Clark, and the Thirty-seventh Illinois Infantry, under Colonel John C. Black, and on arriving at the foot of the ridge, near the scene of the conflict, found the infantry of the third division falling back before a superior force of the enemy. That they had suffered severely in the conflict, was evident from the number of wounded men moving and being borne to the rear.

In order, therefore, to give the decimated regiments time to rally and re-form near Backof's and Foust's batteries, Colonel Huston ordered his two regiments, under Colonels Clark and Black, to charge the Confederate position on the ridge. In advancing up the hill he took the precaution to throw out a company of skirmishers from each regiment to cover its front and guard against a surprise. The two regiments moved steadily forward until they had passed the summit of the hill, when the skirmishers in advance commenced firing upon the enemy, only few of whom could be seen through the thick brush and leaves. In another moment the Confederate infantry arose from where they were lying down, and advancing to the front three ranks deep, poured a destructive fire of musketry into the Federal line at a distance of less than one hundred yards. Anticipating an assault at any moment, and seeing the skirmish line retiring, the Federal infantry were prepared for hot work, and delivered their fire at almost the same instant as the Confederates, and kept it up with great determination and disastrous effect for some time, but were finally forced by superior numbers of the enemy to fall back to a position just in the rear of the Federal batteries.

After repulsing three desperate assaults of the Federal infantry, General Hindman determined to follow up his success by a counter charge, and in a few moments his infantry came pouring over the crest of the ridge in heavy masses, when Foust's and Backof's Federal batteries opened upon them such a destructive fire of grape and canister that they were obliged to fall back out of range into the woods and brush. Captain Murphy's battery and the section of Illinois artillery under Lieutenant Borris were also constantly engaged in this last and the preceding conflicts in throwing shot and shell into the Confederate line, and rendered efficient service in defending the right of the Federal line. When Colonel Huston moved with the Twenty-sixth Indiana and Thirty-seventh Illinois Infantry to the support of the infantry of the third division, he left Colonel Dye, of the second brigade, with the Twentieth Iowa Infantry and Captain Murphy's battery in position on the Federal right.

While the conflict was thus raging with great fury on the ridge to the left and back of the white house, Colonel Dye moved forward Murphy's battery and the Twentieth Iowa Infantry, under Colonel Leake, on the right of it, to a position in the middle of the field, on the right of the main road in front of the white house. From this position his infantry advanced to the timber on the right of the orchard, and attacked and drove back, with the assistance of Murphy's battery, a large Confederate force that were moving against the Federal right. The fine rifled guns of Captain Murphy's battery, in the hands of his well-drilled company, threw percussion shells with the accuracy of sharp-shooters, and after disabling several rebel batteries, kept the others from coming into action in exposed positions.

After the terrible volleys of small-arms had died away along the front, and General Herron's infantry had fallen back upon his artillery, complete silence reigned over the field for a short time, broken at intervals by a shot or shell from the hoarse-throated artillery. General Hindman declined to advance again from his strong position under cover of the timber and brush to attack the Federal troops in the open field, and General Herron did not feel strong enough to make another assault single-handed. His troops were already greatly exhausted by long, forced marches and the fatiguing operations of the day.

About two o'clock, some of his troops on the extreme right heard distant rumbling sounds toward the west that gradually grew more distinct. A moment later, General Blunt was seen approaching at the head of three thousand cavalry and twenty pieces of artillery, through a small prairie at a full gallop. His infantry, having stripped for the fight at Rhea's Mills, were coming up at double-quick a short distance in his rear. Arriving on the field, he soon discovered by rapid inspection that the Confederate forces were in position in his front, and, ordering up a battery, opened fire upon them with shell. General Herron was at once advised of the arrival of the first division on the field, and the booming of artillery on his right announced to his nearly exhausted troops that their eagerly looked-for comrades had come to their assistance, inspiring them with new courage.

Colonel Wickersham, who had moved with his cavalry brigade in advance of the first division from Rhea's Mills, came upon, attacked, and put to flight a detachment of Confederate cavalry who were posted on the extreme left of the Southern army, at the junction of the Cane Hill and Rhea's Mills roads, watching for the approach of General Blunt's division. Finding that he was in front of the position where the Southern forces were drawn up for battle, the Colonel at once deployed skirmishers in his front, and detailed two companies from the First Iowa Cavalry to strengthen his advance guard, and then moved forward in columns of squadrons. On moving forward and passing open ground for a quarter of a mile, and approaching the timber to the southeast, his advance encountered and drew the fire of the enemy near a house on the left of the Confederate line. The Federal cavalry instantly returned the fire with carbines, and after receiving a reinforcement of another squadron of the First Iowa Cavalry, succeeded in driving them back about one hundred and fifty yards.

To further strengthen his advance while forming his brigade in line of battle, Colonel Wickersham sent to its support a section of two-pounder steel howitzers attached to the Tenth Illinois Cavalry, under Corporal Levi Cassity. The Corporal, proceeding down the road, passed a short distance beyond the line of the advance Federal squadrons with his howitzers, when the Confederate force, less than one hundred yards off, fired a volley at him, wounded him in the arm severely, killed one of his horses, and wounded the other. After this mishap, the men in charge of the other gun fell back rapidly with it to the main column, then forming in line and unlimbering, sent several rounds of canister into the Confederate force, causing it to retire into the timber. At the favorable moment, Lieutenant J. M. Simeral, First Iowa Cavalry, took twenty men, rescued and brought the abandoned howitzer and Corporal Cassity, who had remained with it, back into the Federal line.

While General Blunt's cavalry were thus engaged on the right, his three field batteries coming up under whip, galloped into positions pointed out for them by the General and his aides-de-camp, in an open field about four hundred yards to the left and in front of General Hindman's left wing. Captain J. W. Rabb's Second Indiana Battery being in advance, came into position first, and immediately commenced a heavy cross-fire with shot and shell upon the Confederate position, raking it from left to right, and at some points enfilading the rebel lines. Captain M. D. Tenney's First Kansas Battery of the second brigade coming up, took position on the right of Rabb, and Captain Henry Hopkins' Second Kansas (four-gun) Battery was placed in position a short distance to his left. The three batteries of sixteen pieces, supported by part of Colonel Wickersham's cavalry, now hurled a terrible storm of shot and shell into the Confederate lines, and with the assistance of General Herron's eighteen guns, about one half mile to the left, succeeded in driving back the Confederate infantry who were being massed against General Herron's right flank.

His infantry coming up, General Blunt directed Colonel Wickersham to move his brigade of cavalry, consisting of the Tenth Illinois, under Lieutenant-Colonel James Stuart; the First Iowa, under Colonel James O. Gower; the Eighth Missouri, under Colonel W. F. Geiger; and the battalion of the Second Wisconsin Cavalry, under Major W. H. Miller, to the extreme right of the Federal line, to guard it against the movement of the enemy in that direction, and to keep the road open to Rhea's Mills, where General Salomon, with part of the first brigade, was stationed, guarding the first division trains. Colonel E. Lynde, with part of the Ninth Kansas Cavalry, and Major Calkins, with part of the Third Wisconsin Cavalry, also occupied positions on the Federal right flank.

On the arrival of General Blunt's infantry upon the field, the second brigade, commanded by Colonel William Weer, consisting of the Tenth Kansas, under Major H. H. Williams, and the Thirteenth Kansas, under Colonel Thomas Bowen, and forty-four men of the Third Indian Regiment, under Lieutenant William Gallaher, formed in line on the right, in the rear of Captain Tenney's rifle-gun battery. The Tenth Kansas Infantry, with Lieutenant Gallaher's Indians on the right as skirmishers, formed the right wing, a dismounted detachment of Second Kansas Cavalry, under Lieutenant-Colonel Bassett, the centre, and the Thirteenth Kansas Infantry, the left wing of the brigade.

The third brigade, commanded by Colonel W. F. Cloud, consisting of the Second Kansas Cavalry, under Lieutenant-Colonel Owen A. Bassett, the Eleventh Kansas Infantry, under Colonel Thomas Ewing, Jr., and the First Indian Regiment, under Lieutenant-Colonel Stephen H. Wattles, formed on the left of Colonel Weer in the rear of Rabb's and Hopkins' batteries. The Eleventh Kansas Infantry formed the right wing, part of the Second Kansas Cavalry the centre, and the First Indian Regiment the left wing of the third brigade. Colonels Bassett and Wattles dismounted their regiments to fight on foot beside the infantry.

On the left of Colonel Wattles' First Indian Regiment, Colonel Leake's Twentieth Iowa Infantry of the second division formed in line. Very soon after these dispositions were made, the left wing of the Eleventh Kansas Infantry, under Lieutenant-Colonel Thomas Moonlight and Major P. B. Plumb, was detached to support Captain Rabb's battery.

Directly after his batteries were silenced, and his infantry driven back into the woods by Generals Blunt's and Herron's batteries, General Hindman determined to make a desperate effort to crush General Blunt's division, by hurling against it the division of General Frost and part of General Marmaduke's division. These troops, with two batteries, were at once ordered forward to assault the Federal right under General Blunt, while General Shoup's division, consisting of Generals Fagan's and McRae's brigades, and the brigades of McDonald and Shelby, of General Marmaduke's division, were ordered to continue the attack against the Federal left and centre under General Herron. The artillery firing having slackened, the captains of the Federal batteries of the first division having put a generous supply of grape and canister into their caissons, and preparations having been made on both sides for a desperate struggle, the forces of the Confederate left and centre under Generals Frost, Parsons, Roan, and Marmaduke, and of the Federal right under General Blunt, commenced to advance against each other about the same time.

The second and third brigades of General Blunt's first division, in the order described, with skirmish lines thrown out, advanced from the field and prairie, and entering the timber to the south, encountered the Confederate infantry of Generals Parsons' and Roan's brigades. In another moment the opposing forces became engaged in a severe conflict with small-arms, the dreadful roar of which extended along the entire front of the Federal right wing.

The storm of leaden missiles, flying thick as hail, rapidly thinned the ranks of the combatants by death and wounds. In a short time the Confederate line was driven back some distance into the woods, but, receiving reinforcements, advanced again and forced the Federal line to retire almost to the open ground. On seeing his troops falling back before a superior force of the enemy, General Blunt ordered Lieutenant E. L. Stover to move his section of twelve-pounder howitzers attached to the Second Kansas Cavalry into the timber on the right of the Eleventh Kansas Infantry. At the same time Captain Tenney's First Kansas Battery was ordered to a position on the left of that regiment near the edge of the timber. The Federal infantry, having re-formed in line, poured a galling fire of musketry into the advancing line of Confederates, and with the assistance of the howitzers and batteries, which now commenced playing upon the Confederate line with grape and canister, succeeded in checking and driving it back beyond the crest of the hill. But every time the Federal infantry endeavored to pass the summit of the hill they were met with a terrific musketry fire from the enemy, which obliged them to fall back a short distance to a less exposed position. The men were ordered to lie down, and by doing so they not only escaped almost unharmed the volleys of leaden hail hurled at them, but occupied themselves in keeping up an effective fire into the Confederate line the moment it came within range.

Thus the battle with fury raged until the sun, descending behind the mountains, cast a dark shadow over the bloody field. The roar of artillery and small-arms almost died away for a short time. The lingering rays of the sun were growing dim upon the western sides of the high mountain peaks to the eastward, and the leaders of the opposing forces knew that only a short space of time remained for continuing the struggle before the veil of darkness would cover all. A little later, as the shades of evening were fading into twilight, General Blunt ordered his infantry to advance again. They moved forward and reached the crest of the hill, when General Frost's infantry poured out of the woods in overwhelming numbers and charged, and, extending his line beyond the Federal right, commenced a rapid flank movement. The roar of small-arms again burst forth with great fury, but after firing several rounds the Federal infantry were ordered by General Blunt to fall back so as to draw the enemy within range of his guns, which were double charged with grape and canister.

General Hindman ordered two batteries of ten pieces into position on his extreme left to support General Frost's infantry. The Confederate infantry followed close upon the retiring Federal line, and on reaching the summit of the hill, rushed forward with wild shouts in a charge on the Federal batteries. They were permitted to approach near the edge of the timber, within about one hundred yards, when Captain Tenney's battery on the right, Rabb's battery in the centre, Hopkins' battery on the left, hurled a perfect storm of grape and canister into their ranks, and soon sent them in disorder back into the woods. The Federal infantry, by forming on the flanks in the space between the batteries and behind the broken panels of the rail fence near the edge of the timber, also by rapid firing, assisted in repulsing the charge of the enemy. While the conflict was thus raging along the front of the contending forces, the Confederate batteries just referred to as posted on General Hindman's left opened a hot fire upon the Federal position with shot and shell. To neutralize the effect of this artillery fire, General Blunt ordered Captain Tenney to turn his six ten-pounder Parrott rifle guns upon the rebel batteries. The Captain instantly complied, and wheeling his guns into position, commenced throwing percussion shells at them, and in less than ten minutes dismounted two of the rebel guns, and forced the others to leave their position and seek shelter behind the hill in the thick wood.

In this final struggle, two twelve-pound howitzers of the Third Wisconsin Cavalry, posted on the Federal right, by throwing shell and canister shot, did good work in checking and driving back the Confederate force attacking from that quarter. Farther to the Federal left, in the front of Colonel Cloud's brigade, the Confederate infantry commenced collecting in large force behind a farm-house and a stack of straw near the edge of the timber, with the apparent intention of charging Rabb's battery. A detachment of rebel sharp-shooters had also taken shelter in and behind the house and outbuildings, and were endeavoring to pick off mounted Federal officers. Captain Rabb's attention was called to the movements of the enemy behind the straw-pile and buildings, and he at once commenced throwing shell into them. The shells bursting, ignited the straw, and the house was soon in flames. In a few moments the enemy attempted to charge the battery, but were met by such a terrific discharge of grape and canister and volleys of musketry delivered by Lieutenant-Colonel Moonlight's battalion of the Eleventh Kansas Infantry, led by Major Plumb, that they were compelled to fall back into the wood.

Darkness having fallen, the firing of small-arms ceased on both sides, but General Blunt's powerful batteries continued to sweep the brush and wood in front with a storm of shot and shell for some time afterward. Though General Herron's infantry of the second and third divisions, except Colonel Leake's Twentieth Iowa Infantry, were not engaged at close quarters with the enemy after General Blunt came upon the field, his batteries under Murphy, Backof, Foust, and Lieutenant Borris, were constantly engaged from noon until dark in hurling shot and shell and grape and canister into the Confederate lines and position. So effective and destructive was the terrible fire of the Federal batteries, that General Hindman stated "there was no place of shelter upon any portion of the field"; that "wounds were given and death inflicted by the Federal artillery in the ranks of the reserves as well as in the front rank."

In the open fields the Federal batteries changed positions as often as desirable, and still kept up a steady fire into the Confederate position along the wooded ridge. In several instances the captains of these batteries, when closely pressed by the Confederate infantry, attached their guns to the limbers with prolonges and retired firing. The officers of the long-range rifled-gun batteries of Murphy in the centre and of Tenney on the Federal right, were constantly on the look-out for Confederate batteries. The moment one was discovered coming into position, or opening fire, the guns of Captain Murphy's or Captain Tenney's battery were turned upon it, and two or three rounds of percussion shells were generally sufficient to silence it and drive it from the field. It was therefore a source of much satisfaction to the Federal officers that they had by their excellent artillery practice prevented the Confederate batteries from inflicting upon the Federal forces any serious loss or damage.

Night dropped a veil of darkness between the combatants, and apparently left the contest undecided. When the firing ceased at dark, the opposing armies occupied the positions they had taken up on going into action. The Confederate forces bivouacked on the wooded ridge upon which they formed in the morning; and the Federal forces bivouacked in the fields and open ground in front of the ridge. As the fighting was in the timber south of the fields and open ground, some of the Federal dead and wounded fell within the Confederate lines. Although it was a cold, frosty night, neither side ventured to make up fires the early part of the night, so near each other were the combatants resting upon their arms. Assuming that

General Hindman would be in position to renew the conflict the next morning, General Blunt, commanding the three divisions of the Army of the Frontier, determined, under cover of the darkness of the night, to strengthen his line, and have every thing in readiness to renew the battle at daylight. His division trains, which were at Rhea's Mills, five miles west, and exposed to attack, he ordered to Fayetteville, in the rear of the army. General Salomon, commanding the first brigade of the first division, who was guarding the trains with the Ninth Wisconsin Infantry and some detachments of other regiments, was ordered to bring his men to the front immediately. Colonel Wickersham, commanding the cavalry brigade, was directed to detail sufficient cavalry for an escort to the trains.

On the arrival of the cavalry the trains commenced moving out from Rhea's Mills about eight o'clock, and passing to the rear of the army the advance teams reached Fayetteville early the next morning. In the engagement of the afternoon about three thousand of General Blunt's cavalry were not brought into action. The force sent out under Colonel Judson, Sixth Kansas Cavalry, to attack the rear of the Confederate army, did not reach the field until nearly dark. In the rapid movements of the Federal troops from Cane Hill to the battle-field, quite a number of men of the infantry regiments were obliged to drop out of the ranks from exhaustion. The strength of the infantry regiments of General Herron's divisions was also greatly reduced during the three days' marches by the men who were unable to endure the prolonged exertion dropping out of the ranks. The stragglers and men who had thus fallen out of ranks were collected, as far as practicable, and brought to the front during the night to join their proper regiments. In General Blunt's division not one of the regiments had sustained a heavy loss, and in General Herron's second and third divisions only three regiments had suffered severely. By dismounting part of his cavalry to fight on foot, General Blunt could therefore go into battle next morning much stronger than he had gone into the conflict just closed. It would be easier now to properly co-ordinate the movements of the troops than it was in the recent struggle. General Hindman had been permitted to throw the weight of his army first against General Herron's two divisions, and then against General Blunt's first division. He would not likely have an opportunity to do this again, for General Blunt determined to have his three divisions next morning make a simultaneous attack upon the Confederate position.

To satisfy the pinch of hunger, provisions, consisting of hard bread and bacon, were supplied by the commissariat to the Federal troops to prepare them for battle; ammunition was brought up and also distributed to them. The Federal wounded had also, as far as practicable, been taken up and properly cared for by the surgeons and their corps of assistants.

On the Confederate side, General Hindman held a council with his generals, and, after carefully considering the situation, decided to withdraw his army from the field without a further struggle, and to fall back to Van Buren. His troops commenced to withdraw about midnight, and on retiring kindled numerous fires along his front and left them burning for the purpose of deceiving the Federal army. To get his artillery off the field with as little noise as possible, the wheels of the carriages and limbers were muffled with the torn blankets of his soldiers. Having started his infantry and artillery on the retreat to Van Buren, General Hindman remained near the field with two brigades of cavalry, and sent General Marmaduke, accompanied by several members of his staff, under a flag of truce, with a communication to General Blunt, requesting a personal interview for the purpose of making provisions for burying the dead and caring for the wounded of the Confederate army left upon the field. General Marmaduke and his party approached the Federal line on the Fayetteville road, and being halted by the vigilant picket-guards, on whose eyelids sweet sleep sat not, were conducted by the officer of the day to General Herron's headquarters, and held until General Blunt, whose headquarters were about a mile distant, could be communicated with. General Blunt granted the interview, and the next morning, shortly after sunrise, accompanied by General Herron and several officers of their respective staffs and escorts, rode forward to meet Generals Hindman and Marmaduke and members of their staffs.

The interview lasted until about ten o'clock, during which time the commanding generals of the opposing forces entered into a mutual agreement in regard to the exchange of prisoners and the disposition of the wounded left on the field. General Hindman was given six hours to bury his dead, but the two regiments of cavalry detailed for the purpose, instead of attending to that duty, commenced gathering up arms from the field. Their conduct was reported to General Herron, who went in person to the Confederate Colonels and informed them that any of their men found doing any thing else than burying the dead would be held as prisoners of war. This firmness of the Federal General had the effect of stopping them from gathering up any more arms, and the Confederate cavalry soon afterward retired to overtake General Hindman, leaving the Confederate dead to be buried by the Federal forces.

General Blunt reported a loss in his three divisions of 167 men killed, 798 wounded, and 183 missing. On the Confederate side General Hindman reported his casualties at 164 men killed, 817 wounded, and 336 missing. A considerable proportion of the Confederate missing were probably among the wounded, from the fact that the day after the battle General Blunt furnished five thousand rations for one thousand Confederate wounded to keep them from starving.

CHAPTER XXXI.

THE CAPTURE OF VAN BUREN, ARKANSAS.

IN two or three days after the battle of Prairie Grove, the soldiers of both sides who fell upon the field were properly interred. The Federal wounded were removed from the field hospitals to Fayetteville, where the churches and college buildings were turned into hospitals to receive them. And the Confederate wounded were taken to Cane Hill in ambulances furnished by the Federal commanders. The day after the battle the troops of the second and third divisions, under General Herron, went into camp on the battle-field, and the troops of General Blunt's division returned to their former positions at Rhea's Mills and Cane Hill.

The time given General Hindman to inter his dead was made good use of in getting his army over the mountains, safe from the pursuit of the Federal forces. When five o'clock came, the hour at which the flag of truce expired, it was too late in the day, and the Confederate army had got too far from the field, for the Federal forces to commence pursuit. General Blunt did not see until he had granted the flag of truce for six hours, that General Hindman's solicitude for his dead was simply an excuse to gain time for getting his army off the field without a panic.

In the heat of battle it was not unusual for the dead to lie upon the battle-field for several days, and certain it was that in the cool weather of December there was no need of being in a hurry to make the interments of those who fell at Prairie Grove.

After the troops of the second and third divisions had rested two or three days, and several large wagon trains had arrived with supplies for the army, Generals Blunt and Herron had a conference for the purpose of deciding upon a plan of further operations. They had just received information that General Hindman, with the greater part of his army, was still north of the Arkansas River, encamped in the vicinity of Van Buren. They therefore decided to take eight thousand picked men of infantry, cavalry, and artillery from the three divisions; cross the mountains in two columns, one by the telegraph road and one by the Cove Creek road, and after forming a junction south of the mountains, move forward rapidly and attack and rout the Southern forces before they could have time to prepare defensive field-works. But severe winter weather setting in, with a snow-storm and a six-inch fall of snow, caused the Federal generals to postpone the contemplated movement. The few days the stress of weather obliged them to remain in camp at Rhea's Mills and Prairie Grove were usefully employed in strengthening their lines of communication with Fort Scott and Springfield, and in thoroughly scouting the country a day's march east and west of their positions with large detachments of cavalry. It was very evident from the large number of deserters from the Southern army brought in by the detachments of Federal cavalry thus sent out, that General Hindman's army was greatly demoralized. Nearly all these deserters claimed that they were conscripts; that they were at heart Union men, and had been forced into the Confederate army against their wishes. They also stated that in the recent battle Colonel Adams' Arkansas regiment, made up mostly of conscripts, after the first volley threw down their arms, fled from the field, and afterward deserted.

To inspire his troops with desperate courage, and to fill their minds with a fanatical hatred of the Federal troops, General Hindman, on the eve of the battle, issued an address to his army, in which he drew a dreadful and fiendish picture of the foe his men were to engage. Most of the Confederate dead and wounded left on the field had each a printed copy of this coarse address in his pocket.

The weather having moderated, and a second snow having fallen and almost disappeared, Generals Blunt and Herron met on Christmas night and arranged the details for their expedition to Van Buren. At three o'clock on the morning of the 27th, the troops of the second and third divisions, under General Herron and Colonel Huston, were to march from Prairie Grove, taking the telegraph road, and at the same hour the troops of the first division, under General Blunt, were to march from Rhea's Mills, taking the Cove Creek road. The two columns, consisting of eight thousand infantry and cavalry and thirty pieces of artillery, were to form a junction near Lee's Creek south of the mountains.

The day before this expedition started, Colonel W. A. Phillips, with twelve hundred Indian troops, two companies of white cavalry, and a section of artillery, was sent up through the Cherokee nation to Fort Gibson, to attack a Confederate force of Indians and Texans under General Cooper at Fort Davis, on the south bank of the Arkansas River.

Brigadier-General Salomon was left with a regiment of infantry, a battery of artillery, and detachments from different regiments to guard the first division's trains at Rhea's Mills. A considerable force was also left to guard the trains of the second and third divisions at Prairie Grove. While preparations were being made for the expedition to start, a report was purposely given out and circulated through the camps that a demonstration would be made in the direction of Huntsville, so that if any of General Hindman's spies were present, they would be misled in regard to the real destination of the troops.

At three o'clock on the morning of the 27th, the two Federal columns started on the march from Rhea's Mills and Prairie Grove to Van Buren. The night was chilly, with the temperature below the freezing-point, for the puddles in the road were covered with thin sheets of ice. The three or four inches of snow which had recently fallen had not quite disappeared, and as all the slight depressions in the road were filled with slush, the outlook for the infantry and artillery was not very cheerful. A few hours' marching, however, brought the troops daylight, and into a region where the snow and ice had entirely disappeared, and where the road was firmer and inclined to be somewhat rocky.

The advance of General Blunt's division struck the head of Cove Creek about ten o'clock. This stream winds through the mountains in a southerly direction, and of course increased in size as the troops descended it. The rapid melting of the snow in the mountains and the recent heavy rain-fall had started numerous little torrents which, pouring into it, had swelled it to overflowing. In its winding, gurgling course through the mountains, from side to side of the narrow valley, the road crosses it in a distance of twenty miles some thirty-five times. At first the infantry were not much inconvenienced in crossing it, but gradually it became more disagreeable, for every time they waded it, their clothing was wet a little higher. When they bivouacked about ten o'clock that night, nearly all the clothing they had on was wet, for at the different crossings, since dark, the water had been waist-deep. And it was almost ice-cold, for it came mostly from melted snow that had just run down in the mountain torrents.

The infantry stood the terrible day's march with very

little complaint, and suffered less discomfort than one would have supposed. Though their clothing to their waists was wet all the afternoon and evening, the physical exercise of marching kept them from getting chilled. Immediately after halting that night to bivouac on the bank of the raging, foaming creek, they kindled numerous blazing fires and dried their clothing, after which food and a refreshing sleep prepared them for the next day's march.

The bugles sounded reveille at three o'clock the next morning, and in less than half an hour the troops and animals had taken food to satisfy the demands of hunger and resumed the march. The sky had become partly overcast during the night and there was no moon, so that it was pitch dark when the troops moved forward. Colonel Bassett, with part of the Second Kansas Cavalry, led the advance. Then came Colonel Judson with the Sixth Kansas Cavalry and two mountain howitzers. Next in the column was Colonel Barstow with the Third Wisconsin Cavalry and two howitzers, followed by the field artillery and infantry. After crossing Cove Creek five or six times and Lee's Creek once, the cavalry at daylight struck the telegraph road at Oliver's store, eighteen miles north of Van Buren.

A short halt was made for the infantry and artillery to close up. In a few moments General Herron's advance came in sight. That gallant officer had also encountered difficulties in his march over the mountains in the night. He was obliged to use twelve horses to the gun to get his artillery over, and in some places, in addition to these, the assistance of fifty men pulling on a rope was required. On resuming the march Generals Blunt and Herron rode at the head of the column a short distance in the rear of the advance guard. The road was now much wider and better and the cavalry marched by fours.

About three miles south of the junction of the Cove Creek and telegraph roads, the Federal advance came upon the Confederate pickets, who, after exchanging shots with the Federal cavalry, fled in the direction of their camp on the road to Van Buren. An exciting chase ensued, in which the Federal cavalry kept close upon the heels of the flying pickets until they reached the Confederate camp at Dripping Springs, some six miles distant. The report of the shots in front had scarcely died away on the resonant morning air before the entire column of Federal cavalry had struck the gallop, which was kept up until the troops came in sight of the Confederate camp.

To watch the movements of the Federal forces encamped on the north side of the mountains, and to cover Van Buren against attack, General Hindman had posted Colonel Crump with a brigade of Texas cavalry eight miles north of that place at Dripping Springs. Colonel Crump's camp was on the north side of a high hill, west of the main road. In his front, to the north, were open fields with unbroken rail fences. He had very little time to prepare his men for action, for when his pickets came into camp under whip and spurs, the Federal cavalry were coming up in sight.

The clouds had drifted away; the bright sunshine had dispelled the gloom and chill of the night, and it was a lovely Sunday morning. No rumor having reached Colonel Crump of a Federal force being south of the mountains, he allowed his men to breakfast a little later than usual. On coming up on the north side of the field, in sight of the Confederate camp, General Blunt in a moment decided to charge it with his cavalry. Having in a moment thrown down the fence in a number of places, his cavalry came into line in a trot, the Second Kansas on the left, the Sixth Kansas in the centre, and the Third Wisconsin on the right, and dashing across the field at a full gallop, approached within a few yards of the Confederate camp, just beyond the fence, and opened a heavy fire with carbines upon such of the Confederates as had the courage to stand. Most of Colonel Crump's command, however, fled before the Federal cavalry got half across the field, and the remainder, not disabled, fled on receiving the volley from the Federal carbines.

A moment after firing the volley, the fence on the south side of the field was thrown down, and the Federal cavalry formed in the Confederate camp and moved forward rapidly in line over the hill and through the wood in pursuit of the flying foe. In his precipitate retreat, Colonel Crump twice endeavored to form his men in line to check his irresistible pursuers, but was unsuccessful. General Blunt soon saw that the Confederate force was utterly demoralized; that he need not advance farther in line of battle; and drawing his men into the road, moved forward by fours in a gallop, close upon the heels of the Confederate cavalry in their flight to Van Buren, through the streets of the city, and down the bank of the river.

The sight of the Texas cavalry rushing wildly through the streets, bareheaded, barebacked, and half-dressed, closely pursued by two thousand blue-coats, with rattling sabres, greatly astonished the citizens, who hurriedly came out of their houses to ascertain the cause of the confusion. After changing from line of battle to column by fours, General Blunt sent out detachments of cavalry on both sides of the main road to scour the country and pick up stragglers who had fled from Colonel Crump's camp. At the same time, General Herron also sent Major Charles Banzhaf with a battalion of the First Missouri Cavalry to strike the road below Van Buren, with the hope of cutting off any of the Confederate cavalry and trains that should attempt to escape down the north bank of the river.

On arriving upon the heights overlooking the town and river, the Federal generals saw three steamboats, with steam up, leaving the wharf, and endeavoring to escape down the river. When the Federal cavalry reached the river front, the leading boat had got upwards of half a mile off, and was making good time with a fair prospect of getting away. It was soon ascertained, however, that, about two miles below the city, the river made a bend to the north, and that the channel changed to the north side at that point. General Blunt therefore ordered a force of his cavalry and two howitzers to hurry forward and reach the bend, if possible, before the boats, and open fire on them if the officers attempted to pass or refused to land on the north side. Major Banzhaf, with his Missouri cavalry, was also marching toward the bend. Captain Irving W. Fuller's company, being in advance, reached it before the cavalry, which had marched through the city, and seeing the steamer *Rose Douglas* steaming down the river, opened fire on her with their carbines and brought her to a landing. Under the Captain's instructions, one of his officers boarded her with a detachment of soldiers and took her back to Van Buren. Her cargo consisted of four thousand three hundred bushels of corn, six hogsheads of sugar, and a large quantity of molasses, which had just arrived from Little Rock for General Hindman's army. Major Banzhaf's cavalry also captured and brought back to Van Buren a train of twenty-seven wagons loaded with ammunition, baggage, and camp and garrison equipage. In the meantime, General Blunt's cavalry, with the assistance of his mountain howitzers, captured the other two steamers, the *Notre* and *Key West*, and brought them back to the wharf. They were also laden with corn and other supplies for the Southern forces in that vicinity. Another steamer, laid up at the wharf for repairs, was also captured.

The horse-power ferry, while attempting to cross to the opposite side of the river with a number of Southern soldiers and citizens, was struck by a shell thrown by one of the howitzers of the Sixth Kansas Cavalry. The shell exploded, killing the horse at the tread-wheel, and wounding several men. In another moment the boat got into shallow water, and the uninjured men jumped overboard, waded to shore, and escaped. Directly after the captured steamers were brought back to the wharf and made fast, the Federal cavalry commenced bringing in prisoners, wagons, and teams, captured while endeavoring to escape.

Generals Blunt and Herron, with a number of their officers, went aboard the boats to examine their cargoes, and to obtain, if practicable, information of the strength and positions of General Hindman's forces in the vicinity. In a short time, several hundred Federal officers and soldiers, who had dismounted and left their horses a few blocks back to feed them, came down to the river-front to look at the captured boats. While they were thus amusing themselves, and talking over the exciting scenes of the morning, the sound of artillery was suddenly heard from the south bank of the river, and in another instant a solid shot came with a crash, striking the ground only a few yards from a group of soldiers. A moment later, shot and shell from the Confederate battery across the river commenced falling thick and fast along the levee, some striking the boats and some the buildings in the city.

The Federal officers and soldiers at once retired behind some blocks of brick buildings, and soon afterward to the side of the hill in full view of the Confederate battery. About two o'clock two batteries of General Blunt's long-range rifled guns arrived on the heights in the suburbs of the city near the river, and opened fire on the Confederate battery with percussion shells. The artillery duel which now commenced lasted until sunset, when the Confederate batteries and Shaver's brigade of infantry supporting them withdrew. Late in the afternoon the echo of the thundering artillery rolled in undulations down the river to a great distance, growing gradually fainter until it died away.

Having ascertained that General Frost's division was encamped on the south bank of the Arkansas, five miles below Van Buren, General Blunt took part of his artillery down on the north side of the river to a point opposite the Confederate camp, and immediately opened a heavy fire upon it with shot and shell, and in about two hours compelled the Confederate General to break up his camp and retreat south. General Hindman was now getting alarmed at the situation. The two steamboats, *Eva* and *Arkansas*, at Fort Smith, laden with supplies for his army, he ordered burned, after taking from them such stores as he was able to haul away with his limited means of transportation. Knowing that General Blunt had three captured steamers with which he could cross his troops and artillery over the river, and knowing also that his own troops were too much demoralized to fight a battle with the victorious Federal forces, the Confederate leader decided to destroy all the public property which could not be removed, to abandon Fort Smith, and put his army on the retreat southward in the direction of Arkadelphia. The scarcity of transportation, and the disorder and confusion that prevailed, obliged him to leave some six hundred sick soldiers at Fort Smith to take care of themselves.

The retreat of General Hindman's forces during the night of the 28th saved General Blunt the trouble of crossing his troops over the river the next morning to attack them. General Hindman's conduct in ordering his batteries to throw shot and shell all the afternoon into the city filled with women and children was condemned as unwarrantable, for he could not hope to hurt the Federal troops as much as his own people in their houses and on their premises.

On dashing into the city at the head of his two thousand cavalry, General Blunt immediately ordered the telegraph office seized, and found in it some interesting despatches from General Hindman to his officers and to General Holmes, commanding the trans-Mississippi Department. A short time, however, after the arrival of the Federal cavalry, the telegraph wire above and below Van Buren was cut and the line stopped working.

When it was ascertained that the Southern forces had commenced to retreat from their different positions before midnight, the Federal troops returned to Van Buren, went into camp, and regaled themselves with a bountiful supply of the choicest rations from the captured commissary stores. The soldiers were also mindful of the care of their worn and hungry horses, and fed them generously from the large quantity of corn captured on the boats.

While the Federal arms were thus successful under Generals Blunt and Herron, the column sent out under Colonel Phillips crossed the Arkansas River above Fort Gibson on the 27th, and after a short skirmish captured and destroyed Fort Davis, upon which the Confederate Government had expended upwards of one million dollars. On reducing the extensive barracks and commissary buildings to ashes, the Colonel commenced the pursuit of General Cooper's and Colonel Stand Watie's forces in the direction of Scullyville and Fort Smith. General Hindman received information by special courier of the advance of this force under Colonel Phillips down through the Choctaw nation, a few minutes after he heard of General Blunt's arrival in Van Buren, and being thus threatened on the flank and rear, immediately ordered General Cooper to retire to Johnson's Station on the Canadian River, ninety miles southwest of Fort Smith in the direction of the Texas frontier.

Generals Blunt and Herron were now satisfied from their own observations that the Federal arms should take Little Rock and control the navigation of the Arkansas River from that point to Fort Smith, before attempting to maintain a large Federal force in Western Arkansas south of the Boston Mountains. They decided, therefore, to return with their troops to Rhea's Mills and Prairie Grove to report to General Curtis, the department commander, that the Confederate forces had been driven from all that part of the Indian country north of the Canadian River and from Western Arkansas in great demoralization, and that the Army of the Frontier was ready for further aggressive operations.

After the Federal troops and public animals used all the commissary supplies and forage they could, General Blunt ordered as much of the supplies as he could find transportation to haul back with him removed from the boats. Shortly after dark on the evening of the 29th, the four captured steamboats and ferry-boat were set on fire and consumed, together with some fifteen thousand bushels of corn and other stores which had lately been brought up the river for the use of the Confederate army. The tents and camp equipage captured from Colonel Crump's command were also destroyed. In addition to the steamboats and supplies the Federal forces also captured upwards of one hundred Confederate soldiers, sixty wagons and teams, two hundred and fifty fine cattle, and a large number of horses and mules.

The casualties on the Federal side were one killed and five wounded. No official report was made of the Confederate killed and wounded. On the morning of the 30th General Blunt left Van Buren with his troops, and arrived at Rhea's Mills on the afternoon of December 31st. General John M. Schofield, who had relinquished command of the Army of the Frontier in November, on account of sickness, returned to resume command. When he arrived at Prairie Grove he found that nearly all the troops had gone on the expedition to Van Buren. He immediately set out to overtake them, but met them on the return march near Dripping Springs. He then returned with General Herron to Prairie Grove and resumed command of the Army of the Frontier.

CHAPTER XXXII.

GENERAL MARMADUKE'S ATTACK ON SPRINGFIELD, MISSOURI.

On the return of the troops to Rhea's Mills and Prairie Grove from the expedition to Van Buren, General Schofield resumed command of the Army of the Frontier. He had been absent a little more than a month, but from what he saw in his recent trip south of the Boston Mountains, and from information received from officers of his command, he was satisfied that it was impracticable to occupy the Arkansas Valley in his front until the fall of Little Rock and the opening of the Arkansas River to navigation.

The country for one hundred miles below Fort Smith had been so thoroughly drained of supplies for General Hindman's army, that the citizens of that section were on the verge of suffering for food. Forage was so scarce within twenty-five miles of Fort Smith and Van Buren, that on the return of the army from Prairie Grove General Hindman was obliged to ship corn by steamboat from Little Rock for his artillery horses, and to send General Marmaduke's cavalry division in the neighborhood of Lewisburg, one hundred miles below. And the large Federal and Confederate forces operating in Northwestern Arkansas, north of the mountains, during the autumn and early part of the winter, had consumed all the forage and army supplies that could be obtained in that section. As there was no probability that he would soon be threatened in his front by any considerable Confederate force, and as the surrounding country would no longer furnish forage for his cavalry and artillery horses, General Schofield determined to move most of his troops eastward through the northern-border counties of Arkansas, so as to cover Springfield, his main depot of supplies, protect his line of communication, and at the same time watch the movements of the enemy in the Arkansas Valley.

On the morning of January 2, 1863, General Blunt's first division struck tents at Rhea's Mills, and took up the line of march for Elm Springs, twenty-two miles north. The second and third divisions, under General Herron, marched from Prairie Grove to Fayetteville. The cause of this retrograde movement not being understood by the troops, General Schofield was severely criticised for ordering it. Having completed a brilliant campaign, with the enemy driven from the front, it was generally thought strange that the army should commence to retreat.

At Elm Springs General Blunt was relieved of his command, and after issuing a farewell address to his troops, returned to Kansas, where he was enthusiastically received and honored with distinguished consideration for his successful operations against the Confederate forces in his recent campaign.

On the 7th of January General Schofield reviewed the first division at Elm Springs, and on the 8th returned to Fayetteville to review the second and third divisions, under General Herron. The moment the grand reviews were over, the movement of the troops commenced. In the dispositions about to be made, it had been necessary to make some changes in the *personnel* of the army. The Indian brigade, consisting of the three Indian regiments, Captain Hopkins' Third Kansas Battery, and a battalion of the Sixth Kansas Cavalry, were detached under Colonel W. A. Phillips to take position near Maysville, on the line of Arkansas and the Cherokee nation. The First Arkansas Union Cavalry and some detachments of other regiments, under Colonel M. La Rue Harrison, were left at Fayetteville to protect the Federal sick and wounded in the general hospitals at that place, and to scout the country and keep it clear of the enemy as far in the direction of Van Buren as practicable.

Just as the troops of the different brigades were in readiness to march, General Schofield received a despatch from General Brown, commanding at Springfield, that General Marmaduke, with a force of five thousand Confederate cavalry and mounted infantry and a battery of light artillery, had left the Arkansas River and was marching rapidly upon Springfield to destroy the Federal depot of supplies at that place. Knowing that the garrison of Springfield was small, and feeling anxiety for the safety of the place, General Schofield at once ordered Colonel Weer, commanding the first division, to proceed by forced marches to reinforce General Brown. By ten o'clock on the night of the 8th Colonel Weer had his troops in motion and *en route* for Springfield.

The Confederate leaders were well informed of the distribution of the Federal forces in Southern and Southwest Missouri, and of the strength of the stations along the military road from Fayetteville to Springfield and Rolla. They knew, too, that, excepting Springfield, none of the fortified stations in Southern Missouri occupied by the Union militia were armed with artillery, and could not hold out very long against a force provided with artillery. They thought that an expedition sent north would be able to do great damage to the Government, and cause the Federal troops in the Arkansas Valley to hasten toward the northern border of the State to protect their line of communication with their base of supplies. Most of the men of General Marmaduke's division were from Missouri and familiar with the roads and streams in that part of the State which it was proposed to invade. Although in mid-winter, these troops were anxious to start north upon the invasion, because it held out a prospect of giving them an opportunity to return to their homes for a brief season to see their families.

On the day that General Blunt captured Van Buren, but before the telegraph line was destroyed, General Hindman telegraphed General Marmaduke, then at Lewisburg, to move north with his division in the direction of Missouri, and threaten the Federal rear, and if possible destroy the Federal depot of supplies at Springfield, hoping by this movement to cause the withdrawal of the Federal troops from the Arkansas Valley. In compliance with instructions, at daylight on the morning of December 31, 1862, after some preparation, the expedition, under General Marmaduke, consisting of the brigades of Shelby, McDonald, and Carroll, and Bledsoe's three-gun battery, left Lewisburg and started north on the march to Springfield, a distance of two hundred miles. During the first day's march orders were received from General Holmes detaching Colonel Carroll's Arkansas brigade to operate against General Blunt's forces in Western Arkansas. But in its place General Marmaduke was to have Colonel Porter's brigade of Missouri troops then stationed at Pocahontas.

The troops being well mounted and unencumbered with heavy transportation were able to move with great celerity. Nor were their movements likely to be reported to the Federal commanders at once, for their line of march the first three days was over a rough and dreary mountain region, which the Federal scouting parties rarely visited. But in crossing the Boston Mountains Shelby's advance came upon a party of Unionists and conscripts who had escaped from the Southern army, and in the spirited skirmish that ensued several men were killed and wounded on each side. In a short time, however, the Unionists found that they were fighting a large Confederate force, and then they fled to their inaccessible retreats in the mountains. Continuing his march north, General Marmaduke passed into Missouri without further opposition, but not without his advance coming to the knowledge of the Federal officers operating in Southern Missouri.

On the 4th of January Captain Milton Burch, Fourteenth Missouri State Militia Cavalry, left his station at Ozark, Missouri, with a scout of one hundred men for Carroll County, Arkansas, to destroy a powder-mill and to break up a rebel guerilla organization in the vicinity of the mill. At the Widow Fisher's, on Big Creek, six miles from Dubuque, Arkansas, he captured two rebel prisoners, from whom he ascertained that General Marmaduke was near at hand with a Confederate force of five thousand or six thousand men, on the march to Springfield. On the receipt of this information Captain Burch despatched couriers to notify General Brown, commanding at Springfield, and then countermarched his detachment toward Ozark *via* Beaver station, where Major Turner was posted with about two hundred Union militia. As the Major had very little transportation, the station had to be abandoned with the loss of some Government property. Captain Burch had hardly got out of sight of the station when McDonald's regiment came up and opened fire upon him, and took possession of the block-house, and burned it and the other buildings used for quarters.

Finding that the enemy were in large force and pressing him closely, Captain Burch continued to retire toward Ozark, and arrived there about ten o'clock on the night of the 6th, and immediately had all his baggage conveyed across the James River and started on the road to Springfield. A few hours later, under instructions he abandoned the post and fell back to Springfield, a distance of twenty miles. In dividing his command to attack the Federal stations at Beaver and Ozark, General Marmaduke lost some time, which enabled General Brown to make some preparation to meet the attack on Springfield. Though the country from the Arkansas border to within a few miles of Springfield was rough, mountainous, and broken, the roads were generally firm and in good condition for the rapid movement of mounted troops. On account of the scarcity of forage in that region, General Marmaduke was obliged to march his troops in two or more columns, on nearly parallel roads, as far as practicable, with instructions to the commanders of the several columns to form a junction near Springfield on a given day.

The courier from Captain Burch arrived at Springfield about three o'clock in the evening of the 7th, and delivered to General Brown the Captain's despatch reporting the advance of the enemy. Not knowing but that the enemy were advancing close upon the heels of the courier, the General at once telegraphed the situation to General Curtis, commanding the Department at St. Louis, and to General Schofield, commanding the Army of the Frontier in Northwestern Arkansas, and then commenced to take active measures for putting the place in as good a defensive condition as possible. General Curtis immediately ordered General Warren and other officers commanding detachments of troops east of Springfield, to reinforce General Brown by forced marches. Though General Marmaduke and Colonel Shelby spoke of Springfield as the Gibraltar of the Southwest, it was by no means strongly fortified in a military sense. There were four forts under construction to command the approaches to the town, but none of these forts was completed or fully armed.

That he might be as strong as practicable by the next morning, General Brown despatched couriers to all the commanding officers of stations within a radius of twenty-five miles of Springfield, with instructions for them to come to his assistance with every available man by forced marches. Brigadier-General C. B. Holland, commanding the enrolled militia of that district, was also instructed to call into active service and concentrate at that post, at the earliest practicable moment, every available man of the several regiments of his command. When the State was in no immediate danger from an invasion or from an uprising of the secessionists, as was sometimes threatened, the enrolled militia were furloughed and allowed to return to their homes to pursue their usual occupations. But now it was a time of public danger, and all the furloughed men were called in to take their places in line with the regular troops. The news of the approaching foe soon spread through the city and surrounding country, and aids and mounted messengers galloped to and fro with instructions to officers in regard to defensive preparations.

General Brown had received no intimation that a large Confederate force would probably attempt to flank the Army of the Frontier and invade his district, and as frequent requisitions were made upon him for troops to escort trains, for scouting purposes, and to garrison a number of small posts in Southwest Missouri, he had reluctantly and unavoidably allowed the garrison of Springfield to be reduced to a minimum strength of perhaps less than one thousand effective men. In the crisis that was at hand, he determined to arm all the stragglers from regiments in the city, and all the convalescent soldiers from the hospitals, and put them in the forts. These men, to the number of some four hundred, were organized under Dr. S. H. Melcher and Captain C. B. McAfee, and were known as the Quinine Brigade. Many loyal citizens also volunteered, and were furnished with arms to fight in defence of their homes. Detachments of cavalry were sent out on all the roads leading south, to obtain information and report the movements of the enemy. During the night scouts and couriers came in and reported to General Brown that the Confederates were advancing on the Ozark road.

At daylight on the morning of the 8th, Captain Burch arrived, and reported that the enemy's advance had reached that place about midnight, a few moments after he abandoned it, and burned the block-house and other buildings of the post. The flames of the burning buildings darted high into the midnight air and were seen by the citizens for miles around. Though the night of the 7th was so cold that the moisture from the breaths of the soldiers froze on their beards, the Confederate officers decided when they arrived at Ozark that they were too near the prize they so much coveted to spend the night in balmy sleep.

During the night General Brown had three iron twelve-pounder howitzers and one six-pounder gun mounted on wagon-wheels and rolled into Fort No. 4, and two six-pounder brass field-pieces were mounted in Fort No. 1. Wagon trains from Rolla and from the Army of the Frontier arrived during the night, and early on the morning of the 8th the troops from the different stations around Springfield commenced coming in. About ten o'clock the Federal pickets and scouts, some three miles out on the Ozark road, were fired into by the Confederate advance, and fell back upon a detachment of cavalry which had been thrown forward to observe the movements of the enemy. To meet the attack, General Brown had 453 men of Colonel Walter King's Third Missouri State Militia Cavalry, 289 men of Colonel George H. Hall's Fourth Missouri State Militia Cavalry, 223 men of Lieutenant-Colonel John Pound's Fourteenth Missouri State Militia Cavalry, 378 men of Colonel Thomas Z. Cook's Eighteenth Iowa Infantry, 400 stragglers and convalescents under Colonel Benjamin Crabb, Nineteenth Iowa Infantry, and 350 men of Colonel Henry Sheppard's Seventy-second and Colonel Marcus Boyd's Seventy-fourth Regiments Enrolled Missouri Militia.

The near approach of the enemy was at once reported

29

to General Brown. He formed his infantry in line in advance of the forts on the south side of town, and then ordered Colonels King and Hall to move out with the Third and Fourth Regiments Missouri State Militia Cavalry, and meet the advancing foe. For a distance of four miles south and southeast of town, the country was rolling prairie and farms. Proceeding a mile south of town, Colonels King and Hall saw the Confederates advancing in line of battle.

Colonel Shelby had dismounted three regiments to act as infantry, and kept Quantrill's guerilla company and Major Elliott's battalion of scouts mounted to operate on his flanks. McDonald's brigade formed the left of the Confederate line, and remained mounted. When the opposing forces approached within range, they opened fire upon each other with small-arms. But the great length of the Confederate line soon compelled Colonels King and Hall to retire within range of the Federal infantry and forts. General Marmaduke continued to advance his line, and in a few moments opened fire with his three pieces of artillery, throwing shot and shell against the Federal line, the forts, and some houses occupied by the Federal sharp-shooters.

General Brown rode to the front to direct the movement of his troops in person. He soon saw that it was necessary to burn several houses south of the forts, which obstructed the view of the approach of the enemy, and which would, if allowed to remain, afford shelter to the Confederate sharp-shooters. He also saw that he had not a sufficient force to march out and fight the Confederates a pitched battle, and being unable to assume the offensive, he determined to make as good a fight as possible with the troops at his disposal.

The moment the Confederate line came within range, the Federal artillery from the forts opened a vigorous fire upon it with shot and shell. A body of Confederate sharp-shooters endeavored to reach a point of shelter within rifle-range of the fort, but were driven back by the artillery and riflemen from the forts. Gradually the roar of artillery and rattle of small-arms became more constant, showing that the conflict was becoming fiercer, and that both sides were evincing greater determination in the struggle. About one o'clock, part of Shelby's brigade advanced, threatening to turn the Federal left, when Colonel King, with the Third Missouri State Militia Cavalry, charged the Confederates and drove them back upon their artillery and sharp-shooters. In conjunction with this movement, Colonel Hall advanced with the Fourth Missouri State Militia Cavalry and engaged the Confederate centre, but as his regiment and also Colonel King's were exposed in an open field to the concentrated fire of the Confederate artillery and infantry, they were soon ordered to retire under protection of the forts. Shortly after this, Colonel Shelby sent a regiment of cavalry against the Federal left, which appeared unprotected, but they, too, were checked and driven back by the Second Battalion Fourteenth Regiment Missouri State Militia Cavalry, after a few well-directed volleys.

By making a demonstration against one point and then another, General Marmaduke hoped to succeed in drawing the Federal forces out of their fortifications and then crush them by the weight of his superior numbers. He received information before passing Ozark that the town was garrisoned by a small force, and he knew that if he could draw this force from their fortifications, it would be an easy matter to crush the small Federal force, and capture the valuable depot of supplies, without subjecting his command to serious loss of life. Owing to the fact that General Brown had only a small number of experienced artillerymen, his guns were not handled as skilfully and rapidly as could have been desired, but under the eye of Lieutenant Hoffman, First Missouri Light

Artillery, they were served with a fair degree of accuracy and effectiveness, and did good work in repulsing the assaults of the enemy in their efforts to break through the Federal line and capture the forts.

As the fighting up to two o'clock had been indecisive, General Marmaduke determined to mass his forces and hurl them against the Federal centre and right. To co-operate with the troops and artillery in the forts in meeting this assault, General Brown ordered Captain Landis, with one piece of artillery supported by three companies of the Eighteenth Iowa Infantry, under Captains Blue, Van Meter, and Stonaker, to take up a position to the front and right of Fort No. 4. In advancing to the assault, the Confederates saw that the gun was in an exposed position, and with wild yells made a desperate charge upon it, and after shooting down the artillery horses and driving back the support, captured it and bore it to the rear.

After this success, the attack was directed against an unfinished stockade fort occupied by part of the Federal garrison, and as the Confederates advanced to close quarters, the roar of small-arms and artillery burst forth with tremendous fury. As the palisades extended around only three sides of the college building, the Confederate forces soon commenced to flank it on the right and left, in spite of the storm of bullets and shot and shell hurled at them from the forts. This movement of the Confederates made the position untenable and the Federal detachment was obliged to abandon it and seek shelter in the other forts. Having captured the college position, the Confederates became more aggressive and immediately commenced to press the Federal right with much energy.

General Brown saw that the situation was becoming serious and required him to put forth his best efforts if he would check the progress of the enemy. He ordered Colonel Crabb to bring to the front the stragglers and convalescents from the hospitals which had been organized into companies under Captain McAfee, Third Missouri State Militia Cavalry, Lieutenant Root, Nineteenth Iowa Infantry, Lieutenant Wilson, Eighteenth Iowa Infantry, and Lieutenant Bodenhammer, Twenty-fourth Missouri Infantry. The Colonel led these detachments in person and moved to a position behind a fence, to the front and west of the fort, about seventy-five yards from the Confederates, who were also posted behind a fence and in and around a house. He had scarcely got his men into position when the conflict with small-arms commenced and was kept up vigorously for nearly an hour, after which the Confederates retired from that part of the field.

On both sides the men soon found that a moment's exposure would bring them under the eyes and within the range of the rifles of each other's sharp-shooters. A number of men who carelessly exposed themselves in the open ground, feeling that they were at a safe distance from hostile bullets, were struck by leaden missiles from unseen foes, and fell sounding upon their arms.

After being driven from the Federal centre, General Marmaduke determined to concentrate his forces against the Federal right, which he had ascertained was held by the Enrolled Missouri Militia under Colonel Sheppard. A report had been circulated extensively, setting forth that a large percentage of the Enrolled Militia were tainted with disloyalty and would not fight the Southern troops. If they showed an indifference as to the result of the contest, the Southern leader knew that he could easily capture the fort they occupied, which would give him a decided advantage in conducting further operations. His troops moved forward in gallant style, confident that they were about to achieve further success, but when they came within rifle range of the fort, they were met by a perfect storm of bullets from the small-arms of Colonel Sheppard's militia, which checked them for a moment.

General Brown had taken the precaution to order to the support of his centre and right the Third and Fourth Regiments Missouri State Militia Cavalry, the second battalion Fourteenth Missouri State Militia Cavalry, and five companies of the Eighteenth Iowa Infantry, and the timely arrival of these troops enabled them to assist in repulsing the charge of the Confederate forces. In the conflict the Confederates took possession of several houses from which they could not be dislodged, and from which they were pouring volley after volley into the Federal line. They were also closing upon the Federal troops with overwhelming numbers on other parts of the field and gradually forcing them back into the forts. Seeing his troops yielding and believing that the situation was becoming desperate and the result doubtful, General Brown rode forward with his body-guard to encourage his men, and, while leading a charge, was shot from a house by an unseen foe and fell from his horse. Though seriously wounded in the shoulder, he remounted his horse at once and rode back a short distance, but was obliged to be carried off the field.

When he saw that he could no longer keep in the field, he turned the command of the troops over to Colonel Crabb, Nineteenth Iowa Infantry. It was now four o'clock, and though the day was drawing to a close the opposing forces were still fiercely engaged, and the roar of musketry and artillery was incessant. From the first of the action General Brown had kept as many troops outside the forts as could be spared to protect his flanks and to prevent the enemy from forcing an entrance into the city between the forts. The possession of the college position gave General Marmaduke great protection in massing and organizing his forces to charge the Federal line. But in the frequent charges they made, they were as often met with firmness and driven back with decimated ranks by the Federal small-arms and by the storm of shot and shell and grape and canister from the artillery in the forts.

About five o'clock the firing had slackened and almost ceased along the front, but Colonel Crabb, who had assumed command of the Federal forces, soon noticed that the Confederates were preparing to make another assault upon his right and centre. When the Confederate leader saw that it would soon be too dark for conducting further operations, and considered the probability of the Federal commander receiving reinforcements during the night, he determined to make another desperate effort to carry the Federal works, and at once ordered Shelby's and McDonald's brigades forward to the attack. To meet the attacking forces, Colonel Crab ordered up on double-quick time five companies of the Eighteenth Iowa infantry, parts of the Fourth and Fourteenth Regiments Missouri State Militia Cavalry dismounted, part of the Seventy-second Enrolled Missouri Militia Infantry, and the irregular force known as the Quinine Brigade. In a few moments the roar of small-arms showed with what determination both sides had again joined in the conflict.

After gallantly holding out nearly half an hour against a vastly superior force, part of the Federal line began to yield. At this moment an officer commanding a company in the Fourteenth Missouri State Militia Cavalry ordered his men to horse. When they commenced moving to the rear to mount their horses, they were quickly followed by the other companies of the battalion. This movement of these troops was thought by others to be a precipitate retreat and caused some confusion in the Federal line. Colonel Crabb, however, quickly rallied such other of his troops as had begun to give way, and they went into the fight, again gallantly performing their duties. And Colonel Pound re-formed the companies of the second battalion and led them into action on the Federal left and checked an attempted flank movement of the enemy on that part of the field. In this crisis Colonel Crabb ordered to the front five additional companies of the Eighteenth Iowa Infantry under Lieutenant-Colonel Thomas Z. Cook, which had been held in reserve. Colonel Cook brought up his men on the double-quick, cheering as they advanced. The cheering of the reinforcements inspired the Federal troops, who were gallantly maintaining an unequal contest with the enemy with new courage, and they advanced again and drove back the Confederates into the palisades around the college building.

Night coming on drew a veil of darkness over the field, and the firing on both sides gradually ceased. It was a severe disappointment to General Marmaduke to be compelled to ingloriously withdraw from the attack, for in his forced marches of two hundred miles from the Arkansas River over mountains and barren regions in an inclement season, he had promised himself military glory, and his troops a bountiful supply of provisions from the Federal commissary stores. He encamped near Springfield during the night, intending to renew the attack the next morning if Colonel Porter's brigade of reinforcements from Pocahontas, Arkansas, arrived in time. On the march through Arkansas couriers were sent to Colonel Porter with orders directing him to join the expedition against Springfield by forced marches, but the couriers were unable to find him until after the attack had been made.

General Brown's conduct in fearlessly exposing himself on the field until wounded, had a good effect in encouraging his officers and men to do their duty. That night, after the Confederate forces retired from the front, taking off part of their wounded and dead, Colonel Crabb took every precaution to guard against a surprise, and set to work making every possible preparation to continue the fight next morning if General Marmaduke determined to renew the attack. But early the next morning the Confederate forces moved around to the Rolla road about one mile east of town, where part of them were formed in line of battle. Colonel King with the Third and Colonel Hall with the Fourth Missouri State Militia Cavalry were ordered forward to engage them, but General Marmaduke declined to be drawn into another action, and moved off eastward in the direction of Marshfield and Hartville. As General Brown had not received any reinforcements from the Army of the Frontier, the garrison at Springfield was too weak to spare any troops for the pursuit of the enemy.

The Federal loss in the action was 14 men killed, 146 wounded, and 4 missing. General Marmaduke reported the Confederate loss at 20 men killed, and 124 wounded, and Colonel Crabb reported having 60 to 80 of the Confederate wounded, who were left on the field, to take care of. On the Federal side the heaviest loss was in Colonel Sheppard's Seventy-second Regiment Enrolled Missouri Militia. There were nearly two hundred loyal citizens of Springfield who volunteered, received arms, and fought beside the soldiers, and they displayed courage and devotion to the cause that would have been creditable to veterans. Their casualties in killed and wounded were as heavy in proportion to numbers as were the losses sustained by the soldiers.

CHAPTER XXXIII.

ACTION AT HARTVILLE, MISSOURI.

AFTER marching fifteen miles northeast on the Springfield and Rolla road, destroying the telegraph line to St. Louis, General Marmaduke divided his command into two columns, sending McDonald's brigade by a right-hand road to Marshfield, ten miles distant. He then proceeded with Shelby's brigade to Sand Springs, on the main Rolla road, about nine miles distant, where he encamped for the night. On the approach of the Confederates, the company of Missouri State Militia stationed at Sand Springs moved out and met the enemy, and skirmished with and held them as long as possible, to cover the Federal supply train which had been sent back on the road to Lebanon. By showing a bold front to the enemy the militia succeeded in getting the train back to Lebanon without the loss of a wagon. But after they abandoned the station General Marmaduke had the satisfaction of burning it because some of the buildings had been constructed with the view of resisting an attack of small-arms.

Colonel McDonald's force reached Marshfield directly after dark, but the company of militia stationed there, supposing it was General Marmaduke's entire command with artillery advancing, retired toward Lebanon with their baggage and public property. At Marshfield also the block-house and buildings which had been occupied by the Union militia were burned, and all the stores in town sacked by the Confederate troops. On the 10th the brigades of Shelby, McDonald, and Porter formed a junction a few miles south of Marshfield, and marched southeast in the direction of Hartville, from which point General Marmaduke had received information that a Federal force was marching to reinforce General Brown at Springfield.

On the receipt of General Brown's despatch announcing the advance of a large Confederate force from the south, General Curtis immediately, by telegraph and courier, ordered Brigadier-General Fitz Henry Warren, commanding at Houston, in Texas County, to reinforce the Federal garrison at Springfield by forced marches. Houston was about eighty miles east of Springfield, and as it was perhaps forty miles to the nearest telegraph station, General Warren did not receive orders to move until the morning of the 9th. But in a few hours after the arrival of the courier with General Curtis' despatch ordering the movement, his troops were in motion *en route* to Springfield. The force numbered about eight hundred men, and consisted of the available strength of Colonel S. Merrill's Twenty-first Iowa Infantry, the Ninety-ninth Illinois Infantry, under Lieutenant-Colonel L. Park, and a section of Battery L, Second Missouri Light Artillery, under Lieutenant W. Waldschmidt. That the troops might move with all possible speed, a train of Government wagons, each wagon drawn by four mules, was furnished to convey the infantry. As General Warren was unable to accompany this force, he ordered Colonel Merrill, the officer next in rank, to take command.

The troops left Houston at twelve o'clock, and took the road leading to Hartville, thirty-five miles west, where they arrived the next morning at sunrise. At this place, Colonel Merrill was reinforced by one hundred and eighty men of the Third Missouri and Third Iowa Cavalry, who had been sent forward by General Warren to overtake him. Here he also received information from citizens that Colonel Porter's brigade of Confederate mounted infantry, with a two-gun battery, had, on the morning of the 9th, surrounded the town and captured a detachment of thirty-five Union militia, and destroyed the fortifications, and after staying in town until dark, marched west in the direction of Hazlewood and Marshfield. Knowing that the enemy were in his front, the Federal commander, after spending several hours in Hartville to rest and refresh his troops and animals, moved forward again with much caution, and encamped that evening nine miles west on the road to Springfield, intending to resume the march the next morning at two o'clock.

After the Confederate forces formed a junction on the 10th near Marshfield, they marched southeast on the road to Hartville, and encamped that night only a few miles from the Federal force under Colonel Merrill. Having received information that a strong Federal cavalry force was pursuing him, General Marmaduke ordered his brigade commanders to resume the march toward Hartville the next morning, January 11th, at one o'clock. Colonel Porter's brigade was given the advance, followed by McDonald, with Shelby bringing up the rear. About three o'clock the next morning, Colonel Porter's advance, under Lieutenant-Colonel Wimer, were fired upon by the Federal picket, who, in the stillness of the night, had heard the tramping of horses' feet some time before the Confederates came up within easy rifle range. The flashes, quickly followed by the reports, from the discharges of the Federal carbines instantly checked the Confederates. In another moment, Colonel Wimer ordered his men to fall back a short distance, and then he dismounted his regiment and formed line of battle.

Colonel Merrill, on his picket guard reporting the near approach of the enemy, also formed his infantry in line of battle, and sent forward his cavalry, under Captain T. G. Black, Third Missouri Cavalry, to skirmish with and hold the Confederates in check until he could make more satisfactory disposition of his troops for action. In a short time, the Federal cavalry and Colonel Porter's brigade became warmly engaged. Lieutenant Waldschmidt participated in this action with his section of artillery, and by vigorously throwing shot and shell into the Confederate position, assisted materially in forcing the Confederates to retire. In this action, Captain D. G. Bradway, Third Missouri Cavalry, was killed and several members of his company wounded. Not wishing to engage the Federal force in front, with a Federal force ready to attack him in rear, as he believed, General Marmaduke determined to take a right-hand road and march around the hostile force in front, so that he would have an unobstructed way open to retreat south, if defeated. From the prisoners the Federal cavalry took in the action early in the morning, Colonel Merrill ascertained that the combined Confederate forces of Porter, Shelby, and McDonald, under General Marmaduke, estimated at five thousand men, were in his immediate front. And when he found that these forces were endeavoring to turn his left flank and get in his rear, the Federal commander immediately commenced to move back rapidly on the Hartville road.

The opposing forces now pressed forward, each striving to reach the goal before the other, but they both arrived there very nearly at the same time, about half-past ten o'clock, and took up positions on opposite sides of the town, and at once prepared for action. Colonel Merrill formed his line on the brow of the hill, about two hundred yards northwest of town. His position was much sheltered by a heavy growth of small trees and underbrush that covered the slope of the hill from its base to its summit in his front. In the line thus formed, Lieutenant-Colonel Dunlap, with the Twenty-first Iowa Infantry, occupied the centre, Lieutenant-Colonel Park, with the

Ninety-ninth Illinois Infantry, the right, and the detachments of the Third Iowa and Third Missouri Cavalry, dismounted, under Major Duffield and Captain Blake, the left, extending to the Lebanon road. Lieutenant Waldschmidt, with his section of artillery, came up on the gallop, his horses all aglow with excitement. He soon found a suitable position on the hill northwest of town for placing his guns in battery.

In the meantime General Marmaduke had brought up Shelby's brigade and Lieutenant Collins' three-gun battery and placed them in position on the south side of town. Dismounting the brigade, Lieutenant-Colonel Gordon's regiment formed the left of the line, Lieutenant-Colonel Gilkey's the centre, and Colonel Thompson's the right. With skirmishers thrown out to the front, Colonel Shelby ordered his brigade to move forward through town and to the edge of the wood beyond, where the shot and shell from Lieutenant Waldschmidt's guns indicated the Federal troops were posted. Knowing his own weakness in numbers, the Federal commander determined if possible to compel the Confederates to bring on the action. In a few moments, however, he saw the Confederate line advancing to the attack, and he then ordered his men to lie flat down on the ground a short distance from the edge of the wood, and when the Confederates approached within easy rifle range to open fire upon them.

The Federal troops were not held long in suspense, for they had scarcely taken their positions in line when they saw the Confederate line nearing the edge of the wood. In another moment the flash and roar of the discharge of eight hundred Federal muskets burst forth from the dark recesses of the wood, announcing that a storm of leaden hail had been sent forth winged with death and woe. Confederate officers and soldiers dropped to the ground dead or wounded on every side, and the whole line was thrown into confusion, and fell back rapidly to the south side of town, receiving the fire of the Federal infantry as they retired. Colonel Shelby rallied part of his brigade and advanced again to attack the Federal position, but his troops were again driven back with loss. In turning the Federal flank in the morning, Colonel Porter's brigade, which was then in the advance, became the rear of the Confederate column, and, in the circuitous route taken, did not reach Hartville until one o'clock. On his arrival he was informed that the Federal forces were retreating, and was ordered to pursue them. He soon noticed, however, that the Federal troops had not all left their position in the wood near town, and at once dismounted his command and moved forward to attack them. He moved up to within fifty yards of the Federal infantry, when they poured a destructive fire of musketry into his line, throwing it into disorder and wounding him in the hand and leg. Lieutenant-Colonel Wimer was shot dead while leading his regiment, and other officers and men fell dead and wounded.

To support his troops in the attack, Colonel Porter had ordered Captain Brown to bring his two-gun battery into position near the head of the column. But the hot fire of musketry which the Federal infantry poured into the Confederate line, causing it to fall back in confusion, also had the effect of stampeding the horses drawing Captain Brown's caissons, leaving him without ammunition and compelling him to abandon his guns on the field. Later in the day, however, they were recovered and brought off the field by detachments of Green's and Burbage's regiments of Porter's brigade.

Just before Colonel Porter came up, part of Colonel Merrill's command had commenced to retreat on the Lebanon road with the wagon train, and in the next hour or so all his troops had retired from the field except the Twenty-first Iowa Infantry, under Lieutenant Colonel Dunlap. Finding himself left on the field with only his own regiment of two hundred and fifty men, confronted by a division of Confederates, Colonel Dunlap did not deem it prudent to expose his weakness by pursuing the enemy into the open ground every time they were driven back by his well-directed volleys of musketry from his partially concealed position. He soon found that the moment he attempted to emerge from the brush his men would be exposed to the fire of the Confederate sharp-shooters, who had concealed themselves in considerable force behind the houses and fences in town. Though he was wounded himself, and had his horse killed under him, he determined to hold his position until night, when he hoped he would be able to retire in safety under cover of the darkness. But his determination had been more effective than he had anticipated, and he and his troops were much elated when, shortly before the sun sank below the horizon, they saw the Confederate forces retreating over the hills south of town.

In the several attacks made upon the Federal position, the Confederates had lost heavily in officers. Colonel Emmet McDonald, Lieutenant-Colonel Wimer, Major Kirtley, and several other officers were killed, besides a large number wounded. After the repulse of Colonel Porter's brigade, the fighting, until the Confederates retreated, was kept up by the sharp-shooters of both sides. When General Marmaduke saw that his efforts to dislodge the Federal infantry from their position in the wood were unsuccessful, he ordered Major Bennett, commanding McDonald's regiment, which had been sent one and a half miles east of town on the Hartville and Houston road to cut off the Federal retreat, to rejoin the other troops at once. Having collected his troops together, he ordered the retreat, and encamped that night seven miles southeast of Hartville in an open prairie, leaving his dead and severely wounded on the field. The next morning, after sending, under flag of truce, a letter to the Federal commander concerning the care of the Confederate wounded and the interment of his dead, he continued his retreat south into Arkansas, and crossed White River near Batesville.

On the Federal side there were 7 men killed, 64 wounded, 5 made prisoners, and 2 missing. From General Marmaduke's report, his casualties were 12 killed, 96 wounded, and 3 missing. Having been left without provisions for his men, Colonel Dunlap, after making arrangements for the care of the Federal wounded and interment of the dead, was obliged to leave Hartville and rejoin the other troops under Colonel Merrill *en route* to Lebanon.

THE END.

INDEX.

A

B

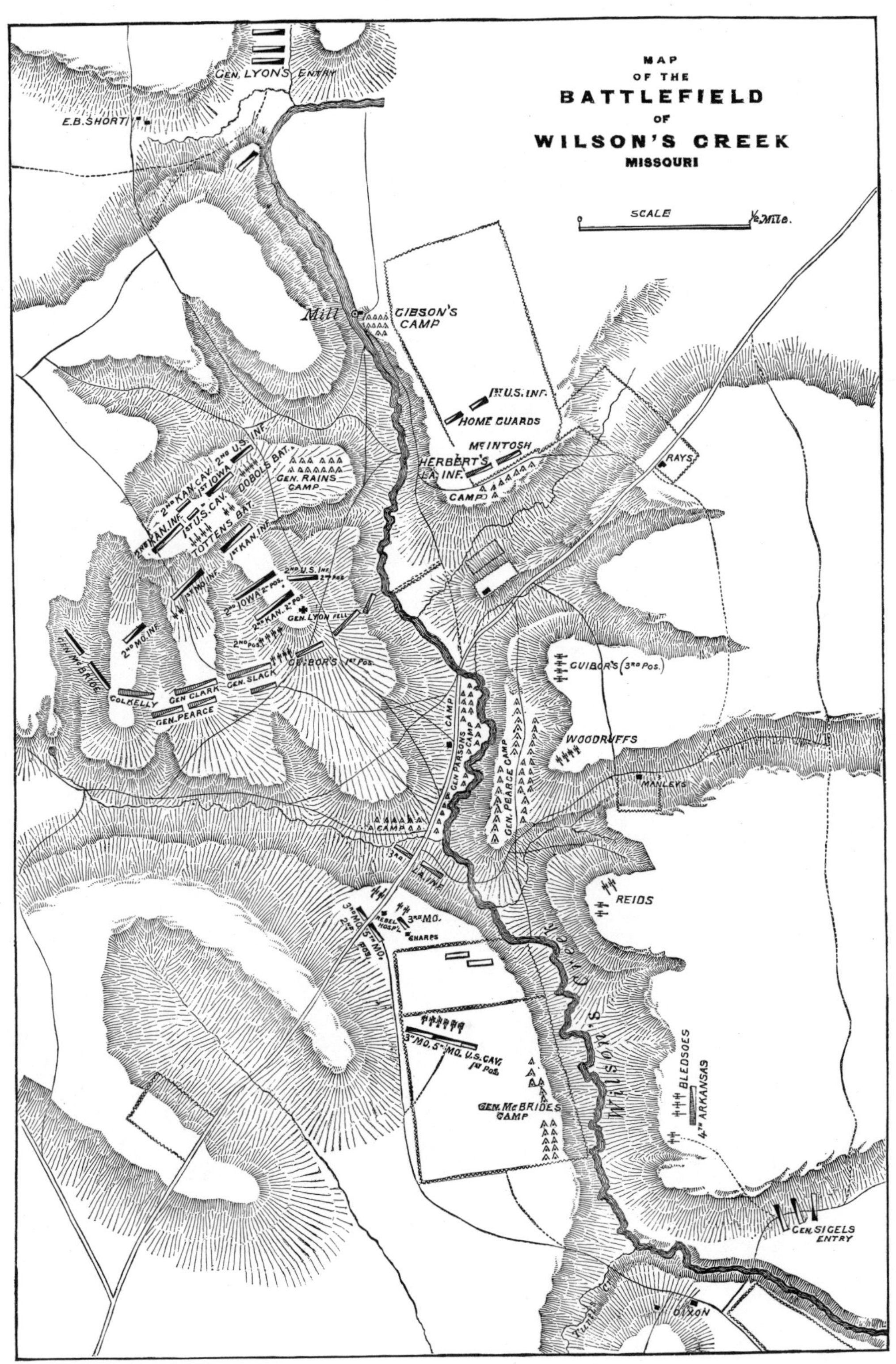
MAP
OF THE
BATTLEFIELD
OF
WILSON'S CREEK
MISSOURI
SCALE
½ Mile.
GEN. LYON'S ENTRY
E.B. SHORT
Mill
GIBSON'S CAMP
1st U.S. INF.
HOME GUARDS
McINTOSH
HERBERT'S LA. INF.
CAMP
RAYS
2nd KAN. CAV.
2nd U.S. INF.
1st IOWA
DUBOIS BAT.
GEN. RAINS CAMP
1st U.S. CAV.
1st KAN. INF.
TOTTEN'S BAT.
1st KAN. INF.
1st MO. INF.
2nd U.S. INF. 2nd POS.
2nd IOWA 2nd POS.
2nd KAN. 2nd POS.
GEN. LYON FELL
2nd MO. INF.
2nd POS.
GUIBOR'S 1st POS.
GUIBOR'S (3rd POS.)
GEN. McBRIDE
COL. KELLY
GEN. CLARK
GEN. SLACK
GEN. PEARCE
CAMP
GEN. PARSONS CAMP
GEN. PEARCE CAMP
WOODRUFFS
MANLEYS
CAMP
3rd LA. INF.
REIDS
3rd MO.
5th MO. 2nd POS.
REBEL HOSP'L
3rd MO.
SHARPS
3rd MO. 5th MO. U.S. CAV. 1st POS.
GEN. McBRIDES CAMP
Wilson's Creek
BLEDSOES
4th ARKANSAS
GEN. SIGELS ENTRY
DIXON

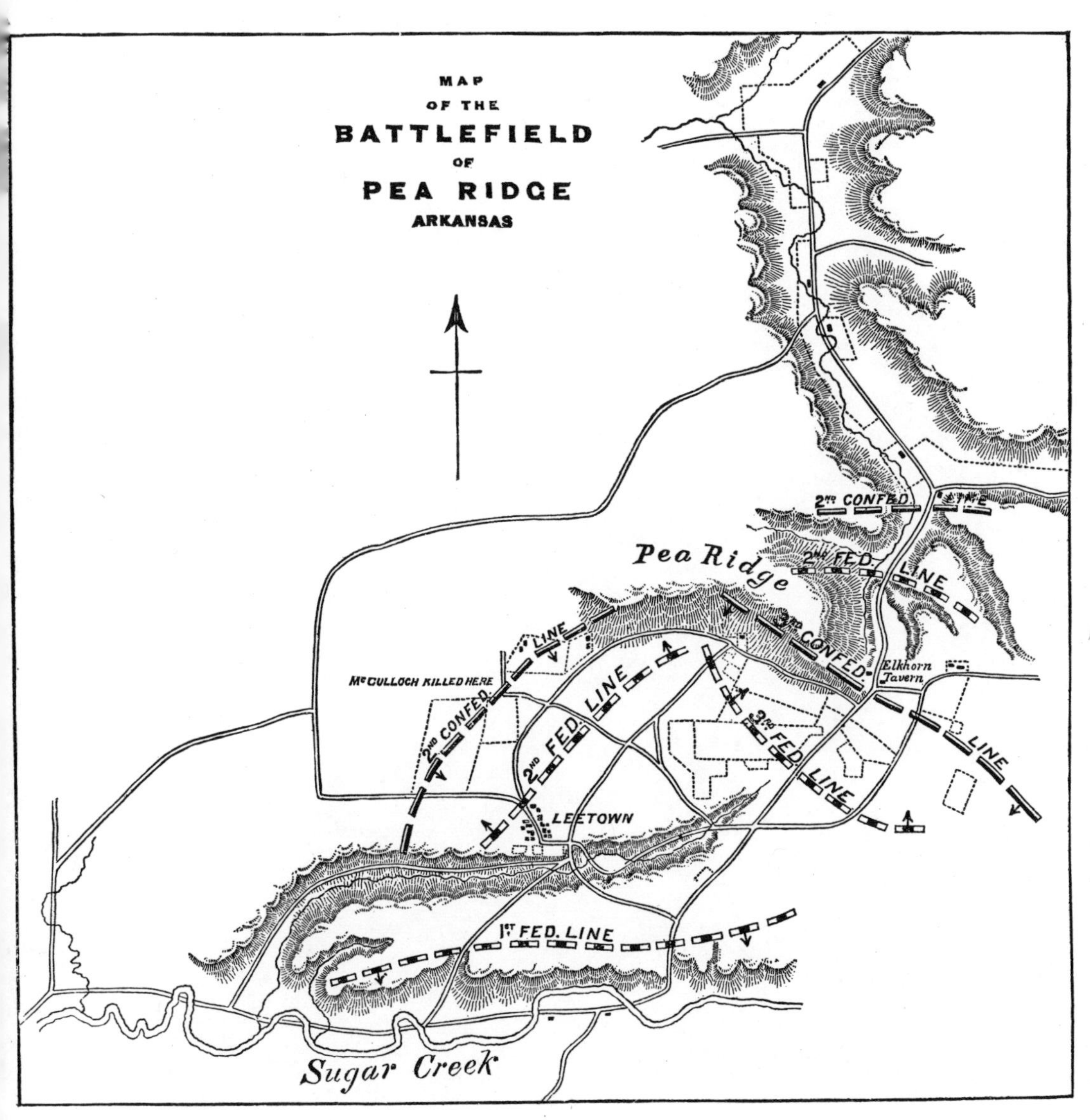
MAP
OF THE
BATTLEFIELD
OF
PEA RIDGE
ARKANSAS
2ND CONFED. LINE
Pea Ridge
2ND FED. LINE
3RD CONFED. LINE
Elkhorn Tavern
McCULLOCH KILLED HERE
LINE
2ND CONFED.
2ND FED. LINE
3RD FED. LINE
LEETOWN
1ST FED. LINE
Sugar Creek